Intelligent Systems for Optical Networks Design:

Advancing Techniques

Yousef S. Kavian
Shahid Chamran University, Iran

Z. Ghassemlooy
Northumbria University, UK

Information Science
REFERENCE

Managing Director:	Lindsay Johnston
Editorial Director:	Joel Gamon
Production Manager:	Jennifer Yoder
Publishing Systems Analyst:	Adrienne Freeland
Development Editor:	Myla Merkel
Assistant Acquisitions Editor:	Kayla Wolfe
Typesetter:	Lisandro Gonzalez
Cover Design:	Jason Mull

Published in the United States of America by
Information Science Reference (an imprint of IGI Global)
701 E. Chocolate Avenue
Hershey PA 17033
Tel: 717-533-8845
Fax: 717-533-8661
E-mail: cust@igi-global.com
Web site: http://www.igi-global.com

Library of Congress Cataloging-in-Publication Data

Library of Congress Cataloging-in-Publication Data

Intelligent systems for optical networks design : advancing techniques / Yousef S. Kavian and Z. Ghassemlooy, editors.
    pages cm
 Includes bibliographical references and index.
 ISBN 978-1-4666-3652-1 (hardcover) -- ISBN 978-1-4666-3653-8 (ebook) -- ISBN 978-1-4666-3654-5 (print & perpetual access) 1. Optical communications-- Design--Research. 2. Intelligent control systems--Research. I. Kavian, Yousef S., 1978- II. Ghassemlooy, Zabih.
 TK5103.59.I5323 2013
 621.382'7--dc23
                            2013007731

British Cataloguing in Publication Data
A Cataloguing in Publication record for this book is available from the British Library.

Yousef dedicates this work to his parents, wife, and daughter.

Zabih dedicates this to his loved ones.

Table of Contents

Detailed Table of Contents

Chapter 1

Bin Wang, Wright State University, USA
Yousef S. Kavian, Shahid Chamran University, Iran

This chapter covers various aspects of optimal optical network design, such as wavelength-routed Wavelength Division Multiplexing (WDM), optical networks, and Spectrum-Sliced Elastic (SLICE) optical networks. As background, the chapter first briefly describes optical ring networks, WDM optical networks, and SLICE optical networks, as well as basic concepts of routing and wavelength assignment and virtual topology design, survivability, and traffic grooming in optical networks. The reader is referred to additional references for details. Many optical network design problems can be formulated as sophisticated optimization problems, including (1) Routing and Wavelength Assignment (RWA) and virtual topology design problem, (2) a suite of network design problems (such as variants of traffic grooming, survivability, and impairment-aware routing), (3) various design problems aimed at reducing the overall energy consumption of optical networks for green communication, and (4) various design optimization problems in SLICE networks that employ OFDM technologies. This chapter covers numerous optical network design optimization problems and solution approaches in detail, and presents some recent developments and future research directions.

Chapter 2

Mina Taheri, New Jersey Institute of Technology, USA
Nirwan Ansari, New Jersey Institute of Technology, USA

This chapter deals with Fiber-Wireless (FiWi) access networks where optical access network is a promising solution to meet the ever-increasing demand for broadband services. Fiber-based technologies, such as Fiber To The Home (FTTH), Fiber To The Building (FTTB), and Fiber To The Curb (FTTC), are well suited to support high bandwidth services and mitigate bandwidth bottlenecks. However, implementing optical fiber to all end points imposes considerable CAPEX. Moreover, fiber cannot directly reach mobile users and devices. Although untethered features of wireless networks are attractive, their limited supported bandwidth cannot answer today's enormous demands. Combining complementary features of these two technologies for broadband access is imminent and meritorious. Thus, integrated Fiber-Wireless (FiWi) access networks are considered as a scalable and economical means for broadband access. In FiWi, end points receive services through a wireless subnetwork, which acts as the front end and is connected to the optical subnetwork, which serves as the back end via gateway nodes.

Chapter 3

Optical Label Processing Techniques for Intelligent Forwarding of Packets in All-Optical Packet Switched Networks 47

Nicola Calabretta, Eindhoven University of Technology, The Netherlands

In this chapter, the authors review several optical label processing techniques providing a comparison based on the potential for each technique to allow for implementation of a scalable and low latency optical packet switching cross-connect node. They present and demonstrate an optical packet switch sub-system employing in-band labeling to allow for transparent forwarding of multi-wavelength packets with multiple data formats at multiple data bit-rates. The optical packet switching sub-system employs a scalable, asynchronous, and low latency label processor. Experimental results are provided that confirm the operation of the label processor in optical packet switching system testbeds. Moreover, the authors discuss applications of the optical packet switching node based on optical label processor and the potential to allow the implementation of intelligent systems for optimal routing of the packets in the optical domain.

Chapter 4

Monitoring Devices for Providing Network Intelligence in Optical Packet Switched Networks 73

Ruth Vilar, Universitat Politècnica de València, Spain
Francisco Ramos, Universitat Politècnica de València, Spain

The objectives of this chapter are addressed to the proposal of new monitoring techniques capable of packet-by-packet monitoring in the optical domain to preserve packet transparency. Moreover, new optical layer functionalities such as dynamic reconfiguration and link level restoration also introduce a level of complexity that may require advanced OPM capabilities. In this chapter, an OSNR monitoring technique and its application for providing network intelligence is explained in detail. In particular, the integration of the monitoring system with the control and management planes is investigated to perform other functions such as quality of service implementation, OSNR-assisted routing, and backup route selection.

Chapter 5

GMPLS for Future Applications: Performance Characterization and Measurements....................... 104

Weiqiang Sun, Shanghai Jiao Tong University, China
Wei Guo, Shanghai Jiao Tong University, China
Yaohui Jin, Shanghai Jiao Tong University, China
Lilin Yi, Shanghai Jiao Tong University, China
Weisheng Hu, Shanghai Jiao Tong University, China

This chapter reviews activities in using GMPLS controlled optical networks in high performance computing environments to identify the benefits, as well as the limitations in such networking practices. It introduces the past and on-going standardization work in the Internet Engineering Task Force (IETF) about GMPLS network performance characterization and measurement. Finally, performance measurement results from a number of deployed GMPLS networks are presented.

Chapter 6

In this chapter, the authors first discuss the background and basic concepts of all-optical regeneration and translucent optical networks. Since all-optical regenerator is much more energy-efficient than traditional O/E/O ones, they investigate translucent lightpath arrangement that involves mixed placement (MRP) of optical inline amplifiers (1R), all-optical 2R regenerators, and O/E/O 3R regenerators for energy-saving. In order to make sure that the end-to-end transmission performance requirement can still be satisfied with this arrangement, the authors analyze the signal BER evolution through fiber links and different types of regenerators, and propose a theoretical model. They then develop search strategies based on exhaustive search and genetic algorithms, and discuss how to use them to optimize the energy-efficiency of lightpaths using MRP. Finally, the authors move to the network design using MRP, in which they considered both offline network design and online network provisioning.

The proliferation of Internet access and the appearance of new telecommunications services are originating a demand for resilient networks with extremely high capacity. Thus, topologies able to recover connections in case of failure are essential. Given the node location and the traffic matrix, the survivable topological design is the problem of determining the network topology at minimum capital expenditure such that survivability is ensured. This problem is strongly NP-hard and heuristics are traditionally used to search near-optimal solutions. The authors present a genetic algorithm for this problem. As the convergence of the genetic algorithm depends on the used operators, an analysis of their impact on the quality of the obtained solutions is presented as well. Two initial population generators, two selection methods, two crossover operators, and two population sizes are compared, and the quality of the obtained solutions is assessed using an integer linear programming model.

Routing and Wavelength Assignment (RWA) of lightpaths in optical WDM networks is a challenging task that belongs to a class of complex combinatorial problems. To solve the RWA problem of realistic size, heuristic or meta-heuristic approaches have to be used. In this chapter, an artificial bee colony metaheuristic approach, known as the Bee Colony Optimization (BCO), is used to solve the RWA problem for static lightpath establishment in wavelength routed optical WDM networks. The BCO metaheuristic is tailored here to solve the Max-RWA problem in which the objective is to maximize the number of established lightpaths for a given number of wavelengths. Behind a comprehensive description of the proposed BCO-RWA algorithm, the numerical results obtained by numerous simulations performed over widely used real world European Optical Network (EON) topology are given and compared with some other approaches used to solve the same problem.

Computational intelligence techniques have been used to solve hard problems in optical networks, such as the routing and wavelength assignment problem, the design of the physical and the logical topology of these networks, and the placement of some high cost devices along the network when it is necessary, such as regenerators and wavelength converters. In this chapter, the authors concentrate on the application of computational intelligence to solve the impairment-aware routing and wavelength assignment problem. They present a brief survey on this topic and a detailed description and results for two applications of computational intelligence, one to solve the wavelength assignment problem with an evolutionary strategy approach and the other to tackle the routing problem using ant colony optimization.

Routing and Wavelength Assignment (RWA) in an arbitrary mesh network is an NP-complete problem. So far, this problem has been solved by linear programming for network topologies with a few nodes, and sub-optimally solved for larger networks by heuristic strategies and the application of optimization algorithms such as Genetic Algorithms (GA), Particle Swarm Optimization (PSO), Differential Evolution (DE), etc. In this chapter, the authors present the use of Ant Colony Optimization (ACO) to find near optimal solutions to the routing and wavelength assignment problem in real sized networks with up to 40 nodes and 65 connecting links. They compare their results to the lower bounds obtained by the Nagatsu's method, finding them to be equal or very close (one wavelength over) to them.

Although some interesting routing algorithms based on HNN were already proposed, they are slower when compared to other routing algorithms. Since HNN are inherently parallel, they are suitable for parallel implementations on parallel platforms, such as Field Programmable Gate Arrays (FPGA) and Graphic Processing Units (GPU). In this chapter, the authors show parallel implementations of a routing algorithm based on Hopfield Neural Networks (HNN) for GPU and for FPGAs, considering some implementation issues. They analyze the hardware limitation on the devices, the memory bottlenecks, the complexity of the HNN, and, in the case of GPU implementation, how the kernel functions should be implemented, as well as, in the case of the FPGA implementation, the accuracy of the number representation and memory storage on the device. The authors perform simulations for one variation of the routing algorithm for three communication network topologies with increasing number of nodes. They achieved speed-ups up to 78 when compared the FPGA model simulated to the CPU sequential version and the GPU version is 55 times faster than the sequential one. These new results suggest that it is possible to use the HNN to implement routers for real networks, including optical networks.

Chapter 12

Firat Tekiner, University of Manchester, UK
Zabih Ghassemlooy, Northumbria University, UK

Antnet is a software agent-based routing algorithm that is influenced by the unsophisticated and individual ant's emergent behaviour. The aim of this chapter is twofold, firstly to introduce improvements to the antnet routing algorithm and then to critically review the work that is done around antnet and reinforcement learning in routing applications. In this chapter a modified antnet algorithm for packet-based networks has been proposed, which offers improvement in the throughput and the average delay by detecting and dropping packets routed through the non-optimal routes. The effect of traffic fluctuations has been limited by applying boundaries to the reinforcement parameter. The round trip feedback information supplied by the software agents is reinforced by updated probability entries in the distance vector table. In addition, link usage information is also used to prevent stagnation problems. Also discussed is antnet with multiple ant colonies applied to packet switched networks. Simulation results show that the average delay experienced by data packets is reduced for evaporation for all cases when non-uniform traffic model traffic is used. However, there is no performance gain on the uniform traffic models. In addition, multiple ant colonies are applied to the packet switched networks, and results are compared with the other approaches. Results show that the throughput could be increased when compared to other schemes, but with no gain in the average packet delay time.

Preface

In the last two decades we have seen an increasing demand for high-speed communication links that has created a growing interest in deployment as well as research and development in optical and all-optical networks. Optical networks have been potentially the most suitable technology for the high speed backbone networks, including Asynchronous Transfer Mode (ATM), Synchronous Optical Networking (SONET), Synchronous Digital Hierarchy (SDH, SONET/SDH) networks, and Internet Protocol (IP) networks. Designing optical networks, subject to quality of service requirements, has become a crucial and complex task. Therefore, meta-heuristic algorithms, which are generally based on some biological and natural processes are employed for solving such problems. Intelligent all optical network is the way forward for the next generation optical networks that offer reliable and fast connections, automatic resource allocation, as well as a number of other intelligent functions. This book contains several chapters that focus on theoretical as well as practical aspects of intelligent methodologies and algorithms applied to real world problems.

Optical networks form the foundation of the global network infrastructure, hence the planning and design of optical networks is crucial to the operation and economics of the Internet and its ability to support critical and reliable communication services. Chapter 1 by Wang and Kavian covers various aspects of optimal optical network design, such as wavelength-routed Wavelength Division Multiplexing (WDM), optical networks, and Spectrum-Sliced Elastic (SLICE) optical networks. As background, the chapter first briefly describes optical ring networks, WDM optical networks, and SLICE optical networks, as well as basic concepts of routing and wavelength assignment and virtual topology design, survivability, and traffic grooming in optical networks. The reader is referred to additional references for details. Many optical network design problems can be formulated as sophisticated optimization problems, including (1) Routing and Wavelength Assignment (RWA) and virtual topology design problem, (2) a suite of network design problems (such as variants of traffic grooming, survivability, and impairment-aware routing), (3) various design problems aimed at reducing the overall energy consumption of optical networks for green communication, and (4) various design optimization problems in SLICE networks that employ OFDM technologies. This chapter covers numerous optical network design optimization problems and solution approaches in detail, and presents some recent developments and future research directions.

Optical access network is a promising solution to meet the ever-increasing demand for broadband services. Fiber-based technologies, such as Fiber To The Home (FTTH), Fiber To The Building (FTTB), and Fiber To The Curb (FTTC), are well suited to support high bandwidth services and mitigate bandwidth bottlenecks. However, implementing optical fiber to all end points imposes considerable CAPEX. Moreover, fiber cannot directly reach mobile users and devices. Although untethered features of wireless networks are attractive, their limited supported bandwidth cannot answer today's enormous demands.

Combining complementary features of these two technologies for broadband access is imminent and meritorious. Thus, integrated Fiber-Wireless (FiWi) access networks are considered in Chapter 2 by Taheri and Ansari as a scalable and economical means for broadband access. In FiWi, end points receive services through a wireless subnetwork, which acts as the front end and is connected to the optical subnetwork, which serves as the back end via gateway nodes.

In Chapter 3, Calabretta gives several optical label-processing techniques providing a comparison based on the potential for each technique to allow for implementation of a scalable and low latency optical packet switching cross-connect node. They present and demonstrate an optical packet switch sub-system employing in-band labeling to allow for transparent forwarding of multi-wavelength packets with multiple data formats at multiple data bit-rates. The optical packet switching sub-system employs a scalable, asynchronous, and low latency label processor. Experimental results are provided that confirm the operation of the label processor in optical packet switching system testbeds. Moreover, the authors discuss applications of the optical packet switching node based on optical label processor and the potential to allow the implementation of intelligent systems for optimal routing of the packets in the optical domain.

The development of all-Optical Packet Switching (OPS) networks brings about new challenges in the topic of Optical Performance Monitoring (OPM). Vilar and Ramos in Chapter 4 have proposed new monitoring techniques capable of packet-by-packet monitoring in the optical domain to preserve the packet transparency. Moreover, new optical layer functionalities such as dynamic reconfiguration and link level restoration that introduce a level of complexity that may require advanced OPM capabilities are outlined. The chapter outlines in detail the OSNR monitoring technique and its application for providing network intelligence. In particular, the integration of the monitoring system with the control and management planes are investigated to perform other functions such as the quality of service implementation, OSNR-assisted routing, and the backup route selection.

Generalized Multiprotocol Label Switching, or GMPLS, is a suite of protocols to enable automated resource discovery, automated service provisioning, and automated failure recovery. In recent years, a considerable number of efforts have been seen in the area of putting GMPLS into advanced networking/service environments. This is exemplified by the various research programs in the US, Europe, and Asia. In such programs, GMPLS has not only been used as a way to reduce management complexity and increase reliability, like the industry is doing right now, but also it is used as a new way for service provisioning. In Chapter 5, Sun et al. first give a review of some activities using GMPLS controlled optical networks in high performance computing environments and outline the benefits as well as the limitations in such networking practices. Also introduced is the past and on-going standardization work in the Internet Engineering Task Force (IETF) about GMPLS network performance characterization and measurement as well as the performance measurement results from a number of deployed GMPLS networks.

Zhu in Chapter 6 outlines the background and basic concepts of all-optical regeneration and translucent optical networks. Since all-optical regenerator is much more energy-efficient than traditional O/E/O ones, they investigate translucent lightpath arrangement that involves mixed placement (MRP) of optical inline amplifiers (1R), all-optical 2R regenerators, and O/E/O 3R regenerators for energy-saving. In order to make sure that the end-to-end transmission performance requirement can still be satisfied with this arrangement, the authors analyze the signal BER evolution through fiber links and different types of regenerators, and propose a theoretical model. They then develop search strategies based on exhaustive search and genetic algorithms, and discuss how to use them to optimize the energy-efficiency of lightpaths using MRP. Finally, the authors move to the network design using MRP, in which they considered both offline network design and online network provisioning.

The proliferation of Internet access and the appearance of new telecommunications services are originating a demand for resilient networks with extremely high capacity. Thus, topologies able to recover connections in case of failure are essential. Given the node location and the traffic matrix, the survivable topological design is the problem of determining the network topology at minimum capital expenditure such that survivability is ensured. This problem is strongly NP-hard and heuristics are traditionally used to search near-optimal solutions. Chapter 7 by Morais and Pinto presents a genetic algorithm for this problem. As the convergence of the genetic algorithm depends on the used operators, an analysis of their impact on the quality of the obtained solutions is presented as well. Two initial population generators, two selection methods, two crossover operators, and two population sizes are compared, and the quality of the obtained solutions is assessed using an integer linear programming model.

Routing and Wavelength Assignment (RWA) of lightpaths in optical WDM networks is a challenging task that belongs to a class of complex combinatorial problems. To solve the RWA problem of realistic size, heuristic or meta-heuristic approaches have to be used. In Chapter 8, Marković outlines an artificial bee colony metaheuristic approach, known as the Bee Colony Optimization (BCO), to solve the RWA problem for static lightpath establishment in wavelength routed optical WDM networks. The BCO metaheuristic is tailored here to solve the Max-RWA problem in which the objective is to maximize the number of established lightpaths for a given number of wavelengths. Behind a comprehensive description of the proposed BCO-RWA algorithm, the numerical results obtained by numerous simulations performed over widely used real world European Optical Network (EON) topology are given and compared with some other approaches used to solve the same problem.

Computational intelligence techniques have been used to solve hard problems in optical networks, such as the routing and wavelength assignment problem, the design of the physical and the logical topology of these networks, and the placement of some high cost devices along the network when it is necessary, such as regenerators and wavelength converters. Martins-Filho et al. in Chapter 9 investigate the application of computational intelligence to solve the impairment-aware routing and wavelength assignment problem by giving (1) a brief survey on this topic, and (2) a detailed description and results for two applications of computational intelligence, one to solve the wavelength assignment problem with an evolutionary strategy approach and the other to tackle the routing problem using the ant colony optimization.

In Chapter 10 Sarmiento et al. outline the use of Ant Colony Optimization (ACO) to find near optimal solutions for routing and wavelength assignment problems in real sized networks with up to 40 nodes and 65 connecting links. Results obtained are compared to the lower bounds obtained by the Nagatsu's method, showing a close match for one wavelength.

Although some interesting routing algorithms based on HNN were already proposed, they are slower when compared to other routing algorithms. Since HNN are inherently parallel, they are suitable for parallel implementations on parallel platforms, such as Field Programmable Gate Arrays (FPGA) and Graphic Processing Units (GPU). In Chapter 11, Bastos-Filho et al. discuss the parallel implementations of a routing algorithm based on Hopfield Neural Networks (HNN) for GPU and for FPGAs. The hardware limitations on devices, memory bottlenecks, complexity of the HNN, and, in the case of GPU implementation, how the kernel functions, should be implemented, as well as, in the case of the FPGA implementation, the accuracy of the number representation and the device's memory storage, are analyzed. The simulation results of one variation of the routing algorithm for three communication network topologies with increasing number of nodes are also compared. The results suggest that it is possible to use HNN to implement routers for real networks, including optical networks.

Antnet is a software agent-based routing algorithm that is influenced by the unsophisticated and individual ant's emergent behaviour. In Chapter 12 Tekiner and Ghassemlooy first introduce improvements to the antnet routing algorithm and then to critically review the work that is done around antnet and reinforcement learning in routing applications. In this chapter a modified antnet algorithm for packet-based networks has been proposed, which offers improvement in the throughput and the average delay by detecting and dropping packets routed through the non-optimal routes. The effect of traffic fluctuations has been limited by applying boundaries to the reinforcement parameter. The round trip feedback information supplied by the software agents is reinforced by updated probability entries in the distance vector table. In addition, link usage information is also used to prevent stagnation problems. Also discussed is antnet with multiple ant colonies applied to packet switched networks. Simulation results show that the average delay experienced by data packets is reduced for evaporation for all cases when non-uniform traffic model traffic is used. However, there is no performance gain on the uniform traffic models. In addition, multiple ant colonies are applied to the packet switched networks, and results are compared with the other approaches. Results show that the throughput could be increased when compared to other schemes, but with no gain in the average packet delay time.

Yousef S. Kavian
Shahid Chamran University of Ahvaz, Iran

Zabih Ghassemlooy
Northumbria University, UK

Acknowledgment

We would like to thank the chapter authors for providing us with the fundamental constituents of this volume and the reviewers who provided detailed and constructive feedback. In addition, thanks are due to members of the staff at the publisher who have guided us through the publishing process.

Yousef S. Kavian
Shahid Chamran University of Ahvaz, Iran

Zabih Ghassemlooy
Northumbria University, UK

Chapter 1
Optical Network Optimization

Bin Wang
Wright State University, USA

Yousef S. Kavian
Shahid Chamran University, Iran

ABSTRACT

Optical networks form the foundation of the global network infrastructure; hence, the planning and design of optical networks is crucial to the operation and economics of the Internet and its ability to support critical and reliable communication services. This book chapter covers various aspects of optimal optical network design, such as wavelength-routed Wavelength Division Multiplexing (WDM) optical networks, Spectrum-Sliced Elastic (SLICE) optical networks. As background, the chapter first briefly describes optical ring networks, WDM optical networks, and SLICE optical networks, as well as basic concepts of routing and wavelength assignment and virtual topology design, survivability, and traffic grooming in optical networks. The reader is referred to additional references for details. Many optical network design problems can be formulated as sophisticated optimization problems, including (1) Routing and Wavelength Assignment (RWA) and virtual topology design problem, (2) a suite of network design problems (such as variants of traffic grooming, survivability, and impairment-aware routing), (3) various design problems aimed at reducing the overall energy consumption of optical networks for green communication, (4) various design optimization problems in SLICE networks that employ OFDM technologies. This chapter covers numerous optical network design optimization problems and solution approaches in detail and presents some recent developments and future research directions.

INTRODUCTION

Optical networking forms the foundation of the global network infrastructure, hence the planning and design of optical networks is crucial to the operation and economics of the Internet and its

ability to support critical and reliable communication services. The optimal design and operation of optical core networks therefore lie in the heart of current and future Internet. Many optical network design problems can be formulated as sophisticated optimization problems.

In this book chapter, we will provide a detailed coverage on the design optimization of optical networks, such as wavelength-routed Wavelength

DOI: 10.4018/978-1-4666-3652-1.ch001

Division Multiplexing (WDM) optical networks, Spectrum-Sliced Elastic (SLICE) optical networks. As background, the chapter first briefly describes ring networks, WDM optical networks, and SLICE optical networks, as well as basic concepts of routing and wavelength assignment and virtual topology design, survivability, and traffic grooming in optical networks.

We will then present a host of network optimization formulations and, whenever applicable, optimal solutions, to a suite of network design problems, such as virtual network topology design, protection and restoration, traffic grooming, energy/impairment-aware routing, and optical layer multicasting. In particular, we will cover some recent developments that deal with solving the Routing and Wavelength Assignment (RWA) problem in large networks with a large number of wavelengths using a decomposition technique which results in computationally efficient formulation for the RWA problem and scalable optimal solutions.

In spite of the fact that optical networks continue to be a critical component of future networks due to their high capacity, low transmission loss, transparency to signal rate and format, and resilience to noise and harsh environmental conditions, less attention has been focused on investigating energy-efficient optical networks. Optical networks consist of components such as optical switches, amplifiers, transponders, regenerators, and wavelength convertors, all of which require considerable energy, and thus maintenance cost, to operate. Furthermore, physical impairments of transmitted optical signals, such as attenuation, dispersion, and cross-talk, can have an adverse impact on the overall system power consumption by increasing the need for equipments to address these impairments. This chapter will cover design optimization problems of new optical network architectures and protocols, aimed at reducing the overall energy consumption in optical core

networks, for example, innovative energy efficient optical grooming routing, traffic grooming, and survivability techniques.

The fixed-size frequency allocation in WDM networks has drawbacks in its coarse granularity, less flexibility and spectral efficiency. Instead of using a single carrier and fixed channel assignment, Spectrum-Sliced Elastic optical path (SLICE) networks (Jinno, Takara, & Kozicki, 2009; Jinno, et al, 2009; Sone, et al, 2009; Takara, et al, 2010) employ OFDM technologies to accommodate traffic more efficiently and alleviate the increase in the cost of capacity in the backbone networks. SLICE networks enable flexible sub-wavelength and super-wavelength accommodation with high spectral and energy efficiency. Power consumption can be reduced by unique features from SLICE networks such as optical sub-carriers bypassing and partial spectrum path shutdown. This chapter will summarize a number of design optimization problems in SLICE networks such as elastic routing and spectrum allocation (RSA) to determine how traffic requests can be best accommodated, virtual networks mapping over SLICE to determine how joint optimization of RSA and virtual network mapping can be achieved, sub-carrier failure recovery, and energy-efficient design in SLICE networks to determine how best constrained network resources can be used in an energy-efficient manner.

OPTICAL NETWORKS AND DESIGN OPTIMIZATION PROBLEMS

Optical fiber transmission has played a key role in increasing the bandwidth of telecommunications networks, especially in recent two decades as the Internet penetrates our daily lives. The evolution of optical communication systems has gone through several generations. In the first-generation of optical networks, optical fibers were used purely as a transmission medium, serving as a replacement for copper wires with all the switching and processing of the bits being handled by electronics. Examples of first-generation optical networks are SONET (synchronous optical network) and SDH (synchronous digital hierarchy) networks (Ramswami & Sivarajan, 2002). Incorporating some of the switching and routing functions that were performed by electronics into the optical part of the network, the second-generation and future generation optical networks were capable of providing more functions than simple point-to-point transmission, for example, lightpath service (a circuit-switched end-to-end all-optical channel) (Chlamtac, Ganz, & Karmi, 1992), dynamic service provisioning, traffic grooming, and so on, in WDM wavelength-routed networks (Ramswami & Sivarajan, 2002). Driven by the increasing demands on communication bandwidth, WDM technology has been widely deployed in the Internet infrastructure. When the bandwidth demand exceeds the capacity in existing fibers, WDM can be more cost-effective than laying more fibers, especially over long distances because more wavelength channels can be lit up as necessary. The tradeoff is between the cost of installation/burial of additional fibers and the cost of additional line terminating equipment.

Overview of Optical Network Technologies

Metro Optical Ring Networks

Much of today's optical ring networks are built around SONET rings. A pair of fibers is used in Unidirectional Path-Switched Ring (UPSR) where one fiber is used as the working fiber and the other as the protection fiber. Traffic from node *A* to node *B* is sent simultaneously on the working fiber in the clockwise direction and on the protection fiber in the counterclockwise direction. As a result, if a link fails on one fiber, node *B* will be able to receive from the other fiber. The bi-directional line-switched ring (BLSR) connects adjacent nodes through one or two pairs of optical fibers, corresponding to BLSR/2 and BLSR/4, respectively. BLSRs are much more sophisticated than UPSRs by incorporating additional protection mechanisms. Unlike a UPSR, working traffic in a BLSR can be carried on different fibers in both directions and is routed along the shortest path in the ring. Half of the capacity of each fiber is reserved for carrying the protection traffic in BLSR/2. In the event of a link failure, the traffic on the failed link is rerouted along the other part of the ring using the protection capacity available in the two fibers. A BLSR with 4 fibers (i.e., BLSR/4) uses a pair of fibers for protection and employs a span switching protection mechanism first. If a transmitter or receiver on a working fiber fails, the traffic is routed on the protection fibers between the two nodes on the same span. BLSRs provide spatial reuse capabilities by allowing protection capacity to be shared between spatially separated connections. BLSRs are significantly more complex to implement than UPSRs due to the extensive signaling required between the nodes. WDM technology has provided the ability to support multiple SONET rings on a single fiber pair by using Wavelength Add/Drop Multiplixers (WADMs) to separate the multiple SONET rings. This tremendously increases the capacity as well as the flexibility of the optical ring networks. However, additional electronic multiplexing equipment is needed which dominates the cost component and needs to be minimized via traffic grooming.

Wavelength-Routed Optical Networks

The massive increase in network bandwidth due to WDM has heightened the need for faster switching at the core of the network (i.e. long-haul networks) to move from point-to-point WDM transmission systems to an all-optical backbone network that eliminates the need for per-hop packet forwarding. Wavelength-routed networks (Stern, Ellinas, & Bala, 2009) have become a major focus area since the early 1990s.

A wavelength-routed network physically consists of a number of Optical Cross-Connects (OXCs) or wavelength routers, taking an arbitrary topology. Each wavelength router takes in a signal at each of the wavelengths at an input port, and routes it to a particular output port, independent of the other wavelengths. The wavelength routers may also be equipped with wavelength converters that allow the optical signal on an incoming wavelength of an input fiber to be switched to some other wavelength on an output fiber link. The basic mechanism of communication in a wavelength-routed network is a *lightpath* (Chlamtac, Ganz, & Karmi, 1992). This is an all-optical communication channel that may span more than one fiber link between two nodes in the network. The intermediate nodes in the physical fiber path route the lightpath in the optical domain using the wavelength routers. If no wavelength converters are used, a lightpath must use the same wavelength on each hop of its physical fiber link. This is known as the wavelength continuity constraint. However, if converters are available, a different wavelength on each fiber link may be used to create a lightpath. A fundamental requirement of a wavelength-routed optical network is that two or more lightpaths traversing the same fiber link must use different wavelengths so that they do not interfere with each other. The end-nodes of the lightpath access the lightpath with transmitters and receivers that are tuned to the wavelength used by the lightpath.

Because of limitations on the number of wavelengths that can be used, and hardware constraints at the network nodes, it is not possible to set up a lightpath between every pair of source and destination nodes. The particular set of lightpaths that are established on a physical network constitutes the virtual topology or logical topology. Careful design of virtual topologies over a WDM network is to combine the best features of optics and electronics. The tradeoff is between bandwidth flexibility and

electronic processing overhead. The traffic on the lightpath does not have to undergo optoelectronic conversion at intermediate nodes. Traffic delay can be reduced through the use of virtual topologies and appropriate routing. However, because lightpaths are circuit-switched, forming lightpaths locks up bandwidth in the corresponding links on the assigned wavelength. A good virtual topology trades some of the ample bandwidth inherent in the fiber to obtain a solution that is the best of both worlds. Different virtual topologies can be set up on the same physical topology, which allows operators to choose or reconfigure a virtual topology that achieves the best network performance given network conditions such as average traffic between network nodes.

As WDM optical networks provide substantial capacity, providing resilience against failures is an especially important requirement for optical networks since the amount of disruption caused by failures is considerable. Therefore, network survivability is a very important issue in WDM optical networks. Network survivability is the ability of a network to recover traffic and services affected by failures (Grover, 2003; Zhou, & Subrammaniam, 2000). There is a large body of literature on survivability in traditional as well as optical networks. Much recent work focuses on survivability in optical WDM networks. Standard 1+1, 1:1, 1:*N* protection, and Automatic Protection Switching (APS) have been well studied (Ramswami & Sivarajan, 2002). These techniques have also been applied successfully in SONET rings (Ramswami & Sivarajan, 2002). However, the techniques used for SONET are not immediately applicable to WDM systems. Survivability in transport WDM mesh networks is more complicated than that in point-to-point links or ring networks, and has been a subject of optimal network design.

Optical networks will essentially serve as Optical Transport Networks (OTNs) that enable "everything over optics" integration, e.g., IP over WDM integration, leading to the building of the next generation optical Internet. In addition, new optical network architectures, such as optical burst switching (Chen, Qiao, & Yu, 2004), optical packet switching (Ramaswami & Sivarajan, 2002), light-trail (Gumaste & Chlamtac, 2004), optical split-and-direct switching, spectrum-sliced elastic optical path (SLICE) networks, and so on, have been proposed, and may potentially change the landscape of future optical networking. Interested readers are referred to the respective references for more details.

Spectrum-Sliced Elastic Optical Path (SLICE) Networks

The state-of-the-art WDM technology allows each fiber to carry numerous wavelengths with bandwidth up to 100 Gbits/s or higher. WDM networks (Figure 1a) use a fixed-size frequency allocation per channel. This is the smallest granularity to accommodate traffic demands. A guide band is left between two optical wavelength channels to ensure no interference from adjacent channels. The drawbacks of WDM networks include coarse channel granularity, less flexibility in bandwidth allocation, and spectrum inefficiency. For example, when the traffic demand (even after grooming) is less than the capacity of one wavelength, an entire wavelength is still required to accommodate the demand in WDM networks. When one traffic demand requires a multi-wavelength rate, guide bands between two adjacent wavelength channels are required, leading to spectral inefficiency.

The Spectrum-Sliced Elastic optical path (SLICE) networks recently proposed (Jinno, Takara, & Kozicki, 2009; Jinno, et al, 2009; Sone, et al, 2009; Takara, et al, 2010) employ Orthogonal Frequency Division Multiplexing (OFDM) modulation technologies to accommodate traffic

more efficiently and alleviate the increase in the cost of capacity in the backbone networks. OFDM modulates data on a group of sub-carriers that can be partially overlapping in the spectrum domain. Using OFDM modulation, SLICE networks can overcome impairments caused by the Chromatic Dispersion (CD) and Polarization Mode Dispersion (PMD) in high-capacity long-haul fiber transmission. SLICE networks enable more flexible sub-wavelength and multi-wavelength accommodation with high spectral and energy efficiency. In the frequency domain, one sub-carrier corresponds to several GHz, and the capacity of one sub-carrier is in the order of Gbps. SLICE networks can naturally accommodate the sub-wavelength traffic in the optical domain. When a traffic demand is larger than the capacity of one sub-carrier, the demand can be satisfied by the combined data rate of a group of sub-carriers, i.e., n consecutive sub-carriers can be allocated without guard-bands as these sub-carriers overlap in the frequency domain. Additionally, the power consumption problem can be addressed by unique features of SLICE networks such as optical sub-carriers bypassing and partial spectrum path shutdown.

OPTICAL NETWORK DESIGN OPTIMIZATION

Routing and Wavelength Assignment (RWA)

Given a set of connections and a network topology, the problem of setting up lightpaths by routing and assigning a wavelength to each connection is called

Figure 1. Comparison of WDM and OFDM systems in the spectrum domain: (a) guard bands in WDM systems; (b) sub-carriers in SLICE networks using OFDM

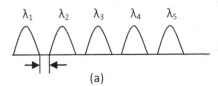

(a)

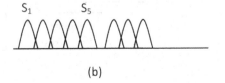

(b)

the Routing and Wavelength Assignment (RWA) problem (Figure 2). Routing and wavelength assignment is a sub-problem of many optical network design problems such as network protection and restoration, traffic grooming, and so on.

A lightpath is used to support a connection in a wavelength-routed WDM network, and it may span multiple fiber links. Nodes in a WDM optical network may or may not have wavelength conversion capability. In the absence of wavelength converters, a lightpath must use the same wavelength on all the fiber links that it traverses. This property is known as the wavelength continuity constraint. A network may have partial wavelength conversion capability where some nodes have wavelength converters.

Various types of connection requests or traffic demands (Figure 2) have been proposed and considered in the literature for the RWA problem, including static, incremental, dynamic, Scheduled Lightpath Demands (SLD) (Kuri, Puech, Gagnaire, & Douville, 2003), sliding scheduled traffic demands (Wang, et al, 2005), and so on.

The RWA problem can then be classified as static RWA and dynamic RWA, depending on whether the set of traffic demands are known in advance. The objective of the RWA optimization problem is either to establish all the lightpaths using a minimum number of wavelengths, or to maximize the number of accepted traffic demands under the constraint that the number of wavelengths is a limit. Both variants have been studied extensively in the literature. Both types of problems are NP-hard.

Many heuristic solution methods have been developed and evaluated under various assumptions and network settings (Zang, Jue, & Mukherjee, 2000, Wang, et al, 2005; Kuri, Puech, Gagnaire, & Douville, 2003; Dutta & Rouskas, 2003, Ramswami & Sivarajan, 1995). Optimal solutions to the static RWA problem have been proposed and studied. Several Mixed Integer Linear Program (MILP) formulations have been proposed for both the minimization and maximization problems. Most formulations can be classified as either link-based or path-based. Common problems that face the ILP based optimal approaches are that

Figure 2. Routing and wavelength assignment in wavelength-routed WDM optical networks

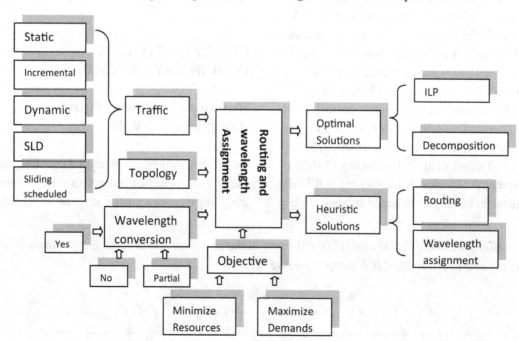

their size increases rapidly with the number of wavelengths and multiple solutions with the same objective value can be obtained by changing the order of wavelengths. As a result, the running time for the ILP based approaches can be very long. These approaches do not scale to networks of practical sizes or a large number of wavelengths per link that are available in current networks (i.e., hundreds of wavelengths).

The combined routing and wavelength assignment problem is a hard problem. It can be simplified by decoupling the problem into two separate sub-problems: the routing sub-problem and the wavelength assignment sub-problem (Zang, Jue, & Mukherjee, 2000). Various existing routing algorithms as well as routing algorithms that specifically take into account the features of WDM optical networks have been proposed and studied, including fixed routing, fixed-alternate routing, adaptive routing, fault-tolerant routing, and so on. The wavelength assignment problem is to assign a wavelength to each lightpath routed along paths determined by a proper routing algorithm such that no two lightpaths share the same wavelength on a common fiber link (Figure 3a). This problem is equivalent to the graph-coloring problem. Consider a network topology (Figure 3a) represented by graph G, and a set of pre-computed

paths between source-destination pairs of G (e.g., 8 lightpaths in Figure 3a). Define a new graph G' (Figure 3b) where each vertex corresponds to a lightpath in G and two vertices are connected to each other in G' if the corresponding lightpaths in G share a common link (Figure 3b). The wavelength assignment problem is then equivalent to assigning separate colors to a vertex in G' for each lightpath established over the corresponding path in G, such that two adjacent vertices in G' are not assigned the same color. Thus, a set of lightpaths in G can use the same wavelength if the corresponding vertices in G' form an independent set. Therefore, the RWA problem can also be formulated based on this graph-coloring approach or maximal independent set based ILP formulation that is independent of the number of wavelengths in a network.

For the case in which lightpaths arrive one at a time, heuristic methods are used to assign wavelengths to lightpaths. Numerous heuristics have been proposed in the literature (Zang, Jue, & Mukherjee, 2000; Chu, Li, & Zhang, 2003), such as (1) Random, (2) First-Fit, (3) Least-Used/ SPREAD, (4) Most-Used/PACK, (5) Min-Product, (6) Least Loaded, (7) MAX-SUM, (8) Relative Capacity Loss, (9) Wavelength Reservation, and (10) Protecting Threshold. These algorithms can

Figure 3. (a) A network G with eight routed lightpaths; (b) the auxiliary graph, G'(V,E), for the lightpaths in the network of (a)

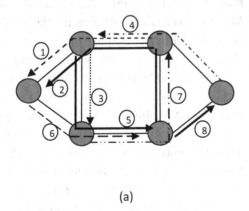

(a)

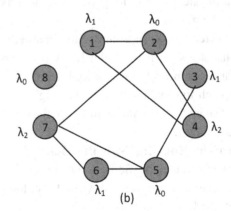

(b)

be combined with different routing schemes, to minimize the connection blocking probability or to maximize the traffic demand accommodated.

Virtual Topology Design

The virtual topology design problem in wavelength-routed optical networks is closely coupled with the RWA problem (Dutta, & Rouskas, 2000; Zang, Jue, & Mukherjee, 2000). Virtual topology design aims at designing a virtual topology on a physical network and deciding the lightpaths to be set up between their source and destination nodes, and assigning a proper wavelength while considering delay, throughput, equipment cost, and reconfigurability. In general, virtual topology design problems can be formulated as optimization problems that maximize network throughput or other performance measures of interest. The exact solutions to the problem quickly grow intractable with increasing size of the network and the problem is NP-hard. The problem can be decomposed into four sub-problems:

1. **Topology Sub-Problem:** This problem determines the virtual topology to be imposed on the physical network, and it figures out the lightpaths and their source and destination nodes;
2. **Lightpath Routing Sub-Problem:** This is a part of the RWA problem that determines the physical paths along which lightpaths will be routed;
3. **Wavelength Assignment Sub-Problem:** This is also a part of the RWA problem that determines the wavelength to be used by each lightpath so that no two lighpaths that share some common links use the same wavelength;
4. **Traffic Routing Sub-Problem:** This problem routes traffic between source and destination node over the virtual topology obtained.

Solving the sub-problems in sequence and combining the solutions may not result in the optimal solution or may even result in no solution to the fully integrated original problem. Exact solutions to all the sub-problems are also not possible since some of the sub-problems (e.g., the RWA problem) are NP-hard as well. Therefore, heuristic algorithms are needed.

To evaluate a solution produced by a heuristic algorithm, some achievable bounds on the optimal solutions are derived from theoretical considerations to determine how close the obtained heuristic solution is to the optimal one. These bounds include lower bounds on congestion, physical topology independent bounds, minimum flow tree bounds, iterative bounds, independent topologies bound, lower bounds on the number of wavelengths, physical topology degree bound, physical topology links bound, and so on (Dutta, & Rouskas, 2000). Heuristics have also been developed for special case network topologies (e.g., regular topologies such as hypercubes or shufflenets) and theoretical results have been derived for such special cases.

Protection and Restoration

Various approaches to provisioning survivability exist for WDM optical networks. These approaches can generally be divided into protection (a.k.a. pre-planned approaches, or proactive approaches) and restoration (a.k.a. reactive approaches) (Mohan & Murthy, 2000) (Figure 4). Specifically, protection refers to techniques that use pre-assigned capacity to ensure survivability while techniques that re-route affected traffic after a failure occurrence using available capacity are referred to as restoration (Mohan & Murthy, 2000). In general, protection based approaches offer faster recovery times while restoration based approaches may be more resource efficient. Various fault-resilient schemes can be designed at IP and/or WDM layers to protect users' traffic from disruptions due to failures.

Figure 4. A taxonomy of survivability provisioning schemes in WDM optical networks

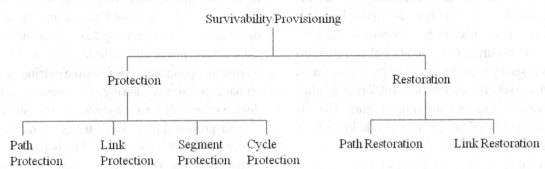

WDM layer survivability is desirable due to its many advantages: speed, simplicity, effectiveness, and transparency (Zhou & Subramaniam, 2000).

A great deal of research has been conducted on survivable service provisioning in WDM optical networks. Previous work has considered several types of traffic models, e.g., static traffic, dynamic random traffic, admissible set, and incremental traffic, where the connection holding-time of demands is not explicitly taken into account for service provisioning. While different traffic models are valid and useful in many circumstances, these models are not able to capture the traffic characteristics of applications that require resources during specific time intervals, for instance, circuit leasing on a short term basis, where a client company may request certain amount of scheduled bandwidth from a service provider to satisfy its communication requirements at a specific time, e.g., between headquarters and production centers during office hours or between data centers during the night when backup of databases is performed, and so on. Many applications require provisioning of scheduled dedicated channels or bandwidth pipes at a specific time with certain duration. These scheduled bandwidth demands (Kuri, 2003) are dynamic in nature. They are not static in the sense that the demands only last during the specified time intervals.

In the work of Kuri et al. (Kuri, 2003; Kuri, Puech, Gagnaire, Dotaro, & Douville, 2003a), a scheduled lightpath demand model was proposed. The routing and wavelength assignment problem

is solved using a branch & bound algorithm and a tabu search algorithm. The issue of diverse routing of scheduled lightpath demands was addressed in another work from the same group (Kuri et al., 2003b). The problem was formulated as an optimization model, which is basically a two-step optimization approach and a simulated annealing based algorithm was proposed to find heuristic solutions to the optimization problem. The work of Tornatore et al. (2005) exploits the connection-holding-time information to dynamically provision shared-path-protected connections using heuristic algorithms. The work of Saradhi, Wei, & Gurusamy (2004) considers the provisioning of fault-tolerant scheduled lightpath demands based on a two-step optimization that uses a set of pre-computed routes for working and protection paths. In (Li & Wang, 2005), given a set of scheduled traffic demands, we provide a set of joint Routing and Wavelength Assignment (RWA) ILP problem formulations that enable the maximum resource sharing in both space and time (i.e., use backup resource sharing and resource sharing that exploits time disjointness among demands). This problem has been shown to be *NP*-hard. We therefore have studied a two-step optimization approach which divides the joint RWA problems into a routing sub-problem and wavelength assignment sub-problems; and then solves them individually (Li &Wang, 2005; Li, Wang, Xin, & Zhang, 2005).

To provide time-efficient solutions, in (Wang & Li, 2006), we have proposed an Iterative Survivable Routing (ISR) scheme that utilizes a capacity provision matrix and processes demands sequentially using different demand scheduling policies. The objective is to minimize the total network resources (e.g., number of wavelength-links) used by working paths and protection paths of a given set of demands while 100% restorability is guaranteed against any single failure. The additional information on connection holding-time offers a service provider a better opportunity to optimize the network resources jointly in space (i.e., backup resource sharing) and in time (i.e., taking advantage of time-disjointness amongst demands). Since a demand is considered accommodated as long as it is provisioned during its holding time, time disjoint demands (working path and protection path alike) can therefore share network resources.

Specifically, we have considered a traffic model termed as scheduled traffic model in (Wang & Li, 2006). The network has an arbitrary topology $G = (N, L)$, where N, L are the set of nodes and the set of directed links, respectively. Each link, represented by a pair of ordered nodes, has a set of wavelengths K. A set of scheduled traffic demands, D, is given, each demand of which is represented by a tuple $(s_r, d_r, n_r, \alpha_r, \beta_r)$, where s_r and d_r are the source and destination nodes of demand r, n_r is the number of requested lightpaths, α_r and β_r are the setup and teardown time of the demand, respectively. The scheduled traffic model is different from the static and dynamic random traffic models generally assumed in the literature. In the static traffic model, all demands are known in advance and do not change over time, while the dynamic random traffic assumes that a demand arrives at a random time, the inter-arrival time and holding time of demands are random or conform to some probability distribution. The scheduled traffic model explicitly considers the time dimension of demands since many demands for bandwidth in ultra high-speed networks will be time-limited rather than permanent. The model is also dynamic in the sense that demands only last during the specified time intervals. Given a set of scheduled demands, some demands may not overlap in time. This motivates us to take into account the time disjointness (if any) among demands along both working and protection paths in addition to optimizing the spatial network resource sharing based on backup resource sharing, to achieve a higher degree of overall network resource shareability.

Our proposed algorithm strives to minimize the total network resources used by both working paths and protection paths of a given set of demands through exploiting network resource reuse in both space and time domains simultaneously. That is, both working capacity and protection capacity are minimized simultaneously. Given a demand, our approach tries to accommodate the demand by finding working and protection paths that will use the least amount of additional network resource after using sharable resources as much as possible. The time relationship among demands is represented by an interval graph. By exploiting the time disjointness among a given set of demands, we transform the problem of finding the minimum total capacity needed on a link to accommodate a set of the demands for their working capacity as well as protection capacity to the problem of finding a maximum weighted clique of the weighted interval graph corresponding to the demand set. Once a working path and a protection path are found for each demand in the given demand set, the total network resources used can be determined. The algorithm then runs iteratively to reduce the total resources used by rearranging the paths of demands. Because the algorithm iteration keeps reducing the objective function, ISR can converges quickly in a stable network (i.e., a fixed topology and a given fixed demand set).

The ISR scheme is evaluated against solutions obtained by integer linear programming (Li & Wang, 2005). The simulation results indicate that the ISR algorithm is extremely time efficient while achieving excellent performance in terms of total network resources used. The impact of demand scheduling policies on the ISR algorithm is also studied. It appears that no significant difference exists among various demand scheduling policies for small demand sets and networks. For large networks and demand sets, in many cases, the ISR algorithm employing the Most Conflicting Demand First (MCDF) policy achieves the best performance, and the one using the Least Conflicting Demand First (LCDF) policy needs more wavelength-links compared with other policies.

In the work of (Jaekel & Chen, 2006), a new ILP formulation for routing and wavelength allocation, under the scheduled traffic model, was presented that minimizes the congestion of the network. Two levels of service were proposed where idle backup resources can be used to carry low priority traffic, under fault-free conditions. When a fault occurs, and resources for a backup path need to be reclaimed, any low priority traffic on the affected channels is dropped. The results demonstrate that significant improvements can be achieved over single service level models. Optimal solutions can also be generated for moderate sized networks, within a reasonable amount of time. The authors also present a heuristic that can quickly generate good solutions for much larger networks.

In the work of (Wang, Li, Luo, Fan, & Xin, 2005), we propose a general scheduled traffic model called the sliding scheduled traffic model. In this model, the setup time α_r of a demand r, whose holding time is τ time units is not known in advance. Rather α_r is allowed to begin in a pre-specified time window $[t_s, t_e]$ subject to the constraint that $t_s \leq \alpha_r \leq t_e - \tau$. We then solve two problems: (1) how to properly place a demand within its associated time window to reduce overlapping in time among a set of demands; and (2) how to route and assign wavelengths (RWA) to a set of demands under the sliding scheduled traffic model in mesh reconfigurable WDM optical networks without wavelength conversion.

As follow-up work, the authors of (Jaekel & Chen, 2007; Jaekel, 2006) present a new ILP formulation for both fixed window model, and the sliding scheduled traffic model. They consider fault-free as well as survivable networks using path protection, and do not require any wavelength conversion. The ILP can jointly optimize the problem of scheduling the demands in time and allocating resources for the scheduled lightpaths. It is shown that the complexity of the ILP formulation for sliding scheduled traffic model, in terms of the number of integer variables, is less than previous ILP formulations for the simpler fixed window model. For very large networks, a fast two-step optimization process is also proposed. The first step schedules the demands optimally in time, such that the amount of overlap is minimized. The second step uses a connection holding-time aware heuristic to perform routing and wavelength assignment for the scheduled demands. The work of (Saradhi & Gurusamy, 2007) develops a time conflict resolving window division algorithm which places a given set of sliding scheduled lightpath demands within their allowed intervals, and two Routing and Wavelength Assignment (RWA) algorithms for routing sliding scheduled lightpath demands in WDM optical networks.

Traffic Grooming

Traffic grooming offers the ability to switch low speed traffic streams into high speed bandwidth trunks so that resources are shared among multiple entities who individually need only a fraction of the resources, which optimizes the capacity utilization by allowing the resource cost to be amortized over the number of users (Dutta, & Rouskas, 2002a; Dutta, & Rouskas, 2002b, Huang, Dutta, & Rouskas, 2006, Dutta, Kamal, & Rouskas, 2008). The traffic grooming problem is a hard optimization problem and, in general, can be logically decomposed into four sub-problems: (1) topology design that determines the virtual topology to be embedded in the physical topology; (2) routing problem that determines the route of each of the high-speed bandwidth trunks (e.g., lightpaths, light-trails, etc.) over the physical topology; (3) connection routing that routes connections over the virtual topology; and (4) wavelength assignment that allocates wavelengths to the bandwidth trunks subject to assignment and continuity constraints.

Much recent work has focused on grooming traffic in mesh networks (Antonakopoulos, & Zhang, 2009; Dutta, Kamal, & Rouskas, 2008; Huang, Dutta, & Rouskas, 2006; Xin, Wang, Cao, & Li, 2006). Existing work on traffic grooming has considered several types of traffic model, such as static traffic model, dynamic random traffic model, incremental traffic model, traffic matrix set model, and scheduled traffic model. In the static traffic model, all traffic demands are known in advance and do not change over time. For instance, a client company may request virtual private network capacity for connectivity among different company sites from a service provider. The objective is typically to minimize the network resources needed or cost, e.g., the amount of Line Terminating Equipment (LTE), or to maximize the network throughput given a resource constraint, and so on. This model does not allow dynamic connection setup and tear-down. In the dynamic random traffic model, a demand is assumed to arrive at a random time and last for a random amount of time. Usually this model assumes a certain stochastic demand arrival process (e.g., Poisson process) and a demand holding time probability distribution (e.g., exponential distribution), as well as a certain spatial traffic distribution (e.g., uniform traffic). The design objective is typically to minimize the percentage of blocked traffic. Other traffic models have been considered for network planning and configuration. The work of (Geary, Antonopoulos, Drakospoulos, & O'Reilly, 2001) on multi-period network planning was based on an incremental traffic model and conducted network planning across several years to incrementally produce a network capable of carrying all traffic predicted up to the end of the planning horizon.

Many applications require the provisioning of scheduled dedicated channels or sub-wavelength bandwidth pipes at a specific time with certain duration. Traffic grooming under scheduled ser-

vice is essential because many applications only need low-rate connections for communication, for instance, connections between corporate sites, scheduled backup between data centers, and occupying a full wavelength for transferring a few megabits or gigabits per second of data results in very poor utilization of network resources. The work on traffic grooming under scheduled service is more recent and relatively limited compared to work on traffic grooming in general. The work by Tornatore et al. (2007) considers dynamic traffic grooming of sub-wavelength connections with known duration where the connection requests arrive one at a time with different starting time and holding time. The objective of grooming is to minimize the network resources used for accommodating each request or implicitly attempt to minimize the overall connection blocking probability.

In (Wang, Li, Luo, & Fan, 2004), we study traffic grooming under a sliding scheduled service model. No wavelength conversion is assumed in the network under consideration. And no traffic bifurcation is allowed. Given a set of sliding scheduled traffic demands, the primary objective of traffic grooming is to minimize the total wavelength-links used while trying to meet demands' timing specifications (i.e., starting time and holding time). Because of the scheduling time flexibility offered by the sliding scheduled service model, the difficulties of the traffic grooming problem lies in the spatial and temporal constraints/flexibilities imposed/offered on the set of demands. In the spatial domain, demands are groomed in a mesh network topology and may share the same wavelength on the same link when the capacity of the wavelength allows. Grooming of demands is also subjected to the wavelength continuity constraint. In the time domain, a demand may slide within its time window and demands may overlap in time, which constrains traffic grooming when combined with the spatial constraints. However, the time-limited nature of demands offers additional opportunities for resource reuse in both time and space during traffic grooming. Obviously, reducing overlapping among demands in time improves temporal resource reuse. A two-step approach to the traffic grooming problem is proposed and studied. First, to maximize the network resource reuse by demands in the time domain, a demand time conflict reduction algorithm is designed to find a proper placement of demand intervals in their associated time windows such that the number of demand pairs that overlap in time is minimized. The second step is to use a time window based algorithm for traffic grooming. The design of this grooming algorithm is based on the following observations. Demands that overlap in time must be groomed with sufficient capacity in the spatial domain if the total capacity of these demands exceeds the wavelength capacity. Network resources used by one demand can be reused by another demand as long as they do not overlap in time. We divide the set of demands into subsets based on the demands' starting time and ending time such that demands in different subsets are disjoint in time except for a few straddling demands. Note that it is not always possible to assign a demand to only one subset because the holding time may result in its being included in multiple subsets. Such a demand is termed as a straddling demand. Specifically, the time conflicts of demands in a set are modeled using a different interval graph. Based on the interval graph representation, an efficient algorithm then divides the demands into subsets. A virtual network topology is constructed to groom each subset of demands. The resources used by demands in one subset can potentially be reused by other subsets. Grooming of a straddling demand, however, requires the same resources be used by it across subsets. Simulation results and comparison with a customized tabu search scheme have shown that the proposed two-step traffic grooming algorithm for sliding scheduled demands is effective in meeting demands' timing specifications as well as reducing the total network resources used.

Optical Layer Multicast/Manycast

Optical layer multicast refers to the support of point-to-multipoint connections directly at the optical layer by employing passive devices capable of splitting the power of an input signal among several outputs (Rouskas, 2003). In this context, the concept of a lightpath is generalized to that of a light-tree, which is an optical channel originating at a given source node and has multiple destination nodes to offer a point-to-multipoint channel. Light-trees may be implemented using power splitters at the OXCs or multicast-capable OXCs. However, splitting operation may result in optical signals to lose power and therefore power amplification may be needed to ensure the quality of outgoing signals.

As we have discussed, the RWA problem is a fundamental control problem in optical networks. The multicast RWA problem also arises in supporting optical layer multicast and becomes more difficult. Similar to point-to-point the RWA problem, the multicast RWA problem is subject to the wavelength continuity constraint in the absence of converters and all light-tree sharing common links must be allocated distinct wavelengths. The problem is also intractable in general as a light-tree instead of a simple path needs to be determined and assigned a proper wavelength. Another significant problem needed to be considered in optimizing the design of optical layer multicast is power-awareness and power-efficiency. Light-tree routing needs to be power-budget-aware. An objective of this optimization process is to minimize any unnecessary power splitting operations. An equally important objective is to minimize the network cost. In a network with only a subset of the nodes that are multicast capable, a design objective is to minimize the number of multicast capable OXCs with minimal effects on the performance experienced by multicast connections, which is also directly related to network cost minimization. Studies have shown that, for a wide range of network topologies and traffic patterns, only about 50% of the OXCs need to be multicast-capable. A closely associated problem is the optimization of the placement of multicast-capable OXCs in the network. Depending on the traffic patterns, for static traffic, the optimal solutions to these problems are often formulated as mixed ILPs. The dynamic multicast RWA problem is encountered during the real-time network operation phase where the dynamic provisioning of light-trees is necessary. Numerous algorithms have been proposed and reviewed in (Rouskas, 2003).

In the work of (Charbonneau & Vokkarane, 2010), the optical layer manycast problem was studied. Manycast is a point-to-multipoint communication paradigm with applications in e-Science, Grid, and cloud computing. A manycast request specifies a candidate set of destinations, of which a subset must be reached. Similar to multicast at the optical layer, a light-tree is established for each manycast request such that the number of wavelengths required is minimized. The exact solution may be again solved using an ILP. Heuristics and tabu search meta-heuristics have been proposed to solve the problem more efficiently.

Virtual Network Embedding

The success of the rigid design principles of the Internet has led to so called ossification problem of the Internet where innovative network designs cannot be easily tested or deployed in the current commodity Internet (Anderson, Peterson, Shenker, & Turner, 2005; Chowdhury, & Boutaba, 2009). Network virtualization has been proposed as a tool for evaluating new architectures, as well as a way of modeling the next-generation networking paradigm that can replace the existing Internet, that is, to eradicate the ossifying forces of the current Internet by introducing disruptive technologies. Network virtualization allows multiple heterogeneous virtual networks to share a common network substrate.

Two major players of network virtualization are infrastructure providers who manage the physical infrastructure, and service providers who create virtual networks by aggregating resources from potentially multiple infrastructure providers and offer end-to-end services. In network virtualization, the resources of the physical infrastructures are shared by multiple virtual networks. A virtual network is a collection of virtual nodes connected together by a set of virtual links to form a virtual topology. Each virtual node is hosted on a particular physical node, and a virtual link spans over a path in the physical network and has a portion of the network resources allocated along the path. Each virtual network is allocated a part of the substrate network resources including virtual routers and virtual links. Different virtual networks may have different topologies, resource requirements or lifetime.

The challenge is how to efficiently map the virtual network requests onto the network substrate (e.g., lightpaths in WDM networks, or spectrum paths in SLICE networks). This includes routing and resource allocation, node mapping, and link mapping. Resource allocation and scheduling of physical resources among multiple virtual networks requests is extremely important in order to maximize the number of co-existing virtual networks and to increase the utilization and the revenue of the infrastructure providers. The allocation of resources with constraints on virtual nodes and virtual links, known as the virtual network embedding problem, can be formulated as a mixed integer program. Existing work has considered the virtual network embedding problem with a single infrastructure provider. There are two flavors of this problem: (1) offline problem where all virtual network requests are known in advance, and (2) online problem where virtual network requests arrive dynamically, and once the resources are allocated for the virtual network request, the virtual network may stay in the infrastructure for a finite duration. The allocated resources are released when the virtual network departs. Various constraints and objectives make this problem computationally intractable. The offline problem can be reduced from the NP-hard multi-way separator problem when all the virtual network requests are given a priori. Heuristic solutions have been proposed and studied for virtual network embedding, and the challenge in the context of WDM/SLICE networks is to jointly optimize the RWA/RSA and resource mapping processes while maximizing the resource utilization in the network. However, virtual network embedding across multiple infrastructure providers has not been studied

As a generalization of the virtual network embedding problem, the work of (Yu, et al, 2010; Yu, et al, 2011) considered the survivable virtual infrastructure mapping problem where the objective is to guarantee survivability of a virtual infrastructure over a wide-area optical network. The problem is solved by provisioning redundant facility nodes at different geographical locations and redundant optical connections such that the virtual infrastructure can still be mapped after the failure. The minimum-cost survivable virtual infrastructure problem is formulated using mixed integer linear programming. Efficient heuristic solutions are proposed.

RECENT DEVELOPMENTS AND FUTURE RESEARCH DIRECTIONS

Design of Green Optical Networks

The energy consumption of the Internet has grown significantly as the Internet has undergone continued expansion, and energy consumption of the Internet has been a cause for concern (Gupta, & Singh, 2003; Baliga, et al, 2009). Various studies showed that, in the US alone, the telecommunication and information technology industries will consume about 5-10 percent of the nation's total energy output in the next 10 years. It is critical to reduce network power consumption and per unit bandwidth cost to achieve efficient use of network resources for future Internet networks as optical networks continue to be the champion of future networks due to their high capacity, low transmission loss, transparency to signal rate and format, and resilience to noise and environmental harsh conditions, and the power consumption of such networks can be substantially high and can incur considerable operational cost.

Little attention has been devoted to the study of energy-efficient optical networks until recently. The work of (Zhang, Chowdhury, Tornatore, Mukherjee, 2010) provides an overview of energy conservation approaches across core, metro, and access levels of optical networks. In core networks, (Wu, Chiaragiglio, Mellia, & Neri, 2009; Idzikowski, et al, 2010) considered a static traffic scenario in which traffic demands are known in advance, energy cost is minimized by routing requests and provisioning resources in a manner that maximizes idle network components, which can then be switched off or placed in a low-power mode. This problem has been proven to be NP-hard, and heuristic solutions are given. Additionally, unused WDM links can be powered off using extended IP routing protocols to support energy-efficient routing in IP over WDM networks. Other researchers have also considered energy-aware traffic grooming. The objective is to groom traffic to minimize the number of interfaces used, thereby minimizing the energy consumption.

Another focus is static energy-efficient network design problems that consider the placement of network equipment. The authors of (Shen, & Tucker, 2009) designed an IP over optical network with the goal of minimizing the total power consumed by routers, transponders, and amplifiers. It is shown that IP routers consume more power than transponders and amplifiers; thus, significant energy savings can be achieved by keeping traffic in the optical domain. It is shown in (Chabarek, et al, 2008) that, to minimize power consumption, the chassis of a node should accommodate large number of line cards, and line card capacities should closely match required bandwidth. The work of (Chowdhury, Tornatore, & Mukherjee, 2010) considered Mixed-Line-Rate (MLR) networks in which different wavelengths may operate at different transmission rates, and they show that such networks consume less energy than single-line-rate networks. Additionally, there have been a few publications that consider energy-efficient routing and traffic grooming for dynamic scenarios in which traffic changes over time. These proposed schemes utilize an auxiliary graph approach to route and groom arriving traffic in a manner that attempts to re-use existing lightpaths and activated components in order to minimize the increase in power consumption.

Despite the recent progress in this area, new architectures and protocols need to be studied and developed to reduce the overall energy consumption in optical networks. Specifically, a few avenues are worthy of further exploration: (1) investigate service differentiation models that can support multiple classes of services to provide a smooth transition to green networks, (2) develop survivability mechanisms for green optical networks, (3) analyze different energy-cost models for nodes and associated power-aware routing mechanisms, (4) develop techniques for providing energy efficiency in optical networks subject to physical-layer impairments, such as energy-efficient impairment-aware routing and wavelength assignment, and (5) explore completely new resource multiplexing paradigm such as the SLICE optical network and develop a host of energy-efficient network control mechanisms.

Routing and Spectrum Allocation (RSA) in SLICE Networks

In SLICE networks, a given traffic demand is accommodated by establishing an optical spectrum path that is an all-optical trail between the source and the destination nodes using one or multiple consecutive sub-carriers. Similar to WDM networks, a challenging problem is how to determine the routes and assign sub-carriers or frequency slots (Jinno, et al, 2010) to satisfy the traffic demands. This is termed as the Routing and Spectrum Allocation (RSA) problem. The allocation of bandwidth in SLICE networks should be carried out on sub-carrier levels or a frequency slot basis where the spectral resources of an optical path are allocated by assigning the necessary number of contiguous frequency slots, considering the client signal spectrum width and an effective filter bandwidth throughout the route.

A number of unique features and constraints make the RSA problem in a SLICE network different from the RWA problem in the wavelength-routed WDM networks. The RSA problem appears to be more challenging than the traditional RWA problem. Specifically,

- The RSA problem in SLICE networks needs to consider the continuous availability of the sub-carriers, and the capacity of the sub-carriers on each fiber. Although OFDM technologies exist and have been extensively studied that can make use of non-contiguous spectrum bands (Zhou, Li, Wu et al, 2010; Wu, Ratazzi, Chakravarthy, & Hong, 2008; Li, Chakravarthy, Wang, & Wu, 2011), current SLICE networks only employ OFDM technologies that use consecutive sub-carriers along a spectrum path. This requirement is termed as the sub-carrier consecutiveness constraint. Further research may be needed to determine if it is effective and economic to employ OFDM technologies that can take advantage of non-contiguous spectrum bands, therefore removing this constraint.
- While the sub-carriers on a spectrum path are consecutive and can overlap in the spectrum domain, different spectrum paths need to be separated in the spectrum do-

main by guard frequencies or guard-carriers when two spectrum paths share one or more common fiber links (Jinno, Takara, & Kozicki, 2009). The guard-carriers may require one or a few sub-carriers, or g sub-carriers in general. Unlike wavelength-routed WDM networks where guard bands are fixed and pre-allocated, in SLICE networks, guard-carriers are not fixed, rather they can be any of the sub-carriers and are dynamically determined in the process of spectrum path establishment. This constraint is referred to as guard-carrier constraint.

In the work of (Jinno, et al, 2009, 2010), the RSA problem is considered in the context of SLICE distance-adaptive spectrum resource allocation, where only the necessary minimum spectral resource is adaptively allocated to an optical path. The allocated spectrum is adapted to the end-to-end physical conditions while ensuring a constant data rate by choosing the most efficient set of transport parameters to minimize the allocated spectrum under a certain optical path condition. The parameters to be adapted include modulation level and optical filter bandwidth. Specifically, for short paths that experience small optical SNR degradation and filter narrowing effect, the most spectrally efficient set of parameters (e.g., 16-QAM and filter width of 37.5 GHz) is selected. For paths with larger number of node hops, a more robust set of parameters (e.g., QPSK and 50 GHz) is utilized. The routing and spectrum-assignment (RSA) problem is solved by calculating route and contiguous frequency slots in a heuristic manner based on a fixed-alternate routing algorithm and a first-fit algorithm under the spectrum-continuity constraint. The fixed-alternate routing algorithm maintains a number of routes for each pair of source and destination. Given a connection request, a route is selected from the available alternate routes. Depending on the number of hops of the route, the number of necessary frequency slots is obtained by searching the available contiguous frequency slots in a lower-to-high order, and the lowest available contiguous slots are selected. If no available contiguous frequency slots are found on the route, an alternate route is attempted.

Wang, Cao, and Pan (2011) studied the routing and spectrum allocation problem in the SLICE network. The RSA problem is proved to be NP-hard. An integer linear programming model is developed to minimize the maximum sub-carrier number on a fiber in the network. Additionally, the authors provide an analysis on the lower/upper bounds of the maximum sub-carrier number for both general and ring networks. Two heuristic algorithms, namely, Balanced Load Spectrum Allocation (BLSA) and Shortest Path with maximum Spectrum Reuse (SPSR), are proposed to efficiently solve the RSA problem in a large network.

The SLICE paradigm realizes the promise of efficient transport by using OFDM flexible-rate transponders and bandwidth-variable WXCs (Jinno, et al, 2009). This architecture enables sub-wavelength, super-wavelength, and multiple-rate data traffic accommodations in highly spectrum-effective manner, as well as provides cost-effective fractional bandwidth service. Additionally, it allows operators to offer cost-effective and highly-available connectivity service through time-dependent bandwidth sharing, energy efficient network operation, and highly survivable restoration with bandwidth squeezing (Jinno, et al, 2010).

However, the study of SLICE network control and management is still preliminary and many issues still remain open, including (1) efficient flexible routing and spectrum allocation algorithms that take into account cross-layer information and allow non-uniform spectrum allocation; (2) multi-granular survivability provisioning in SLICE networks, ranging from sub-carrier failure recovery, link level failure recovery, to shared bandwidth squeezed protection and restoration. (3) energy-efficient design and control of SLICE networks. (4) Virtual network embedding in SLICE networks.

Cross Layer Survivability Optimization

Modern communication systems consist of multiple physical implementations communicating via layered protocols. For example, even a single physical layer (e.g., optical layer) failure may cause multiple cascading failures at the logical layer. Though a rich body of literature on physical layer survivability under multiple failures is available, research on cross-layer survivability and network design optimization deserves some attention. The interdependence between the physical (optical) and logical (IP) layers makes the design of IP over WDM optical networks a very challenging task and has introduced a range of cross-layer optimization problems. Much research is required on the structural characteristics of both physical and logical layers, and their impact on cross-layer survivability. Further research is need to explore the impact of multiple failures in the physical (optical) layer on higher layers, e.g., the IP layer, and to have a better understanding of cross-layer survivability issues, and to advance the general area of cross-layer design and optimization, including cross-layer design of the emerging SLICE networks.

Future-Proof Optimization Solution Approaches

Routing and Wavelength Assignment (RWA) problem is one of the central problems in the design, control, and engineering of WDM networks. Often RWA problem appears as a sub-problem in many WDM network design problems, such as protection and restoration, traffic grooming, light-tree design for supporting optical layer multicast. The static RWA problem is NP-hard and optimal solution approaches have been based on Integer Linear Programming formulations (ILPs). Conventional link and path based RWA ILPs are inefficient due to inherent symmetry in wavelength assignment (Yetginar, Liu, & Rouskas, 2010; Yetginar, Liu, & Rouskas, 2011). The problem size increases quickly with the number of wavelengths. Existing optimization techniques cannot solve optimally instances (even for ring networks with tens of nodes and tens of wavelengths) that arise in practice. Numerous heuristic algorithms have been developed, and in most cases, the performance of these algorithms cannot be definitively ascertained. However, current WDM technologies can support more than 100 wavelengths over a single fiber. It would be highly desirable to efficiently obtain optimal solutions regardless of the number of wavelengths that can be supported in a network of practical sizes, and to have a practical tool that allows network designers to quickly conduct analysis on design alternatives.

Recent work by Yetginar, Liu, and Rouskas (2010, 2011) built on a formulation based on Maximal Independent Sets (MIS), which is independent of the number of wavelengths and does not have the drawbacks of the link or path based ILP formulations. Their approach is to further decompose the set of paths into sets that do not overlap to overcome the exponential growth in the number of variables as the network size increases. Specifically, a new ILP formulation is designed based on the idea of partitioning the path set and representing the MIS in the original network using the independent path sets calculated in each of these partitions. The decomposition can be recursively conducted on the partitions and is exact, which allows trading off the number of variables with the number of constraints. As a result, the new approach achieves a much better scalability in terms of network size and is agnostic to the number of wavelengths. The resulting approach has been shown to be extremely fast (with orders of magnitude of reduction in computational time) and is able to solve ring RWA problems of practical size to obtain the optimal solutions in a few seconds.

This promising new technique needs to be explored and extended to develop efficient MIS decomposition techniques in combination with approaches such as column generation (Jaumard, Meyer, & Thiongane, 2009) to come up with MIS based ILP formulations that can also efficiently and optimally solve the RWA problem in general mesh networks, and once the RWA problem can be solved efficiently with optimal solutions, other important network design problems including dynamic RWA problem, traffic grooming, protection and restoration, multicast, RSA problems in SLICE networks can be further investigated with potentially more efficient optimal solutions approaches.

CONCLUSION

Many optical network design problems can be formulated as sophisticated optimization problems, including (1) Routing and Wavelength Assignment (RWA) and virtual topology design problem, (2) a suite of network design problems (such as variants of traffic grooming, survivability, and impairment-aware routing), (3) various design problems aimed at reducing the overall energy consumption of optical networks for green communication, (4) various design optimization problems in SLICE networks that employ OFDM technologies. This book chapter covers numerous optical network design optimization problems and solution approaches in detail, and presents some recent developments and future research directions

REFERENCES

Anderson, T., Peterson, L., Shenker, S., & Turner, J. (2005). Overcoming the internet impasse through virtualization. *Computer*, *38*(4), 34–41. doi:10.1109/MC.2005.136.

Antonakopoulos, S., & Zhang, L. (2009). Approximation algorithms for grooming in optical network design. In *Proceedings of IEEE INFOCOM*. IEEE.

Baliga, J., Ayre, R., Hinton, K., Sorin, W. V., & Tucker, S. (2009). Energy consumption in optical IP networks. *Journal of Lightwave Technology*, *27*(13), 2391–2403. doi:10.1109/JLT.2008.2010142.

Chabarek, J., Sommers, J., Barford, P., Estan, C., Tsang, D., & Wright, S. (2008). Power awareness in network design and routing. In *Proceedings of IEEE INFOCOM* (pp. 457–465). IEEE. doi:10.1109/INFOCOM.2008.93.

Charbonneau, N., & Vokkarane, V. M. (2010). Routing and wavelength assignment of static manycast demands over all-optical wavelength-routed WDM networks. *IEEE/OSA Journal of Optical Communication and Networking, 2*(7), 427-440.

Chlamtac, I., Ganz, A., & Karmi, G. (1992). Lightpath communications: An approach to high bandwidth optical WANs. *IEEE Transactions on Communications, 40*(7), 1171–1182. doi:10.1109/26.153361.

Chowdhury, N., & Boutaba, R. (2009). Network virtualization: state of the art and research challenges. *IEEE Communications Magazine, 47*, 20–26. doi:10.1109/MCOM.2009.5183468.

Chowdhury, N., Rahman, M., & Boutaba, R. (2009). Virtual network embedding with coordinated node and link mapping. In *Proceedings of IEEE INFOCOM* (pp. 783–791). IEEE. doi:10.1109/INFCOM.2009.5061987.

Chowdhury, P., Tornatore, M., & Mukherjee, B. (2010). On the energy efficiency of mixed-line-rate networks. In *Proceedings of Optical Fiber Communication Conference*, (pp. 1-3). IEEE.

Chu, X., Li, B., & Zhang, Z. (2003). A dynamic RWA algorithm in a wavelength-routed all-optical network with wavelength converters. In *Proceedings of IEEE INFOCOM* (pp. 1795–1802). IEEE.

Dutta, R., Kamal, A. E., & Rouskas, G. N. (2008). *Traffic grooming for optical networks: Foundations, techniques and frontiers*. New York: Springer. doi:10.1007/978-0-387-74518-3.

Dutta, R., & Rouskas, G. N. (2000). A survey of virtual topology design algorithms for wavelength routed optical networks. *Optical Networks*, *1*(1), 73–89.

Dutta, R., & Rouskas, G. N. (2002). On optimal traffic grooming in WDM rings. *IEEE Journal on Selected Areas in Communications*, *20*(1), 110–121. doi:10.1109/49.974666.

Dutta, R., & Rouskas, G. N. (2002). Traffic grooming in WDM networks: Past and future. *IEEE Network*, *16*(6), 46–56. doi:10.1109/MNET.2002.1081765.

Geary, N., Antonopoulos, A., Drakospoulos, E., & O'Reilly, J. (2001). Analysis of optimization issues in multi-period DWDM network planning. In *Proceedings of IEEE INFOCOM*. IEEE.

Grover, W. D. (2003). *Mesh-based survivable transport networks*. Upper Saddle River, NJ: Prentice Hall.

Gupta, M., & Singh, S. (2003). Greening of the internet. In *Proceedings of SIGCOMM*, (pp. 19-26). ACM.

Huang, S., Dutta, R., & Rouskas, G. N. (2006). Traffic grooming in path, star, and tree networks: Complexity, bounds, and algorithms. *IEEE Journal on Selected Areas in Communications*, *24*(4), 66–82. doi:10.1109/JSAC.2006.1613773.

Idzikowski, F., Orlowski, S., Raack, C., Woesner, H., & Wolisz, A. (2010). Saving energy in IP-over-WDM networks by switching off line cards in low-demand scenarios. In Proceedings of Optical Network Design and Modeling (ONDM), (pp. 1-6). ONDM.

Jaekel, A. (2006). Lightpath scheduling and allocation under a flexible schedule traffic model. In *Proceedings of IEEE Globecom*. IEEE.

Jaekel, A., & Chen, Y. (2006). Routing and wavelength assignment for prioritized demand under a scheduled traffic model. In *Proceedings of Broadnets Workshop on Guaranteed Optical Service Provisioning*. IEEE.

Jaekel, A., & Chen, Y. (2007). Demand allocation without wavelength conversion under a sliding scheduled traffic model. In *Proceedings of IEEE Broadnets*. IEEE.

Jaumard, B., Meyer, C., & Thiongane, B. (2009). On column generation formulations for the RWA problem. *Discrete Applied Mathematics*, *157*(6), 1291–1308. doi:10.1016/j.dam.2008.08.033.

Jinno, M., Kozicki, B., Takara, H., Watanabe, A., Sone, Y., Tanaka, T., & Hirano, A. (2010). Distance-adaptive spectrum resource allocation in spectrum-sliced elastic optical path network. *IEEE Communications Magazine*, *48*, 138–145. doi:10.1109/MCOM.2010.5534599.

Jinno, M., Takara, H., & Kozicki, B. (2009). Filtering characteristics of highly-spectrum efficient spectrum-sliced elastic optical path (SLICE) network. In *Proceedings of OFC*. OFC.

Jinno, M., Takara, H., Kozicki, B., Tsukishima, Y., & Sone, Y. (2009). Spectrum-efficient and scalable elastic optical path network: Architecture, benefits, and enabling technologies. *IEEE Communications Magazine*, *47*, 66–73. doi:10.1109/MCOM.2009.5307468.

Kuri, J. (2003). *Optimization problems in WDM optical transport networks with scheduled lightpath demands.* (Unpublished Doctoral Dissertation). ENST Paris, Paris, France.

Kuri, J., Puech, N., Gagnaire, M., Dotaro, E., & Douville, R. (2003). Diverse routing of scheduled lightpath demands in an optical transport network. In *Proceedings of Fourth International Workshop on the Design of Reliable Communication Networks.* IEEE.

Kuri, J., Puech, N., Gagnaire, M., & Douville, R. (2003). A review of routing and wavelength assignment of scheduled lightpath demands. *IEEE Journal on Selected Areas in Communications, 21*(8), 1231–1240. doi:10.1109/JSAC.2003.816622.

Li, T., & Wang, B. (2005). On optimal survivability design in WDM optical networks under a scheduled traffic model. In *Proceedings of DRCN.* DRCN.

Li, T., Wang, B., Xin, C., & Zhang, X. (2005). On survivable service provisioning in WDM optical networks under a scheduled traffic model. In *Proceedings of IEEE Globecom.* IEEE.

Li, X., Chakravarthy, V., Wang, B., & Wu, Z. (2011). *Spreading code design of adaptive non-contiguous SOFDM for cognitive radio and dynamic spectrum access.* IEEE Journal of Selected Topics in Signal Processing.

Mehrotra, A., & Trick, M. A. (1996). A column generation approach for graph coloring. *INFORMS Journal on Computing, 8*(4), 344–354. doi:10.1287/ijoc.8.4.344.

Mohan, G., & Murthy, C. S. R. (2000). Lightpath restoration in WDM optical networks. *IEEE Network, 14*(6), 24–32. doi:10.1109/65.885667.

Ramaswami, R., & Sivarajan, K. N. (1995). Routing and wavelength assignment in all-optical networks. *IEEE/ACM Transactions on Networking, 3*(5), 489–500. doi:10.1109/90.469957.

Ramaswami, R., & Sivarajan, K. N. (2002). *Optical networks: A practical perspective* (2nd ed.). San Francisco: Morgan Kaufmann Publisher.

Rouskas, G. N. (2003, January/February). Optical layer multicast: Rationale, building blocks, and challenges. *IEEE Network*, 60–65. doi:10.1109/MNET.2003.1174179.

Saradhi, C. V., & Gurusamy, M. (2007). Scheduling and routing of sliding scheduled lightpath demands in WDM optical networks. In *Proceedings of OFC.* OFC.

Saradhi, C. V., Wei, L. K., & Gurusamy, M. (2004). Provisioning fault-tolerant scheduled lightpath demands in WDM mesh networks. In *Proceedings of Broadnets* (pp. 150–159). IEEE. doi:10.1109/BROADNETS.2004.70.

Shen, G., & Tucker, R. S. (2009). Energy-minimized design for IP over WDM networks. *Journal of Optical Communications and Networking, 1*(1), 176–186. doi:10.1364/JOCN.1.000176.

Sone, Y., Watanabe, A., Imajuku, W., Tsukishima, Y., Kozicki, B., Takara, H., & Jinno, M. (2009). Highly survivable restoration scheme employing optical bandwidth squeezing in spectrum-sliced elastic optical path (SLICE) network. In *Proceedings of OFC.* OFC.

Stern, T. E., Ellinas, G., & Bala, K. (2009). *Multiwavelength optical networks: Architectures, design, and control.* Cambridge, UK: Cambridge University Press. doi:10.1017/CBO9780511811708.

Takara, H., Kozicki, B., Sone, Y., Tanaka, T., Watanabe, A., Hirano, A., et al. (2010). Distance-adaptive super-wavelength routing in elastic optical path network (SLICE) with optical OFDM. In *Proceedings of ECOC.* ECOC.

Tornatore, M., Baruffaldi, A., Zhu, H., Mukherjee, B., & Pattavina, A. (2007). Dynamic traffic grooming of sub-wavelength connectios with known duration. In *Proceedings of OFC*. OFC.

Tornatore, M., Pattavina, A., Zhang, J., Mukherjee, B., & Ou, C. (2005). Efficient shared-path protection exploiting the knowledge of connection-holding time. In *Proceedings of OFC*. OFC.

Wang, B., & Li, T. (2006). Approximating optimal survivable scheduled service provisioning in WDM optical network with iterative survivable routing. In *Proceedings of IEEE Broadnets*. IEEE.

Wang, B., Li, T., Luo, X., & Fan, Y. (2004). Traffic grooming under a sliding scheduled traffic model in WDM optical networks. In *Proceedings of IEEE Workshop on Traffic Grooming*. IEEE.

Wang, B., Li, T., Luo, X., Fan, Y., & Xin, C. (2005). On service provisioning under a scheduled traffic model in reconfigurable WDM optical networks. In *Proceedings of IEEE Broadnets*, (pp. 15-24). IEEE.

Wang, Y., Cao, X., & Pan, Y. (2011). A study on the routing and spectrum allocation in SLICE networks. In *Proceedings of IEEE INFOCOM*. IEEE.

Wu, Y., Chiaraviglio, L., Mellia, M., & Neri, F. (2009). Power-aware routing and wavelength assignment in optical networks. In *Proceedings of the 35th European Conference on Optical Communication*, (pp. 1-2). IEEE.

Wu, Z., Ratazzi, P., Chakravarthy, V., & Hong, L. (2008). Performance evaluation of adaptive non-contiguous MC-CDMA and non-contiguous CI/MC-CDMA for dynamic spectrum access. In *Proceedings of 3rd International Conference on Cognitive Radio Oriented Wireless Networks and Communications*. IEEE.

Xin, C., Wang, B., Cao, X., & Li, J. (2006). Logical topology design for dynamic traffic grooming in mesh WDM optical networks. *IEEE/OSA. Journal of Lightwave Technology*, 24(6), 2267–2275. doi:10.1109/JLT.2006.874562.

Yetginer, E., Liu, Z., & Rouskas, G. N. (2010). RWA in WDM rings: An efficient formulation based on maximal independent set decomposition. In *Proceedings of IEEE LANMAN*. IEEE.

Yetginer, E., Liu, Z., & Rouskas, G. N. (2011). Fast exact ILP decompositions for ring RWA. *Journal of Optical Communications and Networking*, 3(7). doi:10.1364/JOCN.3.000577.

Yu, H., Anand, V., Qiao, C., & Sun, G. (2011). Enhancing virtual infrastructure to survive facility node failures. In *Proceedings of OFC*, (pp. 1-3). OFC.

Yu, H., Qiao, C., Anand, V., Liu, X., Di, H., & Sun, G. (2010). Survivable virtual infrastructure mapping in a federated computing and networking system under single regional failures. In *Proceedings of IEEE Globecom*, (pp. 1-6). IEEE.

Zang, H., Jue, J. P., & Mukherjee, B. (2000). A review of routing and wavelength assignment approaches for wavelength-routed optical WDM networks. *Optical Networks*, 1(1), 47–60.

Zhang, Y., Chowdhury, P., Tornatore, M., & Mukherjee, B. (2010, July). Energy efficiency in telecom optical networks. *IEEE Communications Surveys and Tutorials*.

Zhou, D., & Subrammaniam, S. (2000). Survivability in optical networks. *IEEE Network*, 14(6), 16–23. doi:10.1109/65.885666.

Zhou, R., Li, X., Wu, Z., Chakravarthy, V., & Li, H. (2010). The demonstration of SMSE based cognitive radio in mobile environment via software defined radio. In *Proceedings of IEEE Globecom Demo Session*. IEEE.

ADDITIONAL READING

Bouillet, E., Mishra, P., Labourdette, J. F., Perlove, K., & French, S. (2002). Lightpath re-optimization in mesh optical networks. In *Proceedings of NOC*. NOC.

Bronand, C., & Kerbosch, J. (1973). Algorithm 457: Finding all cliques of an undirected graph. *Communications of the ACM*, *16*(7), 1081–1096.

Cao, X., Anand, V., & Qiao, C. (2006). A framework for waveband switching in multi-granular optical networks – Part I. *Journal of Optical Networking*, *5*(12), 1043–1055. doi:10.1364/JON.5.001043.

Cao, X., Anand, V., & Qiao, C. (2007). A framework for waveband switching in multi-granular optical networks – Part II. *Journal of Optical Networking*, *6*(1), 48–62. doi:10.1364/JON.6.000048.

Chen, Y., Qiao, C., & Yu, X. (2004). Optical burst switching (OBS): A new area in optical networking research. *IEEE Network Magazine*, *18*(3), 16–23. doi:10.1109/MNET.2004.1301018.

Gori, M., Maggini, M., & Sarti, L. (2005). Exact and approximate graph matching using random walks. *IEEE Transactions on Pattern Analysis and Machine Intelligence*, *27*, 1100–1111. doi:10.1109/TPAMI.2005.138 PMID:16013757.

Gumaste, A., & Chlamtac, I. (2004). Light-trails: An optical solution for IP transport. *Journal of Optical Networking*, *3*(4).

Hindam, T. (2009). Solving the routing and wavelength assignment problem in WDM networks for future planning. *IEEE Communications Magazine*, *47*(8), 35–41. doi:10.1109/MCOM.2009.5181890.

Karasan, E., & Ayanoglu, E. (1998). Effects of wavelength routing and selection algorithms on wavelength conversion gain in WDM optical networks. *IEEE/ACM Transactions on Networking*, *6*(2), 186–196. doi:10.1109/90.664267.

Krishnaswamy, R. M., & Sivarajan, K. N. (2001). Algorithms for routing and wavelength assignment based on solutions of LP-relaxations. *IEEE Communications Letters*, *5*(10), 435–437. doi:10.1109/4234.957386.

Lee, T., Lee, K., & Park, S. (2000). Optimal routing and wavelength assignment in WDM ring networks. *IEEE Journal on Selected Areas in Communications*, *18*(10), 2146–2154. doi:10.1109/49.887934.

Ramamurthy, S., & Mukherjee, B. (1999). Survivable WDM mesh networks, part I – Protection. In *Proceedings of INFOCOM*, (pp. 744-751). IEEE.

Simmons, J. M. (2008). *Optical network design and planning*. Berlin: Springer.

Yetginer, E., & Rouskas, G. N. (2009). Power efficient traffic grooming in optical WDM networks. In *Proceedings of IEEE Globecom*. IEEE.

Chapter 2
FiWi Networks

Mina Taheri
New Jersey Institute of Technology, USA

Nirwan Ansari
New Jersey Institute of Technology, USA

ABSTRACT

Optical access network is a promising solution to meet the ever-increasing demand for broadband services. Fiber-based technologies such as Fiber To The Home (FTTH), Fiber To The Building (FTTB), and Fiber To The Curb (FTTC) are well suited to support high bandwidth services and mitigate bandwidth bottlenecks. However, implementing optical fiber to all end points imposes considerable CAPEX. Moreover, fiber cannot directly reach mobile users and devices. Although untethered features of wireless networks are attractive, their limited supported bandwidth cannot answer today's enormous demands. Combining complementary features of these two technologies for broadband access is imminent and meritorious. Thus, integrated Fiber-Wireless (FiWi) access networks are considered as a scalable and economical means for broadband access. In FiWi, end points receive services through a wireless subnetwork, which acts as the front end and is connected to the optical subnetwork, which serves as the back end via gateway nodes.

INTRODUCTION

Owing to enormous increase in the bandwidth demand for telecommunication services, wireless and copper technologies can not completely meet this challenge. Copper access networks can provide around 50 Mb/s for each user in a short loop length. Increasing the copper length attenuates the provisioned bandwidth rapidly, and could easily limit the bandwidth to 10 Mb/s or less. Hence, noise and signal interference in copper is the major culprit in provisioning high bandwidth for such an access network. On the other hand, wireless technologies such as WiFi and WiMAX can provide users with almost ubiquitous connectivity. WiFi networks can provide local access up to a few hundred feet at a rate of up to 50 Mb/s while a WiMAX antenna can support up to 30 miles at a rate of 70 Mb/s. Essentially, wireless technology does not scale up well in terms of provisioned bandwidth. So far, the best solution for access is fiber (Effenberger, 2007). Although optical fiber cannot

DOI: 10.4018/978-1-4666-3652-1.ch002

reach everywhere, it can provide a large amount of accessible bandwidth. On the other hand, wireless access networks can reach almost anywhere, but with a limited amount of bandwidth. Combining the advantages of these two access networks is a no-brainer to provision tethered Internet access. Thus, Fiber-wireless (FiWi) access networks have been proposed to provision the high capacity of fiber networks along with the mobility of wireless networks into one single infrastructure. FiWi networks hold great promise to change the way we live and work by replacing commuting with teleworking, and thus protect our environment by reducing the carbon footprint of commuting. In this chapter, the distinct and unique characteristics of FiWi broadband networks will be presented.

The rest of the chapter is organized as follows. We will next provide an overview of optical and wireless enabling technologies and introduces related traffic based classes and traffic scheduling. We will then present several architectures that can be used to support the integration of optical and wireless networks. Quality of Service (QoS) provisioning techniques for FiWi networks including integrated path selections, bandwidth allocation, mapping techniques and handover, which supports user mobility, will be discussed next. We will also evaluate energy efficiency of each network as ICT carbon footprints are becoming a serious concern. Methods for greening FiWi networks will also be discussed in this chapter. Then, we elaborate on future research challenges of FiWi networks. Finally, concluding remarks are provided.

BACKGROUND

Merging high capacity of optical fiber networks with the mobility of wireless networks creates a promising technology to support existing and emerging bandwidth hungry services. In this section, enabling technologies of wireless and optical access networks are briefly reviewed.

Wireless Mesh Networks

Wireless Mesh NETWORKS (WMNs) forward traffic to and from wired entry points by using multi hop communications (Bruno, Conti, & Gregori, 2005). These networks can easily, effectively and wirelessly connect entire cities using inexpensive existing technologies. Contrary to WLANS and Mobiles and Adhoc Networks (MANETs), WMNs provide greater flexibility, effective connectivity, and increased flexibility because they can facilitate efficient routing through the mesh that can react dynamically to changes in the topology.

WMNs are categorized into three groups (Akyildiz, Wang, & Wang 2005): infrastructure, client, and hybrid (Figure 1). In an infrastructure WMN, mesh routers form an infrastructure for clients. In a client WMN, client nodes constitute the actual network to perform routing and configuration functionalities. In hybrid WMN, mesh clients can perform mesh functions with other mesh clients as well as accessing the network.

It is worth emphasizing that WMNs can exploit adhoc routing protocols such as AODV (adhoc on-demand distance vector) and DSR (dynamic source routing) because WMNs and MANETs share some commonalities.

Several technologies and routing protocols have been employed to optimize the performance of WMNs. For instance, in the physical layer, in addition to smart antenna, MIMO (Multiple-Input Multiple-Output) and UWB (Ultra Wideband) systems are used to increase the capacity of networks. Besides, wireless gigabit transmission is enabled by synergizing MIMO and OFDM (orthogonal frequency division multiplexing) technologies. On the other hand, bandwidth efficiency of CSMA/CA has been improved by adopting MAC protocols based upon TDMA and CDMA. Moreover, IEEE 802.11 (WiFi) technologies are widely used in commercial products due to their low cost, technological maturity, and high product penetration. However, these protocols are not optimized

Figure 1. Wireless mesh network: a) infrastructure mesh networks, b) client mesh networks, c) hybrid mesh networks

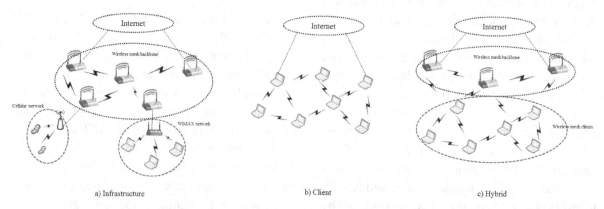

a) Infrastructure   b) Client   c) Hybrid

for WMNs as they are designed for WLANs. To overcome such issues, proprietary wireless technologies and WiMAX have been proposed while IEEE 802.16 is designed for point-to-multipoint wireless transmission.

WMN Class-Based Traffic

Five different classes of service are defined in IEEE 802.16 WiMAX (Kuran, & Tugcu, 2007): Unsolicited Grant Service (UGS), real time Polling Service (rtPS), extended real time Polling Service (ertPS), non-real time Polling Service (nrtPS), and Best Effort (BE). UGS is tailored for real time services with strict delay requirements that generate fixed length packets on periodic intervals. Voice Over IP (VOIP) and T1/E1 voice service employ UGS services. Real time data traffic with variable length packets generated on a periodic basis, such as video, is carried by the rtPS class of service. Minimum reserved traffic rate and maximum delay are two main QoS parameters of this service type. ertPS employsa scheduling mechanism based on the efficiency of both UGS and rtPS. ertPS is designed for real time traffic with variable data rate (such as VOIP service with silence suppression) over the WiMAX network. nrtPS is intended to support delay-tolerant data

streams comprising variable-sized data packets for which a minimum data rate is required. FTP with guaranteed minimum throughput is the typical application of nrtPS service. BE is associated with other services which do not require QoS support.

Optical Access Networks

The most pronouncing advantage of optical fiber is its huge bandwidth potential in comparison to other wireless and wired media. Moreover, optical networks are important due to their low complexity and power consumption. Passive Optical Network (PON) uses a point to multipoint network architecture which reduces the required amount of fiber and central office equipment in comparison with point to point architectures.

FTTX is a generic term for any broadband network architecture using optical fiber to replace all or part of the usual metal local loop used for last mile telecommunications (Hutcheson, 2008). The generic term was initially a generalization for several configurations of fiber deployment (FTTN, FTTC, FTTB, FTTH, etc.), all starting with FTT but differentiated by the last letter, which is substituted by an "X" in the generalization. The central goal of FTTX PLAN is to support the strategic decision process of city carriers and new local operators by performing an objective analysis that considers the varying, but always case-dependent boundary conditions where the "X" ends.

The FTTX approach reduces planning uncertainties, supports a more realistic forecast of costs, and also detects potential technological dead-ends early in the design process. Specifically operators of future FTTX networks for city environments and small regions will benefit from these flexible analyses. To advance a positive business case, the techno-economic dependencies between the total cost of ownership and technical possibilities of the available system technologies need to be well understood. A thorough understanding of photonic technology trends and limitations matched with sophisticated optimization techniques canned in computer-based methods and tools provides a key benefit for network planners of future FTTX networks.

Ethernet Passive Optical Network (EPON)

Ethernet in the First Mile is a standard ratified by IEEE to extend the existing Ethernet technology into the subscriber access area (Kramer, 2005). The key objective of the study was to provide a high performance network with traditional Ethernet while minimizing the deployment, maintenance and operation costs. Ethernet PON is a PON based network using Ethernet frames for encapsulating the data packets as defined in the IEEE 802.3 standard. The standard Ethernet speed is 1 Gb/s in EPON and uses the standard 8b/10b line coding in which 8 bit data are coded to 10 line bits. EPON is applicable for all the data-centric networks and full-service voice, data and video networks.

EPON Class-Based Traffic

In order to support various application requirements, all the incoming traffic to each network and particularly in EPON should be segregated into a limited number of classes to provide differentiated

service (Diffserv) for each class. Below are the supported traffic classifications by IEEE 802.1D (Kramer, Mukherjee, Dixit, Ye, & Hirth, 2002):

1. **Network Control:** Characterized by a "must get there" requirement to maintain and support the network infrastructure.
2. **Voice:** Services with less than 10-ms delay and maximum jitter.
3. **Video:** Services with less than 100-ms delay.
4. **Controlled Load:** Important business applications subject to some form of "admission control". That is, two extremes are to be considered; preplanning of network requirements and bandwidth reservation per flow (when flow is started).
5. **Excellent Effort:** Also known as "CEO's best effort" refers to the best-effort-type services that an information services association distributes to its most important customers.
6. **Best Effort:** No QoS guarantee is needed.
7. **Background:** Bulk transfers and other activities allowed in the network should not affect the use of the network by other users and applications.

Upon receiving a packet, each ONU places it in the appropriate queue based on its classification type. EPON services are classified into three priorities as described in (Kramer 2005): best effort (BE), assured forwarding (AF), and expedited forwarding (EF). Delay sensitive services such as voice which requires bounded delay and jitter are considered as EF services. AF services require bandwidth guarantee instead of bounded delay. BE service such as Email service does not require any warranty for either bandwidth or delay.

EPON Scheduling

As mentioned in the previous section, different classes of services with different quality of service requirements are stored in different priority queues at each ONU. Two scheduling methods are performed to support QoS in EPON: intra-ONU scheduling and inter-ONU scheduling. The former is responsible for arbitrating the transmission of different priority queues in each ONU while the latter is responsible for arbitrating the transmission of different ONUs. Direct scheduling and hierarchical scheduling are two strategies proposed to implement the abovementioned scheduling paradigms (Zheng & Mouftah, 2005).

In direct (single level) scheduling, the scheduler located in the OLT receives information from ONUs and schedules each queue located in ONUs. Hence, the central scheduler can allocate the bandwidth fairly among the queues. Every GATE message sent to ONUs consists of several grants, each specifying the amount of time for a specific class of service allowed for a queue. Assigning a separate logical link to each queue simplifies the implementation of direct scheduling. Therefore, OLT will receive a distinct REPORT message form each unique logical link identifier (LLID) indicating just one queue.

In hierarchical (multi-level) scheduling, each ONU can execute intra-ONU scheduling while OLT executes inter-ONU scheduling. Based on the buffer occupancy, each ONU requests dedicated bandwidth from OLT. After receiving the grant from OLT, allocated bandwidth is divided among different service classes based on QoS requirements. Higher priority traffic is transmitted first in the allocated transmission window, and the remaining time is assigned to lower priority traffic. Hierarchical scheduling is scalable with the number of queues as each ONU sends one single REPORT message and receives a single GATE message to and from OLT, respectively.

Class-Based Bandwidth Allocation in EPON

As the upstream channel of EPON is shared among end users, an efficient medium access control is required to statistically multiplex multiple services from various types of traffic. Luo

and Ansari (2005) provided an overview of the upstream bandwidth allocation for multiservice access over EPON. Owing to Multipoint Control Protocol (MPCP) and bursty traffic prediction, they also proposed a Dynamic Bandwidth Allocation (DBA) scheme to provision QoS guarantees (Luo & Ansari 2005). Multiservice access for different end users is realized by means of class-based traffic estimation.

Class based bandwidth allocation is the most important factor in affecting QoS provisioning of intra ONU scheduling. OLT collects the REPORT messages from all ONUs and then decides the bandwidth allocation. Considering three aforesaid EPON classes of service, OLT first assigns fixed bandwidth to EF traffic. The remaining bandwidth is allocated to AF requests, and the unused bandwidth after serving EF and AF is then disseminated among BE requests. In strict priority scheduling, the high priority traffic arriving during a waiting period will be scheduled ahead of the reported lower priority traffic. Therefore, employing fixed bandwidth allocation increases frame delay for AF and BE traffic since the allocated bandwidth is mostly used for EF traffic. The aforementioned problem is called the light load penalty which can be solved by two strategies proposed in (Assi, Ye, Dixit, & Ali 2003).

The first tactic uses two-stage buffers. A priority queue and a first in first out (FIFO) queue inform the first and second stage, respectively. Transmitting traffic from the ONU side at the allocated transmission window starts from the second stage while the first stage forwards traffic to the second one in a priority order. At the end of the time slot, ONU sends a REPORT message to the OLT based on the current occupancy of its second stage buffer. This approach mitigates the light load penalty problem at the sacrifice of the increase in delay for higher priority traffic (i.e., EF traffic).

The second tactic is called the credit-based slot sizing that requires some prediction methods (Chao, &Liao, 2003). Each ONU knows how much data will arrive in the next specific interval, and the size of the granted slot will be increased by the amount of anticipated additional data. It should be noted that the anticipation is done for constant bit rate (CBR) flows (e.g., EF traffic).

Research by Zhang and Ansari (2010) supports the fairness in bandwidth allocation among applications with different QoS requirements in EPON. The aforementioned differentiated service provisions some queues with higher QoS over others. However, Diffserv can hardly meet any specific QoS requirements imposed by diversified applications in EPON. The authors defined application utilities to quantify users' quality of experience (QoE) as a function of network layer QoS metrics. The fair resource allocation issue is formulated as a utility max-min optimization problem and the optimal value can be achieved by proper bandwidth allocation and queue management.

Resilient Packet Ring (RPR)

A new packet switched ring based architecture called Resilient Packet Ring (RPR) is standardized by IEEE as IEEE 802.17 (Davik, Yilmaz, Gjessing, & Uzun, 2004). It consists of RPR nodes and two counter rotating rings (called ringlet 0 and ringlet 1 in RPR). After receiving a frame by an RPR node located on the ring, the destination address of the frame header will be checked; if the address is not designated to the node, the received frame is forwarded to the next node. Many SONET rings consist of a dual-ring configuration in which one of the rings is implemented as the backup ring, and remains unused in the normal operation, exploited only in the case of failure of the primary ring. RPR inherits the advantages of SONET/SDH rings; unlike SONET rings, the two counter rotating rings in RPR are used for data transmission, thus resulting in much better utilization.

In RPR, each destination node removes frames from the ring, and nodes can concurrently communicate with each other on different ring segments. As a result, the spatial reuse feature is attained.

The main performance objectives of RPR are to achieve high bandwidth utilization, optimum spatial reuse on the dual ring, and fairness. Al-harbi and Ansari (2005) proposed a distributed bandwidth allocation to allocate bandwidth fairly in RPR nodes. .

RPR Class-Based Traffic

RPR provides a three-level class-based traffic priority scheme (Davik *et al.* 2004). Classes requiring low latency and low jittery are considered as high priority services and placed in class A (e.g., voice). Services with predictable latency and jitter (e.g., video) assume medium priority and are considered as class B traffic. The low priority and best effort transport class is known as class C traffic (e.g., Web browsing). Two subclasses are defined for classes A and B; class A is divided into A0 and A1 and class B traffic is divided into classes B-CIR (committed information rate) and B-EIR (Excess information rate). In order to fulfill the service guarantees for class A0, A1 and B-CIR traffic, bandwidth has to be pre-allocated for these traffic classes. Pre-allocated bandwidth for class A0 traffic is called reserved, and each RPR node should make a reservation based on the estimated amount of bandwidth from topology discovery protocol which discovers the initial topology of RPR stations and any changes to that topology. Unused reserved bandwidth that cannot be reclaimed by other nodes is wasted. Pre-allocated bandwidth for class A1 and B-CIR is reclaimable. Bandwidth which is not pre-allocated and unused reclaimable bandwidth can be assigned for class C and B-EIR. The latter classes are called fairness eligible (FE) and their related traffic is controlled by the fairness algorithm.

RPR Scheduling

There are two transit queues in each RPR station. A Primary Transit Queue (PTQ) is mandatory and buffers traffic class A while a Secondary Transit Queue (STQ) is optional and stores in transit traffic of classes B and C. The primary queue has higher priority than the secondary queue. In the absence of packets in PTQ, local traffic is served until the length of stored packets in STQ reaches a specific threshold. Once the threshold is met, STQ starts transferring data. Deploying this mechanism avoids in-transit packets from being dropped due to buffer overflow by midway nodes. Using per class queue scheme causes head-of-line blocking problem. Optionally, the MAC may implement Virtual Destination Queues (VDQs) to reclaim the unused bandwidth and avoid head-of-line blocking probability (Alharbi & Ansari, 2006).

Data traffic from class A is subject to the propagation delay and, rarely, queuing delay related to local packet transmission. As noted earlier, RPR stations do not have the permission to use reserved or reclaimed bandwidth for FE classes. Therefore, data traffic from FE classes experiences high delay when the ring is congested.

FIWI NETWORKS

Two types of FiWi technologies have been studied for many years: Optical Wireless (OW) and Radio Over Fiber (ROF). The former provides end to end communications by modulating infrared or visible beams. Reliability in short range communications and high bandwidth provisioning are two significant characteristics of this type of Line-Of-Sight (LOS) optical communications. Depending on weather conditions, the transmission rate in the full duplex mode covering distances of several kilometers could range from 100 mb/s to 2 Gb/s.

In RoF, a modulated light is transmitted over an analog optical link to facilitate wireless access. Depending on the frequency range of radio signals, two main approaches are considered for RoF systems (Ghazisaidi & Maier 2011):

1. Radio Frequency (RF) over Fiber architecture in which a high radio frequency signal is used for modulating signals before transmitting

over a fiber link. Thus, the wireless signal is distributed directly at high frequencies. There is no need to convert upstream or downstream frequency, thus facilitating cost effective implementation at base stations.

2. IF over fiber architecture in which an IF (intermediate frequency) radio signal with lower frequency is carried on a lightwave signal over the optical link. Hence, the signal should be converted to RF signal at base stations before radiating through the air.

FIWI ARCHITECTURE

In integrated fiber-wireless networks, each gateway is connected to the optical backhaul and creates point to multi-point connection. High scalability and cost effectiveness are two significant characteristics of these kinds of networks. Shaw *et al.* (2007) proposed the hybrid optical wireless access network architecture in which several tree networks are rooted to the ring optical backhaul. Under the proposed architecture shown in Figure 2, the upstream traffic is aggregated at the nearby router and then forwarded to one of the gateway routers. Packets of the downstream traffic are routed to a gateway and then forwarded to the specific router. In Figure 2, for example, the upstream packets are aggregated at router A and then forwarded to routers B and C to reach gateway 1. On the other hand, the downstream traffic are first transmitted to gateway 3 and then forwarded through routers F and A to reach the destination. The routes for upstream and downstream packets are calculated based on the real time situation of the network. Several integrated routing algorithms will be introduced later.

The proposed FiWi architecture combines TDM-PON and WDM-PON for the optical backhaul. Several TDM-PONs are multiplexed by dense wavelength division multiplexing (DWDM). Figure 3 shows the FiWi distribution network. Here, four router gateways are controlled by PON1

Figure 2. Hybrid optical wireless access network architecture

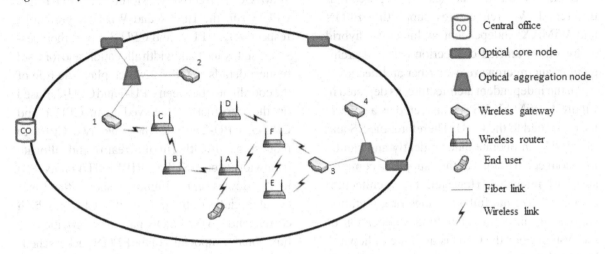

Figure 3. Distribution network and interface between the optical backhaul and WMN

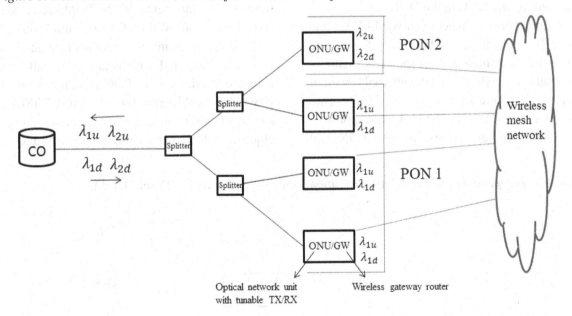

and PON2. The wavelengths of the downstream signals for PON1 and PON2 are denoted as , respectively, while represent the wavelengths of the upstream signals. In this architecture, the backhaul uses Ethernet PON technology, and WiFi technology is deployed to constitute the wireless mesh network. Interoperability between ONU and gateway routers could be facilitated at the network layer by using an IP router or at the data link layer using integrated circuit designed to interpret the format for incompatible packet types. In the proposed network, some PONs may be heavily loaded. In such a situation, some of the ONUs can be deregistered from heavily loaded PONs and reregistered to lightly PONs via multipoint control protocol data unit messages. The proposed architecture aims to achieve the load balance at ONUs and to maximize the network throughput.

Shen, Tucker, and Chae (2007) proposed four different FiWi architectures supporting EPON and WiMAX: independent architecture, hybrid architecture, unified connection-oriented architecture, and microwave-over-fiber architecture.

In the independent architecture, as depicted in Figure 4, WiMAX BS is considered as a generic user attached to the ONU. Therefore, the BS and the ONU can operate independently and can be interconnected as long as they support a common standard interface. However, the architecture does not make the full advantage of integration specifically in optimal bandwidth allocation of the system since the ONU is unaware of how the WiMAX BS schedules the packets and the BS does not know the scheduling of the upstream data sent by the ONU to the OLT.

In the hybrid architecture, a WiMAX BS and an ONU are integrated (both in software and hardware) in a single box, as shown in Figure 4, referred to as ONU-BS and the internal key functional modules are depicted in Figure 5. There are three CPUs; CPU-1 and CPU-3 are responsible for data communications in the EPON and

WiMAX, respectively. Moreover, CPU-1 and CPU-3 run the EPON and WiMAX protocols, respectively. CPU-1 and CPU-3 report their sessions' states and bandwidth allocation, and forward request details to CPU-2 which plays the role of the coordinator between CPU-1 and CPU-3. Based on the information received from CPU-1 and CPU-3, CPU-2 guides the other two CPUs to request bandwidth (in upstream) and allocate bandwidth to each SUBSCRIBER STATION (SS) in the downstream. Figure 5 shows the functional modules of the three CPUs. CPU-1, which corresponds to the EPON part only, provides the functional components of the EPON packet scheduler, priority queues, and the EPON packet classifier. On the other hand, CPU-3 provides the functional components of the WiMAX packet reconstructor and WiMAX upstream scheduler.

Before getting into the details of the unified connection-oriented architecture, we shall first compare WiMAX and EPON from the point of view of bandwidth request and allocation. WiMAX adopts a connection-oriented transmission technique in which bandwidth requests and QoS

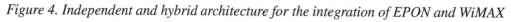

Figure 4. Independent and hybrid architecture for the integration of EPON and WiMAX

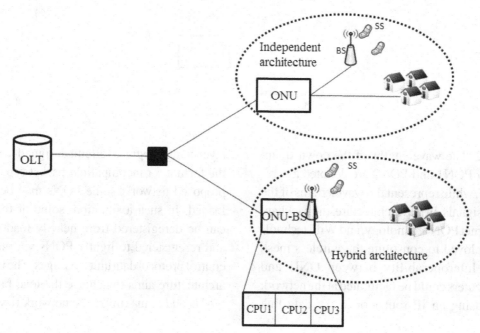

Figure 5. Functional modules of ONU-BS

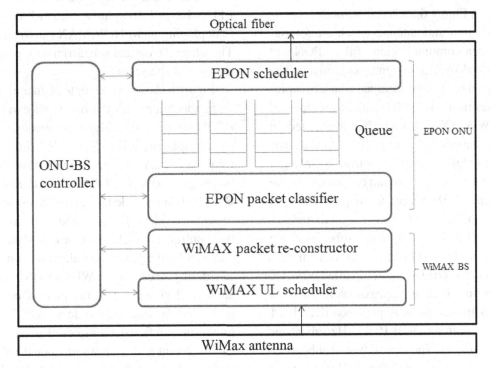

support are connection-oriented. In other words, an aggregate bandwidth is allocated to each SS based on the connection-oriented bandwidth requests. However, in EPON, bandwidth requests are queue-oriented in which an aggregate bandwidth is allocated for each ONU. Each ONU allocates the bandwidth for up to eight different priority queues in the ONU. The two aforementioned types of networks are similar in terms of bandwidth request and allocation. For the sake of comparison, EPON provides better scalability than WiMAX since each ONU has to manage only up to eight priority queues. On the other hand, WiMAX systems generally allocate bandwidth more finely than EPON systems do. Moreover, the connection-oriented bandwidth allocation can provide better QoS than queue-based bandwidth allocation. Consequently, WiMAX is expected to support QoS better than EPON. Based on the above discussion, medium access control (MAC) layer protocols of EPON should be modified to support connection-oriented services

like that of WiMAX. Shen *et al.* (2007) demonstrated the latter modification to enhance the integration. The resulting layout differs from the hybrid architecture in the sense that instead of transporting Ethernet frames in the downstream and upstream direction in EPON, the Ethernet frames are encapsulated as client data in the WiMAX MAC PDUs (Shen *et al.* 2007). Another approach is to adjust a WiMAX network to run the EPON MAC protocols such that all the WiMAX devices are operated under the Ethernet paradigm with unified Ethernet interfaces. However, inadequacies of this modification include: 1) less control of QoS for each service connection, and 2) a need for special extensions to handle coding and modulation of wireless signals (since wireless channels are usually more error prone than fiber media). Unfortunately, both of the above integration architectures are not standardized.

Microwave-over-Fiber Architecture: In order to better exploit the transmission capacity of fiber and reduce the cost of implementing WiMAX and EPON, microwave-over-fiber architecture is proposed. In Figure 6, each remote node consists of an ONU unit and antenna which are responsible for data communication of the EPON and relaying a WiMAX radio signal, respectively. The EPON signal is a baseband signal which occupies frequencies up to 1.25 GHz and is multiplexed with the WiMAX signal which is modulated on a wireless carrier frequency. These two signals are then modulated into an optical wavelength and transmitted to an upstream central node. The modulation of WiMAX carrier frequency over an optical frequency is referred to as Microwave-Over-Fiber (MOF). Two types of subcarriers are considered in this architecture. One is a wireless subcarrier in the WiMAX system, called WiMAX subcarrier, in which an approximately 10 MHz spectrum is divided into multiple subcarriers (1024 subcarriers) with a typical 10.94 kHz subcarrier frequency spacing. The second type of subcarrier is the optical subcarrier in the PON that carries WiMAX signals from an antenna to the central node. It can be easily seen that a WiMAX subcarrier is a subcarrier on an optical subcarrier. Optical subcarrier frequencies from different dumb antennas are chosen to be different in order to make them detectable at the central node. Thus, after each antenna, a frequency shifter is deployed to convert a WiMAX modulation frequency to a higher frequency before being modulated on an

optical frequency. For instance, assume that an EPON has a 1:16 splitter ratio (which is equal to deploying up to 16 WiMAX dumb antennas). Therefore, 16 optical subcarriers are required in the optical spectrum.

Figure 6 shows an example of an optical spectrum allocation with the baseband carrying the EPON signal, and 16 higher frequency subcarriers multiplexing WiMAX signals (with 750 MHz frequency spacing). The central node consists of two major modules, an OLT and a central WiMAX BS. The latter is called a macro-BS, consisting of multiple WiMAX BS units and a macro-BS central controller which processes all data packets and coordinates bandwidth allocation and packet scheduling for each of the WiMAX BS units. Once an optical signal enters the central node, it is converted into an electronic signal. The electronic signal is first demultiplexed into a baseband EPON signal and a group of optical subcarrier signals which are then forwarded to the OLT and WiMAX macro-BS, respectively. Macro-BS architecture benefits from the simplified handover operation for mobile users. However, since the macro-BS needs to handle all the packets received from a large number of SSs in the system, it is a potential bottleneck in the whole WiMAX network. In addition, nonlinearities occurred in practice present two challenging issues: crosstalk among the optical subcarriers modulating a com-

Figure 6. Microwave-over-fiber integration architecture for EPON and WiMAX

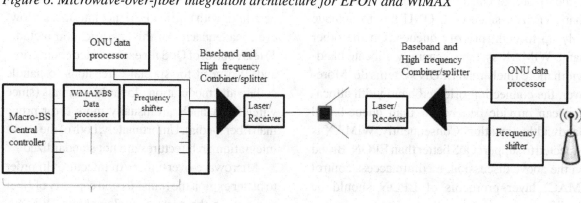

mon active semiconductor component at the central office, and optical beat interference (OBI) between upstream optical subcarrier signals. To overcome this problem, separate wavelengths may be required for each ONU, i.e., the next-generation PON systems (i.e., WDM PONs). WDM PON, which exploits the large capacity of optical fibers, is a promising next generation broadband optical access solution (Zhang, Ansari, Luo, Effenberger, & Ye, 2009).

Lin, Kao, and Chi (2003) proposed a two-level Bidirectional Path-Protected Ring (BPR) architecture for DWDM networks that incooperates the Subcarrier Multiplexing (SCM) technology, as shown in Figure 7, in which many Remote Nodes (RNs) are connected to the central office via a dual-fiber ring. Several Wireless Access Points (WAP), serving many Customer Units (CUs), are cascaded from an RN through Concentration Nodes (CNs). Each RN includes a protection unit, a Bidirectional Wavelength Add Multiplexer (BWAM), and a Bidirectional Wavelength Drop Multiplexer (BWDM), which are built based on dielectric interference filters. Each CN also has a protection unit. Two sets of devices in CO operate

at the two modes: normal and standby mode. In the normal state, downstream traffic is transmitted from CO to WAP through RN and CN in the clockwise direction. The WAP contains an optical transceiver, up/down RF converters, protection unit, and a sleeve antenna. Each WAP provides a 5 MHz channel bandwidth and covers up to 16 CUs by using frequency division multiplexing (FDM) for multiple access. Controllers at CO, RNs and CNs can detect the fiber cut between RNs or CNs by monitoring the received optical signals, and then switch to the other protection ring. If one of the WAPs fails, the retransmitted signals can go through the other optical path. High flexibility, reliability, capacity and self-healing are major characteristics of this architecture.

Bhandari and Park (2006) incorporated optical star and ring into their proposed architecture in which each sub ring is responsible for a small area and accommodates several WiFi-based WAPs. As depicted in Figure 8, each sub ring is connected to two other adjacent sub rings and central office by means of optical switches. The interconnection between WAPs and CO is facilitated by the optical switches which are capable of adapting

Figure 7. Optical fiber ring topology integrated with WiFi based wireless networks

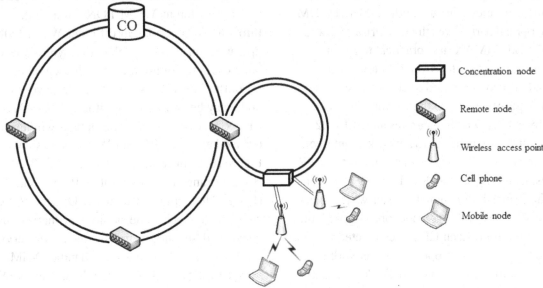

Figure 8. Star-ring optical network integrated with WiFi-based wireless access points

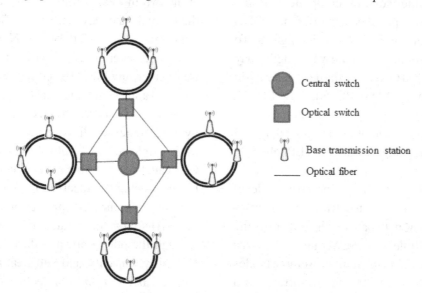

full wavelength. Network monitoring adjusts the proper traffic to the links. When traffic increases, load balancing increases the load of the established low utilization lightpaths. Otherwise, if the lightpaths are highly loaded, new lightpaths need to be established. In the case of a link failure, the affected fiber paths are reconfigured by the redundant paths of the architecture.

Maier, Ghazisaidi, and Reisslein (2008) proposed a FiWi architecture, referred to as Super-MAN, by using both WiFi and WiMAX technology in the wireless part and both TDM and WDM in the optical part. Given the similarities between EPON and WiMAX, it is practical to attain both system advantages to cover different segments instead of being cascaded to cover the same segment. Figure 9 illustrates the network architecture of SuperMAN, which integrates an IEEE 802.17 Resilient Packet Ring metro network by interconnecting WDM EPON networks to the set of RPR nodes. Demonstrated RPR in Figure 9 is an optical dual-fiber bidirectional ring in which every attached WDM PON has a tree topology with the OLT at the root. Each OLT is connected to one of the COs. A passive optical star network is responsible for connecting OLTs/Cos, and the

center hub in the star architecture includes a arrayed waveguide grating (AWG). Each OLT can schedule its transmission and reception to be done on any supported wavelength channel based on WDM extensions to the IEEE 802.3ah MPCP (McGarry, Maier, and Reisslein, 2006). As depicted in Figure 9, is the set of wavelengths used for upstream and downstream transmission between related ONUs and OLT in the same WDM PON. The other set of wavelengths is which facilitates communications between the ONUs located in different WDM PONs in a single hub through AWG. ONUs in different WDM PONs operating on these wavelengths bypass the related OLTs to communicate with each other.

In the SuperMAN infrastructure, every PRP node may be connected to either a WiMAX or a EPON access network. The optical-wireless interface between PRP and WiMAX is shown in Figure 10. Connecting an RPR node to a WiMAX BS is arranged by Integrated Rate Controller (IRC). The Optical-Electrical-Optical (OEO) converter at each node deploys primary transit queue and secondary transit queue for service differentiation. BS controller handles WiMAX related traffic and also arranges handover for SSs.

Figure 9. Super MAN architecture

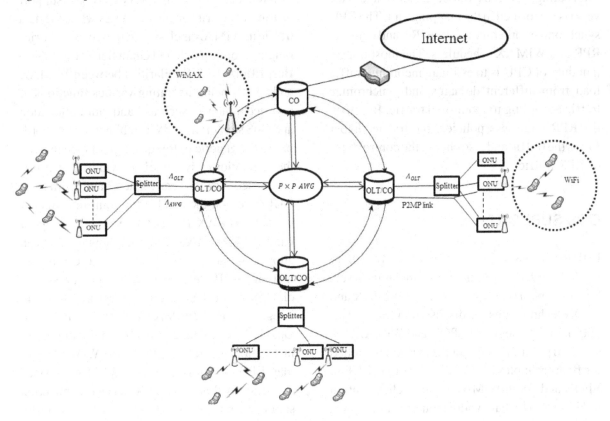

Figure 10. Optical-wireless interface between RPR and WiMAX networks

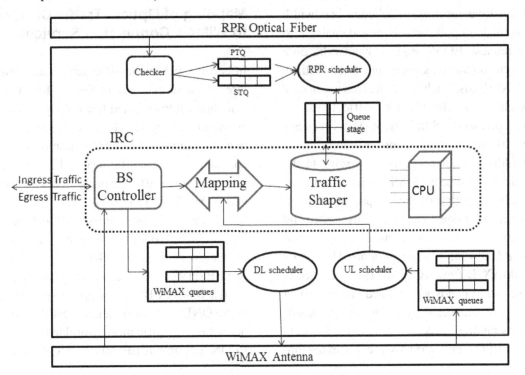

Translating WiMAX traffic to RPR and vice versa is performed in the mapping unit. The CPU synchronizes other units in the IRC and controls RPR and WiMAX schedulers. The most important duty of CPU is to estimate incoming traffic load from different domains and synchronize traffic according to monitored traffic. Based on the RPR's fairness policies, the traffic shaper forms the traffic and also checks the control rates of RPR traffic.

QOS SUPPORT

Efficiently assigning upstream bandwidth to users in FiWi networks is a challenging issue. Some issues arisen from integrated WiMAX and EPON technologies are discussed in (Shen *et al.* 2007). In the integrated EPON and WiMAX, the standard poll/request/grant mechanism is applied for both technologies. A server station (OLT in EPON and BS in WiMAX) polls a client station (ONU or SS) for bandwidth request. After reporting the requests for bandwidth from the client side, the server grants bandwidth. Provisioning delay sensitive services, unsolicited bandwidth grant is made to poll each client and enable it to send a request. EPON requests bandwidth on a per-priority queue basis, but assigns bandwidth on a per-ONU basis. Each ONU decides to allocate bandwidth and schedule for traffic transmission independently. Similarly, WiMAX requests bandwidth on a per-connection basis and allocate bandwidth on a per-SS basis. According to the granted bandwidth, each SS decides locally to allocate bandwidth and schedule packet transmission for each service connection. Unsolicited and upon request bandwidth grants are two types of bandwidth allocation modes supported by EPON and WiMAX. Different QoS level services such as delay sensitive, bandwidth granted, and best effort services are supported by these two aforementioned technologies. As mentioned earlier, data traffic in EPON and WiMAX is categorized into

different classifications. Every ONU can support up to eight priority queues in EPON while the data traffic in WiMAX is classified into five categories ranging from Unsolicited Grant Service (UGS) to Best Effort (BE). Similarities between WiMAX and EPON help integrating various functions of both technologies such as bandwidth allocation and QoS support into FiWi architectures. According to the generic poll/request/grant mechanism, the integration of dynamic bandwidth allocation is performed. An ONU can request bandwidth from OLT based on the bandwidth grant information in each WiMAX BS. After receiving the grant bandwidth, WiMAX BS knows how much it can allocate to each class of service and can assign them in an efficient manner. Detailed procedure of QoS aware bandwidth request and grant in integrated EPON/WiMAX is described in (Yang, Ou, Guild, & Chen, 2009). One of the important factors for integrating EPON and WiMAX is to map EPON priority queues to WiMAX service connections. Each WiMAX service connection should be mapped to one of the EPON priority queue with the equivalent service.

Mapping of Optical Traffic Classes to WiMAX Connection Services

In general, EPON classifies data traffic into differentiated services (DIFFServ) while WiMAX is a connection-oriented technology and follows an integrated service (IntServ) mode. An effective mapping mechanism is required to facilitate conversions between IntServ and DiffServ.

In the proposed traffic mapping between EPON and WiMAX in (Yang *et al.* 2009), five WiMAX service categories are condensed into three: UGS, rtPS and BE. From the prespective of bandwidth allocation, there is no difference between nrtPS and BE services. Hence, these two traffic packets from a WiMAX BS are mapped to the BE queue at the ONU. rtPS also includes ertPS in the new described classification. Similarities between EPON EF and IEEE 802.16 UGS as well as

EPON AF and 802.16 rtPS/ertPS facilitate one to one mapping to the priority queues. Using this kind of mapping technique, all the transmitted packets from 802.16 queues are enqueued in the corresponding ONU queues, and the downstream packets are likewise enqueued in the respective 802.16 and ONU queues.

According to the defined traffic classes for RPR and WiMAX, bidirectional mapping of traffic classes between these two technologies is achieved as follows. RPR traffic classes A0, A1, B-CIR, B_EIR and C are mapped to UGS, ErtPS, rtPS, nrtPS and BE, respectively. In order to provide end to end QoS in the SuperMAN architecture, a hierarchical scheduling algorithm was proposed in (Ghazisaidi, Paolucci & Maier, 2009). As illustrated in Figure 11, different queuing approaches are implemented in the suggested

Figure 11. Hierarchical WiMAX scheduling algorithm of an RPR/WiMAX interface node

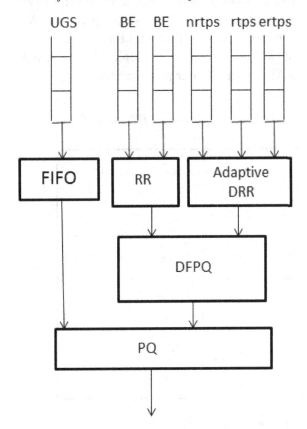

hierarchical scheduling. FIFO queuing, which is used for UGS fixed size packets at a constant data rate, guarantees in-order packet queuing for high priority data traffic. An adaptive deficit round robin (DRR) scheduler is used to schedule ertPS, rtPS and nrtPS traffic classes to fulfill delay as well as fairness performance of real time traffic. It operates in two modes based on traffic status: non-burst mode and burst mode. Delay insensitivity of BE fixed size packets can be readily served by a simple Round Robin (RR) scheduler. Deficit fair priority queuing (DFPQ) organizes the fixed size packet queues in accordance with their priority classes. This method improves the fairness between the outputs of the DRR and RR schedulers in which higher priority packets are scheduled earlier until the queue length reaches the predefined threshold, and then lower priority packets are scheduled. Priority queuing (PQ) is placed at the outputs of FIFO and DFPQ scheduler, and provides service differentiation of higher and lower priority in fixed size packets.

It is worth emphasizing that schedulers are directly controlled by CPU. Based on the requested bandwidth for UGS fixed size packets, the optical-wireless interface node is able to change the reserved bandwidth of traffic class A0 if the UL-requests are received. Moreover, upon reception of an A1 and B-CIR packets by an RPR node, the CPU informs the DFPQ scheduler to dynamically adjust its threshold for ertPS and rtPS. This adaptive interaction between optical and wireless segments facilitates end-to-end QoS provisioned connectivity for the reserved (UGS/A0) and real-time traffic classes over SuperMAN.

Handover

Supporting user mobility, handover should be considered in the situation of crossing the boundary of two WiMAX cells. Overseeing all the microcells connected to the EPON, an OLT can operate as an administrator to handle users handover. The handover central controller should be able to exchange information with the WiMAX BS at each remote node at any time in order to close an old connection between a mobile user and a base station, and initiate a new one with another base station. Hence, a specific control channel should be reserved to guarantee the real time communication between the controller and WiMAX base stations. As described in (Shen *et al.* 2007), the microwave over fiber architecture facilitates a simple handover operation. In this architecture, a central WiMAX macro BS monitors user packets and finds the antenna from which the user traffic is sent as well as its optical subcarrier frequency. Therefore, no specific control channels are needed for communications between the central controller and micro base stations. The central WiMAX macro BS can easily determine whether handover is needed by simply checking if the user traffic comes from a different optical subcarrier..

Congestion Control

A proper routing algorithm plays an important role to improve QoS in FiWi networks. Unidirectional ring/PON architecture (Shaw *et al.* 2008) improvises a new routing algorithm in-

tegrated with congestion control to improve the network delay performance. In this algorithm, each router broadcasts link state information till it reaches the gateways. Using the shortest path algorithm, each gateway computes the best route for every router. Selected routes and related costs are reported to the central office by every ONU. The central office chooses the gateway with the lowest cost for each router. For congestion control, each ONU monitors the flow rate of neighboring routers and continuously checks WMN traffic loading. In the presence of congestion, ONU sends a report message to the central office, and the lowest cost route is recomputed and selected again through neighboring gateways. In (Sarkar, Dixit, & Mukherjee, 2007), various types of routing algorithms such as the shortest path routing algorithm (SPRA), minimum hop routing algorithm (MHRA), predictive throughput routing algorithm (PTRA), delay aware routing algorithm (DARA), and risk and delay aware routing (RADAR) have been proposed for the wireless part of FiWi networks. Table 1 illustrates the pros and cons of various algorithms. As depicted, DARA and RADAR have better performance.

Table 1. Pros and cons of various routing algorithms for the wireless part of a FiWi network

Routing algorithm	Objective	Link prediction used	Alternative path used	Risk awareness	Performance							
					Delay		Throughput		Hop count		Load balancing	
					H	L	H	L	H	L	H	L
MHRA	Hop minimization Unity link weight	No	No	No	+	−	+	−	+	+	−	−
SPRA	Shortest path Inverse capacity Link weight	No	No	No	+	−	+	−	+	+	−	−
PTRA	Throughput Optimization	No	Yes	No	−	−	+	+	−	−	+	+
DARA	Delay Minimization	Yes	Yes	No	+	+	+	+	+	−	+	+
RADAR	Minimize packet loss and delay	Yes	Yes	Yes	+	+	+	+	+	−	+	+
H: High load (0.5-0.95) L: Low load(0.0-0.49) +:algorithm performs well − :Algorithm performs poorly												

In DARA, each wireless router is modeled as a standard M/M/1 queue. Using Link State Prediction (LSP), DARA allocates weights to the wireless links based on the predicted delay. The path with the minimum predicted delay is selected from a router to any gateway and vice versa. Therefore, upstream or downstream packets traverse along the selected path if the predicted delay is less than the specific threshold. On the other hand, RADAR was also proposed to tackle the failures that may happen due to fiber cuts. RADAR can distinguish each gateway to which ONU is connected. A Risk List (LR) in every router keeps track of failures. When no failure occurs, all the paths are marked as "live"; in the presence of a failure, routes leading to the failure gateway are marked as "stale". The suitable path is selected among the live paths.

Ghazisaidi and Maier (2010) introduced an aggregation technique with various types of ONU structures to enhance the throughput, packet loss and delay in FiWi networks. Figure 12 presents the proposed architecture of integrated WLAN and EPON networks.

There are three types of ONU in the aforementioned architecture: ONU, Hyper-ONU, and ONU-HT AP (High Throughput Access Point). A conventional ONU is equipped with a fixed tuned transmitter and receiver. Hyper-ONU is a MAC improved legacy ONU and is compatible to legacy TDM EPON ONUs. An aggregation part shown in Figure 12 is responsible for the aggregation of incoming as well as de-aggregation of outgoing traffic. This type of ONU is not equipped with any wireless extensions. ONU-HT AP provides wireless interface. The configuration consists of a Central Processing Unit (CPU) and HT AP unit rather than Hyper ONU. The HT AP unit contains the wireless equipment, and CPU is responsible for controlling optical and wireless segments. In the proposed scheme, during the registration phase, the OLT informs the participating ONUs and identifies the type of each ONU. Each ONU-HT AP maps the information about the connected HT stations into the reserved fields of the REGISTER_REQ MPCP protocol data unit. Based on this information, Access Point Controller (APC) in the central office and every

Figure 12. Integration of WLAN and EPON

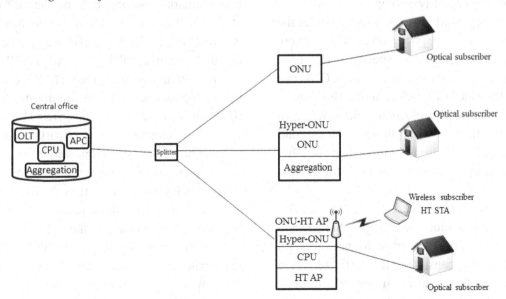

ONU-HP AP create two routing tables. Optical routing table holds the information which is broadcasted by OLT. Wireless routing table includes the information of connected local HT stations and all ONU-HT APs connected to the WMN and related stations. Using the above routing tables, in order to reduce traffic congestion at ONU-HT AP, an integrated dynamic path selection algorithm was proposed in which the status of each ONU-HT AP is buffered. Based on the load of ONU-HT APs, the appropriate path for incoming traffic is selected.

ENERGY SAVING IN FIWI NETWORKS

In order to mitigate global warming and to control the operational expenses, energy efficient solutions become essential. Using energy in an efficient manner for all networks is challenging and is considered as an important and vital concern. So far, all the mentioned FiWi architectures aim to provide high performance, reliability, fault tolerance and robustness, but they rarely consider energy efficiency. Zhang and Ansari (2011) proposed to implement two sleep modes in ONUs to save energy in EPON. The study assumes the availability of multi power level ONUs where each level corresponds to a specific energy consumption level. In the frist scenario, an ONU can sleep within one DBA cycle. An idle_threshold is defined to restrict the maximum time in which an ONU stays idle before going to sleep. In the second scenario, the ONU sleeps for more than one DBA cycle based on the estimated threshold through the downstream traffic profiles of all ONUs.

Considering two different features of FiWi networks, Chowdhury, Mukherjee, Sarkar, and Mukherjee (2010) designed such a network with reduced energy consumption. Traffic rerouting capability of front-end mesh networks through substituted paths protects the network in the case of failures such as fiber cuts. The flexibility

characteristic of wireless front-end facilitates energy saving in the optical part as well. Daily traffic load variation is the other aspect of access networks that should be considered in designing an energy aware network. In view of the different network usage behaviors of different kinds of users (i.e., daily bandwidth demand profiles), some under-utilized parts of the network can enter the sleep mode during low-load hours. In the wireless part, we need to keep all the wireless routers on to ensure availability of the network. The main issue is how to put optical components of a FiWi network into the sleep mode. We will not consider putting OLT into the sleep mode as it connects the FiWi to the rest of the Internet. However, using ring based architecture with several OLTs in a ring setup, a low-load OLT can be put into the sleep mode while rerouting its traffic through other OLTs.

OLT can estimate the traffic load of each ONU at different hours of a day by measuring the length of the corresponding ONU's input queue. When the load falls below the specific threshold, ONU can enter the sleep mode. In FiWi, the centralized sleeping mechanism can be managed by the OLT to put low-load ONUs to sleep. OLT can determine two tidemarks (low and high) for the traffic load at ONUs. The wireless mesh front-end of FiWi will reroute the affected traffic to alternate paths due to the sleep of ONU (Chowdhury, 2011).

Another approach to green a FiWi network is to develop an energy aware routing mechanism (Chowdhury *et al.* 2010). Link State (LS) protocols, which have been discussed earlier, generally vary on how they assign link weights in the link state advertisement. For example, DARA predicts the link delay and then assigns the link weights to achieve several performance objectives. Load balancing, which balances the traffic load in all parts of the network, is one of the attained goals. Load balancing tries to fairly utilize all parts of the network, but it may lead to under-utilization of some parts of the network during low-load hours. To have an efficient network, traffic should be supported by using a small number of devices in the network during low-load hours. The energy-aware LS routing algorithm reported in (Chowdhury *et al.* 2010) uses residual capacity of a link as the link weight. When traffic flows through a link, its next link weight will be updated to be the remaining capacity of that link (original capacity minus traffic flow). To route traffic from the source to the destination, the path with lowest residual capacity is chosen. This kind of path selection may increase hop count and consequently path delay in the network. In order to reduce average path length, the term hop offset is introduced and included in the cost calculation per each hop. Therefore, denoting as the residual capacity of the path with hops and hop offset of , the total path cost is calculated as. The hop offset amount should be determined carefully in order to avoid increasing the average path length excessively from regular shortest-path routing. The optimal amount of hop offset is determined based on the amount of delay the network connection can tolerate. Increasing the average path length may, however, reduce the achieved power savings from putting ONUs to sleep.

FUTURE RESEARCH DIRECTIONS

The current deployment of FiWi assumes that separate data-transfer techniques are deployed for optical and wireless segments, respectively. In the optical part, MPCP-based Dynamic Bandwidth Allocation (DBA) is used while layer-3 routing algorithms are mostly used for the wireless segment. Using layer-3 routing in the wireless mesh also incurs major overhead on the network. Integrated layer-2 routing protocol is a remarkable alternative to reduce layer-3 processing overheads that can route traffic through all segments of the FiWi network in an efficient manner. Latency is also reduced as packets do not need to go beyond layer 2 in the protocol stack in traversing a router.

Hence, as a future work, a hierarchical MPCP-based L2 routing for the FiWi network (multipoint control for an OLT to its downstream ONUs and for an ONU to its downstream gateways) could be developed. One can extend the idea of L2 routing in the optical segment to the wireless mesh network in such a way that one ONU can drive multiple gateways (similar to the case where one OLT drives multiple ONUs). A spanning tree will be used by the wireless mesh for L2 routing. This approach is compatible with the idea of end-to-end L2 capability of FiWi.

The current deployment of wireless mesh network is based on IEEE 802.11g in which wireless routers use the Carrier Sense Multiple Access with Collision Avoidance (CSMA/CA) MAC protocol. As mentioned in (Chowdhury, Mukherjee, Sarkar, Kramer, & Dixit, 2009), the capacity of the wireless mesh can be increased by using TDM-based MAC protocol. TDM-based MAC will also be compatible with the L2 routing protocol. Orthogonal Frequency Division Multiplexing (OFDM) can be combined with TDM in future to increase the wireless capacity.

Note that wireless gateways and routers which are located near gateways carry more traffic than other routers. Therefore, the capacity of these wireless routers can be increased by using some known technologies such as directional antenna, multiple radios, and Multiple Input Multiple Output (MIMO).

CONCLUSION

Fiber Wireless (FiWi) networks are a potent future-proof platform that provides many advantages. Owing to enormously increasing traffic loads generated by new applications, deploying optical fiber as a backhaul can help alleviate bandwidth bottlenecks in wireless access networks. Although FiWi networks provide simultaneous wired and wireless services over the same infrastructure, two integrated technologies are able to work independently of each other, thus resulting in major cost savings. In this chapter, the state of art of FiWi networks has been presented. How to efficiently utilize the high bandwidth provided in the optical subnetwork to improve the throughput of wireless subnetworks remains a great challenge in FiWi access networks. We have reviewed some practical FiWi architectures with emphasis on deployment considerations. We have discussed the network setup, network connectivity, and fault tolerant characteristics of FiWi networks. Moreover, some QoS provisioning techniques including traffic class mapping, scheduling, and resource management have been introduced. In order to improve the integration of optical and wireless access networks, several integrated path selection algorithms have been compared. Finally, we have presented challenges and opportunities for the design of future FiWi networks.

REFERENCES

Akyildiz, I. F., Wang, X., & Wang, W. (2005). Wireless mesh networks: A survey. *Computer Networks*, *47*(4), 31–42. doi:10.1016/j.comnet.2004.12.001.

Alharbi, F., & Ansari, N. (2005). Distributed bandwidth allocation for resilient packet ring networks. *Computer Networks*, *49*(2), 161–171. doi:10.1016/j.comnet.2004.12.004.

Alharbi, F., & Ansari, N. (2006). SSA: Simple scheduling algorithm for resilient packet ring networks. *IEE Proceedings. Communications*, *153*(2), 183–188. doi:10.1049/ip-com:20045232.

Assi, C., Ye, Y., Dixit, S., & Ali, M. (2003). Dynamic bandwidth allocation for quality-of-service over ethernet PONs. *IEEE Journal on Selected Areas in Communications*, *21*, 1467–1477. doi:10.1109/JSAC.2003.818837.

Bhandari, S., & Park, E. K. (2006). Hybrid optical wireless networks. In *Proceedings of the International Conference on Networking, International Conference on Systems, and International Conference on Mobile Communications and Learning Technologies*, (pp. 113–117). IEEE.

Bruno, R., Conti, M., & Gregori, E. (2005). Mesh networks: Commodity multihop ad hoc networks. *IEEE Communications Magazine*, *43*(3), 123–131. doi:10.1109/MCOM.2005.1404606.

Chao, H.-L., & Liao, W. (2003). Credit-based slot allocation for multimedia mobile ad hoc networks. *IEEE Journal on Selected Areas in Communications*, *21*(10), 1642–1651. doi:10.1109/JSAC.2003.815232.

Chowdhury, P. (2011). *Energy-efficient next-generation networks (NGN)*. (Doctoral Dissertation). University of California Davis, Davis, CA.

Chowdhury, P., Mukherjee, B., Sarkar, S., Kramer, G., & Dixit, S. (2009). Hybrid wireless-optical broadband access network (WOBAN), prototype development and research challenges. *IEEE Network*, *23*(3), 41–48. doi:10.1109/MNET.2009.4939262.

Chowdhury, P., Mukherjee, B., Sarkar, S., & Mukherjee, B. (2010). Building a green wireless-optical broadband access network (WOBAN). *IEEE/OSA. Journal of Lightwave Technology*, *28*(16), 2219–2229. doi:10.1109/JLT.2010.2044369.

Davik, F., Yilmaz, M., Gjessing, S., & Uzun, N. (2004). IEEE 802.17 resilient packet ring tutorial. *IEEE Communications Magazine*, *42*, 112–118. doi:10.1109/MCOM.2004.1273782.

Effenberger, F., Cleary, D., Haran, O., Kramer, G., Li, R. D., Oron, M., & Pfeiffer, T. (2007). An introduction to PON technologies. *IEEE Communications Magazine*, *45*(3), S17–S25. doi:10.1109/MCOM.2007.344582.

Ghazisaidi, N., & Maier, M. (2010). Advanced aggregation techniques for integrated next-generation WLAN and EPON networks. In *Proceedings of the IEEE Consumer Communications & Networking Conference (CCNC)*, (pp. 1-5). IEEE.

Ghazisaidi, N., & Maier, M. (2011). Fiber-wireless (FiWi) access networks: Challenges and opportunities. *IEEE Network*, *25*(1), 36–42. doi:10.1109/MNET.2011.5687951.

Ghazisaidi, N., Paolucci, F., & Maier, M. (2009). SuperMAN: Optical-wireless integration of RPR and WiMAX. *OSA Journal of Optical Networking*, *8*, 249–271. doi:10.1364/JON.8.000249.

Hutcheson, L. (2008). FTTx: Current status and the future. *IEEE Communications Magazine*, *46*(7), 90–95. doi:10.1109/MCOM.2008.4557048.

Kramer, G. (2005). *Ethernet passive optical networks*. New York: McGraw-Hill, Inc..

Kramer, G., Mukherjee, B., Dixit, S., Ye, Y., & Hirth, R. (2002). Supporting differentiated classes of service in ethernetpasrive optical networks. *Journal on Optical Networks*, *1*(8), 280–298.

Kuran, M. S., & Tugcu, T. (2007). A survey on emerging broadband wireless access technologies. *Computer Networks*, *51*, 3013–3046. doi:10.1016/j.comnet.2006.12.009.

Lin, W.-P., Kao, M.-S., & Chi, S. (2003). A reliable architecture for broadband fiber-wireless access networks. *IEEE Photonics Technology Letters*, *15*(2), 344–346. doi:10.1109/LPT.2002.806890.

Luo, Y., & Ansari, N. (2005). Bandwidth allocation for multi-service access on EPONs. *IEEE (Optical). Communications Magazine*, *43*(2), S16–S21. doi:10.1109/MCOM.2005.1391498.

Luo, Y., & Ansari, N. (2005). LSTP for dynamic bandwidth allocation and QoS provisioning over EPONs. *OSA Journal of Optical Networking*, *4*(9), 561–572. doi:10.1364/JON.4.000561.

Maier, M., Ghazisaidi, N., & Reisslein, M. (2008). The audacity of fiber-wireless (FiWi) networks. In *Proceedings of the ICST ACCESSNETS*, (pp. 1-10). ICST.

McGarry, M. P., Maier, M., & Reisslein, M. (2006). WDM ethernet passive optical networks. *IEEE Communications Magazine*, *44*, S18–S25. doi:10.1109/MCOM.2006.1593545.

Sarkar, S., Dixit, S., & Mukherjee, B. (2007). HybridWireless-optical broadband-access network (WOBAN): A review of relevant challenges. *IEEE/OSA. Journal of Lightwave Technology*, *25*, 3329–3340. doi:10.1109/JLT.2007.906804.

Shaw, W. T., Wong, S. W., Cheng, N., Balasubramanian, K., Qiao, C., Yen, S. H., & Azovsky, L. G. (2008). Reconfigurable optical backhaul and integrated routing algorithm for load balancing in hybrid optical-wireless access networks. In *Proceedings of the IEEE International Conference on Communications (ICC)*, (pp. 5697-5701). IEEE.

Shaw, W.-T., Wong, S.-W., Cheng, N., Balasubramanian, K., Zhu, X., Maier, M., & Kazovsky, L. (2007). Hybrid architecture and integrated routing in a scalable optical–wireless access network. *Journal of Lightwave Technology*, *25*(11), 3329–3340. doi:10.1109/JLT.2007.909202.

Shen, G., Tucker, R. S., & Chae, C.-J. (2007). Fixed mobile convergence architectures for broadband access: Integration of EPON and WiMAX. *IEEE Communications Magazine*, *45*, 44–50. doi:10.1109/MCOM.2007.4290313.

Yang, K., Ou, S., Guild, K., & Chen, H.-H. (2009). Convergence of ethernet PON and IEEE 802.16 broadband access networks and its QoS-aware dynamic bandwidth allocation scheme. *IEEE Journal on Selected Areas in Communications*, *27*, 101–116. doi:10.1109/JSAC.2009.090202.

Zhang, J., & Ansari, N. (2010). An application-oriented fair resource allocation scheme for EPON. *IEEE Systems Journal*, *4*(4), 424–431. doi:10.1109/JSYST.2010.2082210.

Zhang, J., & Ansari, N. (2011). Toward energy-efficient 1GEPON and 10G-EPON with sleep-aware MAC control and scheduling. *IEEE Communications Magazine*, *49*(2), S33–S38. doi:10.1109/MCOM.2011.5706311.

Zhang, J., Ansari, N., Luo, Y., Effenberger, F., & Ye, F. (2009). Next-generation PONs: A performance investigation of candidate architectures for next-generation access stage 1. *IEEE Communications Magazine*, *47*(8), 49–57. doi:10.1109/MCOM.2009.5181892.

Zheng, J., & Mouftah, H. T. (2005). Media access control for ethernet passive optical networks: An overview. *IEEE Communications Magazine*, *43*, 145–150. doi:10.1109/MCOM.2005.1391515.

Chapter 3
Optical Label Processing Techniques for Intelligent Forwarding of Packets in All-Optical Packet Switched Networks

Nicola Calabretta
Eindhoven University of Technology, The Netherlands

ABSTRACT

In this chapter, the authors review several optical label processing techniques providing a comparison based on the potential for each technique to allow for implementation of a scalable and low latency optical packet switching cross-connect node. They present and demonstrate an optical packet switch sub-system employing in-band labeling to allow for transparent forwarding of multi-wavelength packets with multiple data formats at multiple data bit-rates. The optical packet switching sub-system employs a scalable, asynchronous, and low latency label processor. Experimental results are provided that confirm the operation of the label processor in optical packet switching system testbeds. Moreover, the authors discuss applications of the optical packet switching node based on optical label processor and the potential to allow the implementation of intelligent systems for optimal routing of the packets in the optical domain.

INTRODUCTION

The exponential growth of the Internet data traffic will demand high capacity optical networks (Swanson, (2008). High capacity optical links will carry optical packets at data rates above 100 Gb/s using a variety of data-formats such as OTDM data packets, multi-wavelength optical packets with highly spectral efficient modulation formats such as D(Q)PSK, OFDM, M-QAM. On the other hand, routing of packets by today electronic circuit switching may have fundamental limits due to the speed and the scalability of multi-rack electronic switching fabrics, and the associated power consumption by opto-electronic conversions.

DOI: 10.4018/978-1-4666-3652-1.ch003

Switching of the optical packets transparently in the optical domain eliminates power hungry opto-electronic conversions and improves the latency of the system. However, there are several issues to be addressed for realizing such Optical Packet Switch (OPS) sub-system. The OPS sub-system should be able to handle optical packets with multiple data formats. This implies that both the label processor, which determines the packet destination and controls the switching fabric, as well as the optical switching fabric, should operate independently of the data-format and data rate of the packets. The OPS sub-system should be scalable, that means that the number of input/output ports is not limited by the switch architecture. For instance a large NxN switching matrix based on multi-stage architecture can be realized starting from a 1xN switch. Essential in realizing a 1xN optical switch is the implementation of a scalable label processor. Moreover, the OPS sub-system should introduce little latency for increasing the node throughput. In this architecture the control complexity and the configuration time (latency) is proportional to the label processing time. Therefore, key issue to realize a low latency OPS, scalable, and data format independent OPS is the implementation of an extremely fast label processor (and labeling technique) that allows for processing a large amount of labels for controlling the large port count OPS with a limited increase of the latency.

In this chapter we first review several optical label processing techniques providing a comparison in terms of processing speed (latency), scalability, data format and data rate dependency. Such requirements for the optical label processor are essential to implement a scalable OPS node. After the reviewing of the label processing techniques, we focus on and demonstrate in-band labeling technique that allows for transparent routing of multi-wavelength packets with multiple data formats and at different data bit-rates. The label processor discussed in this chapter is scalable in terms of label bits, operates in asynchronous fashion, and the processing speed and latency is independent of the number of label bits. We present operation of the label processor for multiple data rate and data format and present experimental results that confirms dynamic operation of the label processor in 640 Gb/s dynamic switching and in a cascaded of three optical packet switching nodes spaced by 52 km. The chapter is concluded with a discussion on future research direction in the fields of OPS.

BACKGROUND

To date, several optical labeling techniques have been proposed and demonstrated. Those techniques can be divided in two areas: all-optical label processing techniques, in which all the operation required to recognize the labels are performed in the optical domain, and opto-electronics label processing techniques, in which optical and electronics processing are combined to optimally perform the label recognition.

Several works have been presented in literature that demonstrate all-optical label processing (Vegas Olmos, 2004; Klonidis 2005; Wang 2006, 2010; Takenaka 2006; Wai 2005; Herrera 2008; Calabretta 2004, 2005, 2006, 2007, 2008; Scaffardi 2010; Hamilton 2002; Wada 2007; Le Minh 2006). Despite the ultrafast operation of processing the labels in the optical domain, the main issue in all-optical label processors is the low amount of labels that can be processed and the lack of mature digital photonic circuits (logics) for complex operation required for implementing algorithms and schedulers for routing the optical packets. Moreover, the complexity of those circuits and the lack of mature and generic photonic integration technology prevented the realization of small footprint, and low power consumption circuits for processing large number of labels. Future breakthrough in the field of photonic integration could lead to efficient and scalable all-optical label processing circuits.

A more viable solution is represented by optoelectronic label processing techniques. Here, the main idea is to exploit the optics for efficient pre-processing the optical labels and the flexibility of the electronics for processing a large number of labels and implementing efficiently the routing algorithms. One of the typical schemes is based on serial time multiplexing the optical label at the head of the packets on the same wavelength (Guillemot 1998; Ramos 2005). In order to prevent any degradation of the payload during the label erasure and insertion, guard times must be inserted in between the label and the payload. One drawback is that those labeling techniques require time consuming bit synchronization and clock recovery circuits that introduce large latency. In Chi (2003), Chung-Li (2003), Leguizamon (2009), Bo (2007), Mishra (2006), Tafur Monroy (2004), optical label based Subcarrier Multiplexing (SCM) was employed to deliver the address information. In this approach, the label and the payload are carried in-band within the 100 GHz channel. The optical labels are serial encoded and carried by a high subcarrier frequency with respect to the payload central frequency. For example in Chung-Li (2003), the Subcarrier Multiplexing (SCM) at 18 GHz carries the 155 Mb/s 32 bits serial coded optical label, while the payload had a bandwidth of around 20 GHz. This requires already 206 ns only for acquiring the 32 bits, which is not acceptable for the high speed packets with typically 1500 bytes length (around 120 ns packet length for 100 Gb/s packets). Increasing the data rate of the label can decrease the acquisition time, but the subcarrier frequency would place a limit to the bit rate of the payload in order to avoid any possible overlapping between the payload and the SCM label. In Seddighian (2007), Calabretta (2010), Wavelength Division Multiplexing (WDM) labeling is demonstrated, in which a separate wavelength is exploited to transmit the label. In this case, the optical label is transparent to the payload bit-rate and format,

avoiding any overlapping. In Seddighian (2007), multiple out-band WDM labels in which each label wavelength represents one label bit are exploited for enabling parallel and fast label processing. However, the WDM labeling technique may suffer from the fiber dispersion that causes walk-off between the labels and payload. Besides, it also consumes extra wavelength resources resulting in a poor spectral efficiency.

MAIN FOCUS OF THE CHAPTER

In this chapter, we demonstrate an optical packet switch sub-system employing in-band labeling technique to allow for transparent forwarding of multi-wavelength packets with multiple data formats and at different data bit-rates. The advantage of this labeling technique is that it allows the optical label processor for processing the label bits in parallel. By processing in parallel the label bits, the latency introduced by the optical label processor is constant and independent from the number of label bits.

We will show operation of the label processor for OTDM RZ-OOK and NRZ-DPSK and OFDM multi-wavelength packets, and therefore the label processor and the switch do not need to be reconfigured when changing data format. We will then employ the label processor to demonstrate fast and scalable OPS cross-connect node in networks systems.

In-Band Labeling Technique Concept

Generally, optical packets at high data rate B can be generated in serial by using OTDM techniques, or in parallel by using N colored channels, each channel has bit-rate B/N. Both the OTDM packets and N-channels can be encoded by many modulation formats. We encode the address information of optical packets by in-band labels, i.e. the wavelengths of the labels are chosen within the bandwidth of the payload (see Figure 1a). Each label has a binary value. Thus, 2^N addresses can be encoded by using N labels. This makes this technique scalable within the limited payload bandwidth. In Figure 1a the packet format and the optical spectra are schematically illustrated. The labels have the same duration as the payload. This allows the label processor for operating in asynchronous fashion and with variable packet length. Moreover, the labels can be separated from the payload by using passive wavelength filtering. For 160 Gb/s OTDM packets, the labels were inserted within the spectrum of the OTDM signal (see Figure 1b). For the OOK, DPSK, and OFDM multi-wavelength packets, we use the same label wavelengths, but they are spectrally located in the notches of the spectra of the multi-wavelength payload (see Figures 1 (c-d). We demonstrate that by using the in-band labeling technique, the label processor does not need to be reconfigured to process any packets regardless of the data payload formats.

Optical Label Processing Based on In-Band Labeling

The experimental set-up to demonstrate the OPS operation of packets with multiple modulation formats and in-band labels is shown in Figure 2. At the transmitter side, we generated payloads with different types of modulation formats. First, 160 Gb/s OOK payload centered at 1546 nm is generated by time-multiplexing 40 Gb/s modulated optical pulses. The 1.4 ps optical pulses make the -20dB bandwidth of the payload to be 5 nm. Second, 12x10 Gb/s DPSK multi-wavelength payload with channels from 1544.1 nm to 1548 nm spaced by 50 GHz. The optical address coupled to the payloads was generated by encoding 6 labels with the same duration as the packet payload and with wavelengths L_1=1543.88 nm, L2=1544.36 nm, L3=1545.16 nm, L4=1546.92 nm, L5=1547.72 nm, and L6=1548.2 nm. Note that the labels are located within the optical spectra of the two types of payload (see Figures 1b-c). A similar strategy

Figure 1. a) Schematic of the optical packet format in the time and wavelength domain, optical spectra of the optical packets with multiple modulation format and in-band labels; b) OTDM data packets; c) DPSK data packets; d) OFDM data packets

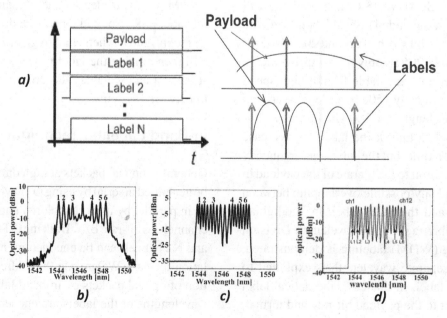

Figure 2. Experimental set-up to demonstrate the OPS operation of packets with multiple modulation formats

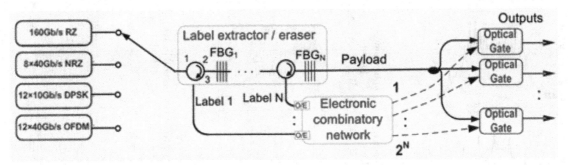

is chosen for the OFDM payload (see Figure 1d). Here, we use Discrete Multitone modulation (DMT), which is the baseband version of OFDM, with up to 64-state quadrature amplitude modulation (64-QAM). To optimize the bandwidth utilization, we use Chow's rate-adaptive bit-loading algorithm (Chow 1995; Yang 2009) to maximize the achievable bit rate. Thus, we are able to transmit more than 40 Gb/s data traffic in less than 10 GHz bandwidth. In the experiment, a computer is used to emulate the digital DMT modulator and the data traffic is then generated by an Arbitrary Waveform Generator (AWG) running at 24 GSamples/s.

The optical packets are fed into the OPS. The schematic of the 1 x N OPS is shown in Figure 2. It consists of an Optical Label Extractor (OLE) that separates the labels and the payload. The separated payload is broadcasted into the optical gates, while the extracted labels are processed by the combinatory network, which provides the control signals for driving the optical gates. The OLE separates the labels and payload by using a cascade of narrow-bandwidth Fiber Bragg Gratings (FBGs) centered at the labels wavelengths and optical circulators. The FBGs have Gaussian profile with 98% of reflectivity and 6 GHz at -3dB bandwidth to avoid significant slicing of the spectrum of the payload that may lead to distortions. The labels output in parallel from the OLE. This avoids complicated packet based clock-re-

covery and high speed electrical serial-to-parallel conversion. The labels are processed by the combinatory network, which is an asynchronous electronic decoder. The output signals control the optical gates. The combinatory network can process a large number of labels without increasing the latency by using several chips in parallel. Note that since the labels have the same duration as the payload, the control signals generated by the combinatory network have duration equal to the payload. This makes flip-flops redundant and allows for operation on packets with variable length. The optical gates are based on electro-optic $LiNbO_3$ switches to guarantee transparent switching of the packets with multiple data formats. The switched optical packets are then received and analyzed by the BER tester.

First, we investigate the compatibility of in-band labels with payloads with multiple modulation formats. We fed into the OPS packets with 6 in-band labels and data payload with different formats. We evaluate the quality of the payloads after filtering the in-band labels. The optical spectra of the packets before and after the label extractor and the BER measurements are shown in Figure 3. For 160 Gb/s RZ-OOK, error-free operation with 0.6 dB power penalty with respect to the back-to-back BER was measured (see Figure 4a). Similarly, less than 0.4 dB of power penalty was measured for the 12 x 10 Gb/s DPSK and 12 x 40 Gb/s OFDM formats (see Figures 4b and 4c).

Figure 3. Optical spectra of the optical packets with different modulation formats: a) OTDM data packets; b) DPSK data packets; c) OFDM data packets

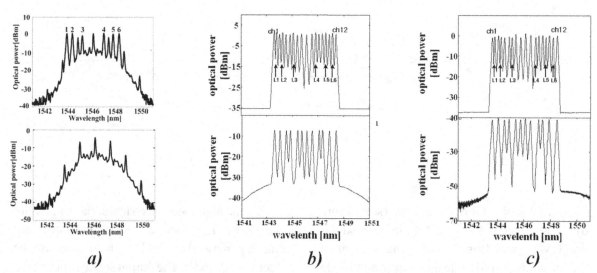

Figure 4. BER measurements of the optical packets with different modulation formats: a) OTDM data packets; b) DPSK data packets; c) OFDM data packets

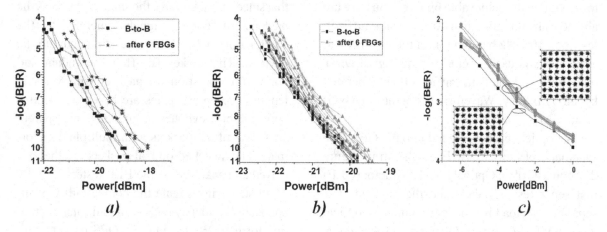

Those results indicate that in-band labeling can be used as universal optical address technique with any payload formats without compromising the signal quality.

Validation of the Labeling Technique in an Optical Packet Switching System

Next, we demonstrate the switching performance of a 1x64 optical packet switch for 160 Gb/s RZ-OOK and 120 Gb/s DPSK packets. The experi-

mental set-up employed is the same as reported in Figure 2. The packets have duration of 6.4 ns and are separated by 3 ns guard band. The optical power of the input packets before the OPS was 3 dBm. In the experiment we investigated the behavior of a 1x64 switch by using only two optical gates and 18 dB attenuator that accounts for the 1 by 64 splitting losses. Using two optical gates is sufficient to evaluate the cross-talk between the output ports as well as the switching dynamics.

Figure 5 shows the time evolution of the optical packets along the OPS for the RZ-OOK and

Figure 5. Measured traces at different points of the OPS for 160 Gb/s RZ-OOK: a) input packets; b) switching control; c) switched packets. A magnification of the traces with 5 ns/div timescale is also reported. Measured traces of the OPS for 120 Gb/s NRZ-DPSK: d) Input packets; e) switching control; f) switched packets.

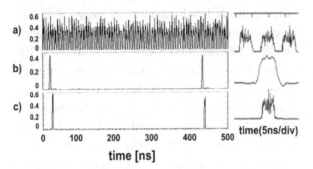
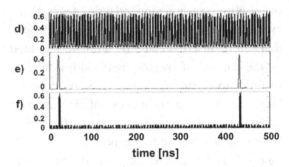

DPSK data packets, respectively. Figures 5a and 5d show the OPS operation with 160 Gb/s RZ-OOK and NRZ-DPSK packets, respectively. The signal produced by the combinatory network, which is used as a control signal of the optical gates is shown in Figures 5b and 5e. The electrical voltage of the control signal generated by the combinatory network was 4.5 V that is sufficient to drive the optical gate without additional amplifiers. The control opens one optical gate, switching the packet to one of the 64 outputs. The 160 Gb/s RZ-OOK switched packet and the NRZ-DPSK switched packet at the output of the gate are reported in Figures 5c and 5f, respectively. The measured cross-talk between the output ports was higher than

18 dB. The measured BER of the switched packet for the 160 Gb/s RZ-OOK and 120 Gb/s DPSK are reported in Figures 6a and 6b, respectively. Error-free operation was obtained with 1.6 dB of power penalty compared to the back-to-back payload BER for the 160 Gb/s RZ-OOK packets, and 0.9 dB of power penalty was measured for the 120 Gb/s NRZ-DPSK packets.

Scaling the In-Band Labeling Technique

In the previous section, we have presented and demonstrated the in-band labeling technique in an OPS subsystem. Essential in this approach is

Figure 6. BER measured at the OPS output: a) 160 Gb/s RZ-OOK and eye diagrams. Time scale is 2 ps/div. b) 12x10 Gb/s NRZ-DPSK of the output packets and eye diagrams. Time scale is 100 ps/div.

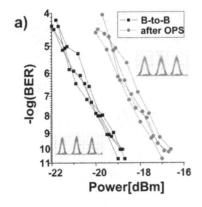
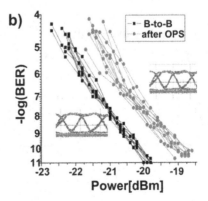

that 2^N addresses could be encoded by N binary coded label wavelengths that are attached within the bandwidth of the payload. This approach allows the OPS to operate asynchronously at the expense of low power consumption and little latency. However, the number of the in-band label wavelengths that can be inserted could be ultimately limited by the amount of spectral bandwidth available. In order to further scale the OPS to address a larger number of ports, it is essential to increase the number of bits delivered by each in-band labels. In this section we propose to use the RF tone in-band labeling technique. In this approach, each of the N in-band label wavelengths carries M binary coded Radio Frequency (RF) tones. In this way, the switch can address $2^{N \times M}$ possible ports (compared to 2^N for the case of only binary coded wavelength labeling (Calabretta 2010). We present the Optical Label Processor (OLP) scheme for the RF tone in-band label, which allows for processing each label wavelength and RF tone in parallel at the expense of little latency. By using the RF tone in-band labeling, we experimentally demonstrated error free OPS operation for packets at data rate of 160 Gb/s and 40 Gb/s. Moreover, we discuss the scalability, the latency and the power fluctuation tolerance of the RF tone in-band labeling technique. We show that this labeling technique is able to deliver 30 label bits in one label wavelength, and introduce an extra latency of less than 7 ns.

Concept

The concept of the RF tone in-band labeling technique is reported in Figure 7. As shown in Figure 7a, N label wavelengths (λ_{Lj}, $j \in [1,N]$) are inserted within the payload spectrum bandwidth, and each label wavelength carries M RF tones (f_1^j to f_M^j). Each of the RF tones is binary coded, and represents one bit of the label (f_i^j represents bit_i^j, $i \in [1,M]$, $j \in [1,N]$). Therefore, N in-band wavelengths with M RF tones are able to provide N×M label bits. This is M times larger than the in-band wavelength labeling technique (Calabretta (2010)). Therefore this labeling technique allows for addressing a larger amount of ports without using extra spectrum to allocate the label wavelenghts. Moreover, as illustrated in Figure 1b, all the label bits have the same duration as the payload length. Thus it allows for handling packets with variable lengths and in an asynchronous fashion.

Figure 8a illustrates the schematic diagram of the Optical Label Processor (OLP) for the RF tone in-band label. At the input of the OPS node, a label extractor/eraser is firstly used to extract the in-band label wavelengths from the input packets. The label extractor/eraser is built up by using a series of the passive narrow band-pass optical filters (e.g. a series of cascading FBGs). The extracted label wavelengths are then processed by the OLP that determines the packet destination

Figure 7. Concept of the RF tone in-band label technique: a) in the spectral domain and b) time domain

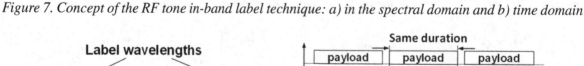

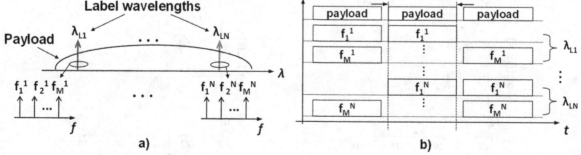

Figure 8. a) The schematic of the optical packet switch subsystem based on RF tone in-band labeling; b) the implementation of the pre-processing block for the RF tone in-band optical label

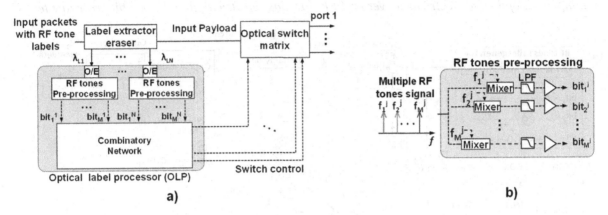

by setting the optical switch. In the OLP, the label wavelengths are separately detected by the optical to electrical converter (O/E), and processed in parallel in the RF tones pre-processing blocks. The RF tones pre-processing blocks are used to extract the baseband label bit from the multiple RF tones signal. The obtained baseband label bits are finally combined together into the electrical combinatory network to generate the switching control signal, which determines the forwarding of the payload in the optical switch matrix.

Figure 8b reports the detailed implementation of the RF tones pre-processing block. The multiple RF tones signal, which is obtained after the detection of the in-band label wavelength, is firstly divided into parallel paths and then baseband down-converted by separately mixing with the local oscillators at f_i^j ($i \in [1,M]$, $j \in [1,N]$). The baseband label bits are selected out by the Low-Pass Filter (LPF) and sent to the electrical combinatory network for the switching control generation. It is worth noting that the RF tones pre-processing blocks process all the RF tones labels asynchronously and in parallel. As a result, the OLP processing time can be kept constant regardless of the number of label wavelengths and RF tones. It is therefore that this technique enables the OPS with an exponential increase of number of ports at the expense of limited increase in latency and complexity.

Demonstration of the Label Technique with Multiple Data-Rate Packets

Figure 9 shows the experimental setup of the optical packet switching for multiple data rate packets using RF tone in-band label technique. The transmitter of the 160 Gb/s and the 40 Gb/s data payload is the same as reported previously. In the RF tone label generator, two in-band label wavelengths at λ_{L1}=1544.3 nm and λ_{L2}=1546.8 nm are generated, each label wavelength carrying three RF tones at f_1^j=420 MHz, f_2^j=510 MHz, and f_3^j=615 MHz (j=1 or 2) to deliver 6 (2×3) label bits. Therefore, maximum 64 ports ($2^{2\times3}$) are able to be addressed by using only two label wavelengths.

Firstly, we investigate the OPS operation with 160 Gb/s OTDM payload. As shown in Figure 10a, two RF tone in-band label wavelengths λ_{L1} and λ_{L2} are inserted within the -20 dB bandwidth of the 160 Gb/s OTDM payload. The optical powers of the label and payload are -3.9 dBm and 3.3 dBm, respectively. At the OPS node, the 160 Gb/s packets with RF tone in-band label is first passing through a label extractor/eraser consisting of two cascaded FBGs before being fed into the optical switch based on LiNbO$_3$ technology (Calabretta 2010). Figures 10b and 10c show the electrical spectra of the multiple RF tones signals after the opto-electrical conversion of λ_{L1} and λ_{L2}, respec-

Figure 9. Experimental setup of the optical packet switching subsystem for multiple data rate packets, MOD: optical modulator, MLFL: mode-locked fiber laser, PG: pattern generator, FBG: fiber Bragg grating, O/E: optical to electrical converter, LPF: low pass electrical filter, BERT: bit error rate tester

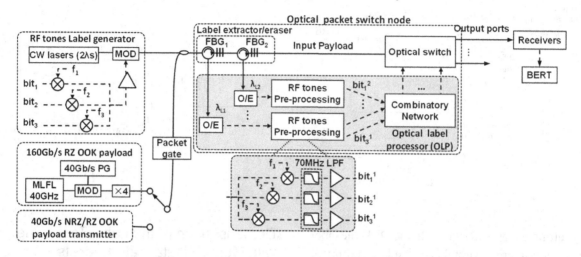

Figure 10. a) Optical spectra of the 160 Gb/s OTDM packets; the electrical spectra of the RF in-band label b) λ_{L1} and c) λ_{L2}

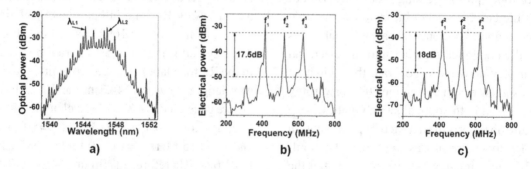

tively. The power ratio between the RF tones and back ground noise peak is 17.5 dB and 18 dB for λ_{L1} and λ_{L2}, which indicates a high electrical signal to noise ratio of the electrical RF tone labels. The 3 label bits for λ_{L1} and λ_{L2} were fed into two separate electrical combinatory networks.

The outputs of the electronic combinatory networks control two separate 1×8 optical switches. Figure 11a and 11b show the corresponding time traces of the switching results. The three graphs at the top shows the time traces of the extracted 3 label bits from λ_{L1} and λ_{L2}, respectively. The label bits have an eye-opening within the range of 0.4 to 0.65. Here, we define the eye-opening of a binary coded signal as (Miller 1994):

$$\text{Eye-opening} = \frac{(L1-\sigma1)-(L0-\sigma0)}{(L1-L0)}. \quad (1)$$

where $L1$, $L0$ is the mean of signal level 1 and level 0, and $\sigma1$, $\sigma0$ is the standard deviation of level 1 and level 0, respectively. The AC coupling behavior is observed in the time traces. This is due to the fact that the employed frequency mixers have the low cut-off frequency of the intermediate frequency (IF) of 5 MHz. A better eye-opening could be obtained if the IF of the mixer starts from DC. The time traces of the switched payload are also reported in Figures 11a and 11b. Figure 11c reports the bit error rate (BER) measurement results after switching the 160 Gb/s

Figure 11. Time traces of the 160 Gb/s OTDM packet switching results when using label bits obtained from a) λ_{L1} and b) λ_{L2}; c) the BER curves of 160 Gb/s OTDM packets

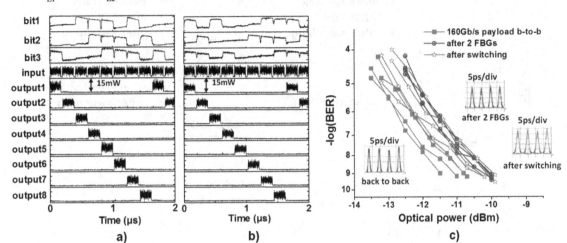

OTDM OOK payload. Error free operation is achieved with a power penalty of 0.5 dB and 0.7 dB after the label extraction and the switching, respectively. Eye diagrams of the 160 Gb/s packets are shown in the insets of Figure 11c. Clear eye diagrams indicate negligible distortion after the label extraction and the switching.

Furthermore, we also carried out optical packet switching operation for 40 Gb/s Non-Return to Zero (NRZ) and RZ OOK packets, which have much narrower spectrum bandwidth. For the 40 Gb/s NRZ and RZ OOK packets, the label wavelength was at λ_{L2}=1546.8 nm which is displaced of 0.26 nm with respect to the central wavelength of payload. The optical powers of the label and the payload are -6.8 dBm and 3.2 dBm, respectively. When the label is located beyond 30 GHz far away to the payload central wavelength, the penalties due to the spectrum carving are less than 1 dB. It indicates that this in-band labeling technique has the potential to be employed even for the data packets with narrow spectrum bandwidth. BER measurements of the 40 Gb/s payload are carried out both after the label extraction and the switching. Figure 12 shows that error free operation of the OPS with penalty of 0.5 dB and 0.4 dB was obtained for 40 Gb/s NRZ and 40 Gb/s RZ pack-

ets, respectively. Open eye diagrams before and after switching can also be found in the insets of Figure 12. One should note that only 0.3 dB and 0.2 dB penalty was measured for 40 Gb/s NRZ and RZ OOK packets after the carving of one FBG, respectively.

Performance of the RF Tone In-Band Labeling Technique

In order to support large scale and low latency OPS, the optical labeling technique is expected to be able to address large number of ports ($>2^{10}$) and introduce little latency during the label processing (~ns). It is therefore important to further investigate the scalability, the latency and the tolerance of the optical power fluctuation of the RF tone in-band labeling. We employed the experimental setup shown in Figure 9. For the simplicity of the discussion, we only assess the performance of generation, extraction and processing of one RF tone in-band label wavelength here, and use a simplified experimental setup during the investigations. As shown in Figure 13, the electrical multiple RF tone label is produced by an Arbitrary Waveform Generator (AWG), and amplified by a 10 Gb/s wideband RF amplifier

Figure 12. BER curves of (a) 40 Gb/s NRZ packets and (b) 40 Gb/s RZ packets

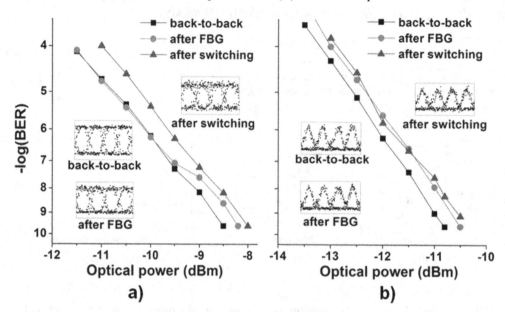

a)   b)

Figure 13. Experimental setup of the investigation on the RF tone in-band label

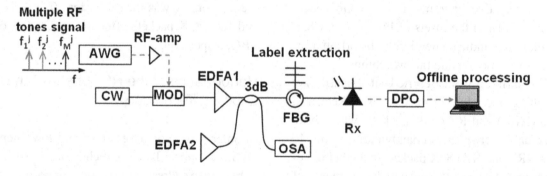

(RF-amp) before driving the optical modulator to generate the optical RF tone label. The optical label is boosted by EDFA1 and then combined with an ASE source produced by EDFA2 to further adjust the OSNR of the optical label. The label extractor/eraser consists of the same FBG that is used in the demonstration in Figure 9.

After extraction, the optical label is detected by a 10 Gb/s optical receiver (Rx). The Rx responses linearly with the input power range from -15 dBm to -3 dBm and introduces significant nonlinear distortion with input power > 4 dBm.

The detected RF label is then sampled by a real time Digital Phosphor Oscilloscope (DPO). The data samples acquired in the DPO are offline processed. Here, Matlab programming is used to simulate the RF tone label processing as is discussed in section II and evaluate the signal quality of the extracted label bits from the RF tone label. During the investigation, the sampling rate of both the AWG and the DPO is 6.25 GSamples/s. The RF tone label used during the investigation has a symbol rate of 10 MSymbol/s, and a duration of 80 ns with 20 ns guard times.

Scalability

The amount of ports of the OPS that can be controlled is determined by the amount of label bits carried by the optical label. As each RF tone is representing one label bit, it is therefore important to investigate how many RF tones can be carried by one in-band wavelength. In this section, we discuss the maximum number of RF tones that can be allocated in one label wavelength based on the setup in Figure 13.

We investigate the optimal frequency spacing between the RF tones to allocate as many as possible tones per label wavelength. It is known that denser is the frequency spacing between RF tones, larger amount of tones can be carried by the in-band wavelength. However, the crosstalk between the RF tones will increase with smaller frequency spacing, and hence require higher order filter to separate them in the OLP. Here, we carry out the investigation using RF tone label carrying 3 RF tones with different frequency spacing. We evaluate the eye opening of the label bits after the label processing with different filter order in the OLP. Similar to the digital filter design, the filter order varies linearly with the sampling rate for the same filter profile. For simplicity, we define the normalized filter order as:

$$\text{Normalized filter order} = \frac{\text{filter order (a.u.)}}{\text{Sampling rate (in GSamples/s)}}. \quad (2)$$

Figures 14a and 14b show the results when varying the frequency spacing of the RF tones and filter order. The figures show that although improved eye-opening of the label bits is given by employing higher order filter, this will cause longer filter delay and slower output rising/falling time. As a result, both the latency and the guard times of the OPS will increase. Besides, Figure14a also indicates that the eye-opening is not improving further when the normalized filter order is over a certain threshold, e.g. the threshold filter order is around 15 at the frequency spacing of 100 MHz. Besides, Figure 14a shows that the minimum eye-opening to recognize the label bits should be larger than 0.4. Figure 14c shows the minimum required normalized filter order for different frequency spacing of the RF tones. According to Figures 14b and 14c, with frequency spacing larger than 100 MHz, normalized filter order around 10 is already sufficient to detect label bits with eye-opening of 0.4 and rising/falling time of less than 6 ns. Therefore, considering RF tones with 100MHz spacing and normalized filter order of 10, potentially more than 25 RF tones in a single wavelength can be allocated within the 3-dB bandwidth of the OLP.

We experimentally investigate the delivering of 30 RF tones in a single wavelength by using the setup shown in Figure 13. In the experiment, the OSNR was 50 dB, the modulator drive voltage was 5.6 V_{pp}, and the frequency spacing of the RF

Figure 14. a) the eye-opening of the obtained label bits when using RF tones of different frequency spacing and filter order in the OLP; b) the rising/falling time of the label bits versus the filter order; c) the minimum required filter order to obtain label bits with eye opening larger than 0.4

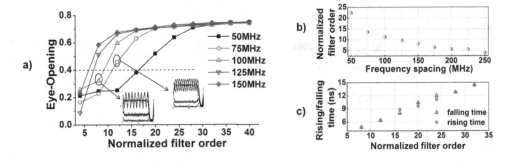

tones is 100 MHz. All the 30 label bits are coded by different $2^{15}-1$ PRBS data to have different combinations. Figure 15 shows the time traces of the received RF tone label (top) and the recovered 30 label bits from the 30 RF tones after the label processing, respectively.

Figure 16a shows that the eye-openings of the 30 label bits are larger than 0.4. The insets show the eye diagrams of the label bits at 100 MHz, 2.4 GHz and 3 GHz. Figure 16b shows the electrical spectra of the 30 received RF tones. It can found

that the peak power of each the RF tone directly determines the eye-openings that can be achieved. The variations of the peak power and the eye opening of the RF tones are mainly due to frequency response of the system. A better performance might be achieved if pre-emphasis of the system frequency response is implemented during the optical label generation.

These results confirm that the RF tone labeling technique is capable of delivering 30 RF tones by a single label wavelength. If we consider more label wavelengths, the number of label bits can increase exponentially. The low penalty indicates that by using 6 in-band label wavelengths, each carrying 30 RF tones, the in-band RF tone labeling technique can potentially deliver 180 (30×6) label bits, and thus coding more than 2^{180} optical addresses.

Figure 15. Time traces of the received RF tone label (top) and extracted 30 label bits (the rest)

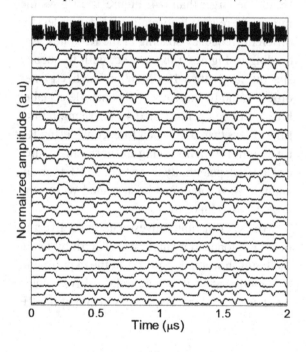

Latency of the Optical Label Processor

The latency of the optical label processor determines the time it required to setup the switch matrix for switching. There are two contributions to the optical label processor latency: one is the pre-processing of the RF tones, which extracts the baseband label bits from the RF tones subcarrier; the other part is the routing controlling which processes the label bits and generates the corresponding switch control signal according the routing algorithm. Both the RF pre-processing and routing controlling will contribute to the total latency of the OLP. We focus on the extra latency

Figure 16. a) Eye opening of the extracted 30 label bits (insets show the corresponding eye diagrams); b) electrical spectra of the RF tone in-band label with 30 tones

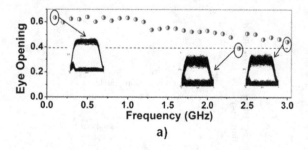
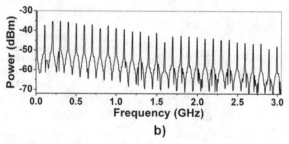

a)

b)

that is introduced by the pre-processing block. The OLP processes the RF tone label in a parallel way. Figure 17a shows the measured delay in each part of the RF tone preprocessing. The delay caused by the pre-processing is 7ns in total, which is mainly contributed by the low pass filter. The delay time is expected to be further reduced by using low pass filter of optimized design (Nayebi 1994). Besides the OLP processes all the RF tones and label wavelength in a parallel and synchronous fashion, the OLP can process RF tone in-band labels carrying large amount of label bits with little latency increase.

Power Fluctuation Tolerance of the Optical Label Processor

The optical power fluctuation of the labels might occur because of the distortion caused by the filtering, or by the switching, or along the transmission system. Therefore it is important to investigate the power fluctuation tolerance of the OLP. For the OLP reported in Figure 13, the power fluctuation tolerance can be assessed by considering the minimum required input optical power at the optical receiver in order to achieve the received label bits with an eye opening larger than 0.4. Figure 17b shows the measured results while increasing the number of the RF tones. It is found that the power fluctuation tolerance decreases as

the number of RF tones increase. For instance, considering ~4 dBm as the maximum allowed input power to the optical receiver in order to avoid significant nonlinear distortion, the power fluctuation tolerance with input OSNR of 35 dB is 6 dB when delivering 13 RF tones, and further decreased to 0.5 dB for delivering 25 tones. With such a small tolerance range, 25 RF tones is the maximum number of tones that can be delivered. While OSNR=50 dB, the power fluctuation tolerance is 11 dB for 13 RF tones and drops to 1 dB for 30 tones. Comparing the two curves at OSNR of 35 dB and 50 dB, it can be found that a larger power fluctuation is tolerated with a higher input OSNR. Besides the tolerance to input power fluctuation also depends on the response linearity of the receiver used in the OLP. It is believed that if a highly linear receiver would be employed, a larger tolerance to the power fluctuation might be obtained.

APPLICATIONS TO OPTICAL PACKET SWITCHING

Experimental results have been provided to confirm the operation of the scalable, asynchronous and low latency in-band label processor in optical packet switching systems. In the next sections, we

Figure 17. a) The time delay introduced by the RF tone pre-processing block; b) the minimum required input optical power to the OLP versus the number of RF tones carried by one label wavelength

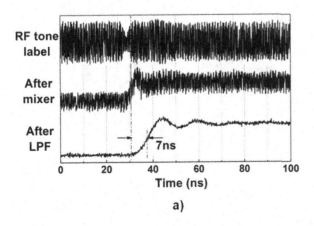
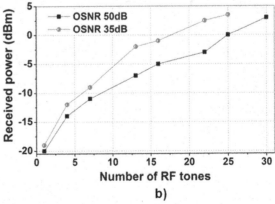

will present two applications of the optical packet switching node based on optical label processor to implement ultra-fast routing of optical packets at 640 Gb/s and systems network operation by routing packets at 160 Gb/s through three optical cross-connect nodes.

Optical Switching of 640 Gb/s OTDM Data Packets

We demonstrate 1×4 optical-packet switching with error-free transmission of 640 Gb/s single-wavelength OTDM data-packets including the in-band label processing technique. The schematic diagram of the OPS concept is shown in Figure 18. The system consists of four main blocks: the transmitter, a 50-km dispersion-compensated transmission link, the optical packet switch and the receiver. In the transmitter, optical pulses are generated by an erbium-glass oscillating pulse-generating laser (ERGO-PGL) at 1542 nm with pulse duration of 1.5 ps and 10 GHz repetition rate. The spectrum is broadened by self phase modulation in 400 m dispersion-flattened highly nonlinear fibre (DF-HNLF dispersion D=-0.45 ps/nm/km and dispersion slope S=0.006 ps/nm²/km

at 1550 nm, nonlinear coefficient 10.5 W/km/1) and filtered at 1545 nm with a 3-dB bandwidth of 9 nm to obtain pulses with duration of 600 fs.

Subsequently, the pulses are encoded by On-Off Keying (OOK) with a 10 Gb/s $2^7 - 1$ PRBS user-pattern to form the payload of the optical packets. The packets have duration of 153.6 ns consisting of 89.6 ns of data payload separated by a 64 ns guard band. The encoded pulses are sent through a fibre interleaver and are time multiplexed to constitute the 640 Gb/s OTDM data-packets. In order to distribute the clock-signal in the system (Gomez-Agis 2010), a clock pilot was generated by modulating a CW laser with a master clock at 10 GHz and inserted in-band with the 640 Gb/s spectrum. To improve the OSNR of the clock pilot, a programmable wave shaper filter with 3-dB bandwidth of 0.4 nm and 30 dB suppression of the rejection band centered at 1552.52 nm, is used to carve a portion of the spectrum where the pilot is inserted.

In order to address the destination of the packets, we employed the in-band labeling technique. Here we use two in-band labels at 1546.62 nm and 1547.28 nm to encode 4 addresses. Figures 19a and 19b show the spectra of the transmit-

Figure 18. Experimental setup: ERGO: erbium-glass oscillating pulse-generating laser, DF HNLF: Dispersion-flattened highly nonlinear fibre, SLA: super large area fibre, IDF: inverse dispersion fibre, FGB: fibre-bragg grating, E/O: electro-optical conversion

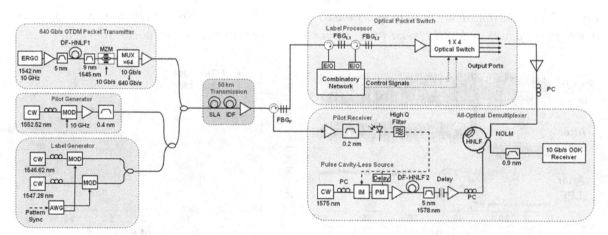

ted signal at the receiver side before and after the labels and pilot are extracted. The 640 Gb/s OTDM packetized data, together with the pilot and labels are transmitted over a dispersion and dispersion-slope compensated fibre span of 50 km optimized at 1545 nm. The transmission link is composed of 25-km SLA (super large area) fibre (D=20 ps/nm/km, S=0.06 ps/nm2/km and PMD=0.04 ps/km1=2) and 25- km IDF (inverse dispersion fiber) (D=-20 ps/nm/km, S=-0.06 ps/nm2/km and PMD=0.02 ps/km1=2) with a total loss of 12 dB. After the 50-km transmission link, the 640 Gb/s data packets are fed into the OPS. The OPS extracts the optical labels by cascading two FBGs (FBGL1 and FBGL2), centered at the label wavelengths, and two optical circulators. The parallel labels are detected and processed by the electrical combinatory network. The combinatory network provides the control signal of the electro-optical switch. Finally, the payload is fed into the 1 × 4 electro-optical switch based on LiNbO3 technology. According to the encoded addresses, one switch is enabled at a time and the switched optical packet is evaluated in the All-Optical Demultiplexer (AOD). Figures 19(c-m) show the dynamic operation of the OPS. The extracted labels and the 640 Gb/s data packets are shown in Figures 19(c-d) and Figure 19e, respectively. According to the packet addresses, the control signals generated by the combinatory network to drive the 1×4 switch are shown in Figures 19(f-i). Figures 19(j-m) show the switched packets from port 1 to port 4 with their respective addresses '11', '10', '00' and '01'.

The switched optical packets are then fed into the receiver to measure the performance of the system. The receiver consists of pilot extraction and the cavity-less pulse source that produces the optical pulse-train required for 640-to-10 Gb/s AOD operation (Hu 2007). The generated optical short pulses serve as clock pulses in a NOLM (nonlinear optical loop mirror)-based AOD.

The quality of the time-demultiplexed signal is analyzed by the Bit-Error-Rate Tester (BERT), which is triggered by the extracted clock. BER curves recorded for the switched packets at each output port are shown in Figure 20a. As reference, we plot the BER curve of the back-to-back (b-to-b) payload (filled-stars). Error-free operation with 1 to 1.5 dB of penalty was measured at output ports 1-4 (filled-squares). As a representative example of the integrity of the total number of channels of the 640 Gb/s payload, we measured the receiver sensitivity at 10^{-9} of 8 of 64 consecutive channels at one of the output ports of the optical switch. As shown in Figure 20b BER < 10^{-9} could be detected for the measured channels before (circles) and after (triangles) transmission. Those results demonstrate the operation of optical packet switching and detection of 640 Gb/s single-wavelength

Figure 19. a-b) Spectra of the 640 Gb/s OTDM signal; c-m) dynamic operation of the optical packet switch

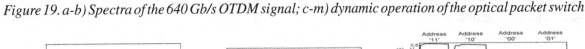

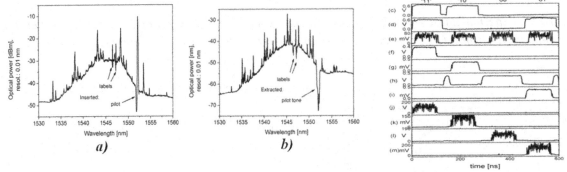

Figure 20. a) BER curves of the payload and switched packets; b) sensitivity of 8 consecutive channels

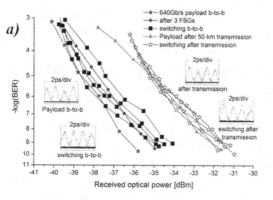 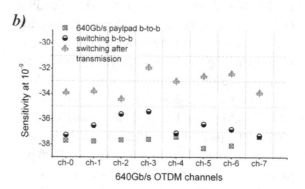

OTDM data-packets based on the in-band label concept including ultra-fast self-synchronization after 50km fibre transmission.

Optical Switching of 160 Gb/s OTDM Data Packets over Multiple Optical Nodes

In this section we present a transparent optical node that includes an asynchronous and optical packet switch sub-system and a packet based clock extraction for data burst detection of 160 Gb/s data packets. We present transmission and dynamic packet switching of 160 Gb/s data packets (single wavelength) through three nodes with a transmission span of 52 Km.

Figure 21 shows the transmission system and the schematic of the optical packet switch. To test the fast operation of the optical packet switch and packet clock extraction, we generate 6.4 ns short

160 Gb/s data packets as discussed previously. We exploit the wide optical spectrum of the OTDM signal to insert in-band a 10 GHz clock pilot and the labels (see spectrum of the packets in Figure 21). In this work both the clock pilot and the packet address are packetized together with the payload and transmitted through the optical nodes. This leads the payload, clock, and address to experience the same dispersion-dependent impairments. Moreover, the clock pilot and the addresses can be asynchronously extracted by passive wavelength filtering and processed, while the payload remains in the optical domain. The burst 10 GHz clock pilot at 1552.52 nm is combined with the payload and the address through an optical coupler. To improve the phase noise of the clock pilot, a portion of the payload spectrum where carved by a Fiber Bragg Grating (FBG1) centered at 1552.52 nm with a 3 dB bandwidth of 0.4 nm and 30 dB suppression of the rejection band. The packet address are in-

Figure 21. Experimental set-up: MLFL: mode-locked fiber laser, AWG: arbitrary waveform generator, PG: pattern generator, O/E: optical-to-electrical converter, DCF: dispersion compensation fiber

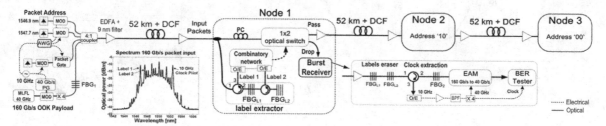

band labeled encoded. We use two in-band labels at λ_{L1}=1546.9 nm and λ_{L2}=1547.7 nm to encode 4 addresses that identify the three optical nodes in the system.

At each optical node the power of the packets is split by a 90:10 coupler. 90% of the power is fed via a polarization controller into the 1x2 electro-optic switch based on LiNbO$_3$ technology. The 10% of the power is fed into the label processor. In the label processor, the labels are extracted by cascading two FBGs centered at the labels wavelengths and two optical circulators. The parallel labels are detected and processed by the electrical combinatory network. The combinatory network provides the control signal of the 1x2 electro-optical switch. The rising and falling time of the control signals that limit the packets guard-time are in the order of 700 ps. According to the encoded address, the packets are then forwarded to the next node or dropped and received.

The burst receiver consists of a packet clock extraction and an 160 Gb/s to 40 Gb/s time demux. First, the labels are erased by using a copy of the FBGs employed in the label processor. Then the payload and the 10 GHz clock pilot are separated via an optical circulator and FBG2, which is identical to FBG1. This allows fast-locking/unlocking times; locking is realised every time a packet arrives at the receiver and unlocking occurs when the packet ends. The history of the previous packet is completely forgotten when the next packets arrive. As the clock and payload are transmitted synchronously and are spectrally in-band, they are affected by the same impairments leading to the same phase drifts. Thus, the relative phase between the clock and the data is preserved. The 10 GHz extracted clock is converted to the electrical domain by a photodetector, amplified and correspondingly quadrupled ($\times$ 4) to drive the 40 GHz Electro-Absorption Modulator (EAM) with a time window of 5 ps to time demux the 160 Gb/s data to 40 Gb/s data. This allows the 40 Gb/s data to be analyzed by commercial BERT system.

The experimental set-up to test the transmission and dynamic switching of the 160 Gb/s packets is shown in Figure 21. The system consists of three nodes with a transmission span of 52 Km of true-wave reduced slope with carefully chromatic dispersion compensation and amplification and filtering at the fibers output to restore signal fidelity. Each node is identified by an address. Optical packets with different addresses are launched in the system (see Figure 22(a-c). Each node let pass or drop the packets according to the packet address. Figure 22 shows the dynamic switching operation of the optical nodes. The control signal generated by the combinatory network provides

Figure 22. Measured traces: a-b) labels of the input optical packets; c) input packet payload; d) control signal generated by node 1; e-f) packets dropped and passed at node 1; g) control signal generated by node 2; h-i) packets dropped and passed at node 2

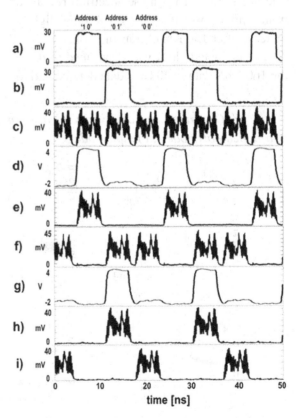

6 Vpp to drive the 1x2 optical switch is shown in Figure 22d. Figures 22(e-f) show the dropped (packet address '10') and passed packets at node 1. The contrast ratio between the dropped and transmitted packets was 18 dB. Similarly, Figures 22(g-h) show switching signal and the dropped packets with address '10' at node 2. The packets with address '00' are detected by the node 3 and are shown in Figure 22i.

Figure 23 shows the optical spectra of the packets at the pass and drop port of different optical nodes. The OSNR reduction due to the in-line amplifiers of the optical packets at node 3 (OSNR= 27 dB) and packets at node 1 (OSNR=35 dB) is around 8 dB.

Open eye diagrams, recorded by using the extracted clock at each node, are clearly visible in Figure 24. To hold the persistence of the clock, we have filtered the clock with a 10 GHz electric filter with 10 MHz bandwidth. The phase noise of the extracted clock is reported in Figure 25. The integration of the noise spectrum reveals a timing jitter lower than 90 fs with only slightly increase after 156 Km of transmission.

The extracted clock was quadruped to drive the 160 Gb/s data to 40 Gb/s data demux, and to

clock the BERT tester. The BERT operation requires a continuous clock. Thus, we supply to the BERT the recovered clock output (a continuous clock) from a Clock-Recovery Data (CRD) receiver, whose input corresponds to the extracted clock. The best case (filled symbol) and worst case (half-filled symbol) BER curves recorded for the switched packets at each node are reported in Figure 26. As reference we report the BER curve of the back-to-back (b-t-b) payload. Error-free operation with 0.65 dB, 1.6 dB, and 3 dB of penalty was measured at node 1, node 2, and node 3, respectively. The penalty is partially attributed to the carving effect of the FBGs (around 0.5 dB) and to the ASE noise accumulated along the transmission system.

CONCLUSION AND FUTURE RESEARCH DIRECTIONS

In this chapter, we have introduced and compared different label processing techniques as critical sub-system for implementing a scalable and low latency optical packet switching cross-connect node. In this respect, we present an in-band opti-

Figure 23. Optical spectra of the packets at: a) input node 1; b) dropped port node 1; c) input node 2; d) dropped port node 2; e) input node 3

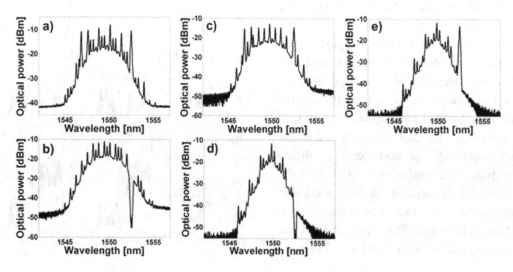

Figure 24. Eye diagrams at different optical nodes

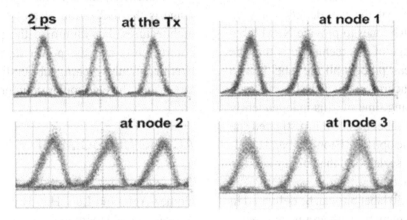

Figure 25. Phase noise and timing jitter of the extracted clock at different optical nodes

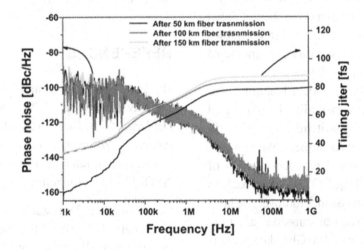

Figure 26. BER curves at different optical nodes

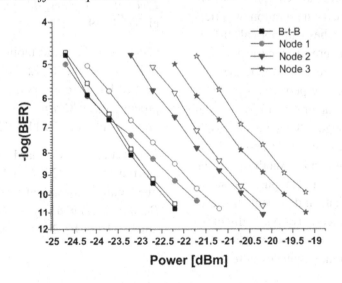

cal labeling technique based on N in-band label wavelengths, each of the wavelength carrying M binary coded RF tones to provide N×M label bits. The advantage of this technique is that the label processor can process all the label bits in parallel and asynchronously. This has allowed very fast processing time of 7 ns independently of the number of label bits. We investigated the performance of the optical RF tone in-band labeling including the scalability, the latency and the optical power fluctuation tolerance of OLP. We show that at least 30 label bits can be delivered in a single label wavelength, with around 7 ns extra latency. These results show that the presented optical RF tone in-band labeling technique has the potential to provide large number of label bits with fast processing time, and thus enables to control an optical switch with large amount of ports at the expense of low latency.

Based on the in-band optical labeling technique, we have experimentally demonstrated error free optical packet switching operations in systems and networks environment. We reported on the operation of optical packet switching of 640 Gb/s single-wavelength OTDM data-packets after 50km fibre transmission. Moreover, we have demonstrated error-free transmission, dynamic switching and detection of 160 Gb/s data packets through three optical nodes.

Possible future directions of exploiting OPS in the optical networks are the integration of optical label processor and switches with optical buffers. However, the lack of mature and generic photonic integration technology prevented the realization of small footprint, and low power consumption circuits for large scale integration of optical devices. Future breakthrough in the field of photonic integration could lead to efficient and scalable optical packet switching circuits. Another potential exploitation of the OPS is in computer interconnecting networks, such as in data centers and in high performing computers networks. In this close environment, large scale OPS cross-connect switch can outperform electronics switches in terms of high bandwidth and low latency. The main challenge is the realization of an optical switching architectures that minimize the packaging and control costs and the power dissipation of the overall optical switching fabric, still substantially larger than the electronics counterpart.

ACKNOWLEDGMENT

The authors wish to thank Wenrui Wang, Fausto Gomez-Agis, Jun Luo, Hau Hu, Hans-Christian Hansen Mulvad for their contributions, and Huug de Waardt, Leif Oxenlowe, and Harm Dorren for the helpful discussions.

REFERENCES

Bo, X., Zuqing, Z., Haijun, Y., Wei, J., Harris, D. L., & Ikezawa, K. … Yoo, S.J.B. (2007). *First field trial of OLS network testbed with all-optical contention resolution of asynchronous, variable-length optical packets*. Paper presented at OFC/NFOEC 2007. Anaheim, CA.

Calabretta, N., Contestabile, G., d'Errico, A., & Ciaramella, E. (2005). All-optical label processor/erasure for label swapping of 12.5 Gbit/s spectrally separated bit-serial DPSK label and payload. *Electronics Letters*, 41, 541–543. doi:10.1049/el:20050449.

Calabretta, N., Contestabile, G., Kim, S. H., Lee, S. K., & Ciaramella, E. (2006). Exploiting time-to-wavelength conversion for all-optical label processing. *IEEE Photonics Technology Letters*, 18, 436–438. doi:10.1109/LPT.2005.863207.

Calabretta, N., de Waardt, H., Khoe, G. D., & Dorren, H. J. S. (2004). Ultrafast asynchronous multi-output all-optical header processor. *IEEE Photonics Technology Letters*, 16, 1182–1184. doi:10.1109/LPT.2004.824993.

Calabretta, N., Jung, H. D., Herrera Llorente, J., Tangdiongga, E., Koonen, A. M. J., & Dorren, H. J. S. (2008). *1 x 4 all-optical packet switch at 160 Gb/s employing optical processing of scalable in-band address labels.* Paper presented at OFC 2008. San Diego, CA.

Calabretta, N., Presi, M., Contestabile, A., & Ciaramella, E. (2007). All-optical asynchronous serial-to-parallel converter circuit for DPSK optical packets. *IEEE Photonics Technology Letters, 19,* 783–785. doi:10.1109/LPT.2007.895895.

Calabretta, N., Wang, W., Ditewig, T., Raz, O., Agis, F. G., de Waardt, S. Z. H., & Dorren, H. J. S. (2010). Scalable optical packet switches for multiple data formats and data rates packets. *IEEE Photonics Technology Letters, 22*(7), 483–485. doi:10.1109/LPT.2010.2040993.

Chi, N., Zhang, J., & Jeppesen, P. (2003). All-optical subcarrier labeling based on the carrier suppression of the payload. *IEEE Photonics Technology Letters, 15,* 781–783. doi:10.1109/LPT.2003.810260.

Chow, P. S., Cioffi, J. M., & Bingham, J. A. C. (1995). A practical discrete multitone transceiver loading algorithm for data transmission over spectrally shaped channels. *IEEE Transactions on Communications, 43,* 773–775. doi:10.1109/26.380108.

Chung-Li, L., Sabido, D. J., Poggiolini, P., Hofmeister, R. T., & Kazovsky, L. G. (1995). CORD-a WDMA optical network: Subcarrier-based signaling and control scheme. *IEEE Photonics Technology Letters, 7,* 555–557. doi:10.1109/68.384542.

Gomez-Agis, F., Calabretta, N., Albores-Mejia, A., & Dorren, H. J. S. (2010). Clock-distribution with instantaneous synchronization for 160 Gbit/s optical time domain multiplexed systems packet transmission. *Optics Letters, 35*(19), 3255–3257. doi:10.1364/OL.35.003255 PMID:20890351.

Guillemot, C., Renaud, M., Gambini, P., Janz, C., Andonovic, I., & Bauknecht, R. (1998). Transparent optical packet switching: the European ACTS KEOPS project approach. *Journal of Lightwave Technology, 16,* 2117–2134. doi:10.1109/50.736580.

Hamilton, S. A., & Robinson, B. S. (2002). 40-Gb/s all-optical packet synchronization and address comparison for OTDM networks. *IEEE Photonics Technology Letters, 14*(2), 209–211. doi:10.1109/68.980524.

Herrera, J., Raz, O., Tangdiongga, E., Liu, Y., Mulvad, H. C. H., & Ramos, F. et al. (2008). 160-Gb/s all-optical packet switching over a 110-km field installed optical link. *Journal of Lightwave Technology, 26,* 176–182. doi:10.1109/JLT.2007.913068.

Hu, H., Yu, J., Zhang, L., Zhang, A., Li, Y., Jiang, Y., & Yang, E. (2007). Pulse source based on directly modulated laser and phase modulator. *Optics Express, 15*(14), 8931–8937. doi:10.1364/OE.15.008931 PMID:19547231.

Klonidis, D., Politi, C. T., Nejabati, R., O'Mahony, M. J., & Simeonidou, D. (2005). OPSnet: Design and demonstration of an asynchronous high-speed optical packet switch. *Journal of Lightwave Technology, 23*(10), 2914–2925. doi:10.1109/JLT.2005.856167.

Koch, B. R., Hu, Z., Bowers, J. E., & Blumenthal, D. J. (2006). Payload-envelope detection and label-detection integrated photonic circuit for asynchronous variable-length optical packet switching with 40-Gb/s RZ payloads and 10-Gb/s NRZ labels. *Journal of Lightwave Technology, 24,* 3409–3417. doi:10.1109/JLT.2006.879221.

Le Minh, H., Ghassemlooy, Z., & Ng, W. P. (2006). OPN06-3: Multiple-hop routing based on the pulse-position modulation header processing scheme in all-optical ultrafast packet switching network. In *Proceedings of IEEE Global Telecommunications Conference 2006 (GLOBECOM '06),* (pp. 1 – 5). IEEE.

Leguizamon, G. P., Ortega, B., & Capmany, J. (2009). Advanced subcarrier multiplexed label swapping in optical packet switching nodes for next generation internet networks. *Journal of Lightwave Technology, 27,* 655–669. doi:10.1109/JLT.2008.926951.

Miller, C. M. (1994). High-speed digital transmitter characterization using eye diagram analysis. *Hewlett-Packard Journal, 45*(4), 29–37.

Mishra, A. K., Ellis, A. D., Cotter, D., Smyth, F., Connolly, E., & Barry, L. P. (2006). Spectrally compact optical subcarrier multiplexing with 42.6 Gbit/s AM-PSK payload and 2.5 Gbit/s NRZ labels. *Electronics Letters, 42,* 1303–1304. doi:10.1049/el:20062414.

Nayebi, K., Barnwell, T. P. III, & Smith, M. J. T. (1994). Low delay FIR filter banks: Design and evaluation. *IEEE Transactions on Signal Processing, 42*(1), 24–31. doi:10.1109/78.258118.

Ramos, F., Kehayas, E., Martinez, J. M., Clavero, R., Marti, J., & Stampoulidis, L. (2005). IST-LASAGNE: Towards all-optical label swapping employing optical logic gates and optical flip-flops. *Journal of Lightwave Technology, 23,* 2993–3011. doi:10.1109/JLT.2005.855714.

Scaffardi, M., Lazzeri, E., Furukawa, H., Wada, N., Miyazaki, T., Potì, L., & Bogoni, A. (2010). 160 Gb/s/port 2x2 OPS node test-bed performing 50 Gchip/s all-optical active label processing with contention detection. *IEEE/OSA. Journal of Lightwave Technology, 28,* 922–930. doi:10.1109/JLT.2009.2035524.

Seddighian, P., Baby, V., Habib, C., Chen, L. R., Rusch, L. A., & LaRochelle, S. (2007). *All-optical swapping of spectral amplitude code labels for packet switching*. Paper presented at Photonics in Switching. San Francisco, CA.

Swanson, B., & Gilder, G. (2008). *Estimating the exaflood*. Seattle, WA: Discovery Institute. Retrieved from http://www.scribd.com/doc/6483200/Estimating_the_Exaflood_012808_by_Bret_

Tafur Monroy, I., Vegas Olmos, J., Koonen, A. M. J., Huijskens, F. M., de Waardt, H., & Khoe, G. D. (2004). Optical label switching by using differential phase shift keying and in-band subcarrier multiplexing modulation format. *Optical Engineering (Redondo Beach, Calif.), 43,* 1476. doi:10.1117/1.1760086.

Takenaka, M., Raburn, M., Takeda, K., & Nakano, Y. (2006). *All-optical packet switching by MMI-BLD optical flip-flop*. Paper presented at: OFC 2006. Anaheim, CA.

Vegas Olmos, J. J., Zhang, J., Holm-Nielsen, P. V., Monroy, I. T., Polo, V., & Koonen, A. M. J. et al. (2004). Simultaneous optical label erasure and insertion in a single wavelength conversion stage of combined FSK/IM modulated signals. *Photonics Technology Letters, 16,* 2144–2146. doi:10.1109/LPT.2004.833084.

Wada, N., Furukawa, H., & Miyazaki, T. (2007). Prototype 160Gbit/s/port optical packet switch based on optical code label processing. *Journal of Selected Topics in Quantum Electronics, 13,* 1551–1559. doi:10.1109/JSTQE.2007.897602.

Wai, P. K. A., Chan, L. Y., Lui, L. F. K., Hwa-Yaw, T., & Demokan, M. S. (2005). 1 x 4 All-optical packet switch at 10 Gb/s. *Photonics Technology Letters, 17,* 1289–1291. doi:10.1109/LPT.2005.846492.

Wang, H., Garg, A. S., Bergman, K., & Glick, M. (2010). *Design and demonstration of an all-optical hybrid packet and circuit switched network platform for next generation data centers*. Paper presented at OFC 2010. Los Angeles, CA.

Wang, J. P., Robinson, B. S., Hamilton, S. A., & Ippen, E. P. (2006). Demonstration of 40-Gb/s packet routing using all-optical header processing. *Photonics Technology Letters, 18,* 2275–2277. doi:10.1109/LPT.2006.884727.

Yang, H., Lee, S. C. J., Tangdiongga, E., Breyer, F., Randel, S., & Koonen, A. M. J. (2009). *40-Gb/s transmission over 100m graded-index plastic optical fiber based on discrete multitone modulation.* Paper presented at OFC 2009. San Diego, CA.

ADDITIONAL READING

Barros, L. A., & Hőlzle, U. (2009). The datacenter as a computer: An introduction to the design of warehouse-scale machines. *Synthesis Lectures on Computer Architecture, 4*(1), 1–118. doi:10.2200/S00193ED1V01Y200905CAC006.

Beheshti, N., Burmeister, E., Ganjali, Y., Bowers, J. E., Blumenthal, D. J., & McKeown, N. (2010). Optical packet buffers for backbone internet routers. *IEEE/ACM Transactions on Networking, 18*(5), 1599–1609. doi:10.1109/TNET.2010.2048924.

Blumenthal, D. J. (2004). *Optical packet switching.* Paper presented at Lasers and Electro-Optics Society, LEOS 2004. Puerto Rico.

Brunina, D., Lai, C. P., & Bergman, K. (2012). A data rate- and modulation format-independent packet-switched optical network test-bed. *IEEE Photonics Technology Letters, 24*(5), 377–379. doi:10.1109/LPT.2011.2179642.

Burmeister, E. F., & Bowers, J. E. (2006). Integrated gate matrix switch for optical packet buffering. *IEEE Photonics Technology Letters, 18*(1), 103–105. doi:10.1109/LPT.2005.860386.

Calabretta, N. (2004). *All-optical header processing based on nonlinear gain and index dynamics in semiconductor optical amplifiers.* (PhD Thesis). Retrieved from http://alexandria.tue.nl/extra2/200411065.pdf

Calabretta, N., Di Lucente, S., Nazarathy, Y., Raz, O., & Dorren, H. (2011). *Scalable optical packet switch architecture for low latency and high load computer communication networks.* Paper presented at 13th International Conference on Transparent Optical Networks (ICTON). Stockholm, Sweden.

Calabretta, N., & Dorren, H. J. S. (2009). *All-optical header recognizer for optical packet switched networks.* Berlin: VDM Verlag.

Calabretta, N., Jung, H.-D., Tangdiongga, E., & Dorren, H. J. S. (2010). All-optical packet switching and label rewriting for data packets beyond 160 Gb/s. *IEEE Photonics Journal, 2*(2), 113–129. doi:10.1109/JPHOT.2010.2044404.

Calabretta, N., Soganci, I. M., Tanemura, T., Wang, W., Raz, O., & Higuchi, K. ... Dorren, H. J. S. (2010). *1×16 optical packet switch sub-system with a monolithically integrated InP optical switch.* Paper presented at Optical Fiber Communications 2010. San Diego, CA.

Chiaroni, D., Simonneau, C., Salsi, M., et al. (2010). *Optical packet ring network offering bit rate and modulation formats transparency.* Paper presented at OFC 2010. San Diego, CA.

Farrington, N., Porter, G., Radhakrishnan, S., Bazzaz, H., Subramanya, V., & Fainman, Y. ... Vahdat, A. (2010). *Helios: A hybrid electrical/optical switch architecture for modular data centers.* Paper presented at: SIGCOMM'10. New Delhi, India.

Gripp, J., Duelk, M., Simsarian, J. E., Bhardwaj, A., Bernasconi, P., Laznicka, O., & Zirngibl, M. (2003). Optical switch fabrics for ultra-highcapacity IP routers. *Journal of Lightwave Technology, 21*, 2839–2850. doi:10.1109/JLT.2003.819150.

Hemenway, R., Grzybowski, R., Minkenberg, C., & Luijten, R. (2004). Optical-packet-switched interconnect for supercomputer applications. *Journal of Optical Networking, 3*, 900–913. doi:10.1364/JON.3.000900.

Herzog, M., Maier, M., & Reisslein, M. (2004). Metropolitan area packet-switched WDM networks: A survey on ring systems. *IEEE Communications Surveys & Tutorials, 6*(2), 2–20. doi:10.1109/COMST.2004.5342236.

Hill, M., Dorren, H. J. S., de Vries, T., Leijtens, X. J. M., den Besten, J. H., & Smalbrugge, B. et al. (2004). A fast low-power optical memory based on coupled micro-ring lasers. *Nature, 432*, 206–209. doi:10.1038/nature03045 PMID:15538365.

Kachris, C., & Tomkos, I. (2011). A survey on optical interconnects for data centers. *IEEE Communications Surveys & Tutorials,* (99), 1-16.

Lam, C. F., Liu, H., Koley, B., Zhao, X., Kamalov, V., & Gill, V. (2010). Fiber optic communication technologies: What's needed for datacenter network operations. *IEEE Communications Magazine, 48*(7). doi:10.1109/MCOM.2010.5496876.

Maier, M. (2008). *Optical switching networks.* Cambridge, UK: Cambridge University Press. doi:10.1017/CBO9780511619731.

Nicholes, S. C., Mašanović, M. L., Jevremović, B., Lively, E., Coldren, L. A., & Blumenthal, D. J. (2009). *The world's first InP 8x8 monolithic tunable optical router (MOTOR) operating at 40 Gbps line rate per port.* Paper presented at OFC 2009. San Diego, CA.

Pan, Z., Yang, H., Zhu, Z., Funabashi, M., Xiang, B., & Yoo, S. J. B. (2006). All-optical label swapping, clock recovery, and 3R regeneration in 101-hop cascaded optical-label switching router networks. *Photonics Technology Letters, 18*, 2629–2631. doi:10.1109/LPT.2006.887360.

Pattavina, A. (1989). *Switching theory: Architectures and performance in broadband ATM networks.* New York: Wiley.

Petrantonakis, D., Kanellos, G. T., Zakynthinos, P., Pleros, N., Apostolopoulos, D., & Avramopoulos, H. (2006). *A 40 Gb/s 3R burst-mode receiver with 4 integrated MZI switches.* Paper presented at OFC 2006. Anaheim, CA.

Porzi, C., Guina, M., Calabretta, N., Bogoni, A., & Potì, L. (2010). Applications of saturable absorption based nonlinear vertical-cavity semiconductor devices for all-optical signal processing. In *Semiconductor Technologies.* Vienna, Austria: In-Tech Education and Publishing KG. doi:10.5772/8554.

Ramaswami, R., Sivarajan, K. N., & Sasaki, G. H. (2010). *Optical networks: A practical perspective* (3rd ed.). San Francisco: Morgan Kaufmann Publishers.

Tanemura, T., Soganci, I. M., Oyama, T., Ohyama, T., Mino, S., & Williams, K. A. et al. (2011). Large-capacity compact optical buffer based on InP integrated phased-array switch and coiled fiber delay lines. *Journal of Lightwave Technology, 29*(4), 396–402. doi:10.1109/JLT.2010.2102338.

Yoo, S. J. B. (2006). Optical packet and burst switching technologies for future photonic Internet. *Journal of Lightwave Technology, 24*, 4468–4492. doi:10.1109/JLT.2006.886060.

Chapter 4
Monitoring Devices for Providing Network Intelligence in Optical Packet Switched Networks

Ruth Vilar
Universitat Politècnica de València, Spain

Francisco Ramos
Universitat Politècnica de València, Spain

ABSTRACT

The development of all-Optical Packet Switching (OPS) networks brings about new challenges in the topic of Optical Performance Monitoring (OPM). The objectives of this chapter are addressed to the proposal of new monitoring techniques capable of packet-by-packet monitoring in the optical domain to preserve packet transparency. Moreover, new optical layer functionalities such as dynamic reconfiguration and link level restoration also introduce a level of complexity that may require advanced OPM capabilities. In this chapter, an OSNR monitoring technique and its application for providing network intelligence are explained in detail. In particular, the integration of the monitoring system with the control and management planes is investigated to perform other functions such as quality of service implementation, OSNR-assisted routing, and backup route selection.

INTRODUCTION

To meet the increasing requirements for higher bandwidth and novel services, an evolution from static optical networks to dynamically reconfigurable architectures is expected. This evolution highlights the importance of providing network

DOI: 10.4018/978-1-4666-3652-1.ch004

solutions putting forward scalability and flexibility as most critical specifications. According to these requirements, Optical Packet Switching (OPS) networks provide high throughput, bandwidth efficiency, and excellent flexibility, as well as offering new capabilities to process packets directly at the optical layer (Jourdan et al., 2001; O'Mahony et al., 2001). However, to support OPS at bitrates up to Terabit/s, networks should reduce the amount of complex electronics by migrating to an all-optical network, where data is switched and routed transparently in the optical domain. At this scenario, All-Optical Label Switching (AOLS) appears to be a solution to avoid the bottleneck imposed by the nodes based on electronic processing (Blumenthal et al., 2000). In such an AOLS scenario, all packet-by-packet routing and forwarding functions of Multiprotocol Label Switching (MPLS) are implemented directly in the optical domain. By using optical labels, the IP packets are routed through the core optical networks without requiring O/E/O conversions whenever a routing decision is necessary. This solution allows the network transparency to be improved but at the expense of increasing the complexity of the network management, being necessary to monitor the parameters affecting the network performance directly in the optical layer.

The need of signal quality monitoring at the physical layer has stimulated interest in Optical Performance Monitoring (OPM) as a potential mechanism for improving the control of transmission and the fault management in the physical layer (Kilper et al., 2004). New optical layer functionalities such as dynamic reconfiguration and link level restoration also introduce a level of complexity that may require advanced OPM capabilities. All of these issues bring focus to OPM as an enabling technology for next OPS networks. In such networks, each optical packet may traverse different paths and different optical components; thereby having its own history and quality. Hence, the key goal for OPM is to develop techniques capable of monitoring the physical impairments with fast response and on a packet basis. Related to this topic, the following questions are of special interest:

- How to perform OPM on a packet basis?
- How to develop a monitoring module with fast response time and wide dynamic range?

- How to associate the monitored parameters with the switch controls and header information?
- How to integrate the monitoring information with the control and management planes to provide some kind of network intelligence?

In this chapter, these questions are addressed and an OSNR monitoring technique suitable for next generation OPS networks is discussed. This technique is based on using a specific data word (monitoring field) inserted into the packet header, which is processed in each intermediate node, for monitoring purpose. Moreover, the integration of the monitoring system with other functions in the packet switching node to take real-time decisions based on quality requirements is also envisaged. This will be a great step forward towards the provision of network intelligence inside optical networks.

This paper explores OPM and its potential for enabling higher reconfigurability, and flexibility in an OPS network, including the issues of what parameters should be monitored in the optical signal. Moreover, this chapter describes the importance of signal quality monitoring on a packet-by-packet basis for next OPS networks and proposes a novel technique based on the use of optical correlation to assess the signal quality at the optical domain with relaxed speed requirements. At the end of the chapter, an overview of the main applications of the proposed monitoring technique is presented.

OPTICAL PERFORMANCE MONITORING

During the last decades, optical transport systems have become the suitable solution to enable the rapid growth of data traffic in the network backbone. Apart from enhancing the network capacity, optical networks allow high bitrates but at the expense of increasing the complexity of the network management.

Many elements can impact on optical signal transmission performance. The dominant impairments for long-haul transmission are broadband noise from fiber amplifiers, e.g., accumulated Amplified Spontaneous Emission (ASE) and fiber dispersions, including Chromatic Dispersion (CD) and Polarization Mode Dispersion (PMD). These elements will limit the transmission capacity and distance, and thus optical performance monitoring is required for managing high capacity optical networks. In addition, as data bitrates and capacity increase to accommodate fast traffic growth, it is more important to incorporate effective OPM into the system in order to simplify system design, facilitate operations, enhance system performance, and reduce overall operational cost (Bendilli, 2000; Kilper et al., 2004).

To enable robust and reliable network operation, the OPM block responsible of signal quality monitoring can play a major role to perform other functions including:

- OPM can provide information for fault management which consists of identifica-

tion, localization, diagnosis, and tracking of faults in a network (Kilper, 2005).

- OPM can be used as a feedback to keep the network operating in an optimal manner (Kilper et al., 2004).
- OPM can perform the signal quality monitoring for quality of service assurance.
- OPM can act as an alarm to predict network failures and allows traffic to be rerouted before failure occurs (Richter, 2002).
- OPM can change routing tables and redirect traffic based on physical layer conditions (Teixeira et al., 2009).

These functionalities allow the integration of OPM into the network management and control system with the goal of providing network intelligence and dynamic reconfiguration. In this scenario, performance information coming from signal quality monitoring module is disseminated by the control plane and shared between network nodes to perform Quality of Service (QoS) provisioning, make routing decisions based on quality requirements, perform fault management or initiate restoration mechanisms. Figure 1 shows the interaction between signal quality monitoring system and the control and management planes.

Figure 1. Interaction between monitoring system and control and management planes

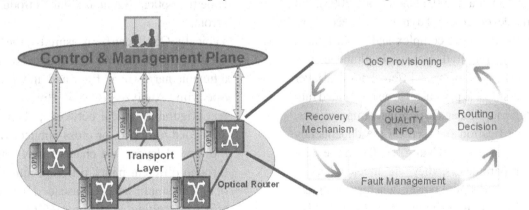

All the desirable features described above require the ability to first monitor the network elements, paths, and data in an accurate and repeatable fashion. Therefore, an ideal optical monitoring method should meet the following criteria:

- Provide meaningful and precise performance data.
- In-service measurement.
- Monitoring technique independent of client's bitrate or data format.
- Fast response to react to changes in the network quickly.
- The cost of monitoring equipment must be low.

The broad spectrum of OPM includes a plethora of parameters to be monitored which can be classified into three categories: signal loss, signal alignment, and signal quality. The first category refers to the monitoring of in-line components failures and fiber cuts that cause the signal loss. Second, signal alignment monitoring concerns with the alignment of signal wavelength, filter position, and pulse carver to ensure proper operation. Finally, signal quality monitoring refers to the monitoring of a multitude of effects degrading the signal that must be minimized or controlled.

OPM started by focusing attention on simple channel parameters, like wavelength and optical power (Chen et al., 2003; Chen et al., 2005), but due to the development of dynamically reconfigurable networks more complex and sophisticated solutions are required, such as simultaneous and independent monitoring of different physical layer parameters. These parameters can be divided into two categories: linear and nonlinear impairments. This classification is based on the dependency on the signal power (Chung, 2000). In the case of linear parameters, they are independent of the transmitted signal power, whereas nonlinear impairments are more complex, and very hard to quantify as they depend on a combination of factors

such as signal power, number of wavelengths per channel, and the channel bandwidth. Commonly, the effect of the linear parameters is dominant. That is why it is usually assumed that the nonlinear impairments are negligible. Hence, the monitoring techniques are focused on the measurement of the following linear parameters: Optical Signal to Noise Ratio (OSNR), Q-factor/Bit Error Rate (BER), CD, PMD, and jitter.

- **OSNR Degradation:** One of the major parameters to monitor is OSNR degradation since it provides direct and important information about the channel quality inside a dynamic network. Optical amplifiers have become essential components in optical networks to compensate the transmission losses. In addition to providing optical gain, these amplifiers add undesired noise onto the amplified signal, which is called amplified spontaneous emission (ASE) noise (Desurvire, 1994). ASE is directly proportional to the signal power and inversely proportional to the amplifier gain and link bandwidth. The spectrum of the background noise is often wide, and thereby some of that noise can cause the signal to get impaired due to the interference between the signal and the noise. This noise affects the receiver ability to properly decode the optical signal and thus introduces errors.

Typically, OSNR can be measured by the linear interpolation between the channels using a tunable narrowband filter and an Optical Spectrum Analyzer (OSA). However, in reconfigurable optical networks, channels are added, dropped, or cross-connected in the optical layer. One channel may travel through different paths, different numbers of optical amplifiers, and cascaded filtering effects, resulting in a non-uniform noise spectrum compared with adjacent channels.

The accumulated noise level may be quite different from channel to channel. As a result, the accurate OSNR of each channel must be monitored in-band.

- **Q-factor/BER:** A bit error occurs when a transmitted signal gets so corrupted that causes the reception of a "0" when a "1" is transmitted or vice versa. The bit error rate (BER) is a statistical measure of how often these errors occur. This parameter is the most preferred one for fault management as it uses the same metric as determining the QoS at end-terminals (Noirie et al., 2002). However, the BER measurements to be statistically significant require a lot of time, several seconds or several minutes, making them inappropriate for future high-speed optical networks.

- **Chromatic Dispersion:** Dispersion is a temporal effect that results in pulse broadening and consequently in errors at the receiver. Chromatic dispersion is the term given by which different spectral components of a pulse travel at different velocities (Ramaswami & Sivarajan, 2002). The chromatic dispersion is caused by the dependence of the refractive index of the transmission medium on the frequency components present in the transmitted signal. Due to the reduced tolerance to CD for the high-data-rate signals (i.e., >40 Gb/s), the accuracy of monitoring becomes increasingly crucial.

- **Polarization Mode Dispersion:** PMD is caused by the asymmetry of the fiber core, in which light polarized in one axis travels slightly faster than light polarized in the orthogonal axis. Pulse spreading arises due to the differential light speed and causes Inter-Symbol Interference (ISI) which results in increased BER. Therefore, PMD has emerged as a key issue for deploying high-speed optical communication systems. Differential Group Delay (DGD),

which is known as the first-order PMD, causes walk-off in time between the two orthogonal polarization states. Moreover, the PMD effects on the data signal are stochastic, time varying, and a random process that acts on each WDM channel differently. Any adaptive PMD compensator must require accurate PMD monitoring in order to dynamically track the degrading effects due to time-varying conditions (Gordon & Kogelnik, 2000). On the other hand, second-order of PMD describes the wavelength dependence of the DGD and has two components: depolarization and polarization-dependent chromatic dispersion. This second-order factor causes the principal polarization modes to broaden.

- **Jitter:** Jitter is defined as a variation in the signal characteristics between consecutive pulses such as a variation in the pulse width and/or phase of the pulse (Fisher, 1956). Commonly, the temporal variations such as the change in the pulse interval or shift in the pulse peak are considered. This parameter is hard to monitor and compensate. The BER measurement is sensitive to this impairment and can be used for identifying the jitter source.

In the literature, numerous optical performance-monitoring techniques have been proposed and demonstrated for monitoring the fiber impairments described above. In current networks, BER is a fundamental performance parameter for signal quality estimation. However, given the increasing transparency and reconfigurability requirements, it is indispensable to propose advanced optical performance monitoring techniques capable of improving monitoring accuracy as well as response time. Indeed, these constraints are especially critical in the frame of the OPS networks since the monitoring must be done on a packet-by-packet basis. In the next section this new challenge to the research in OPM will be addressed.

OPTICAL PERFORMANCE MONITORING IN OPTICAL PACKET SWITCHED NETWORKS

Transport networks are evolving towards reconfigurable optical networks offering a high-bandwidth flexible core. In such a scenario, optical packet switching is particularly attractive as a possible technology for future telecommunication networks, due to its compatibility with Internet Protocol (IP), efficient use of the network resources and flexibility.

With the introduction of new-generation multimedia services, OPS networks transport different types of traffic with different quality requirements so that performance monitoring is especially important to ensure that packets receive appropriate treatment as they travel through the network. In such a dynamic scenario, optical packets are forwarded hop-by-hop based on packet header information, following each packet different routes. Therefore, the concept of OPS brings about new challenges to network performance monitoring and maintenance, adding a new dimension to this topic.

The reasons for the importance of signal quality monitoring on a packet-by-packet basis are:

- As packets are forwarded hop-by-hop based on packet header information, different packets could suffer from different degradations and the data quality may change on the short time of one packet.
- The monitoring information is useful for signal quality management as it can be used for impairment compensation and fault management.
- This quality information can be used for QoS provisioning and packet rerouting in order to fulfil the quality requirements imposed by the client.

The future monitoring techniques must satisfy the requirements of the next-generation high-speed networks which are focused on fast response time, and packet-by-packet operation. The problem of the majority of the techniques reported in the literature is that they require high acquisition time or they have slow response time, being incapable of estimating the signal quality on the short time span of one packet. Therefore, new monitoring techniques on a per-packet basis must be defined. In the literature some works have demonstrated performance monitoring on per-burst/packet basis. These approaches are explained below.

State-of-the-Art of OPM in OPS

All-Optical Time-to-Live using Error-Checking Labels in Optical Label Switching Networks

As packets go through more hops in an optical network, their OSNR decrease, due to repeated attenuation and amplifications at each router and fiber links. Normal packets travel through limited number of router hops and experience limited OSNR degradation. However, when packets are caught in a loop or become errant the OSNR is strongly degraded. J. Yang et al. propose an OSNR-based optical TTL method that utilizes this monotonously decreasing OSNR of abnormal packets to identify all the packets below an OSNR threshold (Yang et al., 2004). The OSNR threshold is reasonably low to leave margin for normal OSNR degradation.

The proposed TTL method uses time division multiplexing (TDM) label to monitor the OSNR of the packet. Each packet has a 48-bit TDM label at the front end. The last 8 bits of the label is a bit interleaved parity (BIP) check field, calculated according to the preceding 40 bits in the label. Each router re-calculates a verifying BIP value when receiving a label, and then the verifying BIP value is compared with the BIP value received in the label field. Bit error in the transmission history causes the two BIP values to differ. The technique finds a sharp OSNR threshold, below which bit errors will occur in the label. This TTL method uses this threshold effect to detect looping packets, dropping the packets in such case.

The error checking experiment presented in (Yang et al., 2004) demonstrates effective dropping of OSNR degraded packets. However, the electronic processing of the label limits the bitrate and also the transparency.

In (McGeehan et al., 2003) an optical time-to-live decrementing module based on gain saturation within an SOA and difference-frequency-generation in a set of waveguide wavelength shifters is proposed. Although this technique overcomes some limitations presented in the previous one, the implementation is too complex.

An OSNR Monitor for Optical Packet Switched Networks

In (Yi et al., 2006) an OSNR monitor capable of direct OSNR monitoring based on radio frequency (RF) noise measurement is presented. Figure 2 shows the principle of operation of the OSNR monitor on a packet basis.

The packet contains an additional performance monitoring segment (PM segment), which consists of ~10 ns of consecutive "1" bits at 10 Gbit/s. At the packet switching node, a part of the input optical signal power is tapped and fed into the OSNR monitor. Inside the OSNR monitor, the PM segment is extracted from the entire packet by using a Mach–Zenhder modulator. The pulse after the PM extractor is fed into a photodiode,

and the optical signal power is then tested. RF spectral components are present at least in a range of 0–10 GHz for the entire packet. In contrast, the RF spectral components are absent at high frequency for the extracted PM segment. By analyzing the optical signal power and RF noise level at the high-frequency range, the OSNR can be calculated. An RF filter is used to filter out the RF noise of the interested frequency range and the RF noise level is then detected by an RF power detector.

The proposed technique has several advantages: a) good immunity to the interference from the payload/label modulation, b) high sensitivity, and c) in-band ASE noise measurements. However, the time duration of the PM segment may be a large overhead for high-speed transmission and therefore may not be feasible for every packet. In addition, the monitoring error is sensitive to imperfect nonlinearity calibration of the photodetector which can lead to high monitoring errors.

Single Technique for Simultaneous Monitoring of OSNR and Chromatic Dispersion at 40 Gbit/s

A technique for simultaneous OSNR and chromatic dispersion monitoring on per-burst basis is proposed in (Meflah et al., 2006). In particular, the proposed method uses an electro-optic

Figure 2. Conceptual diagram of proposed OSNR monitor

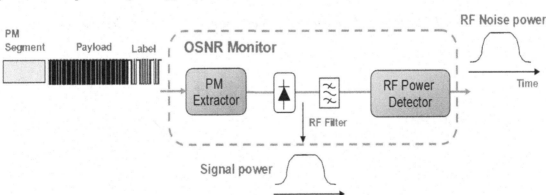

down-conversion technique that simultaneously down-converts multiple WDM channels making it cost-effective for multi-channel operation.

In the proposed scheme shown in Figure 3 the signal is sent through an optical filter in a notch configuration, which simultaneously suppresses one sideband (SSB) from all channels. The multi-wavelength SSB signals are down-converted using two electro-absorption modulators (EAM). These EAMs are driven with a free running local oscillator (LO) using a sinusoidal signal at a frequency, f_{LO}, shifted from the sideband offset frequency, f_o, by 10 KHz. The individual channels are then separated by two wavelength demultiplexers and the down-converted lower and upper sideband signals (LSB and USB) are detected using two low-speed square law detectors. The signals are then digitized for further processing. A Fast Fourier Transform (FFT) is applied to both signals, and the 10 kHz tone is extracted. The phase information extracted from the 10 kHz tone phase of the LSB and USB signals allows CD monitoring. In addition, the amplitude of the tone is only dependent on the average signal power and is independent of the average noise power. Therefore, the ratio between the incoming average signal power and the tone amplitude is proportional to the incoming average noise power, obtaining with this relationship the OSNR value.

The technique provides high accuracy over 30 dB OSNR range and the CD measurements are extremely robust to OSNR. However, PMD re-duces the amplitude of the tone used for monitoring tasks, making the OSNR measurement sensitive to PMD. Another disadvantage of the technique is the acquisition time required to obtain an accurate estimation of the signal degradations (~ 10-100 ms).

Although the above commented techniques are the first step towards the performance monitoring in OPS networks, they still have some limitations in terms of acquisition time, transparency and bitrate operation.

Basis of the Proposed Monitoring Technique

The purpose of this chapter is then to introduce an all-optical approach for OPM suitable for next generation OPS networks, whose main features are:

- Implementation in the optical domain to preserve packet transparency.
- Provision of monitoring information on a packet basis.
- Capability of near-instantaneous error detection based on the quality information obtained from the monitor.
- Association of monitored parameters with switch controls and header information.
- Assistance to the management and control planes in initiating real-time protection schemes and in establishing optical links based on quality requirements.

Figure 3. Multi-channel OSNR and CD monitoring system based on electro-optical mixing

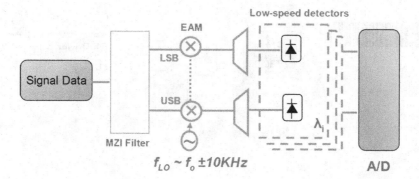

In previous approaches, the signal quality monitoring of the data payload has been demonstrated by monitoring the label bit error rates (Yang et al., 2003). The techniques transmit the payload data in the baseband channel and the label in a sub-carrier channel. As both signals are on the same wavelength travelling the same path in the network, they experience similar impairments in the network. Following this philosophy, the monitoring technique proposed in this chapter is based on using a specific word (monitoring field, Q-field) inserted into the packet header, which is processed in each intermediate node, for monitoring purpose. Instead of using labelling scheme based on wavelength diversity (i.e. sub-carrier multiplexing –SCM- technique), the proposed techniques use serial optical headers travelling at the same bitrate as the payload. The advantage of using the labelling scheme based on time diversity is the avoidance of the interference between the label and the payload, which limits the payload and label bitrates. On the

other hand, all-optical header processing results in a significant added efficiency, transparency and flexibility while overcoming the electronic bitrate limitation.

An optical packet is composed of a payload, which consists of large amount of aggregated data traffic, and a serial optical header with the address keyword information. Between the payload and the header a guard time must be included. In addition to these fields, a monitoring segment is added for monitoring tasks whose format is detailed in next subsection. Thus, when the packet arrives at the node, it enters into a circuit responsible of extracting the monitoring field and the signal quality of the incoming packet is estimated from this extracted Q-field.

Monitoring-Field/Payload Separation Circuit

The monitoring-field extraction circuit is composed of two fundamental building blocks: the

Figure 4. Scheme of the circuit responsible of extracting the monitoring-field (Q) from the payload

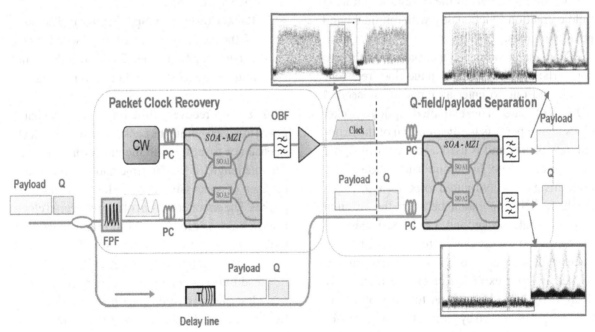

packet clock recovery circuit and the monitoring field extraction circuit itself (Stampoulidis et al., 2005), as shown in Figure 4.

The packet clock recovery circuit consists of a low-Q comb-generating filter (a Fabry Perot filter – FFP), and an all-optical gate operated as a power limiter. The Fabry-Perot filter due to its low Q-factor has a short exponential decaying impulse response that allows for independent packet-to-packet processing. Exploiting the effect of the filter, incoming data packets are transformed to clock-resembling packets with intense amplitude modulation and duration similar to the data packets. This generated clock-resembling signal suffers from intense pulse-to-pulse amplitude modulation that is removed by utilizing an optical power-limiting gate (SOA-MZI). The combination of these two elements results in the self-extraction of a clock packet from each incoming packet, with low rise and fall times (3 bits at 40 Gbit/s). The sub-system responsible of separating the monitoring field from the payload is based on the packet clock recovery and an additional high speed SOA-MZI optical gate. Proper interconnection between the two circuits leads to the desired monitoring field extraction functionality with minimal band guard penalties.

Then, the incoming data packets are split into two parts: one used as input in the clock recovery circuit and one to enter as input in the second SOA-MZI gate. The extracted optical packet clock signal persists for the duration of the original data packet and is used as the control signal in the second gate. For monitoring field separation, this gate is configured to perform a simple Boolean AND operation between the original incoming data packet and a delayed version of the recovered packet clock after optical filtering. Successful separation is obtained if the original packet and the extracted clock are temporally delayed by an amount equal to the monitoring field length increased by the rise time required for clock acquisition. As such, only the payload bits

fall within the switching window of the recovered clock and are therefore switched at the gate output, as shown in the insets of Figure 4.

Monitoring Field Definition

The packet clock recovery subsystem and the monitoring-field separation circuit impose some restrictions when defining packet format as well as the monitoring field. These requirements are detailed below:

- **Preamble Field (T_p):** Necessary for the synchronization;
- **Label/Monitoring/Payload Band Guard (T_r):** In order to prevent optical switching with the imperfect recovered clock bits (rise time). For the previous circuit is equal to 3 bits.
- **Payload Data:** The payload traffic type is defined so as to contain a maximum number of successive zeros depending on the selected recovered clock tolerance. This traffic is quantitatively characterized by PRBS sequences.
- **Packet-to-Packet Spacing (T_e):** The sum of the label size and the recovered clock persistence (fall time, T_f) defines the minimum allowed spacing between packets.

The clock recovery time impacts on the band guard imposed within the packet whereas the clock persistence together with the clock tolerance define the length of the fall time and the maximum number of successive zeros allowed within the packet. The exponential tail of the recovered clock imposes a constraint on the minimum spacing of the packets contributing to the overall band guard requirements imposed by the circuit.

In addition to taking into account the restrictions described above, the length of the monitoring field should be defined in order to obtain a good balance between the overhead introduced by this field and the accuracy in the measurements. At this point, there is a trade-off between the efficiency, in favour of shorter lengths, and the measure accuracy, in favour of longer lengths. According to the previous comments, the packet format including the monitoring field is illustrated in the Figure 5.

Once presented the key basis of the signal quality monitoring proposed in this chapter, an OSNR monitoring technique suitable for OPS networks will be presented in next section.

OSNR MONITORING TECHNIQUE

In previous sections the importance of implementing optical performance monitoring for managing OPS networks was stated (Wen & Chan, 2005; Kilper, 2002).

As previously mentioned, the BER is a fundamental performance parameter in determining the signal quality (Shake et al., 1998; Ding et al., 2004; Ye & Zhong, 2007). In fact, BER monitoring based on the evaluation of signal amplitude histograms has emerged as an attractive scheme since it provides the same metric that is used at each network end-terminal for QoS functions. However, BER measurements require O/E conversions which limit the signal bitrate so that

new technologies to perform fast signal quality monitoring directly at the optical physical layer should be defined.

The OSNR is one of the most useful parameters for estimating the quality of a signal directly in the optical layer. This is mainly because the OSNR can be correlated to the end-terminal BER of the transmitted optical signal. In addition, since the OSNR is transparent to both the bit rate and the modulation format of the optical signal, it is ideally suited for use in dynamically reconfigurable optical networks in which OSNR can also be used for QoS implementation, Service-Level Agreement (SLA) verification, the setup of an early signal degradation alarm, resilience mechanism activation, rerouting and new routes establishment based on quality estimation, and so on.

Therefore, OSNR is a significant factor for the quality of any optical systems including even OPS networks. In such networks, optical packets are forwarded hop-by-hop based on optical packet header information. These packets may traverse a number of optical packet switching nodes and long fiber segments and thus the use of amplifiers is necessary to compensate the losses incurred by the packet in all these nodes and fiber segments. The problem is that the optical amplifiers introduce ASE noise into the optical packets, degrading the

Figure 5. Packet format including the monitoring field

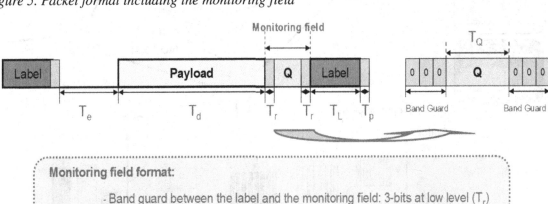

OSNR. In addition, the noise background is modified by optical filtering and contains contributions from signals with different transmission histories so that OSNR can change on a packet-by-packet basis, as shown in Figure 6.

Figure 6 shows how the quality of three packets can be different depending on their routes followed along the network. Packets 1 and 3 are generated from the same source, while packet 2 originates from a different source. The three packets pass through diverse optical links and switches, then exit on the same node (node A). The bottom of Figure 6 depicts the optical intensity of the output packets from node A, showing that the ASE noise level in each packet is different. Therefore, in order to determine the

health of optical signals in OPS networks, the optical packets in each intermediate node must be monitored.

Therefore, for the proper management of OPS network, a novel technique based on the use of optical correlation to assess the signal quality at the optical domain with relaxed speed requirements with respect to typical techniques is presented. In this technique, a specific data word (i.e. monitoring field) is inserted into the packet header and is processed by means of an optical correlator based on Fiber Bragg Gratings (FBGs). From the noise statistics of the resulting autocorrelation pulse, the OSNR of the incoming packets is estimated.

In the following parts of this section, the principle of operation of the OSNR monitor is

Figure 6. Packets with different OSNR in an OPS network

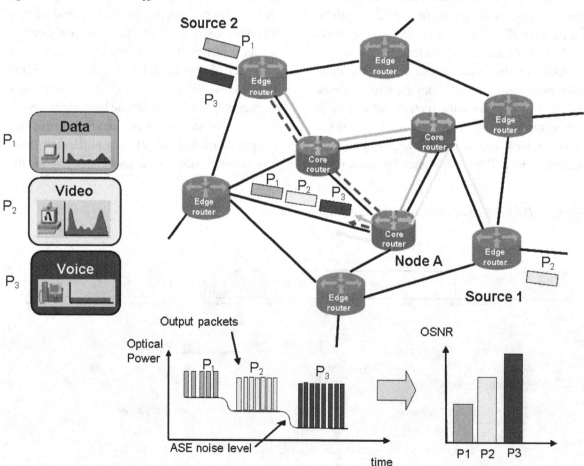

described and the basis of the use of the optical correlation as an OSNR estimator for OPS networks is presented.

Description of the OSNR Monitor

Figure 7 shows the block diagram of the proposed monitor for optical packets (Vilar et al., 2007). The signal quality monitoring method is based on sending a specific data word inserted into the packet header, which is called monitoring field (Q). This monitoring field is comprised of a set of bits with a value either '0' or '1' with a peak power of P_1, $Q = [q_0 \, q_1 \, q_2 \, ... \, q_{n-1}]$ with $q_i = 0$ or 1 and $i = 0, .., n-1$.

At the packet switching node, the monitoring field is extracted from the header and processed for monitoring purpose. The circuit responsible for this task was explained in more detail in previous section. Once the monitoring field is extracted, the optical correlator allows signal quality to be monitored with high fidelity and in real time.

Optical correlation is an important signal-processing function. In the definition of this function, two variable of interest are considered: the transmitted signal $s(t)$ over the fiber optical link and the received signal $r(t)$. The correlation function $c(t)$ is defined by the integral (1) and is a measure of how similar $r(t)$ and $s(t)$ are:

$$c(t) = \int_{-\infty}^{\infty} s(\tau) r(t - \tau) d\tau \qquad (1)$$

The infinite limits indicate that the correlation function is continuous over an infinite data stream. In the discrete domain, the function $c(t)$ can be re-written for a finite number of bits of the received signal by the following summation:

$$c(t) = \sum_{k=0}^{n-1} s(k\tau) r(t - k\tau) \qquad (2)$$

where n is the number of bits in the correlation sequence, τ is the bit period, $s(k\,\tau)$ represents the reference signal as the k weights that multiply each of the delayed received signals, and $r(t - k\tau)$ is the received signal delayed by k bit times.

In temporal optical correlation, a time-varying signal (e.g. intensity or phase) is compared to a reference time-varying signal. The result of the comparison is then summed or integrated to produce the correlation output. Let us suppose that the optical correlation is configured to match with a reference signal comprised of N bits with $q_i = 1$. If the two signals, $r(t)$ and $s(t)$, are identical, Equation (1) becomes an autocorrelation and the output correlation pulse appears as a single sharp peak in the center with an amplitude equal to NP_1. If the signals are less well matched, then the peak

Figure 7. Block diagram of the OSNR monitor

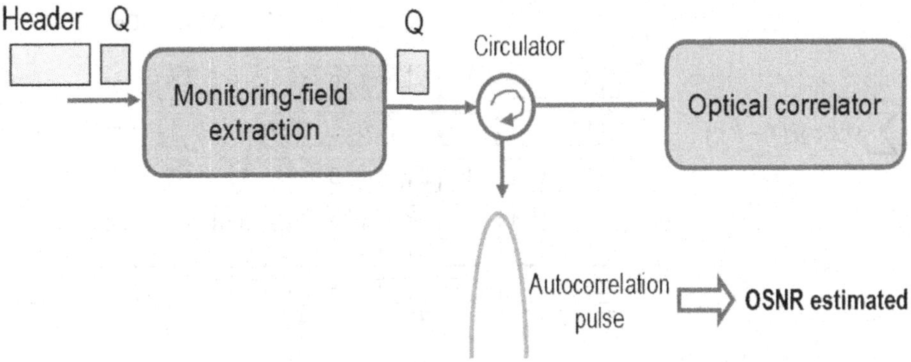

85

decreases and the information on either side of the peak increases. Figure 8 schematically shows how to perform the correlation for three input signal when correlated with a reference 4-bit monitoring field Q = [1 1 1 1]. As can be seen, the autocorrelation peak with higher amplitude corresponds to the first input signal. Figure 9 shows the output signal from the optical correlator for this case.

For monitoring purpose, the monitoring field suffering from impairments that the link imposes is correlated with an undegraded version of this reference signal. At the correlator output, a maximum autocorrelation peak will be produced if the input signal is an exact match to the store one. The amplitude and the shape of this optical pulse directly measure the degree of degradation. Considering noise degradation, noise produces an amplitude variation in the autocorrelation pulse peak. Figure 10 shows the effect of noise on correlation function for different noise levels (The noise is assumed to be Gaussian). In particular, the noise causes an increase in the floor of the correlation output as well as affecting the amplitude of the autocorrelation pulse.

Then, by using the statistics of the autocorrelation pulse peak power the OSNR of the incoming packets can be calculated. The OSNR is defined as:

$$OSNR = \frac{mean^2}{\sigma^2} \tag{3}$$

Figure 9. Output signal from the optical correlator corresponding to Q = [1 1 1 1]

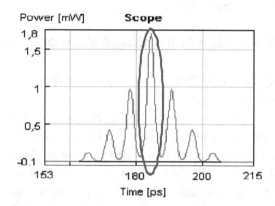

where *mean* is the mean value and σ is the standard deviation of the autocorrelation pulse peak power. Equation (3) shows that the monitored OSNR depends on the shape of the correlator's output as commented before.

Simulation results presented in Figure 11 show the OSNR estimation using the autocorrelation pulse for different bitrates. As can be seen, the estimated OSNR adjusts perfectly to the "real" OSNR value and it is independent of the bitrate.

As commented previously, the traditional monitoring techniques based on BER measurements are not appropriate for future ultra high-speed optical networks due to the O/E conversion unless it is preceded by optical demultiplexing.

Figure 8. Principle of operation of the optical correlation

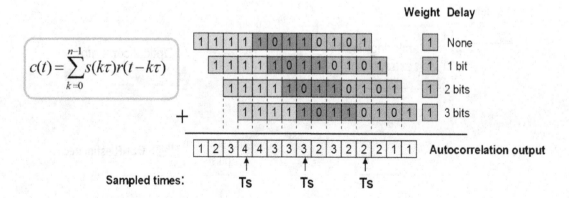

Figure 10. Effect of the noise on correlation function for different noise levels (correlation corresponding to Q=[1 0 1 1])

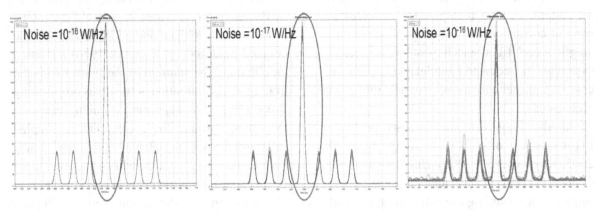

Figure 11. Simulation results of OSNR for different bitrates

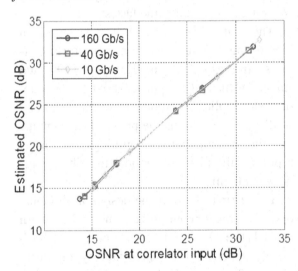

The proposed technique estimates the OSNR value from the noise statistics of the autocorrelation pulse. Despite using a sampling oscilloscope for extracting the statistics parameters, the technique allows high-speed bit rate operation as it only measures the autocorrelation pulse, so the system works well at the packet rate and thereby alleviating speed requirements with respect to typical BER techniques. For example, if packets at 160 Gb/s are travelling along the network, the monitoring system will generate an autocorrelation pulse each time a packet is received. Therefore, successive packets will produce autocorrelation pulses delayed the duration of the payload, i.e. the system will work at packet rate.

FBG-Based Optical Correlator Design

Now that the optical correlation as an OSNR monitor has been introduced, this subsection shows several implementations of optical correlators at the optical domain. A common implementation of an optical correlator is the tapped delay line (Chang et al., 1977; Jackson et al., 1985; Euliss & Athale, 1994).

In this implementation the received signal is sent to a tapped delay line which requires one tap for each bit in the desired sequence that are weighted by the factors '1' or '0' depending on the value of the bit of the sequence. The weights can either be phase shifts or amplitude weights or both (amplitude weights of 1s or 0s are implemented by placing a switch in each path that is closed for weight=1 and opened for weight=0). The received signal is equally split among the delay lines. Each successive delay line adds one additional bit of delay to the received signal before the combiner, where the signals are added to yield the correlation output function. The problem of this implementation is that the optical tapped-delay-line structure requires a separate fiber branch and an optical switch for each bit in the desired bit pattern, making it impractical to construct bank of correlators of many bits. Moreover, the length of each fiber branch must be cut precisely to provide the requisite 1-bit delays between successive branches and that is extremely difficult at high speeds.

Another implementation is based on Planar Lightwave Circuits (PLCs) (Takiguchi et al., 2002; Koyama et al., 2007). But this solution is disadvantageous in cost and packaging losses (input/output coupling losses). A simpler, easily manufactured, and manageable correlator may be constructed by writing a series of fiber Bragg grating mirrors into a single length of fiber (Petropoulos et al., 2001; Hauer et al., 2003). Indeed, in order to validate the proposed OSNR monitoring technique a FBG-based correlator is designed and characterized by simulations.

In this type of correlator a series of FBGs is written into a single length of fiber. In these applications the array of gratings reflects back part of the signal at different times, resulting in multiple replicas of the input signal spaced in time with the delay increment τ. The reflectivities of the FBGs provide the same weighting function as the optical correlation and their values are designed so that the light reflecting of each FBG has equal power when it exits the correlator, following this recursive equation:

$$\frac{R_n}{(1-R_n)^2} = R_{n+1} \qquad (4)$$

Since the light makes a double pass through the array, the spacing between FBGs must match half the bit period to produce a round-trip delay of 1-bit.

In order to properly design the optical correlator, the response of the array of gratings was modelled and simulated by means of the matrix transfer approach (Yamada & Sakuda, 1987; Meltz et al.,

1989; Lemaire et al., 1993). Different theoretical models are used to analyze the optical properties of Bragg gratings written in optical fibers. One of the most developed and widely utilized is the coupled-mode theory (Kogelnik, 1976). It is based on obtaining the solution of the fields inside the grating as a perturbation of the fields propagating inside a fiber without grating, by linking ones with the others through the corresponding coupled differential equations. However, this approach is time-consuming. In the case of considering more complex structures as the proposed correlator, it is better to analyze the optical properties of such structures by using matrix methods, such as the transfer matrix approach, since such a method is simple to implement, almost always sufficiently accurate, and generally the fastest.

The matrix transfer approach is based on identifying 2x2 matrices for each uniform grating section as defined in (Kashyap, 1999) and calculates the FBG response taking into account the field amplitude of modes travelling in +z and −z directions and thus the phase of the signals. For the spacing between gratings, we insert a phase-shift matrix to model the fiber spans between them.

In the first phase of the design, a 40 Gbit/s optical correlator configured to match the pattern [1 1 1 1] (i.e. Q = [1 1 1 1]) was considered. Each '1' of the pattern was represented by a uniform grating. The optical fiber length between two successive FBGs was proportional to the bit period in order to recognize the desired pattern. Therefore, the optical correlator was composed of 4 uniform FBG properly spaced to produce a round trip delay of 1-bit between two successive FBGs. By using Equation (4), the reflectivities were set so that the reflecting signals of each grating had equal power at the correlator output. As a result, the reflectivities were set to $R_1 = 16\%$, $R_2 = 23\%$, $R_3 = 38\%$, and $R_4 = 100\%$. Simulation results showed that secondary reflections strongly affected the correlator output even masking the autocorrelation pulse.

In order to reduce this effect, the proposed correlator is designed with unequal grating spacing, i.e. with different time intervals, which is a novelty with respect to other correlators proposed in the literature (Hauer et al., 2003). By means of simulations, a study of the correlator output as function of the pattern is carried out in order to decide which one provided better performance and less overhead.

Figure 12.(a), (c), (e), and (g) show the correlator response to a single input pulse for the patterns [1111], [101011], [10001011], and [10000010011], respectively, all with $N=4$. As the spacing increases, secondary reflections have less amplitude and less impact on the autocorrelation pulse. Figure 12 (b), (d), (f), and (h) show the autocorrelation output for the patterns mentioned earlier. In the cases (b) and (d), the presence of secondary reflections causes the increase of the sidelobes, reducing the contrast between the central peak and these sidelobes and even hiding it. The cases (f) and (h) provide good performance at the expense of increased overhead. Therefore, the pattern [10001011] is set to obtain the better performance with less overhead.

Should be noted that during the simulations the autocorrelation function is considered in complex amplitude basis and consequently optical interferences can be observed. For this reason, in the proposed design the spacings between gratings, i.e. the phase differences, have been properly adjusted to maintain the pulse phase along the correlator avoiding the interference effects commented previously (Fsaifes et al., 2006a).

FBG-Based Optical Correlator Fabrication

In the previous section, the pattern [10001011] was chosen for offering better performance in comparison with symmetric patterns. Then, to demonstrate the feasibility of the monitoring system, a 40-Gbit/s correlator is configured to match the said pattern. As explained before, each '1' of the pattern is represented by a uniform grating and the spacing between successive gratings are proportional to T_b, $2T_b$, and $4T_b$ (where T_b is the bit period) to recognize the desired pattern. The design is shown in Figure 13.

The FBG-based correlator fabrication process is based on the exposure of the fiber to ultraviolet (UV) laser light with the phase mask method (Anderson et al., 1993; Hill & Meltz, 1997). Phase masks are fabricated using lithography techniques. A silica plate is exposed to electron beams, and using techniques such as plasma etching, a one-dimensional periodic surface relief pattern is produced with well defined spacing and etched depth. The phase mask works in transmission. When a UV beam is incident normally to the phase masks surface, the beam is diffracted into the -1, 0 and +1 orders. Appropriate choice of etch depth allows the intensity of the zero order to be as low as < 5%, so that up to 40% of the UV energy is diverted in the ±1 orders (Kashyap, 1999). The overlap between the ±1 orders close to the phase mask produces the interference pattern that is inscribed into the fiber. Using the phase mask in close proximity to the fiber, the inscribed period is equal to half of the period of the phase mask. The use of the phase mask allows highly reproducible fabrication of FBGs with fixed characteristics determined by the phase mask properties. This technique offers easier alignment and imposes a less stringent requirement on the coherence of the writing source.

All the FBGs are tuned to the same wavelength ($\lambda = 1553.8$ nm). Bragg wavelength shift can occur due to environment conditions and due to technological considerations, so all the FBGs cannot be tuned to the same wavelength. In particular, FBG wavelength is sensitive to temperature. To avoid this effect, the FBG-based correlator should be packaged and stabilized by using thermal paste and heat sink. In those conditions, the temperature variations have no significant impact on correlator response. As far as technological considerations are concerned, Bragg

Figure 12. Correlator output as function of the pattern. (a)-(b) Correlation response to a single pulse and correlation output for the pattern [1111], respectively; (c)-(d) Correlation response to a single pulse and correlation output for the pattern [101011], respectively; (e)-(f) Correlation response to a single pulse and correlation output for the pattern [10001011], respectively; (g)-(h) Correlation response to a single pulse and correlation output for the pattern [10000010011], respectively.

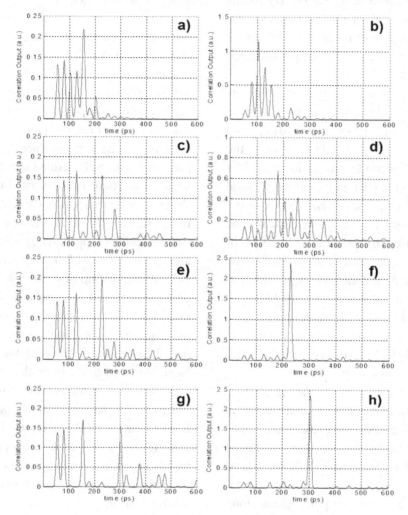

Figure 13. FBG-based correlator configured to match the pattern [10001011]

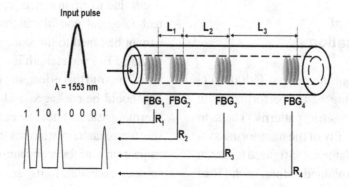

wavelength mismatches are produced by writing the FBGs with different refractive-index modulation amplitude. Due to this fabrication process, Bragg wavelengths are detuned from each other. Moreover, different errors or imperfections during the writing could also produce detuning. This mismatch can impact on the autocorrelation pulse reducing the optical power and therefore increasing the monitor error. To overcome Bragg wavelength detuning, the FBGs should be written with the same index modulation depth and the reflectivity can be adjusted by varying the FBG physical length as it is explained in (Fsaifes et al., 2006b). According to this requirement, the index modulation used in the correlator is set to $5 \cdot 10^{-4}$.

A FBG-based optical correlator is commonly constructed by using thermally controlled FBGs as tunable-reflectivity mirrors (Hauer et al., 2003). The thermal control consists of a series of thin-film microheaters onto the surface of a single uniform grating which cause a shift in the grating spectrum towards longer wavelengths in response to the rise in temperature. Then, FBGs are fabricated to act as high reflectivity mirrors. By tuning the FBG thermally, the grating passband is shifted so that the signal wavelength intersects with the rising or falling edge of the grating response to obtain the desired reflectivities given by Equation (4). However, tuning the grating reflectivity by operating it in the edge of the reflectivity is quite sensitive and has some disadvantages associated with polarization dependence, time-delay variation with reflectivity and dispersion. As each subgrating is tuned to a different reflectivity by operating them at the band edge, each grating will introduce some non-negligible polarization dependent loss, causing distortion in the correlation output. Moreover, the time delay of a signal reflected from a FBG varies for different points along the edge. These unwanted time delay variations between subgratings degrades the correlation. Also, as the edge is steep, the signal can be affected by dispersion. To solve these problems, the proposed correlator

is also constructed by writing a series of uniform FBGs into a single length of fiber but each grating has the desired reflectivity thereby avoiding the thermal tuning and the inconvenience associated with operating at the edge of the FBG spectrum. In particular, the reflectivities are fixed to 16%, 23%, 38% and 100% (using Equation (4)). Fabricating low reflectivity gratings with high precision is not an easy task because of the reflectivity dependence on the $\tanh^2(kL)$ function. This means that when the grating is not saturated, a slight deviation of the refractive index will have a large impact on the reflectivity. However, for reflectivity deviations of $\pm$ 10% the impact on the correlator response is almost negligible.

The fabrication process is as follows. The grating with the highest reflectivity, FBG_4 (R_4=100%), is firstly written. Then, the fiber is moved along its axis over a length corresponding to the required '0' in the pattern and the FBG_3 grating (R_3=38%) is written. The FBG_2 (R_2=23%) and FBG_1 (R_1=16%) gratings are written following a similar process. The optical fiber length between the successive gratings are L_1= 2.5810 mm, L_2= 5.162 mm and L_3= 10.324 mm, measured from the beginning of one grating to the beginning of the following one, as shown in Figure 13. These lengths correspond to time intervals of T_b, $2T_b$ and $4T_b$ at 40 Gbit/s. The length of the gratings are L_{FBG1}= L_{FBG2}= L_{FBG3}= 1 mm and L_{FBG4}= 4 mm. The accuracy of the FBG positioning along the fiber is in the micrometer range. The bandwidth of the FBGs corresponds to a Full Width at Half Maximum (FWHM) of 10 ps.

The correlation functionality is validated by introducing the appropriate sequence into the correlator, i.e. Q= [10001011]. The correlator output for this sequence is shown in Figure 14. As the incoming signal matches with the pattern stored in the array of FBGs, an autocorrelation pulse appears. The amplitude level of the sidelobes is almost the same at both sides of the autocorrelation pulse and some residual peaks appear at the end

Figure 14. Correlator output for the incoming sequence Q= [10001011]

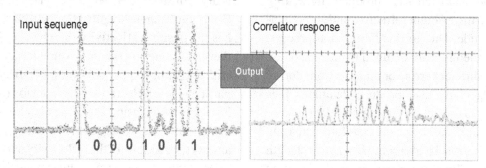

of the correlation function due to the secondary reflections produced inside the subgratings. These residual peaks suffer from larger time delays and attenuation.

Experimental Validation

After the characterization of the fabricated correlator, experimental demonstration of the monitoring system is carried out in the laboratory as a proof-of-concept. The principle of operation of the OSNR monitoring technique is validated experimentally by means of the setup shown in Figure 15.

The monitoring-field, Q = [10001011], is generated through external modulation of a Return-to-Zero (RZ) Gaussian pulse source at 1553.8 nm. The modulating signal driving the Mach-Zehnder Modulator (MZM) is obtained from a 40 Gbit/s electrical PRBS equipment. The signal

out from the transmitter is coupled with a second EDFA to simulate the link noise. Thus, the OSNR of the optical signal can be changed by combining the signal with different ASE noise levels adjusting the gain of the EDFA pump laser. The optical signal degraded with the noise passes through a 1-nm bandwidth filter and then is split in two branches for OSNR measurements. One branch uses an Optical Spectrum Analyzer (OSA) as reference and the other branch goes to the OSNR monitor. Inside the OSNR monitor, an optical circulator is placed at the correlator input to route the counter-propagating correlation output to the sampling scope.

The optical correlator output is sensitive to the fluctuations in the received signal due to the fiber impairments and it can be used to estimate the OSNR of the optical packets from the statistics of the autocorrelation pulse. By using the mean value and the standard deviation, the OSNR value

Figure 15. Experimental setup

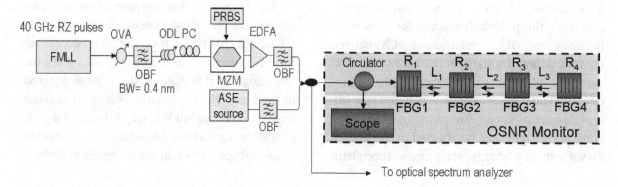

is calculated. These values are extracted by means of a high-speed sampling scope. Despite using a sampling scope, the technique allows high-speed bitrate operation as it only measures the autocorrelation pulse, so the system works at the packet rate and thereby alleviating speed requirements with respect to typical BER techniques, as mentioned in previous sections.

To demonstrate the feasibility of the proposed OSNR monitoring technique, the OSNR from the OSA is measured and compared with the value extracted from the noise statistics from the autocorrelation pulse. This reference OSNR (i.e. OSNR from OSA) is calculated as follows:

$$OSNR = \frac{P_S}{P_{ASE}} \tag{5}$$

where P_S is the signal peak power and P_{ASE} is the ASE noise floor level for the channel bandwidth. Figure 16 depicts the measured OSNR from the autocorrelation pulse using the proposed technique as a function of the actual OSNR measured by the OSA. As can be seen, the estimated OSNR values agree well with the results extracted from the OSA.

The OSNR monitoring errors are the difference between the OSNR measured from the OSA and from the autocorrelation output pulse. From the

curve the maximum error for the measurement of different OSNR values is 0.5 dB in the 15 dB to 25 dB OSNR range (Figure 16). The slight deviation in lower OSNR values can be explained by the noise filtering behavior of the FBG-based correlator. The optical signal degraded with the noise passes through a 1-nm bandwidth filter and enters the optical correlator whose bandwidth is approximately 0.6-nm. Therefore, for lower OSNR values the output of the correlator is less sensitive to the degradation than the input, primarily due to the narrower optical passband of the FBG-based correlator providing a smaller noise background. Conversely, for higher OSNR values, where the noise background is practically negligible, the difference is due to the insertion loss of the gratings which slightly affects the power of the correlator response. Therefore, monitoring errors are caused by noise at lower OSNR values and by insertion loss at higher OSNR values.

APPLICATIONS OF OPTICAL PERFORMANCE MONITORING SYSTEM

Apart from the monitoring function itself, the monitoring system has other applications. Indeed, the proposed monitoring system can be integrated with other functions in the packet switching node to take immediate actions when the signal quality is strongly degraded. On one hand, the monitoring information can be used as part of QoS implementation to keep the level of QoS promised to customers (Boudriga et al., 2008). On the other hand, this performance information can be used to establish new optical paths or select backup paths when recovery mechanisms are needed. Next, these applications are explained in more detail.

Monitoring for QoS Implementation

With the introduction of new generation multimedia services, OPS networks transport different types of traffic with different quality requirements

Figure 16. OSNR monitoring: OSNR measured using an OSA and using the proposed technique

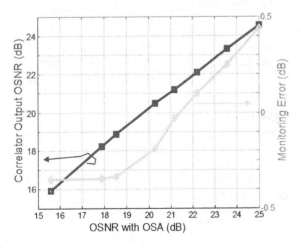

so that performance monitoring is especially important to ensure that packets receive appropriate treatment as they travel through the network. Packets entering the network must be analyzed to determine their QoS requirements depending on the kind of network service and then the signal quality must be monitored in each intermediate node to guarantee certain level of performance.

In this scenario, the monitoring-field (i.e. Q) inserted into the packet header for monitoring functions specifies the QoS requirement of the incoming packet. In other words, this QoS field fixes the signal quality requirement for each packet flow coming from a specific service. Optical headers of packets with the same QoS requirements (i.e. the same monitoring-field associated with the same kind of service) are then processed in each intermediate node to check if the estimated quality fulfils the terms of QoS and to guarantee the required level of performance. Figure 17 shows the block diagram of the proposed monitor as a part of the QoS implementation (Vilar et al., 2009).

The monitor is composed of M correlators, each of which is configured to produce a "match" signal for a specific QoS. The number of correlators, M, defines the number of type of services or QoS levels provided by the carriers. The correlator is composed of a series of gratings written into a fiber whose principle of operation is similar to the FBG-based correlator explained in this chapter.

Three basic levels are usually defined in the network: best-effort service, differentiated service and guaranteed service (Cisco Press, 2003), each of which is defined by a different monitoring-field (i.e. Q_1 for best effort, Q_2 for differentiated, and Q_3 for guarantee). Thanks to the definition of different Q values, each intermediate node can monitor packet flows with the same QoS requirement independently since the autocorrelation peak activates the OSNR process. In other words, the output of the correlator is compared with a defined threshold so that when the amplitude of the autocorrelation pulse exceeds the threshold level, the monitoring process is activated. Then, from the OSNR value estimated with the correlator, each intermediate node can control whether the transmission meets the QoS and performance requirements specified by the carrier, providing a consistent treatment for each QoS class at every hop. Figure 18 shows the correlator output for three QoS levels. Only in the case where the input signal matches the pattern written into the fiber, an autocorrelation pulse appears and the OSNR monitor is activated. Otherwise, the peak decreases and the OSNR monitoring for the corresponding Q values is inhibited. As commented previously, the definition of different Q values allows the network to offer differentiated services with specific quality requirements. Although no standards for the quality parameters have been

Figure 17. Block diagram of the OSNR monitor for QoS implementation

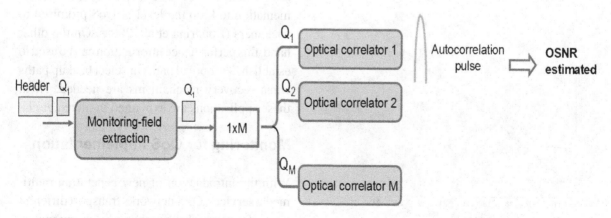

Figure 18. Independent treatment for each QoS class in the intermediate nodes by means of the use of an optical correlator

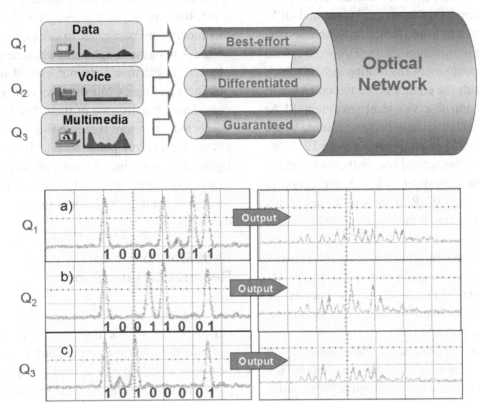

defined yet, BER degradation is usually considered as the parameter to be monitored as some applications may tolerate degraded BER and others will not. In case of guaranteed service, the BER value should be lower than 10^{-12}. In case of differentiated service, some BER degradation is allowed and the BER values vary between 10^{-12} and 10^{-6}. Finally, best-effort service establishes the connectivity with no guarantees so the required BER is not too strict. The corresponding OSNRs for each service depend on the optical receiver. For example, for a typical optical system a BER $< 10^{-12}$ corresponds to an OSNR value higher than 20 dB (Cisco).

In addition, the proposed monitoring system can be integrated with other functions in the packet switching node to take immediate actions when the signal quality is strongly degraded. The

beauty of using performance monitors close to the intermediate switching nodes is that the monitored parameters can be associated with the switch controls and label information. Therefore it is possible to integrate the optical performance monitors with switching nodes for providing network intelligence and fast impairment mitigation.

Monitoring for OSNR-Assisted Routing

The combination of the increasing demand for capacity and the trend towards OPS networks creates new challenges to QoS provisioning. In this fully reconfigurable scenario, the optical packets are no longer regenerated in the networks nodes and the changing nature of the traffic demand requires dynamic path computation taking into account the impact of physical impairments on the feasibility of the lightpaths (Kilper, 2002). Therefore, a solution for the integration of the control plane and OPM functions must be implemented. In this context the monitoring information obtained from the optical correlator could assist the routing system which interacts with the control plane to contribute to the supervision of service level agreement (SLA) fulfilment and efficiently perform routing based on signal quality requirements. Figure 19 shows the proposed interaction between the control plane and the monitoring system. The monitoring system is based on the OSNR monitor proposed in this chapter, but instead of processing a specific word, Q, inserted into the packet header, a set of test packets are periodically sent along the network following different paths (e.g. paths P_1, P_2, P_3, and P_4 shown in Figure 19). These packets are processed in each intermediate node to monitor the network performance.

The link performance information coming from this monitor is then disseminated by the control plane and shared between network nodes to assess the status of all connections. Moreover, the OSNR estimation is added as an additional factor in the routing decision. Then, every link, i, is characterized by a parameter α_i which includes the signal quality estimated. Since the impairments are additive, the quality degradation of a path is determined by the sum of the α_i of the traversed

links. A maximum value α_{MAX} associated with QoS requirements is defined. For a dynamic path setup, the control plane investigates the value of this monitoring parameter to calculate potential routes. Among them, lightpaths whose accumulate physical impairments do not exceed α_{MAX} are possible candidate while the others are no longer considered. Finally, one of these feasible routes is selected. Therefore, this OSNR-assisted routing allows the control plane to establish or select lightpaths taking into account physical impairments and thereby sustaining reliability requirements and keeping the level of QoS promised to end users.

Path Monitoring for Restoration Functions

As mentioned, the monitoring information obtained by the OSNR monitor can be used for assisting the routing system in order to establish new optical paths based on quality requirements. Apart from this application, the extracted quality parameter could be used by the fault management system to start the recovery mechanisms and also to establish backup paths taking into account performance requirements.

The proposed signal quality monitoring system is based on periodically sending test packets over a supervisory wavelength. The supervisory

Figure 19. Interaction between the proposed monitoring system and the control plane

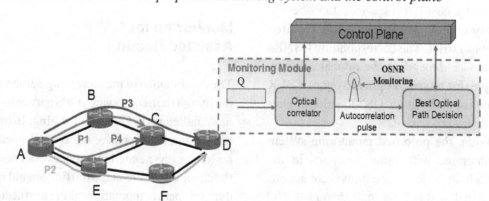

wavelength is reserved in each link between two adjacent nodes to transmit the test packet, allowing immediate failure detection when the node does not receive any signal. When a failure occurs, the node reports this fault condition to the control plane to start the recovery actions. These packets are processed by the FBG-based correlator in the end nodes to assess the quality of a set of backup paths. Then, the network state is inferred from the result of a set of end-to-end measurements, providing a cost-effective recovery solution. For restoration to be feasible, disjoint backup paths are defined, concept widely used for the design of a survivable WDM optical network because it may be faster, simpler and easier than other restoration techniques (Kodialam, 2003).

Figure 20 shows the principle of operation of the proposed monitoring system. In this figure, some packets are transported over the working paths P1 and P2, and two disjoint backup paths (dashed lines), which do not share the same links, are also defined. The test packets transmitted over each of these backup paths are labelled with a specific data word, B_1 and B_2, defined in a similar way to the monitoring-field used in the OSNR monitoring technique. Then, the test packets are processed in the destination node to monitor the

quality of these backup paths by means of a bank of optical correlators. As in the case of the QoS implementation, each correlator is configured to monitor a specific backup path.

With this solution the fault management system is able to detect transmission failures, start recovery mechanism, and monitor the network performance in a cost-effective way.

CONCLUSION AND FUTURE WORK

As other networks, optical impairments degrade the performance of OPS networks and, therefore, monitoring of the optical signal quality is becoming critically important. In fact, OSNR monitoring is essential for signal quality management in such networks.

Unlike circuit switching, OPS technology routes optical packets over independent paths to their destination so that each packet suffers from different level of degradation. As a result, OPS networks require new technologies to perform OSNR monitoring with fast response directly at the optical physical layer.

In this chapter, a novel OSNR monitoring technique based on optical correlation has been

Figure 20. Path monitoring system for restoration functions

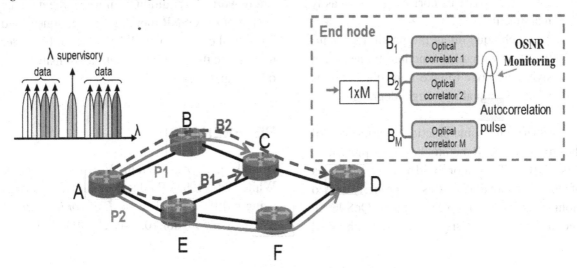

proposed and demonstrated experimentally. To this end, a specific monitoring field is inserted into the optical label and is processed in each intermediate node. The monitoring system is composed of a circuit responsible of extracting the monitoring field and the monitor itself based on a FBG-based correlator. Along this chapter, the principle of operation of the OSNR monitoring technique has been described and the basis of the FBG-based correlator has been presented. Simulations have been carried out to properly design the parameters of the correlator. After characterization of this device, the monitoring technique has been experimentally demonstrated. By measuring the noise statistics of the autocorrelation pulse peak power, the OSNR has been estimated with an error lower than 0.5 dB. Thereby the autocorrelation peak can be a feasible indicator of the signal impairments in high-speed optical networks.

The advantages of the proposed OSNR monitoring technique are the following:

- The technique provides in-band measurements. It eliminates the extrapolation uncertainty using the out-band approach.
- The technique performs the signal quality monitoring with relaxed speed requirements with respect to typical techniques as the correlator works at the packet rate.
- The FBG-based correlator is easily manufactured.
- The technique offers the possibility of integration with other functions in the packet switching node to take immediate actions when the signal is strongly degraded.

Furthermore, some practical applications of the proposed OSNR monitor have been presented. First, the OSNR monitor could be deployed as part of QoS to ensure that packets are properly treated along the network according to their QoS level. Second, the monitoring information obtained from the optical monitor could be included when calculating new routes for data signals. Indeed, signal quality monitoring information could be added as an additional factor in the routing decision. Additionally, the OSNR information could also be utilized for path monitoring for restoration functions.

In the proposed OSNR monitoring technique presented in this chapter, the FBG-based correlator was designed with unequal grating spacing, i.e. with different time intervals. By means of simulations, a study of the correlator output as function of the pattern written into the FBG array was carried out in order to decide which pattern provided better performance and less overhead. At this point, the pattern can be also chosen to improve the auto/cross-correlation properties. This means that the proper selection of codes with special properties can lead to an increase in the difference between the autocorrelation output and the cross-correlation outputs, allowing the provision of QoS applications. In the literature, longer and sparser aperiodic Quadratic (QC) and Extended Quadratic Congruence (EQC) codes have been used because they have better performances than other typical codes (Maric, 1993). Experiments using QC and EQC codes for the pattern written into the FBG-correlator are currently under investigation and will be presented in future works. In addition, an improvement on the design of the OSNR monitoring technique based on optical correlation will be addressed in order to enhance the correlation output's sensitivity to other impairments.

REFERENCES

Anderson, D. Z., Mizrahi, V., Erdogan, T., & White, A. E. (1993). Production of in-fiber gratings using a diffractive element. *Electronics Letters*, 29(6), 566–568. doi:10.1049/el:19930379.

Bendilli, G. (2000). *Optical performance monitoring techniques*. Paper presented at 26th European Conference on Optical Communication (ECOC'00). Munich, Germany.

Blumenthal, D. J., Olsson, B. E., Rossi, G., Dimmick, T. E., Rau, L., & Masanovic, M. et al. (2000). All-optical label swapping networks and technologies. *IEEE/OSA. Journal of Lightwave Technology, 18*(12), 2058–2075. doi:10.1109/50.908817.

Boudriga, N., Lazzez, A., Khlifi, Y., & Zghal, M. (2008). *All optical network switching: A new scheme for QoS provision and virtual memory control*. Paper presented at 10th International Conference on Transparent Optical Networks (ICTON'08). Athens, Greece.

Chang, C. T., Cassaboom, J. A., & Taylor, H. F. (1977). Fibre-optic delay-line devices for R. F. signal processing. *Electronics Letters, 13*(22), 678–680. doi:10.1049/el:19770481.

Chen, W., Tucker, R. S., Yi, X., Shieh, W., & Evans, J. S. (2005). Optical signal-to-noise ratio monitoring using uncorrelated beat noise. *IEEE Photonics Technology Letters, 17*(11), 2484–2486. doi:10.1109/LPT.2005.858100.

Chen, W., Zhong, S., Zhu, Z., Chen, W., & Chen, Y. J. (2003). Adding OSNR and wavelength monitoring functionalities on a double resolution AWG-based power monitoring circuit. *IEEE Photonics Technology Letters, 15*(6), 858–860. doi:10.1109/LPT.2003.811138.

Chung, Y. C. (2000). *Optical monitoring technique for WDM networks*. Paper presented at IEEE/LEOS Summer Topical Meetings 2000. New York, NY.

Cisco. (2003). *Internetworking technologies handbook*. Indianapolis, IN: Cisco Systems, Inc.

Cisco. (n.d.). *Data sheet: OC-192/STM-64 line card portfolio for the Cisco ONS 15454 SONET/SDH multiservice provisioning platforms*. Indianapolis, IN: Cisco.

Desurvire, E. (1994). *Erbium-doped fiber amplifiers, principles and applications*. New York: John Wiley & Sons, Inc..

Ding, L., Zhong, W. D., Lu, C., & Wang, Y. (2004). A new bit error rate monitoring method based on histograms and curve fitting. *Optics Express, 12*(11), 2507–2511. doi:10.1364/OPEX.12.002507 PMID:19475088.

Euliss, G. W., & Athale, R. A. (1994). Time-integrating correlator based on fiber-optic delay lines. *Optics Letters, 19*, 649–651. doi:10.1364/OL.19.000649 PMID:19844401.

Fisher, R. A. (1956). *Statistical methods and scientific inference*. Edinburgh, UK: Oliver and Boyd.

Fsaifes, I., Lepers, C., Lourdiane, M., Gabet, R., & Gallion, P. (2006). *Pulsed laser source coherence time impairments in a direct detection DS-OCDMA system*. Paper presented at Conference on Lasers Electro-Optics (CLEO'06). Long Beach, CA.

Fsaifes, I., Lepers, C., Obaton, A., & Gallion, P. (2006). DS-OCDMA encoder/ decoder performance analysis using optical low-coherence reflectometry. *IEEE/OSA. Journal of Lightwave Technology, 24*(8), 3121–3126. doi:10.1109/JLT.2006.878039.

Gordon, J. P., & Kogelnik, H. (2000). *PMD fundamentals: Polarization-mode dispersion in optical fibers*. Washington, DC: National Academy of Sciences. doi:10.1073/pnas.97.9.4541.

Hauer, M. C., McGeehan, J. E., Kumar, S., Touch, J. D., Bannister, J., & Lyons, E. R. et al. (2003). Optically assisted Internet routing using arrays of novel dynamically reconfigurable FBG-based correlators. *IEEE/OSA. Journal of Lightwave Technology*, *21*(11), 2765–2778. doi:10.1109/JLT.2003.819144.

Hill, K., & Meltz, G. (1997). Fiber Bragg grating technology fundamentals and overview. *IEEE/OSA. Journal of Lightwave Technology*, *15*(8), 1263–1276. doi:10.1109/50.618320.

Jackson, K. P., Newton, S. A., Moslehi, B., Tur, M., Cutler, C. C., Goodman, J. W., & Shaw, H. J. (1985). Optical fiber delay-line signal processing. *IEEE Transactions on Microwave Theory and Techniques*, *33*, 193–209. doi:10.1109/TMTT.1985.1132981.

Jourdan, A., Chiaroni, D., Dotaro, E., Elienberger, G. J., Masetti, F., & Renaud, M. (2001). The perspective of the optical packet switching in IP-dominant backbone and metropolitan networks. *IEEE Communications Magazine*, *39*(3), 137–141. doi:10.1109/35.910601.

Kashyap, R. (n.d.). *Fiber Braggs gratings*. San Diego, CA: Academic Press.

Kilper, D. C. (2002). Optical performance monitoring. *IEEE/OSA. Journal of Lightwave Technology*, *22*(1), 294–304. doi:10.1109/JLT.2003.822154.

Kilper, D. C. (2005). *Optical performance monitoring applications in transparent networks*. Paper presented at International Conference on Wireless and Optical Communications (WOCC'05). New York, NY.

Kilper, D. C., Bach, R., Blumenthal, D. J., Einstein, D., Landolsi, T., & Ostar, L. et al. (2004). Optical performance monitoring. *IEEE/OSA. Journal of Lightwave Technology*, *22*(1), 294–304. doi:10.1109/JLT.2003.822154.

Kodialam, M. (2003). Dynamic routing of restorable bandwidth-guaranteed tunnels using aggregated network resource usage information. *IEEE/ACM Transactions on Networking*, *11*, 399–410. doi:10.1109/TNET.2003.813044.

Kogelnik, H. (1976). Filter response of non-uniform almost-periodic structures. *The Bell System Technical Journal*, *55*, 109–126.

Koyama, K., Hashimoto, J. I., Tsuji, Y., Ishizuka, T., & Katsuyama, T. (2007). Optical label encoder/correlator on GaAs-based photonic integrated circuit for photonic networks. *SEI Technical Review*, *65*, 11–14.

Lemaire, P. J., Atkins, R. M., Mizrahi, V., & Reed, W. A. (1993). High pressure H2 loading as a technique for achieving ultrahigh UV photosensitivity and thermal sensitivity in GeO2 doped optical fibres. *Electronics Letters*, *29*(13), 1191–1193. doi:10.1049/el:19930796.

Maric, S. V. (1993). New family of algebraically designed optical orthogonal codes for use in CDMA fibre-optic networks. *Electronics Letters*, *29*(6), 538–539. doi:10.1049/el:19930359.

McGeehan, J., Kumar, S., Gurkan, D., Motaghian Nezam, S. M. R., Willner, A. E., & Fejer, M. M. et al. (2003). All-optical decrementing of a packet's time-to-live (TTL) field and subsequent dropping of a zero-TTL packet. *IEEE/OSA. Journal of Lightwave Technology*, *21*, 2746–2751. doi:10.1109/JLT.2003.819131.

Meflah, L., Thomsen, B., Savory, S., Mitchell, J., & Bayvel, P. (2006). *Single technique for simultaneous monitoring of OSNR and chromatic dispersion at 40Gbit/s*. Paper presented at 32nd European Conference on Optical Communication (ECOC'06). Cannes, France.

Meltz, G., Morey, W. W., & Glenn, W. H. (1989). Formation of Bragg gratings in optical fibers by a transverse holographic method. *Optics Letters*, *14*(15), 823–825. doi:10.1364/OL.14.000823 PMID:19752980.

Noirie, L., Cerou, F., Moustakides, G., Audouin, O., & Peloso, P. (2002). *New transparent optical monitoring of the eye and BER using asynchronous undersampling of the signal*. Paper presented at 28th European Conference on Optical Communication (ECOC'02). Copenhagen, Denmark.

O'Mahony, M. J., Simeonidou, D., Hunter, D. K., & Tzanakaki, A. (2001). The application of optical packet switching in future communication networks. *IEEE Communications Magazine*, *39*(3), 128–135. doi:10.1109/35.910600.

Petropoulos, P., Wada, N., The, P. C., Ibsen, M., Chojo, W., Kitayama, K. I., & Richardson, D. J. (2001). Demonstration of a 64-chip OCDMA system using superstructured fiber gratings and time-gating detection. *IEEE Photonics Technology Letters*, *13*(11), 1239–1241. doi:10.1109/68.959376.

Ramaswami, R., & Sivarajan, K. N. (2002). *Optical networks - A practical perspective*. San Francisco: Morgan Kaufmann Publishers.

Richter, A. (2002). Optical performance monitoring in transparent and configurable dwdm networks. *IEEE Proceedings, 149*(1), 1–5.

Shake, I., Takara, H., Kawanishi, S., & Yamabayashi, Y. (1998). Optical signal quality monitoring method based on optical sampling. *Electronics Letters*, *34*(22), 2152–2154. doi:10.1049/el:19981465.

Stampoulidis, L., Kehayas, E., Avramopoulos, H., Liu, Y., Tangdiongga, E., & Dorren, H. J. S. (2005). *40 Gbit/s fast-locking all-optical packet clock recovery*. Paper presented at Optical Fiber Communication Conference (OFC'05). Anaheim, CA.

Takiguchi, K., Shibata, T., & Itoh, M. (2002). Encoder/decoder on planar lightwave circuit for time-spreading/wavelength-hoping optical CDMA. *Electronics Letters*, *38*(10), 469–470. doi:10.1049/el:20020314.

Teixeira, A., Costa, L., Franzl, G., Azodolmolky, S., Tomkos, I., & Vlachos, K. et al. (2009). An integrated view on monitoring and compensation for dynamic optical networks: From management to physical layer. *Photonic Network Communications*, *18*, 191–210. doi:10.1007/s11107-008-0183-5.

Vilar, R., Garcia, J., Tremblay, G., Kim, Y., LaRochelle, S., Ramos, F., & Marti, J. (2009). Monitoring the quality of signal in packet-switched networks using optical correlators. *IEEE/OSA. Journal of Lightwave Technology*, *27*(23), 5417–5425. doi:10.1109/JLT.2009.2028034.

Vilar, R., Ramos, F., & Marti, J. (2007). *Optical signal quality monitoring using fibre-Bragg-grating-based correlators in optical packet-switched networks*. Paper presented at 33rd European Conference on Optical Communication (ECOC'07). Berlin, Germany.

Wen, Y. G., & Chan, V. W. S. (2005). Ultra-reliable communication over vulnerable all-optical networks via lightpath diversity. *IEEE Journal on Selected Areas in Communications*, *23*(8), 1572–1587. doi:10.1109/JSAC.2005.851763.

Yamada, M., & Sakuda, K. (1987). Analysis of almost-periodic distributed feed-back slab waveguide via a fundamental matrix approach. *Applied Optics*, *26*(16), 3474–3478. doi:10.1364/AO.26.003474 PMID:20490085.

Yang, J., Jeon, M. Y., Pan, J. C. Z., & Yoo, S. J. B. (2003). *Performance monitoring by sub-carrier multiplexing in optical label switching network*. Paper presented at Optical Fiber Communication Conference (OFC'03). Atlanta, GA.

Yang, J., Zhu, Z., Yang, H., Pan, Z., & Yoo, S. J. B. (2004). *All-optical time-to-live using error-checking labels in optical label switching networks*. Paper presented at 30th European Conference on Optical Communication (ECOC'04). Stokholm, Sweden.

Ye, D., & Zhong, W. D. (2007). Improved BER monitoring based on amplitude histogram and multi-Gaussian curve fitting. *Journal of Optical Networking*, 6, 584–598. doi:10.1364/JON.6.000584.

Yi, X., Chen, W., & Shieh, W. (2006). An OSNR monitor for optical packet switched networks. *IEEE Photonics Technology Letters*, 18(13), 1448–1450. doi:10.1109/LPT.2006.877571.

KEY TERMS AND DEFINITIONS

Bit Error Rate (BER): In digital transmission, the number of bit errors is the number of received bits of a data stream over a communication channel that has been altered due to noise, interference, distortion or bit synchronization errors. The bit error rate (BER) is the number of bit errors divided by the total number of transferred bits during a studied time interval. BER is a unitless performance measure, often expressed as a percentage.

Chromatic Dispersion (CD): Of an optical medium is the phenomenon that the phase velocity and group velocity of light propagating in a transparent medium depend on the optical frequency. The CD for a uniform medium can be calculated as: $CD = -\frac{\lambda}{c}\left(\frac{d^2 n}{d\lambda^2}\right)$, where λ is the wavelength of the transmitted signal, c is the speed of the light, and n is the refractive index of the uniform medium.

Fiber Bragg Grating (FBG): Is a type of distributed Bragg reflector constructed in a short segment of optical fiber that reflects particular wavelengths of light and transmits all others. This is achieved by creating a periodic variation in the refractive index of the fiber core, which generates a wavelength specific dielectric mirror. A fiber Bragg grating can therefore be used as an inline optical filter to block certain wavelengths, or as a wavelength-specific reflector.

Optical Performance Monitoring (OPM): Is a potential mechanism to improve control of transmission and physical-layer fault management in optical transmission systems. In a general perspective, OPM is responsible of physical layer monitoring of the signal quality, i.e., monitoring of the health of the signal in the optical domain.

Optical Signal-to-Noise Ratio (OSNR): Ratio between the signal power and the noise power in a given bandwidth. Most commonly a reference bandwidth of 0.1 nm is used. This bandwidth is independent of the modulation format, the frequency, and the receiver.

Packet-Switched Networks: Packet-switched describes the type of network in which relatively small units of data called packets are routed through a network based on the destination address contained within each packet.

Polarization Mode Dispersion (PMD): Is a form of modal dispersion where two different polarizations of light in a waveguide, which normally travel at the same speed, travel at different speeds due to random imperfections and asymmetries, causing random spreading of optical pulses. Unless it is compensated, which is difficult, this ultimately limits the rate at which data can be transmitted over a fiber. The first-order PMD is called differential group delay (DGD) and measures the temporal delay between the principal polarization modes of the fiber. The DGD of the fiber is described by: $DGD = \Delta\tau = D_{PMD}\sqrt{L}$ where L is the fiber link, and D_{PMD} is the fiber PMD parameter measured in $ps/\sqrt{km}$. The unit for DGD is ps.

Quality of Service (QoS): Is a set of technologies for managing network traffic in a cost effective manner to enhance user experiences for home and enterprise environments. QoS technologies allow you to measure bandwidth, detect changing network conditions (such as congestion or availability of bandwidth), and prioritize traffic. For example, QoS technologies can be applied to prioritize traffic for latency-sensitive applications (such as voice or video) and to control the impact of latency-insensitive traffic (such as bulk data transfers).

Chapter 5
GMPLS for Future Applications:
Performance Characterization and Measurements

Weiqiang Sun
Shanghai Jiao Tong University, China

Yaohui Jin
Shanghai Jiao Tong University, China

Wei Guo
Shanghai Jiao Tong University, China

Lilin Yi
Shanghai Jiao Tong University, China

Weisheng Hu
Shanghai Jiao Tong University, China

ABSTRACT

Generalized Multiprotocol Label Switching, or GMPLS, is a suite of protocols to enable automated resource discovery, automated service provisioning and automated failure recovery. In recent years, a considerable number of efforts have been seen in the area of putting GMPLS into advanced networking/service environments. This is exemplified by the various research programs in the US, Europe, and Asia. In such programs, GMPLS has not only been used as a way to reduce management complexity and increase reliability, like the industry is doing right now, but also it is used as a new way for service provisioning. In this chapter, the authors first review activities in using GMPLS controlled optical networks in high performance computing environments. They try to identify the benefits, as well as the limitations in such networking practices. Then they introduce the past and on-going standardization work in the Internet Engineering Task Force (IETF) about GMPLS network performance characterization and measurement. Finally, the authors present the performance measurement results from a number of deployed GMPLS networks.

INTRODUCTION

Generalized Multiprotocol Label Switching, or GMPLS, is a suite of protocols to enable automated resource discovery, automated service provisioning and automated failure recovery. Driven by the

DOI: 10.4018/978-1-4666-3652-1.ch005

benefit of improved network reliability (through protection or fast failure recovery) and reduced network OPEX, an increasing amount of GMPLS enabled networks are now being deployed in metro area and even in national backbones. In the short run, the deployment of such networks will enable network operators to provide new value added services such as Bandwidth on Demand (BoD) at a reduced OPEX. In the long run, GMPLS networks have the potential of carrying a big variety of services.

Starting from 2001, the time when the key concepts and features of GMPLS are gradually being standardized, a considerable number of efforts have been seen in the area of putting GMPLS into advanced networking/service environments. This is exemplified by the various research programs in the US, Europe and Asia. In such programs, GMPLS has not only been used as a way to reduce management complexity and increase reliability, like the industry is doing right now, but also it is used as a new way for service provisioning. For example, the GMPLS control plane is often integrated with the application to realize seamless on-demand circuit provisioning, so that dynamic data intensive applications may be served with dedicated bandwidth pipes in an efficient manner.

But before GMPLS can be fully utilized to its potential, it is important that we have good ways to characterize and measure its performance. What seem obvious performance measures include LSP dynamic provisioning performance, failure recovery performance, singling and routing scalability etc. What seems less obvious is the consistency between control plane and data plane.

In this chapter, we will first review activities in using GMPLS controlled optical networks in high performance computing environments. We try to identify the benefits, as well as the limitations in such networking practices. Then we will introduce the past and on-going standardization work in the Internet Engineering Task Force (IETF) about GMPLS network performance characterization and measurement. Finally, we will present our performance measurement results from a number of deployed GMPLS networks. These results are obtained during a time span of more than 6 years, over devices from three different vendors.

APPLYING GMPLS IN HIGH PERFORMANCE COMPUTING ENVIRONMENTS

Distributed storage, high performance computing and next generation e-science applications have long been research interests of the networking and computing communities. Such applications generally require large volumes of data be transferred from one place to another, or a set of steering and control operations from a centralized node be distributed to visualization/computing nodes in a timely manner. Although researches in grid computing has made tremendous advances in connecting widely distributed resources using ubiquitous Internet infrastructure, the fact that Internet is a shared packet switched network and is thus unable to provide the required bandwidth or QoS guarantee has intrigued much interests in building dedicated networks for that purpose. Circuit switched optical networks, because of its huge bandwidth and the guaranteed QoS performance, are regarded as excellent transport infrastructures for such applications.

Given the dynamic and heterogeneous nature of applications, the following requirements make the problem of provisioning circuits to applications even more challenging:

- Meeting the arbitrary communication needs of applications, while at the same time maintaining a high level of efficiency.
- Providing an user-friendly interface, such that no or little additional complexity incur in application design.
- Providing optimized performance for a variety of applications with different requirements.

A finely tuned provisioning model that couples the applications with the network management system or control plane is essential to meet such requirements. Intensive research and development efforts on provisioning optical circuits for such applications have been witnessed in the recent literature. Testbeds using either all optical or hybrid electronic/optical switches are being deployed. Efforts have been made to address the challenges mentioned earlier. For example, in all the reported testbeds (projects), optical circuits either in the forms of wavelength channels (St Arnaud, Bjerring, 2004; Taesombot & Uyeda, 2006) or Ethernet connections (Rao & Wing, 2005; Zheng & Veeraraghavan, 2005; Lenhman & Sobieski, 2006; Mambretti & Lillethun, 2006) are provisioned dynamically upon request. This enables bandwidth sharing in the core network between potentially a large number of users. Dynamic provisioning is done through GMPLS distributed control plane (Zheng & Veeraraghavan, 2005; Lenhman & Sobieski, 2006), or through centralized Web service platforms (St Arnaud, Bjerring, 2004; Taesombot & Uyeda, 2006). Through standardized User Network Interface (UNI) or Web service invocation interface, it is

not necessary for end hosts to implement complex intelligence of optical networks, thus simplifies deployment. In general, the tighter a provisioning model is coupled with specific applications, the better performance it is likely to achieve (Zheng & Veeraraghavan, 2005). However, a loosely coupled provisioning model may provide more flexibility in deployment (St Arnaud, Bjerring, 2004). Hardware accelerated provisioning is reported in (Veeraraghavan & Zheng, 2006) to achieve better performance. We summarize these testbeds (projects) in Table 1.

THE CHALLENGES

Dedicated Connectivity Interface vs. Multiple Connectivity Interface

Among the above efforts, a widely and often implicitly adopted assumption is that communications in such applications are generally single-

Table 1. Testbeds (projects) of provisioning circuits to end hosts (users)

	Networking Technology	Provisioning Method	Provisioned Channel capacity	Applications
USN	SONET/10 Gigabit Ethernet (core) and Multi-Service Provisioning Platform (edge)	Centralized scheduling and signaling within a VPN	10Gbps, 1Gbps and high-precision channels such as SONET OC-1	Large data transfer
CHEETAH	SONET (core) and Multi-Service Provisioning Platform (edge) with packet switching for dual homing	GMPLS with hardware-accelerated signaling	10Gbps and 1Gbps	Large file transfer and remote visualizations
UCLP/ CA*net4	Lightpath Switching	Centralized provisioning through Web Service	Wavelength (10Gbps) and sub-wavelength	High performance computing
DRAGON	DWDM switching (core) and Ethernet, TDM, IP (edge)	GMPLS with centralized broker	Wavelength, Ethernet and IP	e-VLBI
SURFnet6	Lambda switching and packet switching	User controlled provisioning	Wavelength	Large data transfer
OptiPuter	Lambda Switching with packet switching for dual homing	Client-provisioning through Web Service	Wavelength	Distributed Virtual Computer (DVC)
OMNInet	DWDM switching and L2/L3 devices	GMPLS with OIF UNI	10/100/1000Mbps	Grid applications
3TNet	SONET (core) and Multi-Service Provisioning Platform (edge)	GMPLS with OIF UNI	1000Mbps	Large data transfer

task based. At any specific time, there exists only one communications task in an end system and it will consume all the provisioned bandwidth. When a circuit is provisioned between a pair of interfaces, e.g., two Ethernet network interfaces, the connected end systems will be able to take full advantage of the dedicated bandwidth. This addresses a wide arrange of applications, characterized by large data transfer from one site to another. We refer to interfaces with exclusive usage as Dedicated Connectivity Interface (DCI) and the corresponding service model as DCI model. DCI enables end hosts to take advantage of huge bandwidth that circuit provides. However, it also inhibits them from communicating with different remote systems simultaneously. At the same time, DCI model exhibits little flexibility in provisioning finer granularity circuits.

The limited connectivity problem introduced by DCI can be partially resolved by a dual-homing strategy (Zheng & Veeraraghavan 2005; Taesombot & Uyeda, 2006). Besides one interface that connects each end host to a circuit switched network, another interface connects it to a packet switched network. Different routing policies can be applied to determine which interface to use when communication requests are generated. This strategy has two interesting features. First, as packet switched networks provide "always on" connectivity, the limited connectivity of circuit switched networks can thus be remedied. Second, as bandwidth of provisioned circuits is equal to interface capacity and may be well beyond the need of a single communication task, falling back to the packet switched network can improve bandwidth efficiency. However, due to the fact that packet switched networks have neither bandwidth nor QoS guarantee, this strategy is actually a tradeoff between connectivity and the provisioned QoS.

One other way to circumvent this problem is scheduling multiple communication requests onto the dedicated interface. The basic idea of scheduling is to arrange local data transfer requests in time domain, and at any specific time only one of them is served. The objective is to achieve least resource consumption, minimized overall finishing time, maximized throughput or other performance metrics alike (Sun & Guo, 2008; Taesombot & Uyeda, 2006; Kuri & Puech, 2003). As provisioning latency may incur significant overhead in the performance, it is also desirable to reduce provisioning latency (Veeraraghavan & Zheng, 2006). Although the scheduled model is suitable for applications in which data transfer requests can be re-arranged so that they have no overlap in time, it is not adequate for applications that have concurrent communication requests.

In a provisioning model called V-STONES, we have presented a Multiple Connectivity Interface (MCI) scheme. This scheme takes advantage of VLAN tagging mechanism on the end systems, and VLAN switching mechanisms on network devices. By tagging departing packets with different VLAN ID on end systems, and dynamically mapping them into different circuits, MCI may be implemented. The MCI model provides more flexibility in circuit provisioning. But it requires that both the end system and edge network devices support VLAN based mechanisms (Sun & Xie, 2008).

Performances of Dynamic Provisioning

It has been widely agreed that GMPLS can provide the necessary signaling and routing functions to realize connection establishment in an on-demand fashion. But it is still largely unknown to the industry and the academia how GMPLS-enabled optical networks will perform under varied traffic patterns. The gap between the network provisioning performance and application needs is apparent. The lack of performance characterization will result in either degraded application performance, or lower network utilization. In commercial networks, the lack of detailed and standard performance information will also prevent Service Providers from defining differentiated Service Level Agreements (SLAs).

One example of dynamic LSP provisioning is Bandwidth on Demand (BoD). Gao and Li (2008) showed typical time-varying bandwidth requirements from enterprises and home users. By dynamically adjusting the reserved bandwidth, BoD services can potentially reduce the bandwidth leasing cost while increasing the bandwidth efficiency in a Service Provider's network. In general, the bandwidth fluctuation from such users is slow and usually in the order of hours. The reliability performance, e.g., very low failure probability when setting up/releasing/modifying a connection, is more important than the provisioning delay.

Habib & Song (2006) conclude that near-real-time connection setup is desirable in certain applications that require instant scheduling. More recently, joint scheduling of computing and network resources have also been reported to improve application performance in grid environments (Wang & Jin, 2007; Sun & Guo, 2008). In the current literature, the connection provisioning delay is assumed to be constant or is simply ignored. This leads to a relatively simple application model and may reflect the system's statistical or sometimes, the worst-case performances. However the current state of the art GMPLS networks exhibit very dynamic behavior in provisioning performance. A practical model must take into account this variability and randomness. To bridge this gap, work in measurement and characterization of GMPLS network performance is imperative.

STANDARDIZATION OF LSP DYNAMIC PROVISIONING

Standardization Efforts in MPLS-TE Convergence and Protection Performance

The community, as seen from the IETF standardization efforts, has partly identified the need for common benchmarking and quantification of GMPLS/MPLS performance. Notably in IETF's

Benchmarking Working Group (BMWG), in the draft "Motivation of benchmarking of MPLS-TE scalability and performance," Vapiwala and Ratnam (2008) proposed the performance and scalability metrics to benchmark MPLS Traffic Engineering (TE) convergence. The document identified a number of factors that may affect the MPLS-TE performance, including RSVP-TE refresh reduction, RSVP authentication, CPU and memory etc. Benchmarking the signaling performance under different factors can help network operators to benchmark IP/MPLS networks properly to meet specific service level agreement needs.

In another draft, Rajiv Papneja et al proposed to benchmark MPLS protection mechanisms in terms of failover packet loss, reversion packet loss, failover time, reversion time and additive backup delay (Poretsky, Papneja & Vapiwala, 2011). The proposed metrics can be used to characterize performances of sub-IP layer (i.e., layer 2 or below) protection mechanisms such as Automatic Protection Switching (APS), Virtual Router Redundancy Protocol (VRRP), Stateful High Availability (HA), and Multi-Protocol Label Switching Fast Reroute (MPLS-FRR). The benchmarking is performed in the IP layer and is thus independent of the specific protection mechanisms being used. It is worth noting that the failover time may vary when the number of existing/affected LSPs differs upon a link or node failure. The document suggests that such numbers are recorded when performing the procedures. It may be worthwhile that standalone benchmarking of scaling performance is performed as well, to reflect the need for the potentially large number of co-existing LSPs in an MPLS-TE network.

Standardization Efforts for LSP Provisioning Performance

Motivated by the above discussion, and also by our involvement in building and testing a GMPLS network testbed, we proposed to define a set of metrics to characterize the LSP provisioning performance of GMPLS networks. A draft was first submitted to IETF Common Control and Measurement Plane (CCAMP) working group in Feb. 2007 and was published as RFC 5814 in March 2010 (Sun & Zhang, 2010). In the document, we define three performance metrics: (1) uni-directional LSP setup delay, (2) bi-directional LSP setup delay, and (3) LSP graceful release delay. These metrics are believed to be the most fundamental performance parameters specific to GMPLS networks and can be used to depict the dynamic provisioning performance of GM-PLS networks where the signaling protocol is RSVP-TE.

The necessity in defining LSP setup delay as one of the key parameters is straightforward. When designing an application that takes advantage of GMPLS provisioning, the designer must take into account how quickly a circuit can be provisioned. This is especially true when the circuit holding time is comparable to the LSP setup delay. A better match in between the application requirement and the network provisioning capability will lead to higher network resource utilization and better application performance. At the same time, the designer must also take into account the probability with which a setup attempt may fail. When the network is properly dimensioned, i.e., when the available bandwidth is sufficient to satisfy the requests, this probability is basically determined by the processing capability of the control plane. The LSP setup delay can therefore characterize the performance of the control plane under different traffic load pressure.

LSP release delay is defined separately for two different LSP release procedures. In one procedure LSP release is initiated by ingress nodes and in the other, it is initiated by egress nodes. Graceful release delay itself is a helpful metric because it is not only part of the total cost of dynamic LSP provisioning but also is more preferred in a GM-PLS controlled network (Swallow & Drake, 2008).

The document also suggests a set of statistics definitions to report for each metrics above. These include minimum, median and percentile of metric and failure probability. These metrics are useful in drawing certain conclusions of a GMPLS network. For example, for signaling delays, the median is more stable than average in the presence of a few outliers. The minimum of metric reflects the best-case performance and can be very stable in a given implementation.

In measuring each metrics, a given methodology will have to include a way to determine whether a latency value is infinite or whether it is merely very large. Simple upper bounds may be used, but GMPLS networks may accommodate many kinds of devices. For example, some photonic cross-connects (PXCs) have to move micro mirrors. This physical motion may take several milliseconds, but electronic switches can finish the nodal processing within several microseconds. So the LSP setup delay may vary drastically from one network to another. In the process of LSP setup, if the downstream node overrides the label suggested by the upstream node, the setup delay may also increase. Thus, in practice, the upper bound should be chosen carefully. Up till now, two version of measurement software have been implemented and used in the tests discussed below.

Standardization Efforts for LSP Data Path/Control Plane Consistency

It is worth noting that for GMPLS, the control plane is separate from the data plane. As elaborated by Shiomoto and Farrel (2011), the RSVP protocol specification defined standard behavior for cross connection programming. It suggests that for unidirectional LSPs, cross connection should in place and ready to forward traffic before RESV message is sent upstream. For bi-directional LSPs, the protocol specification requires that upstream nodes must be ready to forward data in the reverse direction before the egress node finishes processing the Path message. It is desirable that prior to the signaling delay measurement, a data plane testing is performed to verify the availability of the data path. The standardization of such measurements has started in IETF. In (Sun & Zhang, 2012), we define five performance metrics to characterize the performance of data path provisioning with GMPLS/MPLS-TE signaling. These metrics complement the metrics defined in RFC5814, in the sense that the completion of the signaling process for a Label Switched Path (LSP) and the programming of cross connections along the LSP may not be consistent. The five metrics are:

1.   **RRFD:** The delay between RESV message received by ingress node and forward data path becomes ready for use.
2.   **RSRD:** The delay between RESV message sent by egress node and reverse data path becomes ready for use.
3.   **PRFD:** The delay between PATH message received by egress node and forward data path becomes ready for use.
4.   **PSFD:** The delay between PATH message sent by ingress and forward data path becomes ready for use.
5.   **PSRD:** The delay between PATH message sent by ingress and reverse data path becomes ready for use.

The performance metrics in RFC5814 characterize the performance of LSP provisioning from the pure signaling point of view, while the metric in this document takes into account the validity of the data path. It is worth noting that the accuracy of the defined metrics depends on the clock resolution of both the ingress and egress nodes. In measuring some of the metrics, clock synchronization between the ingress and egress nodes may be required. The accuracy of measurement is also dependent on how the error free signal is received and may differ significantly when the underline data plane technology is different. For instance, for an LSP between a pair of Ethernet interfaces, the ingress node may use a rate based method to verify the connectivity of the data path and use the reception of the first error free frame

as the error free signal. In this case, the interval between two successive frames has a significant impact on accuracy. The document recommends that the ingress node use small intervals, under the condition that the injected traffic does not exceed the capacity of the forward data path. The value of such intervals should be reported.

PERFORMANCE MEASUREMENT OF LSP DYNAMIC PROVISIONING

A testbed consisting of 13 synchronous digital hierarchy cross-connects was deployed in Eastern China from 2002 (Sun & Hu, 2011). Each of these cross-connects were equipped with a GMPLS control entity to provide on-demand Gigabit Ethernet connectivity to routers and media servers. There had been an essential uncertainty in designing the provisioning model due to the lack of performance information of the network testbed. A fairly pessimistic estimate with both LSP setup and release delay of 1 second was finally adopted, resulting in a network utilization of less than 80%. Later tests showed that the value could be as low as 1/3 of the estimate with small but non-zero failure probability. Apparently having beforehand a set of performance statistics will help designers to design more efficient and robust application models.

From 2004, we performed a number of tests on several SDH based GMPLS networks/testbeds. For better understanding of the results, only linear topologies are considered. For all topologies, the length of each link is small and contributes only an insignificant portion to the overall delay. In each test, the GMPLS network organized in linear topology is connected to two UNI client devices (UNI-C) acting as measurement endpoints. An LSP is a gigabit Ethernet connection carried by a group of SDH VC-4 paths. The ingress UNI-C node generates LSP setup requests periodically according to specified arrival rate. Each LSP is held for some fixed duration of time and released again by the ingress UNI-C. By comparing the timestamp of sending the Path message and receiving of the corresponding RESV message, we obtain the setup delay of an LSP. LSP release delay is obtained by comparing the timestamp of the outgoing Path (with D&R bits set) message and returning PathErr message. The process of setting up, holding and releasing an LSP is repeated in each test to get multiple samples. For simplicity, in the following discussions, we will focus on LSP setup delay and most of the observations are applicable to release delay as well.

It is assumed that an LSP setup fails when the ingress UNI-C doesn't receive the corresponding RESV message after a relatively long time or receive the PathErr message. In the testing, the time out value for 2 nodes topology is set to 3 minutes and this value increases proportionally with the number of nodes in a topology. As in RFC 5814, the setup delay of a failed attempt is deemed to be infinite and is not counted in the results below.

It is worth noting that measuring GMPLS provisioning performance is a difficult task, provided that such performance is subject to many factors. By presenting the results below, we are trying to draw a sketch of the performance of the state of the art GMPLS implementations. Further conclusions cannot be made until more measurements considering specific factors are conducted.

Decomposition of LSP Setup Delay

The LSP setup delay is composed of the propagation delay, the transmission delay and the nodal processing delay. It is reasonable to assume that given the network configuration, the propagation and transmission delay are constant for each request. The nodal processing delay can be further decomposed into message processing delay and some times, the cross connection programming time. The message processing delay can be affected by the number of routing and signaling messages being processed in the control plane at the time the LSP is being setup. It also can be affected by operating system routines that coincide with the LSP setup process. The cross connection programming time is the time from when an initial attempt (to configure the data plane) is made by the control plane, until a confirmation is passed back. As will be revealed later, this part of delay can sometimes dominate the overall LSP setup delay.

Performances vs. Time:
The Big Picture

Figure 1 shows the measured minimum average LSP setup delay in milliseconds from the year 2004 to 2006. The time span coincides with the R&D phrase of GMPLS controlled SDH network

Figure 1. Measured minimum average setup delay vs. time. The time span illustrated above coincides with the R&D phrase of GMPLS controlled SDH network elements from tested vendors. The steady decrease of setup delay reflects that implementation of GMPLS signaling is getting mature. It is also partly due to the continual requests from application designers to reduce connection setup delay.

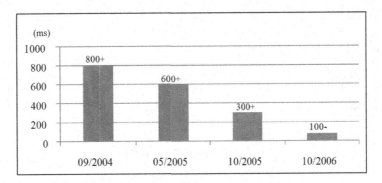

elements of tested vendors, from early lab testing to field trial till the network became operational in mid 2006. The minimum average delay is the minimum value among the tested vendors. Each value is obtained by collecting a large number of samples and calculating their average. The minimum average delay can thus reflect the best achievable setup performance from multiple vendors at the time of measurement. The steady decrease of setup delay indicates that the vendors' experiences in GMPLS implementation increased dramatically during that period. It was also partly due to the continual requests from application designers to reduce connection setup delay. It is also observed that under similar traffic arrival rate, blocking probability decreased from a typical value of more than 10% to a best case of 0% in a continuous testing lasted longer than 72 hours during the same period.

In the following sub-sections, we will look into recent measurement results in a more microscopic way and try to analyze the possible cause of various phenomenons. It is possible that recent setup delay is longer than the value presented in Figure 1 because the minimum value in Figure 1 was obtained from data sets of multiple vendors and releases, while the results that follow are measured on specific releases.

Average Setup Delay and Variance vs. Nodes

Figure 2 illustrates the average setup delay against the number of hops along an LSP. Good linear relationship between the average setup delay and the number of hops is observed. This can be explained by the fact that the nodal processing of signaling messages are the same hence each node exhibits the same statistical behavior. By linearly fitting the data, it appears that introducing an additional node along the LSP path imposes an extra delay of around 156 milliseconds. We also find that the intercept of the fitting is around 68 milliseconds. This can be attributed to the measurement end

Figure 2. Average setup delay/Setup delay variance vs. number of nodes. There is a good linear relation between the LSP setup delay and number of nodes along the LSP. The variance increases as the number of hops in an LSP increases. The intercept of the linear fitting is caused by measurement end points.

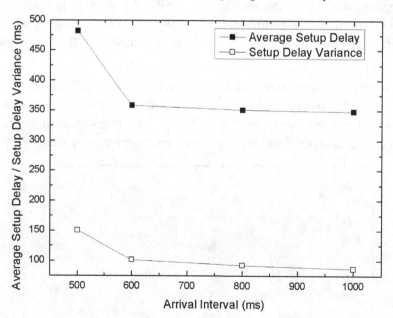

points connected to each side of the control channel. Note this part of the delay is fixed and does not affect the analysis.

Also shown in Figure 2 is the variance against number of hops. The variance increases as the number of hops in an LSP increases. This is because in terms of LSP setup delay, the nodal processing is itself a random process and the overall signaling process is the combination of a series of dependent additive processes. The more hops an LSP traverses, the larger variance the overall setup delay will exhibit.

Setup Performance vs. Traffic Load

As discussed in the previous sections, the setup performance of GMPLS networks is dependent on traffic load. This is because the control channel and control plane processor have to handle more messages when setup/release requests arrive at a higher rate. In a scenario if multiple setup path requests arrive in parallel, the cross connection

programming of the requests need to be queued, which further increases the overall setup delay. Figure 3 illustrates the average and standard error of setup delay versus arrival interval in a 2-hop network. It can be concluded that the arrival rate has little impact on setup delay when the arrival interval is more than two times the minimum delay. However, as the arrival interval approaches the minimum delay, the setup delay will increase dramatically. This implies that in testing a GMPLS network according the methodologies listed in RFC 5814, the request arrival rate must be carefully selected so that this dependency is sufficiently observed.

Regular Patterns in Measured Data Sets

We now present some results that are somewhat unintuitive. Figure 4(a) shows a section of the setup delay sequence from one test. In this sequence, most setup delay samples distribute around only

Figure 3. Setup delay/variance vs. arrival interval. The typical setup delay under very light traffic load reflects the minimum time needed to setup an LSP in this test. The arrival rate has little impact on setup delay when the arrival interval is more than two times the minimum delay. However, as the arrival interval approaches the minimum delay, the setup delay will increase dramatically.

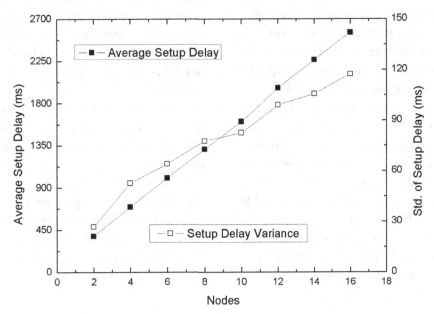

Figure 4. Regular patterns in measured data sets. The regular patterns in LSP setup delay sequence indicate that there are dominant factors in the overall LSP setup process. One possible dominating factor is the cross connection programming. To get an accurate stochastic model, one must first decouple the deterministic factors that cause regular patterns. (a) Setup delay sequences exhibiting step-wise behavior in one test (b) Setup delay sequences exhibiting step-wise behavior in another test

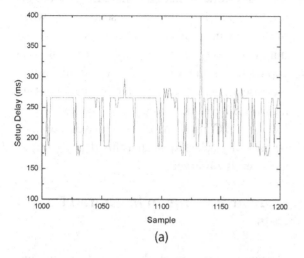

(a)

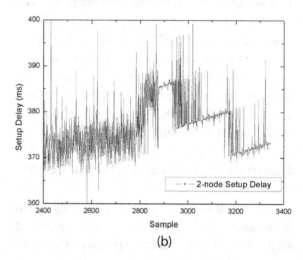

(b)

a few values and the neighboring values have same difference of approximately 15 ms. Successive samples with very close delay value are observed, followed by samples with a different value, but the differences are multiples of 15 ms. This clearly indicates that in the network under test, the randomness in nodal processing time is negligible and the LSP setup delay is dominated by factors that are highly stable over time. The former can be explained by the fact that in the network under test, the control plane was implemented in a separate box which provided more computing power and higher memory access speed.

Although it cannot be confirmed due to the proprietary control plane implementation is not disclosed, the authors believe the predominant factor can be attributed to the cross connection programming and the interaction between the control plane and data plane. In one possible implementation, the data plane may pass the configuration results back to the control plane every 15 milliseconds. It may take zero or more 15-millisecond slots before one result is success-

fully passed back. Apparently, by making further improvements to the control plane/data plane interface, the message passing overhead between the control plane and data plane can be kept at a minimum and the overall setup delay can be reduced significantly.

Figure 4(b) shows another setup delay sequence obtained from a different network. This sequence exhibits larger degrees of randomness, while at the same time shows easily recognizable patterns. This can be caused by similar reasons but detailed explanation is outside the scope of this article.

There is no universal significance in the sequences discussed above, since both of them are obtained from specific networks. But they remind us that the behavior of LSP setup delay is highly implementation dependent. The statistical modeling of LSP setup delays must take into account specific implementation model. To get an accurate stochastic model, one must first decouple the deterministic factors that cause regular patterns from the random ones.

CONCLUSION AND FUTURE RESEARCH DIRECTIONS

Despite the fact that more and more GMPLS enabled optical networks are being deployed worldwide and automated connection provisioning of GMPLS is being used in high performance networks, the measurement and characterization of its provisioning performance is still under-explored. This results in a gap between network performance and application needs. This article first introduces the pioneering efforts on this topic in IETF. Then, by presenting the testing results from a number of GMPLS networks, it also tries to provide some insights into the provisioning performance of the state of the art GMPLS networks. The main finding of the tests include: 1) Implementation of GMPLS is getting mature over time; 2) LSP setup delay exhibits high variance, especially under high traffic load and when the number of hops along the LSP is large; 3) LSP setup delay can be highly implementation dependent; 4) the delay in cross connection programming and data plan/control plane interaction can be dominating factors in the overall LSP setup delay. As both the interest and understanding in this topic are increasing in the community, it is expected that more issues will be identified. To sum up this article, we try to list below a few topics that need to be considered in the near future.

The standardization of GMPLS/MPLS-TE performance measurement has just started and apparently has a long way to go. As the number of applications that take advantage of GMPLS/MPLS-TE continues to grow, and their requirements being increasingly demanding, the standardization needs that cover various aspects of GMPLS/MPLS-TE performance will surely be identified. In this process, the standardization of IP performance metrics and benchmarking technologies can be good examples. But due to the fact that GMPLS networks normally have separate control plane and data plane, the measurement and characterization of its performance are more complicated in nature.

The statistical modeling of the provisioning performance is very difficult. On the one hand, this is because GMPLS control plane is totally distributed. The difficulty can easily be understood if one thinks about delay modeling in IP networks. On the other, as mentioned previously in this article, provisioning performance can be highly dependent on implementations. Although it may be virtually impossible to derive a universally applicable model for different implementations, a model with general enough assumptions is still desirable to provide insights into the provisioning performance of GMPLS networks.

Blocking performance may be device vendors' primary concern at the beginning of this century, but it is now far from enough. As shown in this article, the need for faster connection setup urged device vendors to optimize their implementations and significant reduction in setup delay has been achieved in only a few years. Meanwhile, the results presented in this article show that setup delay is highly dependent on implementations and still exhibits high variances. The need for further improvement will grow as the number of demanding applications grows. Executing the control plane on more powerful hardware platforms may be one lightweight solution, but in the long run, fine tuning protocol design/implementation and the interaction between the control plane and data plane are important to achieve high performance provisioning.

REFERENCES

Gao, J., & Li, D. (2008). *BoD service with VCAT/LCAS and GMPLS signaling*. Paper presented at NOMS Workshops 2008. Salvador da Bahia, Brazil.

Habib, I., & Song, Q. (2006). Deployment of the GMPLS control plane for grid applications in experimental high-performance networks. *IEEE Communications Magazine, 44*(3), 65–73. doi:10.1109/MCOM.2006.1607868.

Kuri, J., & Puech, N. (2003). Routing and wavelength assignment of scheduled lightpath demands. *IEEE Journal on Selected Areas in Communications, 21*(8), 1231–1240. doi:10.1109/JSAC.2003.816622.

Lenhman, T., & Sobieski, J. (2006). DRAGON: A framework for service provisioning in heterogeneous grid networks. *IEEE Communications Magazine, 44*(3), 84–90. doi:10.1109/MCOM.2006.1607870.

Mambretti, J., & Lillethun, D. (2006). Optical dynamic intelligent network services (ODIN), an experimental control-plane architecture for high-performance distributed environments based on dynamic lightpath provisioning. *IEEE Communications Magazine, 44*(3), 92–99. doi:10.1109/MCOM.2006.1607871.

Papneja, R., & Vapiwala, S. (2011). *Methodology for benchmarking MPLS protection mechanisms. Internet draft, draft-ietf-bmwg-protection-meth-09.txt, work in progress*. IETF.

Poretsky, S., & Papneja, R. (2011). *Benchmarking terminology for protection performance*. RFC 6414.

Rao, N. S. V., & Wing, W. R. (2005). Ultra-science net: network testbed for large-scale science applications. *IEEE Communications Magazine, 43*(11), s12–s17. doi:10.1109/MCOM.2005.1541694.

Shiomoto, K., & Farrel, A. (2011). *Advice on when it is safe to start sending data on label switched paths established using RSVP-TE*. RFC 6383.

St Arnaud, B., & Bjerring, A. (2004). Web services architecture for user control and management of optical Internet networks. *Proceedings of the IEEE, 92*(9), 1490–1500. doi:10.1109/JPROC.2004.832948.

Sun, W., & Hu, W. (2011). *Distributing digital TV over a hybrid packet- and circuit-switched network*. Retrieved January 5, 2011, from http://spie.org/x17175.xml?ArticleID=x17175

Sun, W., & Xie, G. (2008). A cross-layer optical circuit provisioning framework for data intensive IP end hosts. *IEEE Communications Magazine, 46*(2), S30–S37. doi:10.1109/MCOM.2008.4473084.

Sun, W., & Zhang, G. (2010). *Label switched path (LSP) dynamic provisioning performance metrics in generalized MPLS networks*. RFC 5814.

Sun, W., & Zhang, G. (2012). *Label switched path (LSP) data path delay metric in generalized MPLS/MPLS-TE networks. draft-ietf-ccamp-dpm-06.txt, Internet draft, work in progress*. IETF.

Sun, Z., & Guo, W. (2008). Scheduling algorithm for workflow-based applications in optical grid. *Journal of Lightwave Technology, 26*(17), 3011–3020. doi:10.1109/JLT.2008.923935.

Swallow, G., &, Drake, J. (2008). *Generalized multiprotocol label switching (GMPLS) user-network interface (UNI), resource reservation protocol-traffic engineering (RSVP-TE) support for the overlay model*. RFC 4208. IETF.

Taesombot, N., & Uyeda, F. (2006). The OptIPuter: High-performance, QoS-guaranteed network service for emerging E-science applications. *IEEE Communications Magazine, 44*(5), 38–45. doi:10.1109/MCOM.2006.1637945.

Vapiwala, S., & Ratnam, K. (2008). *Motivation for benchmarking MPLS TE scalability and performance*. Internet Draft, draft-bmwg-rsvpte-convergece-motivation-01.txt, work in progress.

Veeraraghavan, M., & Zheng, X. (2006). On the use of connection-oriented networks to support grid computing. *IEEE Communications Magazine*, *44*(3), 118–123. doi:10.1109/MCOM.2006.1607874.

Wang, Y., & Jin, Y. (2007). Joint scheduling for optical grid applications. *Journal of Optical Networking*, *6*(3), 304–318. doi:10.1364/JON.6.000304.

Zheng, X., & Veeraraghavan, M. (2005). CHEE-TAH: Circuit-switched high-speed end-to-end transport architecture testbed. *IEEE Communications Magazine*, *43*(8), s11–s17. doi:10.1109/MCOM.2005.1497551.

KEY TERMS AND DEFINITIONS

GMPLS: The Generalized Multi-Protocol Label Switching (GMPLS) is a protocol suite extending MPLS to manage further classes of interfaces and switching technologies other than packet interfaces and switching, such as time division multiplex, layer-2 switch, wavelength switch, and fiber-switch.

IETF: The Internet Engineering Task Force (IETF) is a large open international community of network designers, operators, vendors, and researchers concerned with the evolution of the Internet architecture and the smooth operation of the Internet. It is open to any interested individual.

LSP: In MPLS networking, a Label Switched Path (LSP) is a path through an MPLS network, set up by a signaling protocol such as LDP, RSVP-TE, BGP or CR-LDP. The path is set up based on criteria in the forwarding equivalence class (FEC).

MPLS-TE: An extension to MPLS for selecting the most efficient paths across an MPLS network, based on both bandwidth and administrative rules.

RSVP-TE: Resource Reservation Protocol - Traffic Engineering is an extension of the resource reservation protocol (RSVP) for traffic engineering. It supports the reservation of resources across an IP network. Applications running on IP end systems can use RSVP to indicate to other nodes the nature (bandwidth, jitter, maximum burst, and so forth) of the packet streams they want to receive. RSVP runs on both IPv4 and IPv6.

UNI-C: User-to-Network Interface, Client side.

Chapter 6
Energy–Efficient Optical Transport Networks with Mixed Regenerator Placement

Zuqing Zhu
University of Science and Technology of China, China

ABSTRACT

In this chapter, the authors first discuss the background and basic concepts of all-optical regeneration and translucent optical networks. Since all-optical regenerator is much more energy-efficient than traditional O/E/O ones, they investigate translucent lightpath arrangement that involves mixed placement (MRP) of optical inline amplifiers (1R), all-optical 2R regenerators, and O/E/O 3R regenerators for energy-saving. In order to make sure that the end-to-end transmission performance requirement can still be satisfied with this arrangement, the authors analyze the signal BER evolution through fiber links and different types of regenerators, and propose a theoretical model. They then develop search strategies based on exhaustive search and genetic algorithms, and discuss how to use them to optimize the energy-efficiency of lightpaths using MRP. Finally, the authors move to the network design using MRP, in which they considered both offline network design and online network provisioning.

INTRODUCTION

Over the last decade, Internet traffic has been growing at an annual rate of more than 70% (Odlyzko, 2003), and various network applications continue to require for more bandwidth. With the Dense Wavelength Division Multiplexing (DWDM) technology, over 10 Tb/s capacity can be provided over a single strand of fiber (Fukuchi et al., 2001).

In order to facilitate efficient and flexible access to such a wide bandwidth, researchers are still looking for ways to automate and expedite bandwidth provisioning in the optical layer. These ongoing efforts indicate the inevitable trends of the development of more flexible, intelligent, and energy-efficient optical layer, especially for core and transport networks. While the remarkable growth of Internet bandwidth demands have spurred intensive research on efficient optical networking systems, the major technical difficulties are still

DOI: 10.4018/978-1-4666-3652-1.ch006

caused by the physical layer limitations, such as signal-to-noise degradation, fiber dispersions, crosstalk, and nonlinearities. In opaque optical networks, optical-electronic-optical (O/E/O) 3R (Re-amplification, Re-shaping, and Re-timing) regenerators overcome physical layer limitations at every switching node to increase transmission reach. However, since devices are usually expensive and power-hungry (Leclerc et al., 2003). For example, the state-of-the-art optoelectronic core router, a Cisco CRS-3 16-slot single-shelf system for 4.48 Tb/s aggregate switching capacity, has dimensions (H x W x D) of 213.36 x 59.94 x 91.44 cm, with a maximum power consumption of 13.2 kilowatts http://www.cisco.com/en/US/products/ps5763/prod_models_comparison.html). To support over 300 Tb/s throughput, it has to use a multi-shelf configuration that may consume more than one million watts. These factors limit the scaling of the transport network infrastructure. Therefore, network operators have to mitigate their network infrastructure from opaque to translucent, for reducing capital expenditures (CAPEX) and operational expenditures (OPEX) (Saradhi et al., 2010).

Translucent network design aims to minimize the number of O/E/O 3R, without compromising transmission performance. Recently, all-optical 2R (Re-amplification and Re-shaping) regenerators have been demonstrated for operation speed at 40 Gb/s and beyond (Leclerc, et al., 2003), and commercially available devices have been released (Maxwell, 2008; Zhu et al., 2005). Compared to O/E/O 3R, these devices are much more energy-efficient and cost-effective, and can achieve wavelength conversion simultaneously with signal regeneration (Leclerc, et al., 2003). Therefore, if we introduce all-optical 2R in translucent lightpath design, we can solve the signal quality and wavelength contention issues in optical networks with a more energy-efficient and cost-effective way. To explore these benefits, we will discuss on translucent lightpath arrangement that involves mixed placement (MRP) of optical

inline amplifiers (1R), all-optical 2R regenerators, and O/E/O 3R regenerators. It is well known that the estimation of quality of transmission (QoT) in optical transport networks is usually time consuming, especially for the cases with mixed regenerator placements (Zhu, 2011). We will focus on search strategies based on exhaustive search and genetic algorithm, discuss how to use them to find the optimized solutions of MRP for lightpaths, and compare the performance of these strategies. By the end of this chapter, we move to network design with MRP, in which we will consider both offline network design and online network provisioning.

The rest of the chapter is organized as follows: Introduction discusses the background and basic concepts. The analytical model of signal transmission through translucent lightpaths with Mixed Regenerator Placement (MRP) is presented afterwards. We propose several regenerator location search algorithms to design energy-efficient translucent lightpaths. The MRP-based green translucent network design and provisioning methods are then discussed. Finally, we summarize this chapter and draw conclusions.

BACKGROUND AND BASIC CONCEPTS

All-Optical Regeneration

The major task of optical transport networks is to deliver high-speed data over long transmission distance across a large number of switching nodes. While the combination of wavelength division multiplexing (WDM), optical amplification and modulation techniques keeps pushing the fiber transmission capacity to heroic numbers (Becouarn et al., 2004; Borne et al., 2006; Yoshikane et al., 2004), the main technical difficulties for improving the optical transport networks' scalability remain to be physical layer limitations from signal-to-noise ratio degradation, Chromatic Dispersion

(CD), Polarization Mode Dispersion (PMD), fiber nonlinearities, and other impairment mechanisms. The state-of-the-art commercial systems resolve these limitations by combining optical fiber amplifiers, dispersion management, modulation format engineering, and 'receive-and-retransmit' based O/E/O regeneration. Nevertheless, O/E/O regenerators typically involve bulky and power-hungry high-speed electronics. The dispersion compensation typically has bandwidth limitations, and dynamic PMD and CD compensation is difficult to achieve across a wide wavelength range. More importantly, these degradation mechanisms can interact with each other to induce unexpected impairments. Thus, a more robust and tolerant solution is desired. The O/E/O regeneration has been prevalent in the current optical transport networks, however, its power consumption and physical size have affected the scalability of the next generation transport networks. Alternatively, all-optical regeneration can potentially work with lower power consumption and much more compact size relative to its O/E/O counterpart, and can provide transparency to protocol and format (Dupas et al., 1998; Karlsson et al., 2004; Leclerc, et al., 2003; Leuthold, 2002).

All-optical regenerators using combinations of re-amplification (1R), reshaping (2R), and retiming (3R) have been studied intensively. Figure 1

shows working principle and design requirements of all-optical regenerators. The Optical re-amplification (1R) compensates for the propagation loss of optical signals and supplies sufficient optical power beyond the receiver sensitivity. However, linear amplification adds noise to degrade the Optical-Signal-to-Noise-Ratio (OSNR) (Marcuse, 1990). Therefore, optical reshaping with nonlinear power transfer function becomes necessary to clamp the amplitude noise. Optical reshaping together with the re-amplifying provides optical 2R capability. When retiming is absent, timing jitter generated from pattern dependence of bandwidth limited optical components (Stephens, 2004), environmental variations, etc. can accumulate through the fiber transmission and induce major impairments even when the amplitude domain noise is well suppressed (Raybon et al., 2002). The retiming function in optical 3R regeneration suppresses the timing jitter from accumulating at the expense of additional system complexities in clock recovery and timing re-alignment.

Translucent Optical Networks

As shown in Figure 2, in a transparent optical network, the optical signal will not go through any O/E/O regeneration in a lightpath. The lightpaths are thus set up with different wavelength channels

Figure 1. Working principle and design requirements of all-optical regenerators

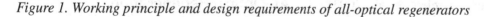

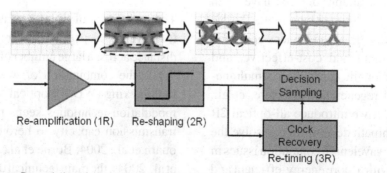

■ Degradations to overcome: amplifier noise, dispersion, fiber nonlinearities, crosstalk, and etc.
■ Various modulation formats to support: RZ, NRZ, NRZ-DPSK, RZ-DPSK, and etc.
■ Burst-mode operation is necessary to support packetized data.

Figure 2. Transparent optical network infrastructure

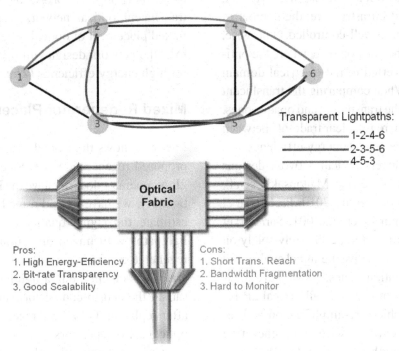

that traverse multiple switching nodes, and wavelength continuity has to be considered. For optical transport networks, this kind of infrastructure is famous for its high energy-efficiency, good scalability, and bit-rate transparency. However, due to the fact that the optical signal will not be regenerated from the source to the destination, signal distortions can accumulate and eventually limit the transmission reach and the number of switching hopes. It also makes performance monitoring difficult due to the lack of electrical processing inside the lightpaths. Moreover, to maintain wavelength continuity, bandwidth fragmentation can be generated. The idea of translucent optical network is to find a balance between network performance and energy-efficiency. As shown in Figure 3, in the translucent optical network, the optical signal can be O/E/O regenerated when its quality is low, or

Figure 3. Translucent optical network infrastructure

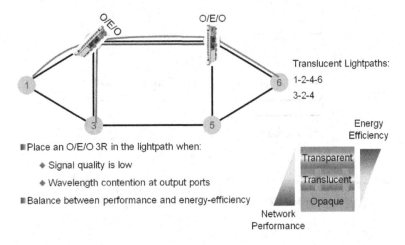

when there is a need for wavelength conversion. In this translucent infrastructure, the number of O/E/O regenerators is well-controlled. Otherwise, the network can become opaque, where the optical signal is converted to the electrical domain too frequently. When comparing the translucent infrastructure to the transparent and opaque ones, we can see that there is a clear trade-off between network performance and energy-efficiency.

Current translucent optical network designs (Azodolmolky et al., 2011; Manousakis et al., 2010, 2009; Martinez et al., 2010; Pachnicke et al., 2008; Ramamurthy et al., 2001; Saradhi, et al., 2010; Shinomiya et al., 2007) rely solely on O/E/O regenerators to solve the signal quality and wavelength contention issues. As we have mentioned in the previous section, all-optical 2R regenerators can achieve re-amplification and re-shaping functionalities with a regenerative all-optical wavelength conversion. And therefore, they can also resolve the signal quality and wavelength contention issues. Current advances on all-optical 2R regeneration show that devices operating at 40 Gb/s have already become commercially available (Maxwell, 2008; Zhu, et al., 2005). Compared to O/E/O 3R regenerators, all-optical 2R regenerators usually have compact sizes and relatively low power consumption. Therefore, if we use all-optical 2R regenerators

to partially replace O/E/O 3R regenerators in translucent optical networks, and introduce a mixed placement of optical 1R/2R/3R regenerators, the network design will become promising for high energy-efficiency (Zhu, 2011a, 2011b).

Mixed Regenerator Placement

Figure 4 shows the hybrid configuration of our proposed regeneration site. Since an all-optical 2R regenerator does not have the Re-timing functionality, we have to find a method to precisely estimate the signal quality evolution through lightpaths with mixed operations of 1R/2R/3R regenerators. Then, we can figure out the regenerator placement along a lightpath that can still satisfy the end-to-end performance requirement after replacing O/E/O 3R regenerators with all-optical 2R regenerators.

It is well known that the origin overlapping between the noise distributions associated to the space- and mark-levels of a noisy signal cannot be removed but only minimized even through regeneration using an ideal step function at the optimal sampling point (Mork et al., 2003; Ohlen et al., 1997). Thus, the optimal BER of a regenerated signal is the same as that before the regeneration if measured directly after the regenerator without forward error correction (FEC). Conse-

Figure 4. Hybrid configuration of regeneration site

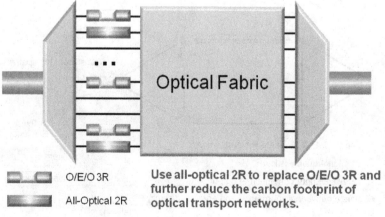

quently, measurements right at the output are insufficient to quantify the regenerative performance of an optical regenerator (Leclerc, et al., 2003). Inline, multi-hop regeneration experiment is necessary to show the benefit of slower BER increasing through the regeneration stages and to estimate the ultimate cascadability of the regenerators. As an indication of the system scalability and the maximum transmission reach, the cascadability of an optical regenerator becomes the ultimate factor to evaluate its performance to against physical limitations. Optical signal-to-noise (OSNR) degradation caused by optical amplifiers limits the cascadability of optical 1R regenerators (Marcuse, 1990). Optical 2R regenerators utilize nonlinear transfer functions to prevent amplitude noise from accumulation. When the retiming is absent, timing jitter accumulates and eventually imposes the necessary for full optical 3R regeneration (Raybon, et al., 2002).

Previous work in (Mork, et al., 2003; Ohlen, et al., 1997) has theoretically investigated how the degree of nonlinearity affects the cascadability of all-optical 2R regenerators when ignoring the timing jitter effects. However, experiments have found that jitter accumulation limits the cascadability of an optical 2R regenerator in a most interesting way (Funabashi et al., 2006; Ohlen et al., 2000; Poulsen et al., 1997). Timing jitter usually consists of noise-induced random jitter and systematic jitter caused by bandwidth limitation, memory effect, and other system imperfections (Stephens, 2004; Takasaki, 1991; Trischitta et al., 1989). For all-optical 2R regenerators, experimental investigation indicated that systematic jitter dominates the jitter accumulation (Funabashi, et al., 2006; Ohlen, et al., 2000; Poulsen, et al., 1997). And the situation becomes even worse when the systems employ the non-return-to-zero (NRZ) format and the memory-effect reduction technologies, such as differential operation (Joergensen et al., 1997) and spectrum slicing (Raybon, et al., 2002), are difficult to apply. Previous proposed theoretical models for simulating the jitter accumulation

through cascaded optical 2R regenerators either only considered the noise-induced random jitter (Green et al., 1996; Weinert et al., 1999), or depended on the assumption of linear jitter increment (Ohlen, et al., 2000; Ohlen et al., 1998). As it will be seen below, the systematic jitter increases nonlinearly when the regenerative nonlinearity is insufficient or the pattern-dependence from the memory effect is severe. In the next section, we systematically investigate the jitter and amplitude noise accumulation in cascaded optical 2R regenerators with theoretical simulations and experimental measurements. The simulation model studies the individual and combinational effects from the degree of regenerative nonlinearity, bandwidth limitation and pattern-dependence and how they limit the cascadability of all-optical 2R regenerators. The simulation results show a good match with the experimental results.

ANALYTICAL MODEL OF MIXED REGENERATOR PLACEMENT

Optical 2R Regeneration Using SOA-MZI

Monolithic integration (Mikkelsen et al., 1996) makes the semiconductor optical amplifier based Mach-Zehnder interferometer (SOA-MZI) a compact building block for optical 2R regeneration. The interferometric property of a SOA-MZI provides a nonlinear transfer function for the suppression of the amplitude noise. As shown in Figure 5, the 2R regeneration is based on the cross-phase modulation (XPM) effect. The on-off modulation of the input signal changes the carrier density in the SOA. This carrier density change affects the refractive index, which in turn modulates the phase of the CW probe light. This phase modulation is then converted into an intensity modulation at the output of the Mach-Zehnder interferometer. Due to the nature of the interferometer, the power transfer function of XPM is a nonlinear function as shown

Figure 5. Working principle of all-optical 2R regeneration using a SOA-MZI

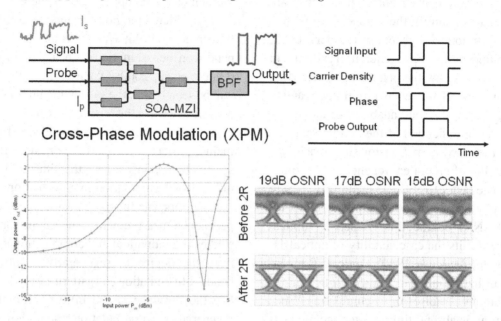

in the inset of Figure 5. With proper input power biasing, the device can regulate the noise on the mark- and space-levels with this transfer function and thus achieve optical 2R regeneration. The eye-diagrams in Figure 5 show the 10 Gb/s input at different OSNR levels, and the corresponding 2R-regenerated outputs. It can be seen that the amplitude noise gets suppressed well.

Theoretical Model of Optical 2R Regeneration

Figure 6(a) shows the diagram of a simplified optical 2R regenerator model (Mork, et al., 2003; Ohlen, et al., 1997) that considers only the signal levels for noise analysis and ignores dynamic effects, memory effects and jitter. The model decomposes an all-optical 2R regenerator into a linear amplifier and a nonlinear reshaping element. The reshaping element is represented by a nonlinear transfer function (Mork, et al., 2003; Ohlen, et al., 1997):

$$\begin{cases} f(x) = a \cdot \tanh(b(x - 0.5)) + 0.5 \\ \quad\quad f(0) = 0 \\ \quad\quad f'(0.5) = 1 / \gamma \end{cases} \quad (1)$$

Here, x represents the input signal level ranging from 0 to 1, a and b are constants that normalize $f(x)$ within (0, 1), and γ is the parameter characterizing the degree of the nonlinearity. The γ parameter changes $f(x)$ from a step-function (perfect nonlinear thresholding) when $\gamma = 0$ to a linear-slope (no nonlinear thresholding) when $\gamma = 1$ (Mork, et al., 2003). Figure 6(b) plots the nonlinear transfer functions with different γ parameters. With this model and the noise analysis method proposed in (Mork, et al., 2003), we simulate the BER accumulation through 2R regeneration stages with different γ parameters. We assume the initial BER is $3.31 \times 10\text{-}14$ after the first optical 2R regenerator. Figure 6(c) plots the simulation results. The results indicate that the evolution of the BER induced by amplitude noise is critically dependent on the γ parameter.

Figure 6. (a) Simplified all-optical 2R regenerator model for noise analysis, (b) normalized nonlinear transfer functions with different γ parameters, and (c) BER evolution for 2R regenerator with different γ parameters

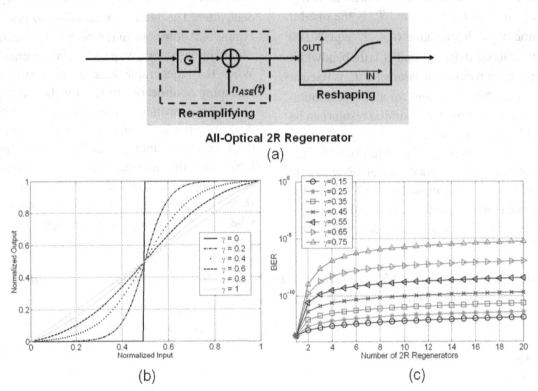

Figure 7 shows the diagram of the simulation model that includes the frequency response of the optical 2R regenerator. Here, $H_1(j\omega)$ represents the transfer function of the device. For the noise entering into the reshaping element to be restricted, $H_1(j\omega)$ should possess a low-pass filtering property (Ohlen, et al., 1998). In practical optical 2R regenerators, the device properties, such as carrier dynamics, can intrinsically limit the bandwidth (Durhuus et al., 1996; Joergensen, et al., 1997). To isolate problems, we assume that $H_1(j\omega)$ only induces minimal pattern-dependent jitter. One practical realization of $H_1(j\omega)$ as a means of validating the assumption is Bessel

Figure 7. Simulation model of all-optical 2R regenerator that considers the bandwidth limitation of the device

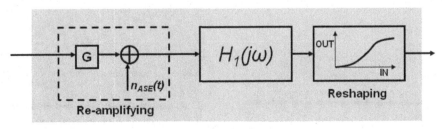

filtering function (Trischitta, et al., 1989). In the following simulation, $H_1(j\omega)$ takes the shape of a fifth-order Bessel filter with a 3-dB cutoff frequency of $f_1 = \beta / T_0$. Here, T_0 is the one-bit duration of the input signal (*e.g.* T_0 equals 100 ps for 10 Gb/s simulation), and β is the bandwidth enhancement factor. The parameter T_0 is fixed at 100 ps (10 Gb/s operation) for all of the simulations in this Section, while similar results can be applied to other bit-rates.

Figure 8(a) shows the simulated 10 Gb/s eye-diagrams after 20 cascaded optical 2R regenerators with $\beta = 1$ for input Pseudo-Random Bit Sequence (PRBS) lengths of 2^7-1 and 2^{31}-1. The eye-diagrams for signals with different PRBS lengths are almost identical when the γ parameter is the same. This result verifies our assumption that $H_1(j\omega)$ induces minimal pattern-dependent jitter. The jitter accumulation observed in Figure 8(a) comes from the waveform distortion caused by cascaded low-pass filtering operations. When the regenerator does not have sufficient reshaping nonlinearity to recover the waveform distortion, it can induce severe jitter accumulation. And this jitter accumulation comes solely from the bandwidth limitation of the device. Figure 8(b) shows the jitter peak-to-peak evolution for PRBS lengths of 2^7-1 and 2^{31}-1. The simulation shows that the jitter accumulation is nonlinear when the γ parameter is larger than 0.65. Sev-

Figure 8. (a) Simulated 10 Gb/s eye-diagrams after 20 cascaded optical 2R regenerators with $\beta = 1$, (b) jitter peak-to-peak evolution for PRBS lengths of 2^7-1 and 2^{31}-1

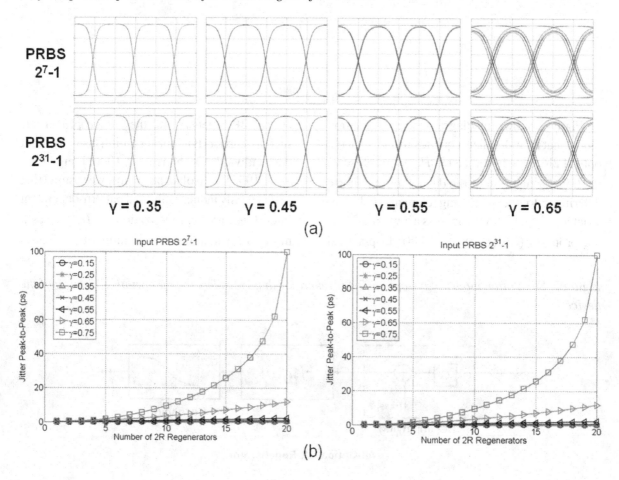

eral previously proposed jitter models relied on the assumption that the jitter accumulation is linear through cascaded optical 2R regenerators (Ohlen, et al., 2000, 1998). The results in Figure 8(b) indicate that the linear jitter accumulation assumption is applicable only when the 2R regenerators have sufficient nonlinearity (*i.e.* $\gamma < 0.65$). The simulation shows that the jitter accumulation is also critically dependent on the γ parameter when the pattern-dependence is minimized.

The BER simulation uses an ideal integrate-and-dump receiver to recover the bit-stream. The receiver sampling-clock is assumed to be jitter-free. We ignored the clock imperfection caused by the receiver synchronization mechanism. More sophisticated and complicated receiver models that consider receiver-timing imperfections from clock recovery and sampling are available in (Trischitta, et al., 1989). Note that due to the jitter discussed above, the signal integral over an one-bit duration is no longer identical for all '1' bits. As $H_1(j\omega)$ achieves minimal pattern-dependent jitter, we can consider the closest bit-neighbors only (Ohlen, et al., 1998). For a '1' bit, there are four sequences with equal possibility: 010, 011, 110, and 111. Simulation obtains the integral of the '1' symbol in these sequences after cascaded 2R operations. With the integral results defined as $E_{n,010}$, $E_{n,011}$, $E_{n,110}$, and $E_{n,111}$ for the '1' symbol in different sequences after n all-optical 2R regenerators, the BER can be written as

$$
\begin{cases}
BER_1 = \dfrac{1}{4}[Q(\dfrac{E_{1,010}-D}{\sigma_1}) + Q(\dfrac{E_{1,011}-D}{\sigma_1}) \\
\quad + Q(\dfrac{E_{1,110}-D}{\sigma_1}) + Q(\dfrac{E_{1,111}-D}{\sigma_1})] \\
BER_n = \dfrac{1}{4}[Q(\dfrac{E_{n,010}-D}{\sigma_n}) + Q(\dfrac{E_{n,011}-D}{\sigma_n}) \\
\quad + Q(\dfrac{E_{n,110}-D}{\sigma_n}) + Q(\dfrac{E_{n,111}-D}{\sigma_n})] + BER_{n-1}
\end{cases}
$$

$$(2)$$

Here, D is the decision threshold and

$$Q(x) = \frac{1}{2}erfc(\frac{x}{\sqrt{2}})$$

is the Q function. For simplicity, a fixed $D = E_0 / 2$ is used in the simulation and

$$E_0 = \int_0^{T_0} g(t)dt$$

is the integral of an initial '1' symbol. In the 2R regeneration operation, the amplifier noise term is approximated using a linear transformation with slope γ (Mork, et al., 2003):

$$
\begin{cases}
\sigma_1^2 = \sigma_{ASE}^2 \\
\sigma_n^2 = \gamma^2 \sigma_{n-1}^2 + \sigma_{ASE}^2
\end{cases}
\tag{3}
$$

where n represents the number of cascaded all-optical 2R regenerators and σ_{ASE}^2 is the variance of the amplifier noise. Previous work in (Mork, et al., 2003) has demonstrated that this approximation is an appropriate representation for modeling the dominant noise component in optical regenerators when the re-amplification gain is reasonably large (> 10 dB), as in most cases (Mork, et al., 2003; Ramaswami et al., 2002). Figure 9 shows the BER simulation results for $\beta = 1$ and input PRBS length of 2^{31}-1. Figure 9(a) plots the BER evolution when the jitter effect from bandwidth limitation is included. Figures 9(b) and (c) compare the BER curves in Figure 9(a) to the simulation results that ignore the jitter effect (as in Figure 6(c)). The BER comparisons indicate that, when the γ parameter is relatively small (*e.g.* 0.15 or 0.25), errors from amplifier noise are dominating the BER and that the jitter effect can be ignored without affecting the simulation accuracy. However, when the γ parameter is larger

Figure 9. BER simulation results for $\beta = 1$ *and input PRBS length of* 2^{31}-1, *(a) BER evolution when including the jitter effect from bandwidth limitation, (b) BER comparison for* $\gamma = 0.25$, *and (c) BER comparison for* $\gamma = 0.65$

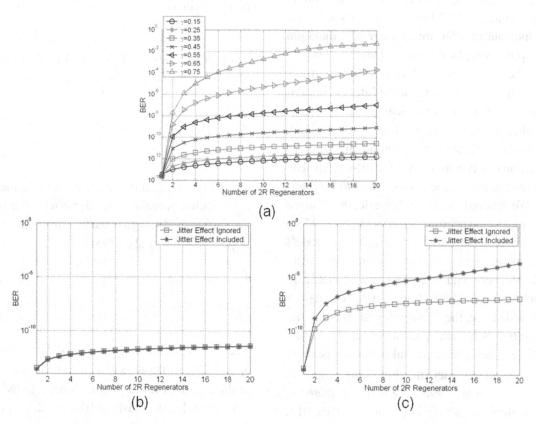

(a)

(b)

(c)

than 0.65, errors from the jitter effect will dominate the BER, so jitter can no longer be ignored.

The above simulations demonstrate that bandwidth limitation induces jitter and limits the cascadability of all-optical 2R regenerators. However, any increase in bandwidth corresponds to a decrease in the Signal-to-Noise Ratio (SNR). If we assume that the noise spectral density is constant and σ^2_{ASE} is the noise variance when the bandwidth enhancement factor $\beta = 1$, then the noise variance for a 2R regenerator with an arbitrary bandwidth is:

$$\sigma^2_{ASE,\beta} = \beta \cdot \sigma^2_{ASE} \qquad (4)$$

Substituting σ^2_{ASE} in Equation (2) with $\sigma^2_{ASE,\beta}$, we can simulate the trade-off between bandwidth limitation and SNR degradation. Figure 10 plots the effects of the bandwidth enhancement factor β on BER evolution. Narrowing the regenerator bandwidth limits the amplifier noise entering into the reshaping element and thus decreases the initial BER and BER increment due to amplitude noise in each hop. On the other hand, small regenerator bandwidth speeds up the jitter accumulation resulting from waveform degradation. Figure 11 shows the BER after 20 optical 2R regenerators for the combinations of γ and β. With the respect to BER after 20 2R regenerators, the optimal value of β is less than 1 when

Figure 10. Effects of bandwidth enhancement factor β on BER evolution, γ parameter of optical 2R regenerators are (a) 0.25, (b) 0.35, (c) 0.55, and (d) 0.65

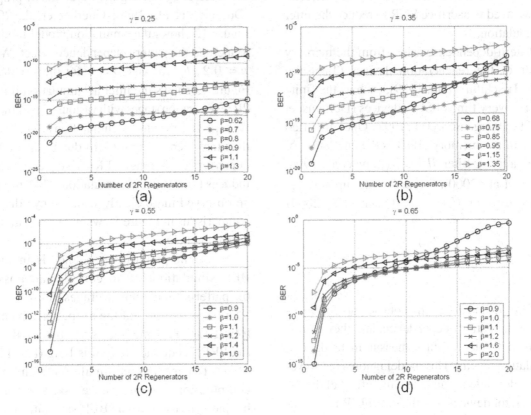

Figure 11. BER after 20 optical 2R regenerators for the combinations of γ and β

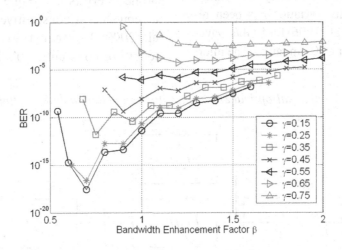

$\gamma < 0.55$, while optimal β is larger than 1 when γ equals 0.65 and 0.75. This observation is consistent with the results in Figure 9. For small γ parameters, errors from amplitude noise dominate the BER. Narrowing down bandwidth can efficiently restrict amplifier noise, and the extra jitter-tolerance margin from the regenerator nonlinearity can overcome the jitter accumulation resulting from the bandwidth limitation. A large γ parameter makes the jitter-tolerance margin insufficient, and we need to sacrifice SNR to reduce the jitter accumulation.

Pattern-dependence arises from the memory effects of the regeneration devices (Takasaki, 1991; Trischitta, et al., 1989), such as the finite gain recovery time of SOA devices (Durhuus, et al., 1996; Joergensen, et al., 1997). One simplified model of the memory effect is the emulation of it with a linear filter $H_2(j\omega)$ (Kang et al., 1996; Ohlen, et al., 2000). We define the impulse response $h_2(t)$ of $H_2(j\omega)$ as (Ohlen, et al., 2000)

$$h_2(t) = \begin{cases} a \cdot e^{-t/bT_0}, & t \geq 0 \\ 0, & t < 0 \end{cases} \quad (5)$$

Here, a and b are the coefficients for quantifying the pattern-dependence, and they can be obtained through fitting measurement data to simulation results. This model ignores the wavelength-dependence and the chirp effect of the 2R regenerator devices. For the optical 2R regenerators based on SOA-based interferometers, the wavelength dependence is relatively small, and a 0.5 dB receiver-penalty variation has been reported in (Durhuus, et al., 1996) for 5 Gb/s wavelength conversion over a 30 nm range. The inter-

ferometric SOA regenerator can also optimize the chirp effect by biasing the input signal properly (Durhuus, et al., 1996; Guerber et al., 2000). Figure 12 shows the simulation model modified to include the pattern-dependence effect. We fix $a = 0.2$, $b = 5$, and $\beta = 1$ for the simulation. Figure 13 shows the jitter accumulation through 2R regeneration stages with various γ parameters. As expected, the jitter accumulation is much worse than that seen in Figure 8(b) due to the pattern-dependence. A longer PRBS sequence length induces larger jitter accumulation. This trend can be observed more clearly with the eye-diagram comparisons in Figure 14 when the γ parameter is fixed at 0.55.

Since the pattern-dependence is included, BER simulation has to consider all possible bit-patterns and then averages the error-rate over the possibility of the bit-pattern to get the total BER. This method is not practical when the PRBS sequence length is long (*e.g.* PRBS 2^{31}-1). To carry out the simulation with limited computational resources, we have to refine the bit-patterns used for the BER simulation. It has been demonstrated that the '1' bit that is most prone to errors is a single '1' bit preceded by a sequence of consecutive '0' bits (Ohlen, et al., 2000; Takasaki, 1991). Since the greatest length of consecutive 0's is $M-1$ in a 2^M-1

Figure 12. Block diagram of an all-optical 2R regenerator model that includes pattern-dependence effect

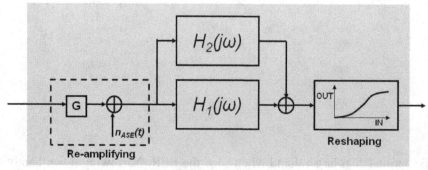

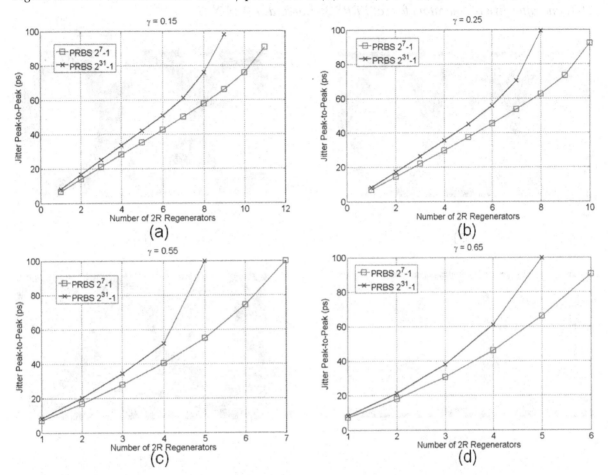

Figure 13. Jitter accumulations when γ parameter is (a) 0.15, (b) 0.25, (c) 0.55, and (d) 0.65

PRBS sequence, we can consider only these $M-1$ sequences to estimate the total BER. We define the possibility of m consecutive '0' bits as $P_M(m)$ in a 2^M-1 PRBS sequence and the integral result of the following single '1' symbol as $E_m(n, \gamma)$. Here, n represents the number of 2R regenerators the signal has experienced. Then, the total BER can be approximated as shown in Box 1.

Figure 15 shows the BER simulation results for PRBS 2^7-1 and PRBS 2^{31}-1 with $a = 0.2$, $b = 5$, and $\beta = 1$. Figure 16 shows the BER evolution comparisons between PRBS 27-1 and PRBS 231-1.

When the optical reshaping device is absent, the optical regenerator becomes a '1R' regenera-

tor, only with an optical amplifier. In this Section, we compare the cascadability of optical 1R and 2R regenerators with simulations. In most cases, the optical reshaping device is also an active device associated with noise addition (Leclerc, et al., 2003). Thus, we cannot simply remove the filters and the reshaping element in Figure 17 to model an optical 1R regenerator. Given the noise contribution from the optical amplifier and the optical reshaping device, the variance of the noise can be written as

$$\sigma^2_{ASE} = \sigma^2_{reamplifying} + \sigma^2_{reshaping} \qquad (7)$$

We assume

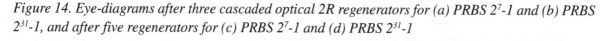

Figure 14. Eye-diagrams after three cascaded optical 2R regenerators for (a) PRBS 2^7-1 and (b) PRBS 2^{31}-1, and after five regenerators for (c) PRBS 2^7-1 and (d) PRBS 2^{31}-1

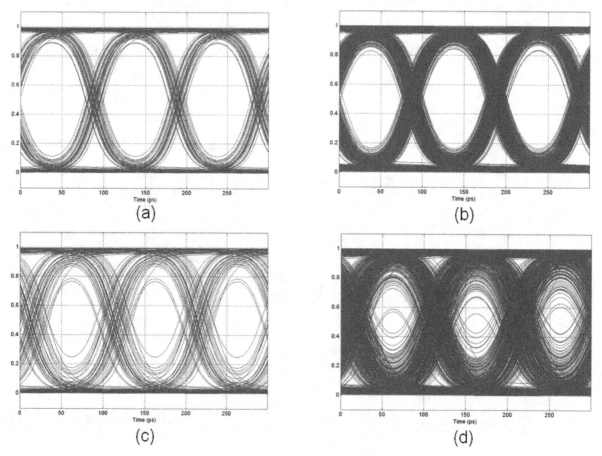

(a)   (b)

(c)   (d)

Box 1.

$$
\begin{cases}
BER_1 = \dfrac{1}{4} \displaystyle\sum_{m=1}^{M-1} P_M(m) \cdot Q\left(\dfrac{E_m(1,\gamma) - D}{\sigma_1}\right) + \dfrac{3}{4} Q\left(\dfrac{E_0}{2\sigma_1}\right) \\[3mm]
BER_n = \dfrac{1}{4} \displaystyle\sum_{m=1}^{M-1} P_M(m) \cdot Q\left(\dfrac{E_m(n,\gamma) - D}{\sigma_n}\right) + \dfrac{3}{4} Q\left(\dfrac{E_0}{2\sigma_n}\right) + BER_{n-1}
\end{cases}
\tag{6}
$$

$\sigma^2_{reamplifying} = \sigma^2_{reshaping}$

for the simulations in the remainder of this Section. Figure 17 shows the cascadability comparisons for optical 1R and 2R. When the pattern-dependence is large ($a = 0.2$), the optical 2R regenerator must have an almost ideal

nonlinear transfer function ($\gamma \leq 0.15$) to over-perform the optical 1R. With a smaller pattern-dependence ($a = 0.02$), the optical 2R regenerator can over-perform the optical 1R with a γ parameter of 0.65. These results indicate that the pattern-dependence can severely decrease the cascadability of an optical 2R regenerator

Figure 15. BER evolution for (a) PRBS 2^7-1 and (b) PRBS 2^{31}-1

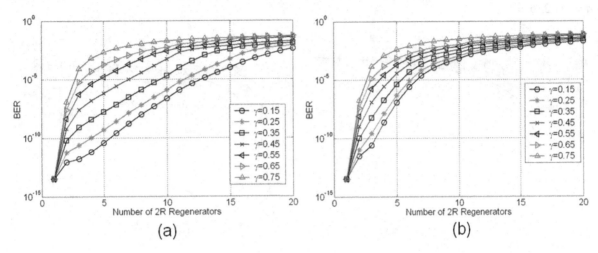

(a)
(b)

Figure 16. BER evolution comparisons when $\beta = 1$, $a = 0.2$, $b = 5$, and γ is (a) 0.15, (b) 0.25, (c) 0.55, and (d) 0.65

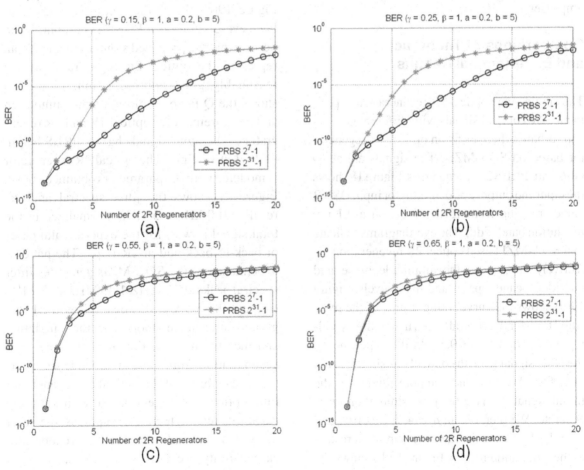

(a)
(b)
(c)
(d)

Figure 17. Cascadability comparison for optical 1R and 2R, (a) $\beta = 1$, $a = 0.2$, $b = 5$ and (b) $\beta = 1$, $a = 0.02$, $b = 5$

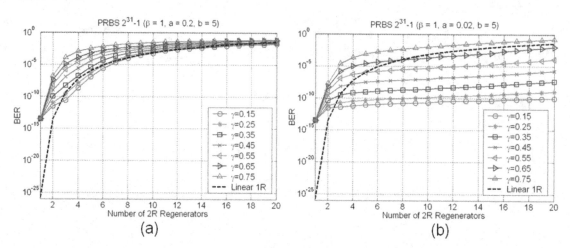

(a)   (b)

and make it perform worse than a linear optical amplifier.

Comparisons of Theoretical and Experimental Results

The single-stage optical 2R regeneration experiment takes optical signals with different OSNRs and reshapes them using an optical 2R regenerator based on SOA-MZIs. The signals are at 10 Gb/s with PRBS 2^{31}-1 sequences. Figure 18 shows the input and output eye-diagrams for input OSNR values ranging from 15 to 27 dB on a 0.1 nm resolution bandwidth. The eye-diagrams indicate that SOA-MZI based optical 2R regeneration effectively suppresses the amplitude noise and provides cleaner space- and mark-levels. Figure 19(a) shows the curve fitting results of the measured transfer function after normalization, yielding a γ parameter of 0.55. In the experiments, the NRZ signal from the optical transmitter is not jitter-free. We introduce random jitter onto the initial signal to make the jitter simulation more accurate. We then obtain $a = 4$, $b = 0.108$, and $\beta = 1.0$ by fitting the jitter measurement results to the simulation results. Figure 19(b) shows the comparison of the measured and simulated jitter

accumulations on a 10 Gb/s optical NRZ signal. Figure 19(c) shows the measured and simulated eye-diagrams for PRBS 2^{31}-1 input. It can be seen that the proposed simulation model can represent the optical 2R regenerator with a reasonably good approximation. Figure 20 shows the Q factor evolution from simulation and measurement for optical 1R and 2R regenerators. The input signals have a PRBS length of 2^{31}-1 at 10 Gb/s. The optical 2R regenerator is modeled with the parameters obtained above. Figure 21 shows the jitter spectral analysis results (100 kHz ~ 5 GHz, normalized to the total signal power) for the experimental cases of back-to-back and at 2R Lap3. The pattern-dependence of the SOA-MZIs generates jitter spectral peaks at 714 kHz, 1.43 MHz, 2.14 MHz etc, and the SOA ASE noise raises the background jitter noise floor. Both the simulation and measurement results show that the jitter accumulation from pattern-dependence limits the cascadability of the optical 2R regenerator. Full optical 3R regeneration with retiming capability can effectively suppress the jitter accumulation and improve the regenerator cascadability (Leclerc, et al., 2003).

Figure 18. Input and output eye-diagrams of an optical 2R regenerator based on SOA-MZIs

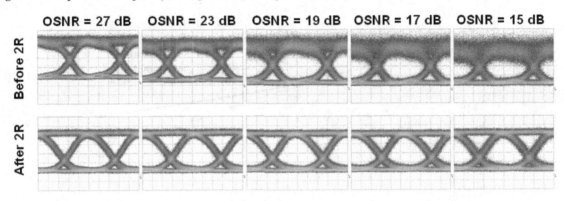

Figure 19. (a) Curve fitting of the measured optical 2R transfer function after normalization, (b) measured and simulated jitter accumulation, and (c) measured and simulated eye-diagrams for PRBS 2^{31}-1

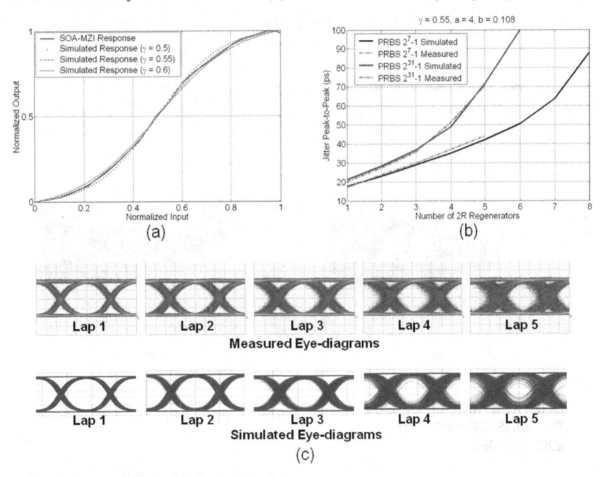

Figure 20. Q factor evolution from simulation and measurement for optical 1R and 2R regeneration

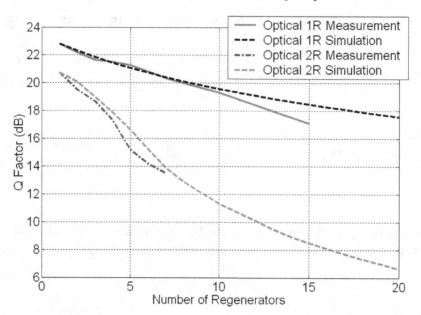

Figure 21. Jitter spectral analysis results for (a) back-to-back and (b) 2R Lap3

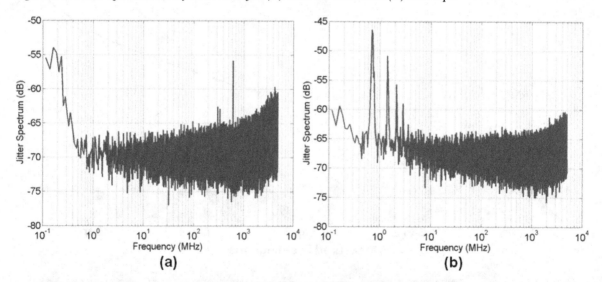

THEORETICAL MODEL OF MIXED OPERATIONS OF 1R/2R/3R REGENERATORS

To precisely estimate the signal quality evolution with the theoretical model we develop above, we model the BER evolution in mixed operations of 1R/2R/3R regenerators as (Zhu, 2011):

$$BER_n = BER_{n-1} + Err(L_{n-1,n}, R_n(\gamma, \sigma_{regen}^2, i)) \tag{8}$$

where BER_n is the signal BER value after the current regenerator, n is the ID of the current regenerator (e.g. the number of the regenerators the signal experienced along the lightpath), $Err(\cdot)$

is the error function to calculate the incremental BER caused by the current regenerator, $L_{n-1,n}$ represents the link characteristics of the fiber link between the current and previous regenerators (such as length, noise, dispersion and etc), $R_n(\cdot)$ represents the characteristics of the current regenerator, $\gamma \in [0,1]$ is the degree of amplitude regenerative nonlinearity, σ^2_{regen} models the noise generated by the current regenerator, i can be 1, 2, or 3 to distinguish the current regenerator as 1R, 2R or 3R regenerator, respectively. Figure 22 shows the numerical simulation results with this model. The data rate is 40 Gb/s. We simulated three scenarios: the red curve is for the transparent case where only inline fiber amplifiers are included in the lightpaths, referred as 1R-only case; the pink one is for the case with 1R and 2R regenerators included; and the blue one is for the translucent case with mixed placement of 1R, 2R, and 3R regenerators. These curves illustrate the accumulation of jitter and amplitude noise through the fiber spans, and their effects on signal BER. In these simulations, the regenerators are simply placed in a periodic way. More sophisticated algorithms need to be developed to optimize the mixed regenerator placement for high energy-efficiency.

Mixed Regenerator Placement Algorithms

To optimize the mixed regenerator placement along lightpaths, we develop two algorithms. The first one is exhaustive search, in which the placement is divided into two steps based on certain constraints, such as maximum number of different regenerators, minimum regenerator spacing and etc. The first step is for all-optical 2R regenerator placement, and the second one is for O/E/O regenerator placement. The algorithm scans all possible locations along a lightpath for optimal positions. Figure 23 shows an example of regenerator placement with exhaustive search. We need to setup a 7-hop lightpath for 40 Gb/s operation, the fiber length between each adjacent switching node is identical as 160 km. In each optimization round, the algorithm places one all-optical 2R regenerator and calculate the end-to-end BER with Equation (8). After three rounds, the end-to-end BER is below the pre-set BER threshold at $1 \times 10\text{-}4$, and there is no need to place any O/E/O 3R regenerator in the lightpath. For the cases when O/E/O 3R regenerator placement is necessary, the algorithm starts to search for the optimal positions of O/E/O 3R regenerators based

Figure 22. Performance estimation for mixed operation of optical 1R/2R/3R regenerators

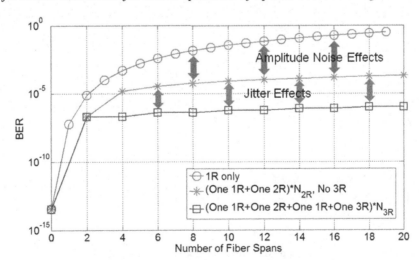

Figure 23. Optical 2R regenerator placement optimization with the exhaustive search algorithm

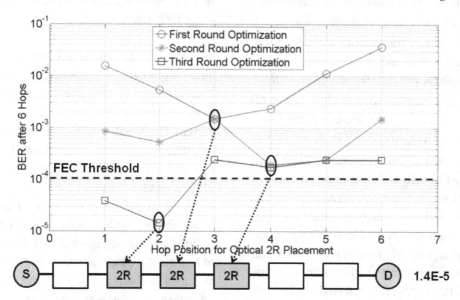

on the output of all-optical 2R regenerator placements. Similar to the 2R regenerator placement,
one 3R regenerator is placed in the lightpath in
each round to minimize the end-to-end BER until
it is below the pre-defined threshold. Figure 24
shows the 1R/2R/3R regenerator placements for
lightpaths with lengths of 10 to 21 hops, where the
data-rate is still 40 Gb/s and the fiber length for

a hop is 160 km. To emulate a practical network,
we also run simulations to consider the situation
where the link characteristic is random. Figure
25(a) shows the link noise characteristic with
random generated values. The noise characteristic is normalized with the fixed value we use for
Figure 24. By applying our regenerator placement
algorithms, we get the optimized placements as

Figure 24. 1R/2R/3R regenerator placements for lightpaths with lengths of 10 to 21 hops

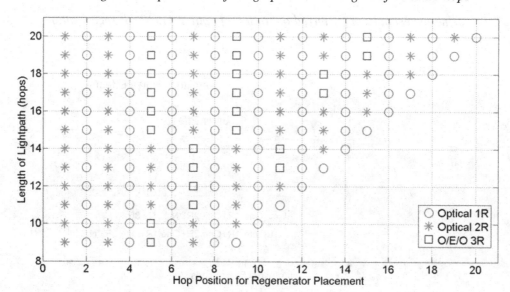

Figure 25. (a) Link noise characteristic with random generated values, (b) 2R and 3R regenerator placement results, and (c) 3R regenerator placement results without any 2R regenerator involved

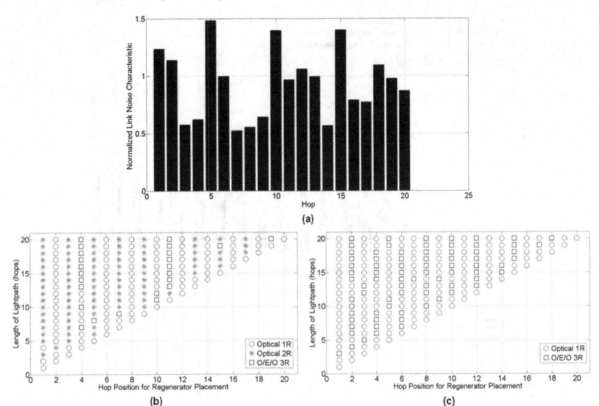

shown in Figure 25(b). As a reference, Figure 25(c) shows the placements without any all-optical 2R regenerator. Our proposed algorithms effectively reduce the number of O/E/O 3R regenerators by using all-optical 2R regenerators as replacements. The comparison in Figure 26(a) illustrates that our proposed scheme reduces the 3R regenerators' number to less than 50% for all of the lightpath lengths. Another benefit from replacing O/E/O 3R regenerators with all-optical 2R regenerators is energy saving. The power consumption of a 40 Gb/s O/E/O 3R regenerator is usually hundreds of Watts (e.g. 250 W (Murakami et al., 2009)) due to high-speed electronics, while that of an all-optical 2R regenerator can be calculated as 20 W from DC current injections (Murakami, et al., 2009). Figure 26(b) shows the power saving achieved by the proposed scheme.

This exhaustive search algorithm is simple enough, but it is very time consuming and will become impractical when the number of candidate positions is large, or the Routing and Wavelength Assignment (RWA) algorithm afterwards requires multiple candidate placements. Genetic Algorithms (GA) are stochastic search optimization methods that mimic the process of natural evolution (Koza, 1992). They have been recently used for solving topological design (Morais et al., 2011), impairment-aware RWA (Monoyios et al., 2011), and other complicated problems in optical network designs. A set of possible solutions (individual chromosomes) is first generated as the initial population. The GA then applies a fitness function to select relatively good individuals for the next generation. A pair of individuals may crossover to create offsprings, and individuals may mutate

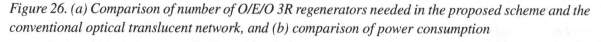

Figure 26. (a) Comparison of number of O/E/O 3R regenerators needed in the proposed scheme and the conventional optical translucent network, and (b) comparison of power consumption

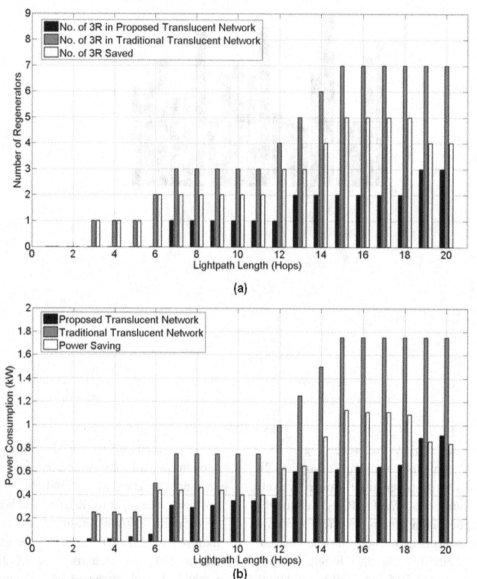

their genes to increase population diversity. By applying these operations iteratively, the GA modifies the population consistently, until good solutions that satisfy the optimization requirement of the problem have been found. Figure 27 shows the genetic encoding scheme for solving the Mixed Regenerator Placement (MRP) problem. For a lightpath with N hops, there are N-1 intermediate nodes for MRP. Hence, an individual chromosome with N-1 genes will be generated as an array. Each gene can be 1, 2, or 3, corresponding to a placement of 1R, 2R, or 3R regenerator at the intermediate node. The fitness function consists of two objective functions: 1) the end-to-end BER of the lightpath after the MRP, and 2) the total energy cost on regeneration after MRP. Our genetic algorithms can consider the tradeoff between these two objective functions in the optimization.

Figure 27. Genetic encoding for solving the MRP problem

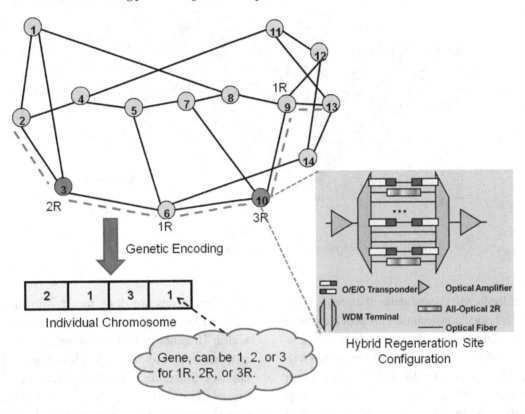

The GA starts with generating an initial population with an appropriate size randomly. To improve the convergence performance of the GA, we implement an initial filtering process to kill individuals with apparently low fitness (e.g. either the end-to-end BER or the total energy cost is too high). We then use the Selection Operator (SO) for two operations: 1) to select pairs of individuals from the current generation for crossover, and 2) to select individuals for the next generation. Two SO are proposed for different evolution directions of the population corresponding to various balance between the two objective functions. The first is BER-Preferred SO (BPSO) that sets a upper boundary on the energy cost, and uses a roulette-wheel method to obtain individuals with the lowest end-to-end BER. The second is Energy-Preferred SO (EPSO) that operates similarly as the first one until the average value of the individuals' BER is below a preset threshold. And

then, it directs the evolution to obtain individuals with the lowest energy-cost, using a modified strategy. In the crossover operation, the individuals are first sorted based on their fitness (i.e. from fittest to less fit). We then take pairs in a descending order and apply a common multiple-point crossover on them. The crossover genes are randomly selected with either a fixe possibility (UFCO) or a self-adaptive one (SACO) that is proportional to the individuals fitness. The mutation also utilizes two operators: 1) fixe-rate MO (FRMO), and 2) adaptive-rate MO (ARMO).

Figure 28 shows the optimized MRP results for lightpaths with different lengths. The results are obtained by applying the GA that uses the combination of EPSO, SACO, and ARMO. For the longest lightpath with 28 hopes, the GA gets the optimized results within 32 generations. Even though we only plot one best result in Figure 28 for each lightpath length, the GA actually ob-

Figure 28. MRP results from GA for lightpaths with lengths of 9 to 28 hops

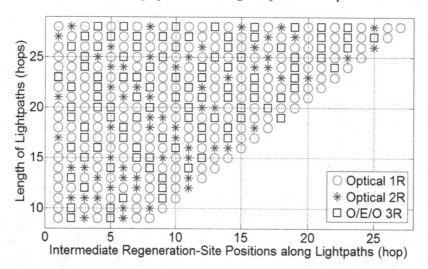

tains multiple MRP candidates that can satisfy the performance constraints. This provides more flexibility for the network design afterwards (e.g. Routing and Wavelength Assignments [RWA]). Figure 29 plots five qualified MRP results and their corresponding end-to-end BER for a 21-hop lightpath. The GA obtains these MRP results in the 19-th generation. Figure 30 show shows the convergence performance of the adaptive and uniform schemes for crossover and mutation.

The simulations are done for 26-hop lightpath with BPSO. Both schemes start to converge within 10 generations from when the first good individual (end-to-end BER is less than $1 \times 10\text{-}4$) appears. Since the self-adaptive scheme adjusts the possibility of the crossover and mutation intelligently based on the fitness of the individuals, it can obtain larger percentage of good individuals (~60%), while the percentage from the uniform case saturates at ~50%.

Figure 29. MRP results for a 21-hop lightpath obtained by the GA in the 19-th generation

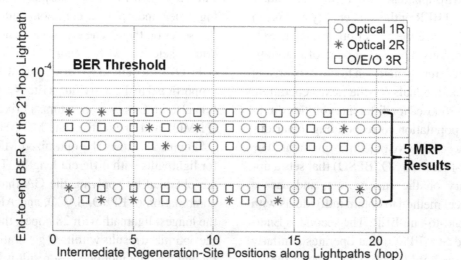

Figure 30. BER histograms of MRP results for a 26-hop lightpath, from GA using (a) adaptive scheme (BPSO-SACO-ARMO), and (b) uniform scheme (BPSO-UFCO-FRMO)

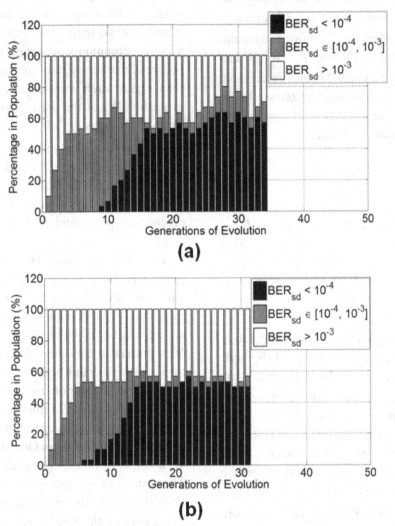

ENERGY-EFFICIENT NETWORK DESIGN AND PROVISIONING WITH MRP

With the mixed regenerator placement algorithms, we can design energy-efficient network planning and provisioning. Given a set of connection requests, the network planning problem of setting up lightpaths by assigning routing path, and wavelength channels (RWA) under the wavelength-continuity constraint is known as non-polynomial (NP)-complete. This problem is also considered as static planning since all the bandwidth requests are known a priori.

We consider a WDM network physical topology $G(V, E)$, where V is the node set, and E is the fiber link set. Each link supports wavelength set W. $L_{s,d}$ is the number of lightpath requests from node s to d, $s, d \in V$. The wavelength connection flag is $f_{s,d}^{(u,v)}(w)$. Its value is 1 if wavelength w is used on link (u, v) for a lightpath from node s to d; otherwise, it is 0. The BER threshold is

BER_t, and $BER_{s,d,k}$ denotes the end-to-end BER for the *k-th* lightpath from node s to d. $R2_u$ and $R3_u$ denote the number of 2R and 3R regenerators at node u, respectively. The power consumption per regenerator is P_{2R} and P_{3R}, for 2R and 3R regenerator, respectively. The energy-efficient network design problem is summarized as: choose routing path, place regenerators and assign wavelengths for lightpaths, such that:

$$\sum_{s \in V} \sum_{d \in V} \sum_{w \in W} f_{s,d}^{(u,v)}(w) \leq |W|, \forall (u,v) \in E \quad (9)$$

$$BER_{s,d,k} \leq BER_t, \forall s \in V, \forall d \in V, k \in [1, L_{s,d}] \quad (10)$$

$$\min(P_{3R} \sum_{u \in V} R3_u + P_{2R} \sum_{u \in V} R2_u) \quad (11)$$

For each lightpath request from node s to d, our network design algorithm first finds N shortest paths $R_{s,d}^{(1)}, R_{s,d}^{(2)}, ..., R_{s,d}^{(N)}$. The regenerators are then placed for each path using the algorithms developed in the previous section. Here, we consider the mixed placement of 2R and 3R (2R&3R-MP) and the 3R-only placement (3R-OP). After this first-round regenerator placement, we perform wavelength assignment for $R_{s,d}^{(1)}, R_{s,d}^{(2)}, ..., R_{s,d}^{(N)}$. Note that both 2R and 3R regenerator can work as a wavelength converter. Therefore, we only need to consider the wavelength continuity constraint for the transparent path segments between regenerators. The first-fit wavelength assignment (FF-WA) algorithm assigns wavelengths based on local information and can work in a distributed way. However, it may require more regenerators for wavelength conversion when there is wavelength contention inside transparent segments. We insert a 2R regenerator for wavelength conversion for the 2R&3R-MP approach to save energy. To minimize unnecessary wavelength conversions, we propose a maximum segment

length wavelength assignment (MSL-WA) algorithm. In this approach, we assign wavelength based on the information of nodes along each transparent segment, test whether there is an available common wavelength for the segment, and readjust regenerator placement along the whole path when wavelength contention is unavoidable. When the wavelength assignment is finished for paths $R_{s,d}^{(1)}, R_{s,d}^{(2)}, ..., R_{s,d}^{(N)}$, we validate their availabilities by verifying wavelength continuity and recalculating the end-to-end BER. We then choose the path with minimum power consumption from Equation (11), and commit the regenerator placement and wavelength assignment.

In order to evaluate the performance of the proposed network design algorithms, we perform simulation experiments for two network topologies: a ring network with 21 nodes in Figure 31(a), and a grid network with 121 nodes in Figure 31(b). We assume that the signal bit-rate is 40 Gb/s, and the length of fiber link between two adjacent nodes is 160 km in both topologies. Each link in Figure 31 represents one pair of fiber between two nodes, and each fiber link supports 40 wavelengths. The power consumption of an O/E/O 3R is set as 250 W, and that of an all-optical 2R is set as 20 W. The number of shortest paths *N* is set as 2 in the simulations. The lightpath requests are generated by picking up the source and destination nodes randomly. Figure 32 and 33 show the number of regenerators required for different volumes of lightpath requests in the ring network. For each data point, we simulate 16 times and average the results for statistical accuracy. The simulation results show that the 2R&3R-MP approaches require much less O/E/O 3R regenerators comparing to the 3R-OP ones, and the MSL-WA algorithm effectively reduces the number of 2R and 3R regenerators in the network. Figure 32 also shows that the number of 3R regenerators are almost identical for 2R&3R-MP-FF-WA and 2R&3R-MP-MSL-WA. This is due to the reason that we only

Figure 31. (a) Ring network topology, (b) grid network topology

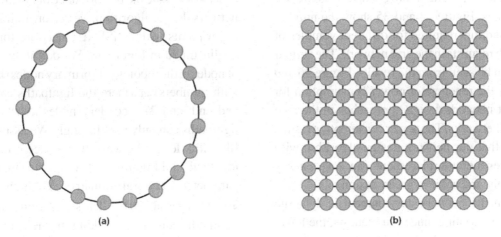

Figure 32. Average number of 3R regenerators and needed in ring network

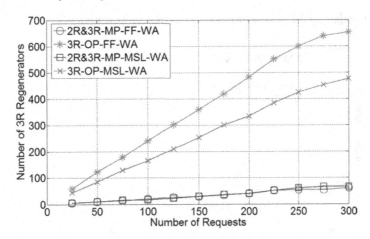

Figure 33. Average number of 2R regenerators needed in ring network

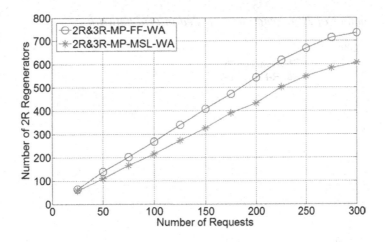

place 2R for wavelength conversion in 2R&3R-MP approaches. Figure 34 and 35 show the number of regenerators required for different volumes of lightpath requests in the grid network. The similar trend can be seen from the results. Figure 36 and 37 show the regenerator power consumption for different network design approaches in the ring and grid networks. The power consumption results verifies that our network design algorithm with mixed regenerator placement can save energy effectively and achieve green design.

When the network environment is dynamic with time-variant connection requests, the RWA becomes a network provisioning problem. In order to evaluate the performance of the proposed network design algorithm, we perform simulation experiments with a NSFNET network topology as illustrated in Figure 38. We define two types of nodes in the topology, 1) primary nodes (labeled with numbers) at where the lightpaths can start and end, and 2) secondary nodes at where the lightpaths can only pass through. We assume the fiber link length between two adjacent nodes is identical, and Figure 39(a) shows the simulation parameters. The traffic matrix Λ_{sd} is in Figure 39(b) (Nag et al., 2010). The simulation generates lightpath requests by picking up the source and destination nodes with a probability normalized

Figure 34. Average number of 3R regenerators and needed in grid network

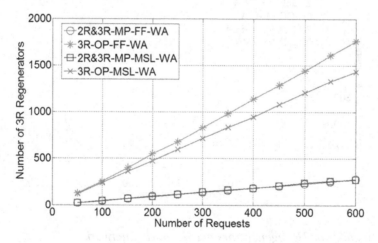

Figure 35. Average number of 2R regenerators needed in grid network

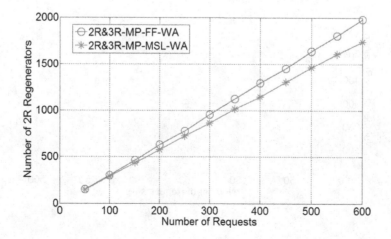

Figure 36. Comparisons of regenerator power consumption for different design approaches in the ring network

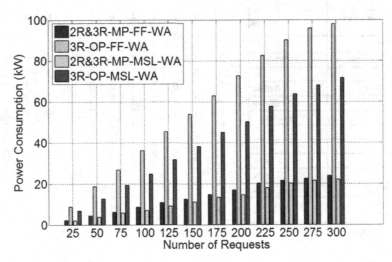

Figure 37. Comparisons of regenerator power consumption for different design approaches in the grid network

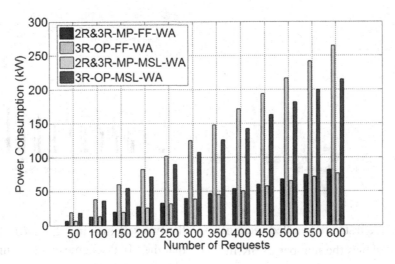

Figure 38. NSFNET network topology for numerical simulations

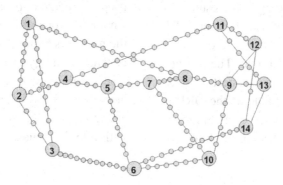

Figure 39. (a) Simulation parameters, (b) traffic distribution matrix

Data Rate	40 Gb/s
Link Length between Two Adjacent Nodes	300 km
End-to-end BER Threshold	10^{-4}
Data Sequence for BER Estimation	PRBS 2^{31}-1
Wavelengths per Link	40
Output Power per Wavelength	0 dBm
Fiber Loss	0.25 dB/km
PMD	0.1 ps/(km)$^{1/2}$
EDFA Noise Figure	6 dB
EDFA Spacing	75 km
Energy Cost per 2R	2 units
Energy Cost per 3R	25 units
N, Number of Path Candidates	3
M, Number of Regenerator Placement Schemes per Path	5

(a)

Node	1	2	3	4	5	6	7	8	9	10	11	12	13	14
1	0	2	1	1	1	4	1	1	2	1	1	1	1	1
2	2	0	2	1	8	2	1	5	3	5	1	5	1	4
3	1	2	0	2	3	2	11	20	5	2	1	1	1	2
4	1	1	2	0	1	1	2	1	2	2	1	2	1	2
5	1	8	3	1	0	3	3	7	3	3	1	5	2	5
6	4	2	2	1	3	0	2	1	2	2	1	1	1	2
7	1	1	11	2	3	2	0	9	4	20	1	8	1	4
8	1	5	20	1	7	1	9	0	27	7	2	3	2	4
9	2	3	5	2	3	2	4	27	0	75	2	9	3	1
10	1	5	2	2	3	2	20	7	75	0	1	1	2	1
11	1	1	1	1	1	1	1	2	2	1	0	2	1	61
12	1	5	1	2	5	1	8	3	9	1	2	0	1	81
13	1	1	1	1	2	1	1	2	3	2	1	1	0	2
14	1	4	2	2	5	2	4	4	0	1	61	81	2	0

(b)

Figure 40. Simulations results on (a) number or 3R regenerators required, and (b) energy consumption in the network

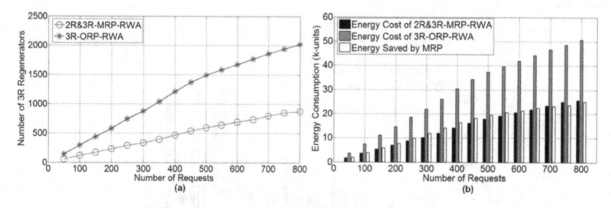

from Λ_{sd}, and the requests are handled sequentially. Figure 40(a) shows the number of 3R required for different volumes of lightpath requests in the NSFNET topology. For each data point, we simulate 16 times and average the results for statistical accuracy. It can be seen that the MRP scheme requires much less 3R regenerators, comparing to the traditional ORP one. The average number of 3R regenerators per request in MRP scheme is ~1.2, while this value of the ORP is ~2.5. Using the values of energy costs in Figure 39(a), we plot the total energy consumption for

the two schemes in Figure 40(b). It can be seen that the MRP scheme can save up to 50% energy consumption on regeneration.

To further evaluate the performance of the proposed network design algorithm, we perform simulations on online network provisioning with the networks being designed. With a desired regeneration energy cost, the regenerators have been placed in the networks according to the algorithms described in the previous section. We then generate lightpath requests based on a Poisson process with rate λ requests/time-unit. The source and destination of a request are randomly chosen based on the probability normalized from Λ_{sd}. The holding time of each lightpath is set according to an exponential distribution with an average of μ time-unit. Therefore, the traffic load can be defined as $\lambda \cdot \mu$ Erlangs. For network provisioning, we also finds N shortest routing paths for each lightpath request. For each of the routing paths, we first allocate regenerators to keep the end-to-end BER below BER_t. Similar to that in network design, the wavelength assignment afterwards tries to maximize transparent segments and minimize regeneration energy cost. During the wavelength assignment, the regenerator allocation may be readjusted when wavelength contention is unavoidable. When the wavelength assignment has been done for all routing paths, we validate their availabilities by verifying wavelength continuity and recalculating the end-to-end BER. The available paths are then sorted based on their lengths and we pick the shortest path to carrier the lightpath request. If there is no available path, the request will be blocked. Figure 41 shows the simulation results of the network provisioning. For each data point, we simulate 16 times and average the results for statistical accuracy. For each simulation, 10000 lightpath requests are processed. The MRP scheme achieves lower blocking probability when the energy cost on

regeneration is fixed. This is due to the reason that 2R regenerators in the MRP scheme help solve more signal quality and wavelength contention issues. Therefore, more lightpath requests can be set up.

CONCLUSION

In this chapter, we started with the background and basic concepts of all-optical regeneration and translucent optical networks. We found that all-optical regenerator is much more energy-efficient compared to traditional O/E/O ones. To explore these benefits, we discussed on translucent lightpath arrangement that involves mixed placement of optical inline amplifiers (1R), all-optical 2R, and O/E/O 3R regenerators (MRP). In order to make sure that the end-to-end transmission performance requirement would still be satisfied with this arrangement, we analyzed the signal BER evolution through fiber links and different types of regenerators and proposed a theoretical model. The numerical results with this model showed good match with the experimental results. We then focused on search strategies using exhaustive search and genetic algorithm, and discussed how to use them to optimize the energy-efficienty of

Figure 41. Blocking probability for networks designed with regeneration energy cost as (a) 15k-units, and (b) 27k-units

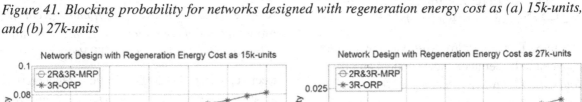

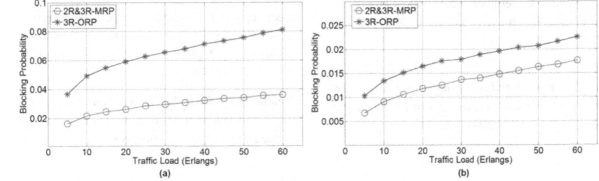

lightpaths using MRP. Toward the end of this chapter, we moved to network design of translucent optical networks with MRP, in which we considered both offline network design and online network provisioning. Network-level results for regenerator placement and routing and wavelength assignment (RWA) were shown to illustrate the effectiveness of the proposed algorithms for high energy-efficiency.

REFERENCES

Azodolmolky, S. et al. (2011). Experimental demonstration of an impairment aware network planning and operation tool for transparent/translucent optical networks. *Journal of Lightwave Technology*, 29, 439–448. doi:10.1109/JLT.2010.2091622.

Becouarn, L., et al. (2004). *42 x 42.7 Gb/s RZ-DPSK transmission over a 4820 km long NZDSF deployed line using C-band-only EDFAs*. Paper presented at the OFC'04. Los Angeles, CA.

Borne, D., et al. (2006). *1.6-b/s/Hz spectrally efficient 40 x 85.6-Gb/s transmission over 1,700 km of SSMF using POLMUX-RZ-DQPSK*. Paper presented at the OFC'06. Los Angeles, CA.

Dupas, A. et al. (1998). 2R all-optical regenerator assessment at 2.5 Gbit/s over 3600 km using only standard fibre. *Electronics Letters*, 34(25), 2424–2425. doi:10.1049/el:19981621.

Durhuus, T. et al. (1996). All-optical wavelength conversion by semiconductor optical amplifiers. *Journal of Lightwave Technology*, 14(6), 942–954. doi:10.1109/50.511594.

Fukuchi, K., et al. (2001). *10.92-Tb/s (273*40-Gb/s) triple-band/ultra-dense WDM optical repeatered transmission experiment*. Paper presented at the OFC 2001. Los Angeles, CA.

Funabashi, M. et al. (2006). Optical clock recovery and 3R regeneration for 10-Gb/s NRZ signal to achieve 10,000-hop cascadability and 1,000,000-km transmission. *IEEE Photonics Technology Letters*, 18(20), 2078–2080. doi:10.1109/LPT.2006.883247.

Green, P. E. et al. (1996). WDM protocol-transparent distance extension using R2 remodulation. *IEEE Journal on Selected Areas in Communications*, 14(5), 962–967. doi:10.1109/49.510920.

Guerber, P., et al. (2000). *Chirp optimised operation of an optical 3R regenerator*. Paper presented at the ECOC'00. New York, NY. Retrieved from http://www.cisco.com/en/US/products/ps5763/prod_models_comparison.html

Joergensen, C. et al. (1997). All-optical wavelength conversion at bit rates above 10 Gb/s using semiconductor optical amplifiers. *IEEE Journal on Selected Topics in Quantum Electronics*, 3(5), 1168–1180. doi:10.1109/2944.658592.

Kang, K. I. et al. (1996). Comparison of Sagnac and Mach-Zehnder ultrafast all-optical interferometric switches based on a semiconductor resonant optical nonlinearity. *Applied Optics*, 35(3), 417–426. doi:10.1364/AO.35.000417 PMID:21069026.

Karlsson, M., et al. (2004). *PMD compensation using 2R and 3R regenerators*. Paper presented at the ECOC'04. New York, NY.

Koza, J. (1992). *Genetic programming: On the programming of computers by means of natural selection*. Cambridge, MA: MIT Press.

Leclerc, O. et al. (2003). Optical regeneration at 40 Gb/s and beyond. *Journal of Lightwave Technology*, 21(11), 2779–2790. doi:10.1109/JLT.2003.819148.

Leuthold, J. (2002). *Signal regeneration and all-optical wavelength conversion*. Paper presented at the LEOS'02. New York, NY.

Manousakis, K. et al. (2009). Offline impairment-aware routing and wavelength assignment algorithms in translucent WDM optical networks. *Journal of Lightwave Technology, 27*, 1866–1877. doi:10.1109/JLT.2009.2021534.

Manousakis, K. et al. (2010). Joint online routing, wavelength assignment and regenerator allocation in translucent optical networks. *Journal of Lightwave Technology, 28*, 1152–1163. doi:10.1109/JLT.2010.2041527.

Marcuse, D. (1990). Derivation of analytical expression for the bit-error probability in lightwave systems with optical amplifiers. *Journal of Lightwave Technology, 8*, 1816–1823. doi:10.1109/50.62876.

Martinez, R. et al. (2010). Experimental translucent-oriented routing for dynamic lightpath provisioning in GMPLS-enabled wavelength switched optical networks. *Journal of Lightwave Technology, 28*(8), 1241–1255. doi:10.1109/JLT.2010.2043335.

Maxwell, G. (2008). *Hybrid integration technology for high functionality devices in optical communications.* Paper presented at the OFC 2008. Los Angeles, CA.

Mikkelsen, B. et al. (1996). All-optical noise reduction capability of interferometric wavelength converters. *Electronics Letters, 32*(6), 566–567. doi:10.1049/el:19960343.

Monoyios, D. et al. (2011). Multiobjective genetic algorithm for solving the impairment-aware routing and wavelength assignment problem. *Journal of Optical Communications and Networking, 3*, 40–46. doi:10.1364/JOCN.3.000040.

Morais, R. et al. (2011). Genetic algorithm for the topological design of survivable optical transport networks. *Journal of Optical Communications and Networking, 3*, 17–26. doi:10.1364/JOCN.3.000017.

Mork, J. et al. (2003). Analytical expression for the bit error rate of cascaded all-optical regenerators. *IEEE Photonics Technology Letters, 15*(10), 1479–1481. doi:10.1109/LPT.2003.818059.

Murakami, M., et al. (2009). *Power consumption analysis of optical cross-connect equipment for future large capacity optical networks.* Paper presented at the ICTON'09. New York, NY.

Nag, A. et al. (2010). Optical network design with mixed line rates and multiple modulation formats. *Journal of Lightwave Technology, 28*, 466–475. doi:10.1109/JLT.2009.2034396.

Odlyzko, A. M. (2003). Internet traffic growth: sources and implications. *Proceedings of the Society for Photo-Instrumentation Engineers, 5247*, 1–15. doi:10.1117/12.512942.

Ohlen, P. et al. (1997). Noise accumulation and BER estimates in concatenated nonlinear optoelectronic repeaters. *IEEE Photonics Technology Letters, 9*(7), 1011–1013. doi:10.1109/68.593383.

Ohlen, P. et al. (1998). BER caused by jitter and amplitude noise in limiting optoelectronic repeaters with excess bandwidth. *IEE Proceedings. Optoelectronics, 145*(3), 147–150. doi:10.1049/ip-opt:19981963.

Ohlen, P. et al. (2000). Measurements and modeling of pattern-dependent BER and jitter in reshaping optoelectronic repeaters. *IEE Proceedings. Optoelectronics, 147*(2), 97–103. doi:10.1049/ip-opt:20000289.

Pachnicke, S., et al. (2008). *Physical impairment based regenerator placement and routing in translucent optical networks.* Paper presented at the OFC 2008. Los Angeles, CA.

Poulsen, H. N., et al. (1997). *Transmission enhancement by deployment of interferometric wavelength converters within all-optical cross connects.* Paper presented at the OFC'97. Los Angeles, CA.

Ramamurthy, B., et al. (2001). *Translucent optical WDM networks for the next-generation backbone networks*. Paper presented at the GLOBECOM 2001. New York, NY.

Ramaswami, R. et al. (2002). *Optical networks a practical perspective* (2nd ed.). San Diego, CA: Academic Press.

Raybon, G., et al. (2002). *40 Gbit/s pseudo-linear transmission over one million kilometers*. Paper presented at the OFC'02. Los Angeles, CA.

Saradhi, C., et al. (2010). *Practical and deployment issues to be considered in regenerator placement and operation of translucent optical networks*. Paper presented at the ICTON 2010. New York, NY.

Shinomiya, N. et al. (2007). Hybrid link/path-based design for translucent photonic network dimensioning. *Journal of Lightwave Technology*, 25, 2931–2941. doi:10.1109/JLT.2007.905224.

Stephens, R. (2004). Analyzing jitter at high data rates. *IEEE Communications Magazine*, 42, 6–10. doi:10.1109/MCOM.2003.1267095.

Takasaki, Y. (1991). *Digital transmission design and jitter analysis*. Norwood, MA: Artech Housen.

Trischitta, P. R. et al. (1989). *Jitter in digital transmission systems*. Norwood, MA: Artech House.

Weinert, C. M. et al. (1999). Measurement and modeling of timing jitter in optoelectronic repeaters and frequency converters. *IEEE Photonics Technology Letters*, 11(2), 278–280. doi:10.1109/68.740729.

Yoshikane, N., et al. (2004). *1.14 b/s/Hz spectrally-efficient 50 x 85.4 Gb/s transmission over 300 km using copolarized CS-RZ DQPSK signals*. Paper presented at the OFC'04. Los Angeles, CA.

Zhu, Z. (2011). Mixed placement of 1R/2R/3R regenerators in translucent optical networks to achieve green and cost-effective design. *IEEE Communications Letters*, 15(7), 752–754. doi:10.1109/LCOMM.2011.051011.110519.

Zhu, Z. (2011). *Design green and cost-effective translucent optical networks*. Paper presented at the OFC 2011. Los Angeles, CA.

Zhu, Z., et al. (2005). *43 Gb/s 264 km field fiber transmission using 2R regeneration in a tunable all-optical signal regenerator*. Paper presented at the CLEO 2005. New York, NY.

Chapter 7
Topological Design Using Genetic Algorithms

Rui Manuel Morais
*Department of Electronics, Telecommunications and Informatics, University of Aveiro, Portugal &
Instituto de Telecomunicações, Aveiro, Portugal*

Armando Nolasco Pinto
*Department of Electronics, Telecommunications and Informatics, University of Aveiro, Portugal &
Instituto de Telecomunicações, Aveiro, Portugal*

ABSTRACT

The proliferation of Internet access and the appearance of new telecommunications services are originating a demand for resilient networks with extremely high capacity. Thus, topologies able to recover connections in case of failure are essential. Given the node location and the traffic matrix, the survivable topological design is the problem of determining the network topology at minimum capital expenditure such that survivability is ensured. This problem is strongly NP-hard and heuristics are traditionally used to search near-optimal solutions. The authors present a genetic algorithm for this problem. As the convergence of the genetic algorithm depends on the used operators, an analysis of their impact on the quality of the obtained solutions is presented as well. Two initial population generators, two selection methods, two crossover operators, and two population sizes are compared, and the quality of the obtained solutions is assessed using an integer linear programming model.

INTRODUCTION

We are currently living in an information era, where most people use devices with advanced multimedia applications to obtain and exchange information. These trends are creating a demand for flexible, scalable, and reliable transport networks with minimum Capital Expenditures

(CAPEX) and Operational Expenditures (OPEX). Optical networks that employ Wavelength Division Multiplexing (WDM) are currently the first choice for transport networks. Wavelength division multiplexing is a technology that aggregates multiple wavelengths into a single optical fiber offering a transmission bandwidth of terabits per second. With such huge amount of traffic traversing a single optical fiber a link failure may lead to catastrophic consequences affecting critical applications from governmental agencies, banks

DOI: 10.4018/978-1-4666-3652-1.ch007

or health services. Therefore, a network providing enough capacity to recover connections in case of failure is essential.

The node location is one of the first pieces of information that the network designer has, corresponding to the location of the central offices where the traffic is added and dropped. The first stage of the overall network design process is the topological design; at this stage the connections between the nodes are established. The network topological design should guarantee a reliable network, and this depends on which links are going to be implemented (Kerivin & Mahjoub, 2005). The traffic to be transported by the network is hard to forecast and is continuously changing (Klopfenstein, 2009). In practice, several traffic scenarios are defined and evaluated, then the lowest cost network that will remain feasible for the majority of the scenarios is implemented (Klopfenstein, 2009). Therefore, the utilization of methods to quickly design physical topologies ensuring the routing of the required traffic and guaranteeing the network survivability at minimum cost is crucial. In optical networks, the failure of multiple fibers at the same time is extremely rare (Ramamurthy et al., 2003). The majority of failures regard single-link failures. Thus, we consider that the network should be survivable against any single link failure. Hence, the underlying topology is a 2-connected graph (Jungnickel, 2008). The topological design of minimum cost 2-connected graphs, not allowing the use of parallel edges, is strongly NP-hard (Kerivin & Mahjoub, 2005; Garey & Johnson, 1979); thus Integer Linear Programming (ILP) models only lead to optimal solutions, within reasonable time and computational effort, for small networks. Consequently, heuristics are commonly used to search for near-optimal solutions.

A 2-connected graph is required to ensure survivability in optical networks, however it is not sufficient. In order to guarantee survivability, protection schemes have to be implemented. We focus on path dedicated protection, where a link disjoint backup path is used to protect each opti-

cal channel (Ramamurthy et al., 2003). In this scheme the backup path has dedicated resources that cannot be shared with others working and backup paths. When a working path link fails all the affected demands are switched to the respective dedicated backup path.

In this chapter, we address the problem of jointly designing the physical topology, ensuring survivability, and minimizing the network CAPEX of an opaque optical transport network (Bouillet et al., 2007). In order to deal with this problem we propose a genetic algorithm. As the convergence of the genetic algorithm depends on the used genetic operators, we analyze their impact on the quality of the obtained solutions. Two initial population generators, two selection methods, two crossover operators, and two population sizes are compared within the genetic algorithm. The performance of the proposed heuristic is evaluated using an ILP model. We use a simplified cost model to calculate the CAPEX of an optical network to obtain exact results that can be compared with the heuristic solutions. The computational results are obtained using the node location of nine real telecommunications networks.

BACKGROUND

The most cost effective way to connect a set of nodes is known to be the minimum spanning tree (Cieslik, 2009). The minimum spanning tree ensures that between any pair of nodes exists, at least, one path, thus exists connectivity. An efficient algorithm to compute the minimum spanning tree is, for example, the Kruskal's algorithm (Cieslik, 2009). In this algorithm the tree is generated link by link, starting with links with the lower cost and ensuring that cycles are not created. The minimum spanning tree problem does not consider capacity constraints in the links nor survivability requirements, however in most of real telecommunication problems, besides being necessary to connect all the nodes it is also necessary to consider these types of restrictions. When constraints like these are considered, the minimum spanning tree is not the optimal solution of the problem because a single link failure disconnects the network. This type of problem is usually modeled using flows (Cieslik, 2009). Formulations for flows in networks were introduced by Ford and Fulkerson to model the problem of sending a flow of an origin node to a destination node through a network with capacity constraints on the links (Ford & Fulkerson, 1962). However, optimization problems that rely on flow formulations are usually very time and memory consuming.

We intend to design the topology that minimizes the capital expenditures, ensuring survivability and considering link capacity constraints. To ensure the network survivability, connectivity requirements are needed such as a pre-specified number of disjoint paths between any pair of nodes. The disjoint paths can be disjoint by links or by nodes, depending on the type of failures in analysis. By Menger's theorem (Jugnickel, 2009) we know that in a graph $G = (V, E)$, with V vertices (nodes) and E edges (links), there is no cutting links of cardinality less or equal than $n-1$ that disconnects two nodes, if and only if there are at least n link disjoint paths between them (Jugnickel, 2009). As we aim to protect the network against single link failures two link disjoint paths between each pair of nodes are necessary. The problem of determining the minimum cost network topology where there are two disjoint paths between all pairs of vertices is sometimes designated as 2-connected network design problem (Kerivin & Mahjoub, 2005; Soni et al., 1999). In the remaining, we are going to call this problem as simply the survivable topological design problem.

The survivable topological design problem has attracted the attention of many researchers (Kerivin & Mahjoub, 2005; Soni et al., 1999; Caenegem et al., 1998; Soni & Pirkul, 2002; Balakrishnan et al., 2004; Balakrishnan et al., 2009). A survey on ILP models, decomposition methods, and heuristics for the topological design of survivable networks can be found in (Kerivin & Mahjoub, 2005; Soni et al., 1999). In (Soni & Pirkul, 2002; Balakrishnan et al., 2004; Balakrishnan et al., 2009) ILP models and heuristics are analyzed to minimize the total number of links. Optimization methods to minimize the CAPEX of an optical WDM network can be found in (Pluntke et al.,2009; Duelli et al., 2008; Jarray et al., 2009; Miguel et al., 2010). In (Pluntke et al, 2009), ILP models are presented to obtain the least-cost network in terms of CAPEX, for various network architectures, and in (Duelli et al., 2008), deterministic and greedy heuristics are presented to optimize the lightpath routing with and without protection. A tool to jointly minimize the CAPEX and the OPEX is presented in (Jarray et al., 2009). In (Miguel et al., 2010; Buriol et al. 2007; Chaves et al., 2010) genetic algorithms are used in the design of telecommunication networks. In (Miguel et al., 2010), a genetic algorithm is presented to route and dimension dynamic optical networks, without considering the network survivability. In (Buriol et al. 2007), a genetic algorithm is used to design survivable networks, assuming that the topology is given. The genetic algorithm presented in (Chaves et al., 2010) minimizes the CAPEX of an all-optical network, considering physical impairments. To contour the NP-hardness nature of the problem, the physical topology and the traffic model are assumed to be known in advance in (Pluntke et al.,2009; Duelli et al., 2008; Jarray et al., 2009; Miguel et al., 2010; Buriol et al. 2007). In (Bouillet et al., 2007; Labourdette et al., 2005) simplified models are developed to estimate the optical network CAPEX without the knowledge of the network topology.

Network Architecture

We consider a multilayered network, with an electrical and an optical layer. The electrical layer is responsible for the traffic grooming and protection. The optical layer as the function of multiplexing, transmitting, and switching wavelength signals to establish end-to-end paths (Bouillet et al., 2007). An optical transport network can be seen as a set of nodes connected by bidirectional links. We assume that the traffic is bidirectional and follows the same path in both directions. Figure 1 presents the node architecture considered.

We assume that all network nodes are equipped equally with an Electrical Cross Connect (EXC) and an Optical Cross Connect (OXC). The traffic enters into the transport network via the EXC, with different granularities. It is subsequently groomed into the fundamental units of capacity used in the WDM transmission systems and sent to the OXC. To ensure survivability, each groomed signal is routed through two link-disjoint paths. The optical signal traverses two or more OXCs in the path from the source to the destination node. In the intermediary nodes, the optical signal is bypassed at the optical layer (see dashed line in Figure 1). In the terminal node it is switched to the EXC (see solid line in Figure 1). In this way, the EXC only processes the local traffic. However, for regeneration purposes, we assume that optical signals suffer an Optical–Electrical–Optical (OEO) conversion at every node (Bouillet et al., 2007; Azodomilky et al., 2009; Batchellor & Gerstel, 2006).

The transponders mark the end points of wavelength signals and comprise a short-reach interface and a long-reach interface. At the node side the transponder has a short-reach interface, whereas at the line side it has a long-reach interface to send the optical signal along the transmission system. The transponders also have the function of wavelength assignment. The transmission system is composed of WDM terminals, optical amplifiers, and the optical fiber; see Figure 2. The WDM terminal is capable of multiplexing/demultiplexing multiple wavelength signals into/from a single optical fiber. Besides this, the WDM terminal also has a booster amplifier and a preamplifier. Optical line amplifiers are installed along the transmission system to amplify the optical signal. We assume that the node location and the traffic are inputs of the model. We are also assuming that the EXC and the OXC switching matrices are able to process all the required traffic. Therefore, the number of EXCs, OXCs, tributary ports, and ports between the EXC and the OXC are fixed.

Figure 2. Transmission system architecture: transponders, WDM terminal, optical line amplifiers, and optical fibers

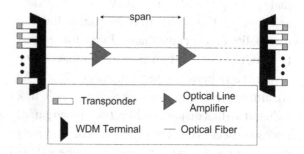

Figure 1. Node architecture: bidirectional electrical tributary ports, bidirectional short-reach optical ports, electrical cross connect (EXC), and optical cross connect (OXC).

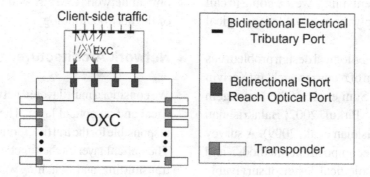

For a better understanding of the structure of an optical network, an example of a survivable network using the dedicated protection scheme will be presented detail. The network is presented in Figure 3. In this network, the links between nodes one and two, three and one, two and four, three and four, have 500 km and the link between nodes one and four has 707 km. The assumed traffic is a uniform and unitary matrix. The required spacing between amplifiers is of 80 km, giving a total of 32 optical line amplifiers used. The routing scheme is the shortest path in number of hops.

As the network survivability is provided by dedicated protection, each demand needs capacity for the working path and extra dedicated resources for the backup path. The solid lines represent the working path of each demand and the dashed lines represent the backup path. As an example consider the demand between the nodes

Figure 3. Dimensioned network using a dedicated protection scheme

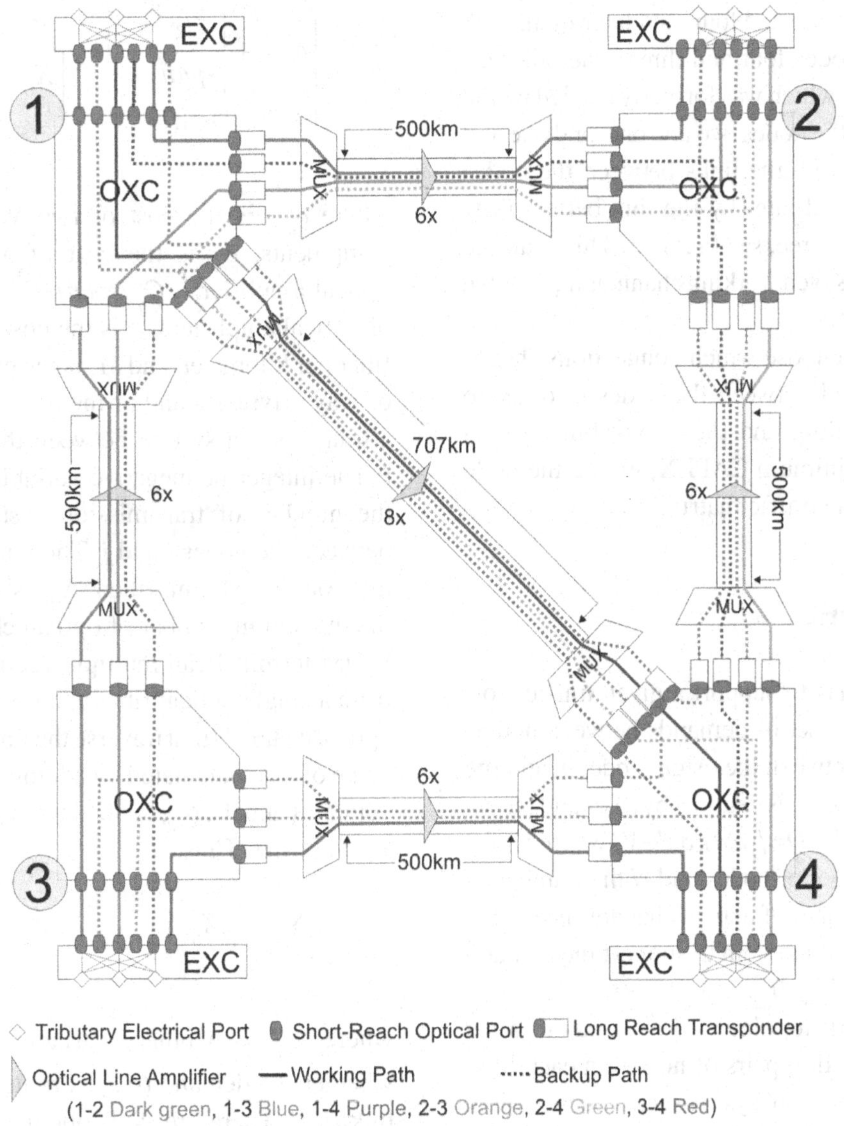
EXC
EXC
1
2
OXC
OXC
500km
6x
MUX
MUX
707km
8x
6x
6x
500km
500km
OXC
OXC
3
4
6x
500km
EXC
EXC
Tributary Electrical Port
Short-Reach Optical Port
Long Reach Transponder
Optical Line Amplifier
Working Path
Backup Path
(1-2 Dark green, 1-3 Blue, 1-4 Purple, 2-3 Orange, 2-4 Green, 3-4 Red)

one and three (shown in blue) and the demand between the nodes two and three (shown in orange) in Figure 3. Since there is a direct connection between the nodes one and three, the demand will be sent directly through this link. Note that the same connection also transports the demand between the nodes two and three and belongs to the backup path of the demand between the nodes three and four. If the link $\{1,3\}$ fails, the demands between the nodes one and three and two and three will be affected, requiring a backup path that not go through that failed link. The demand between one and three is re-routed by the links between nodes one and four, and later in the link between the nodes four and three. The other affected demand which was formerly carried by the links between the nodes two and one, and one and three is carried by the links between the nodes two and four and later by the link between the nodes four and three, see Figure 3. This example takes a total of seven working channels and twelve backup channels.

We aim to choose which connections should be implemented between the nodes in order to ensure the routing and the survivability of all demands at minimum CAPEX, giving the node location and the traffic matrix.

COST MODEL

The network has to support a given traffic, corresponding to a set of demands between nodes. The demand between the origin node, *o*, and the destination node, *d*, is denoted by *(o,d)* and the set of all demands by $D=\{(o,d):o,d\in V\}$ where $V=\{1, ..., N\}$, is the set of nodes and *N* the number of nodes. The number of optical channels needed in each transmission system to support the demand *(o,d)* is denoted by B_{od}.

The network topology corresponds to a set of links connecting pairs of nodes. In each link, several transmission systems can be installed.

The cost of all transmission systems in the link *{i,j}* without transponders, F_{ij}, is the cost with its deployment plus the cost with the WDM terminal equipments, optical amplifiers, and optical fibers. The cost with the optical fiber is proportional to the length C_{ij} between the nodes. The number of optical amplifiers depends on C_{ij} and on the *span*, which is defined as the maximum allowed distance between consecutive optical amplifiers. Moreover, two WDM terminal equipments are needed per transmission system, one in each end. Therefore, *Fij* can be assumed to be given by

$$F_{ij} = \left(c_{term} + \left\lceil \frac{C_{ij}}{span} - 1 \right\rceil c_{oa} + C_{ij}c_f + M_{ij} \right) X_{ij},$$ (1)

where c_{term} is the cost of two WDM terminal equipments, c_{oa} is the cost of a bidirectional optical amplifier, $\lceil (C_{ij}/span)-1 \rceil$ is the number of optical amplifiers, c_f is the cost of the optical fiber per kilometer, and M_{ij} is the cost with right-of-way privileges and/or method used to deploy a transmission system between the nodes *i* and *j*. The integer nonnegative variable X_{ij} indicates the number of transmission systems installed between the nodes *i* and *j*. The number of transmission systems installed, X_{ij}, is dependent on the maximum number of optical channels that a WDM terminal can multiplex/demultiplex into/from a single optical fiber and on the number of optical channels that traverse the link *{i,j}*, L_{ij}. The value of L_{ij} is calculated by adding the number of optical channels, B_{od}, for all demands that traverse the link *{i,j}*. Thus,

$$L_{ij} = \sum_{(o,d)\in D} B_{od} Z_{ij}^{od},$$ (2)

where Z_{ij}^{od} is a binary variable that indicates whether the demand *(o,d)* is routed through the link *{i, j}*. Therefore, X_{ij} is obtained by

$$X_{ij} = \left\lceil \frac{L_{ij}}{K_{ij}} \right\rceil, \tag{3}$$

where K_{ij} is the capacity of each transmission system in the number of optical channels. The cost with transponders, O_{ij}, corresponds to two transponders per optical channel that traverses the link. Given that ct is the cost of a pair of transponders, O_{ij} can be calculated by

$$O_{ij} = c_t L_{ij}. \tag{4}$$

Therefore, the transmission cost, T_c, is given by the sum of the cost F_{ij} plus O_{ij} for all links,

$$T_c = \sum_{\{i,j\} \in E} \left(F_{ij} + O_{ij} \right), \tag{5}$$

where $E=\{\{i, j\}: i, j \in V, i<j\}$, is the set of edges that represents all possible bidirectional links.

The main goal of this work is to search for the physical topology that minimizes T_c. The topology and the paths of each demand can be obtained by the values of the variables X_{ij} and Z_{ij}^{od}, respectively. The topological design problem is characterized by being hard in complexity, time consumption, and memory requirements.

Consequently, exact solutions within reasonable time can only be obtained for small networks. As optical transport networks can have more than 100 nodes, ILP models are prohibitive for larger networks. In the following, a heuristic approach and an ILP model to obtain solutions that minimize expression (5) with survivability requirements is presented. The ILP model is used to evaluate the quality of the solutions obtained using the genetic algorithm in terms of accuracy and time consumption, for small networks.

GENETIC ALGORITHM

Genetic algorithms are search algorithms based on the mechanics of natural selection (Goldberg, 1989). In every generation (iteration), a new set of artificial individuals (solutions) is created, using pieces of the previous generation. A genetic algorithm has the following steps: generation of an initial population, encoding, evaluation, selection, crossover, mutation, and decoding (Goldberg, 1989; Dréo et al., 2006). Figure 4 presents a flowchart of a generic genetic algorithm.

A set of initial feasible solutions of the problem (individuals) is generated, forming the initial population. Afterwards, the genetic algorithm

Figure 4. Flowchart of a generic genetic algorithm

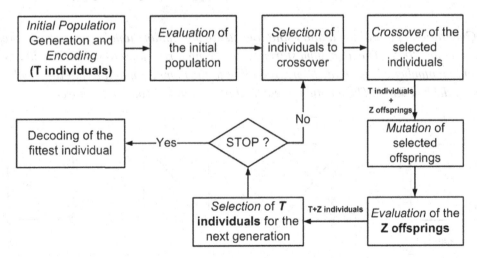

modifies this population repeatedly. A pair of individuals is chosen under selection rules based on the evaluation (cost) of each individual. After, pairs of individuals are combined under crossover rules, giving rise to another pair of individuals (offsprings). To increase the population diversity, mutations can also be applied.

The convergence of a genetic algorithm is dependent on the used operators. In the following, two initial population generators, two selection methods, and two crossover operators are presented within the genetic algorithm.

Initial Population

A feasible problem solution is a network topology with at least two link-disjoint paths between any pair of nodes. In this contribution we use two topology generators to create the initial population set. One generates completely random topologies, based on (Labourdette et al., 2005). The other generates topologies that preserve the main characteristics of real telecommunication networks, based on (Pavan et al., 2010).

The random topology generator starts by designing a ring topology connecting all nodes of the network, thus guaranteeing that all initial solutions are feasible (Labourdette et al., 2005). The ring topology is randomly generated for each individual of the initial population. Afterwards, *t* links are added to the ring topology, connecting

t pairs of randomly selected nodes. The number *t* of additional links is randomly generated and ranges from 0 to *N(N-3)/2*, i.e., from a ring to a full mesh network. Figure 5 presents some possible topologies generated using this method for a four nodes network. The ring topology is displayed as a black line. Additional links are presented as dashed grey lines.

The topology generator presented in (Pavan et al., 2010) models a survivable transport network as a set of interconnected smaller sub-networks and introduces constraints to guarantee the characteristics showed by real ones, see Figure 6. The topology generator is based on the Waxman approach, where the probability of a pair of nodes being directly connected depends on the Euclidian distance between them (Waxman, 1988). The method starts by placing the nodes into a plane that is divided into regions of equal size, see Figure 6(a). Afterwards, four situations may occur: the region does not have any node; it has one; two; three or more nodes. When a region has two or more nodes an additional procedure is required: if two nodes are located into a region they will be directly connected; if three or more nodes exist they will be connected as a closed cycle, see Figure 6(b). As aforementioned, the link selection follows the Waxman link probability (Waxman, 1988; Pavan et al., 2010). The probability, $P(i,j)$, of a link existing between the node i and the node j is given by (Waxman, 1988)

Figure 5. Generation of initial population solutions using the random topology generator presented in (Labourdette et al., 2005). The algorithm starts by designing a ring topology (black solid lines). Afterwards a random number t is generated corresponding to the number of additional links to be added to the ring (grey dashed lines). The location of each additional link is randomly chosen.

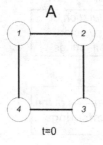 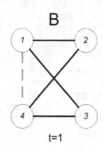 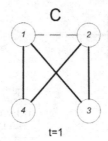 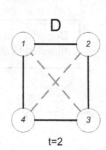

Figure 6. Generation of initial population solutions using the topology generator that resembles the properties of real world networks (Pavan et al., 2010): (a) the plane and the nodes placed into regions; (b) intra-region survivability; (c) region interconnection; (d) a possible network topology over a six-region plane

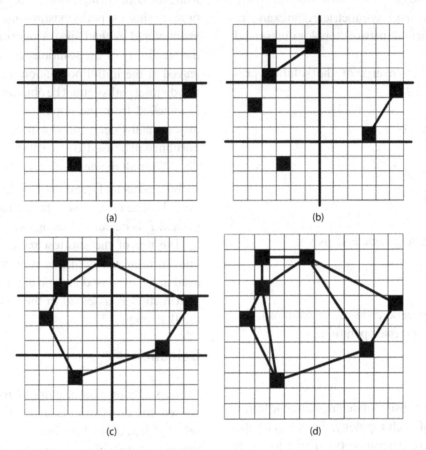

(a)　　　　　　(b)

(c)　　　　　　(d)

$$P(i,j) = \beta \exp \frac{-C_{ij}}{\alpha L}, \qquad (6)$$

where C_{ij} is the distance, in kilometers, between the node i and j; L is the maximum distance between any two nodes in the network; and following (Pavan et al., 2010), β and α are both assumed to be 0.4.

After this initial procedure the network survivability is ensured by connecting each region to two other regions, see Figure 6(c). If a region has only one node, it must be connected to at least two nodes of neighbors regions. If the region has two nodes each one is connected to one node located in a neighbor region. If a region has three or more nodes, at least two nodes must be connected to other two nodes in the neighbor regions. This process also follows the Waxman link probability. At this time the network survivability is ensured. Afterwards, a random number of additional links are added to the network; see Figure 6(d).

Encoding and Decoding

The encoding corresponds to the creation of a genetic code that uniquely represents a solution. To encode the solutions, we used the concatenation of the rows of the upper triangular matrix of the adjacency matrix. The adjacency matrix is an $N \times N$ matrix in which an element in position i, j is 1 if node i is directly connected to node j, and 0 otherwise. As the network links are bidirectional, the adjacency matrix is symmetric. As an example, consider the four node network topology presented in Figure 7.

The adjacency matrix of the solution presented in Figure 7 is

$$[g] = \begin{bmatrix} 0 & 1 & 1 & 1 \\ 1 & 0 & 1 & 0 \\ 1 & 1 & 0 & 1 \\ 1 & 0 & 1 & 0 \end{bmatrix},$$

and the respective genetic code is

1 1 1 | 1 0|1.

Given the genetic code of the solutions, the decoding is the inverse operation.

Evaluation

The evaluation consists of determining the transmission cost of each topology. To calculate the network cost we determine two paths for each demand (a working and a backup path) and use them to calculate the number of optical channels needed in each link. We assume that the working path is the shortest path (in number of hops) and the backup path is the second-shortest path. The working path is determined using the Dijkstra

Figure 7. Network topology with 4 nodes

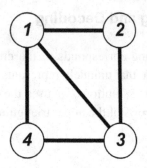

algorithm. To obtain a second link disjoint shortest path, the links in the working path are overweighted, and the backup path is determined using the Dijkstra algorithm a second time. If two or more shortest paths exist, we use the first path encountered by the Dijkstra algorithm. Note that the feasibility of the solutions can only be guaranteed at the initial population. Later on, if the two disjoint paths cannot be obtained, the solution is removed from the population. The two link-disjoint paths determined using the Dijkstra algorithm will be used to give values to the variables Z_{ij}^{od}. After all the demands have been routed, O_{ij} is obtained using Equation (4) and X_{ij} using Equation (3). The cost F_{ij} is obtained using Equation (1) and T_c is calculated using expression (5).

The use of the shortest paths in number of hops to route the demands is an approximation used in the proposed genetic algorithm. This approximation is assessed in the following, using the ILP model.

Selection

In the selection phase, pairs of individuals are chosen for crossover. Usually, individuals are selected based on their fitness, i.e., the cost of the respective solution, emphasizing the fitter individuals expecting that their offspring will have higher fitness. However, a strong selection can reduce the diversity of the population, leading to suboptimal solutions; contrariwise, a weak selection can result in slow evolution (Goldberg, 1989; Dréo et al., 2006). Two different selection methods that differ in the selection pressure are used: the roulette wheel and the tournament method (Goldberg, 1989).

In the roulette wheel method solutions are chosen based on their fitness. The lower cost solutions have higher probability to be chosen for crossover than solutions with higher cost. After all solutions are evaluated, the total generation cost is determined by adding all the solution costs. The next step is the calculation of the solution fitness. The fitness of each solution is the difference between the total generation cost and the cost of the solution. In this way, the solutions with lower cost will have higher fitness than the solutions with higher cost. Finally, the selection probability is calculated by the ratio between the solution fitness and the sum of the fitness of all individuals. Therefore, solutions with lower cost have greater probability of being selected for crossover. Table 1 shows an example of the crossover probability calculation using the roulette wheel method. As can be seen solution A has the smaller cost and therefore the highest probability to be chosen. The opposite happens in solution D whereas its higher cost leads to the smallest probability.

In the tournament method, the fitness of each solution is not considered to choose the individuals for crossover. The selection is done randomly. Four individuals are randomly selected from the population and grouped two by two. Afterwards, two numbers, r_1 and r_2, ranging between 0 and 1 are randomly generated. If $r_1 < 0.75$, the solution with the smaller cost from the first group is selected for crossover; otherwise the less-fit individual is selected. The same occurs for the second group.

Crossover and Mutation

In the crossover operation, pairs of individuals previously selected are combined, giving rise to another pair of new individuals. Usually the crossover operators respect the following properties (Goldberg, 1989; Dréo et al., 2006):

Table 1. Example of the crossover probability determination using the roulette wheel selection method

Individual	Genetic Code	Cost	Fitness	Probability
A	101101	20	100	0.28
B	111101	30	90	0.25
C	101111	30	90	0.25
D	111111	40	80	0.22
TOTAL	---------	120	360	1

- The crossover of two equal individuals will lead to a new pair of individuals like the previous ones.
- The crossover of two individuals that are in the nearby of the search space will generate individuals next to them.

There is no guarantee that the crossover of two individuals with good fitness will generate a high quality individual as well. A crossover is called lethal when produce individuals with low fitness and this comes from two highly adapted individuals. To assess the impact of the crossover operator in the quality of the obtained solutions two crossover operators are analyzed: the single point crossover and the uniform crossover (Goldberg, 1989; Dréo et al., 2006).

In the single point crossover, a border between two elements of the genetic code is randomly selected. The two left sides of progenitor 1 and progenitor 2 are copied to offspring 1 and offspring 2, respectively. The right sides of each code shall be exchanged, i.e., the right side of progenitor 1 is copied to offspring 2 and the right side of progenitor 2 is copied to offspring 1. An example is displayed in Table 2. In this example, the border is placed between the fourth and the fifth element of the genetic code for the two progenitors.

In the uniform crossover, a mask is randomly generated. If the crossover mask bit i is 1, the offspring 1 receives the bit i from progenitor 1 and offspring 2 receives the bit i from progenitor 2. If the mask bit i is 0, offspring 1 inherits the bit i from progenitor 2 and offspring 2 inherits it from progenitor 1. The example in Table 3 illustrates this process.

Table 2. Example of the single-point crossover

Individual	Genetic Code					
Progenitor 1	1	1	1	1	0	1
Progenitor 2	1	0	1	1	1	1
Offspring 1	1	1	1	1	1	1
Offspring 2	1	0	1	1	0	1

Table 3. Example of the uniform crossover

Individual	Genetic Code					
Progenitor 1	1	1	1	1	0	1
Progenitor 2	1	0	1	1	1	1
Mask	0	1	1	0	0	1
Offspring 1	1	1	1	1	1	1
Offspring 2	1	0	1	1	0	1

The mutation operation consists of a simple exchange of 0's to 1's, or vice versa, at random locations of the genetic code, for a randomly selected number of individuals. This operation has the goal of increasing the diversity of the population.

After the individuals are evaluated, selected, and reproduced, the next generation is created. The selection of the individuals to form the next generation is made from the present generation and the generated offspring. We consider that a maximum of 20% of individuals are selected from the present generation, the remaining 80% are offspring, to make available for crossover the maximum number of different links as possible.

INTEGER LINEAR PROGRAMMING MODEL

In this section, we present an ILP model to minimize the cost of a survivable optical transport network. In order to formulate the flow conservation constraints the binary variable Z_{ij}^{od} is divided into two binary variables Y_{ij}^{od} and Y_{ji}^{od}. The variable Y_{ij}^{od} indicates if the demand *(o,d)* is routed through the link *{i,j}* in the direction from *i* to *j*, $Y_{ij}^{od} = 1$, or not $Y_{ij}^{od} = 0$. The variable Y_{ji}^{od} indicates if the demand *(o,d)* is routed through the link *{i,j}* in the direction from *j* to *i*, $Y_{ji}^{od} = 1$, or not $Y_{ji}^{od} = 0$. The ILP model is the following:

$$\min\ T_c = \sum_{\{i,j\}\in E} \left(F_{ij} + O_{ij} \right)$$

subject to

$$\sum_{j\in V\setminus\{o\}} Y_{ij}^{od} - \sum_{j\in V\setminus\{d\}} Y_{ji}^{od} = \begin{cases} 2, & i = o \\ 0, & i \neq o,d \\ -2, & i = d \end{cases}$$

$$\forall (o,d) \in D, \forall \{i,j\} \in E, \tag{7}$$

$$\sum_{(o,d)\in D} B_{od} \left(Y_{ij}^{od} + Y_{ji}^{od} \right) \leq K_{ij} X_{ij}$$

$$\forall \{i,j\} \in E,\ X_{ij} \in \mathrm{N}_0 \tag{8}$$

$$\forall \{i,j\} \in E,\ Y_{ij}^{od}, Y_{ji}^{od} \in \{0,1\} \tag{9}$$

$$\forall (o,d) \in D, \forall \{i,j\} \in E. \tag{10}$$

The objective function, to be minimized, is expression (5), already presented. Constraints (7) are the usual flow conservation constraints and ensure that, for each *(o,d)* pair, we route two units of flow from node *o* to node *d*. These constraints together with constraints (8) guarantee the connectivity between all pairs of nodes. Constraint set (8) connects the sets of variables, guaranteeing that the total number of optical channels that crosses the link *{i,j}*, in both directions, does not exceed the maximum capacity, K_{ij}, of the number of installed transmission systems, X_{ij}. Constraint set (9) defines the variables X_{ij} as nonnegative integer variables, allowing the installation of more than one pair of transmission systems in each link. The disjointness of the two flows, to ensure survivability, is enforced by constraints (10). As the variables Y_{ij}^{od} and Y_{ji}^{od} are binary, the two flows cannot traverse the same links. Hence, the existence of two link-disjoint paths for each origin destination pair is guaranteed.

Figure 8 shows an example of a two units flow from the origin node o to the destination node d. The source node sends two units of flow and the destination node has to receive those two units of flow. In the remaining nodes, being neither origin nor destination, the receive flow have to be send, constraints (7). As the variables Y_{ji}^{od} are binary, the two flows are sent through disjoint links, see Figure 8.

The number of variables and constraints of the ilp model increases exponentially with the increase of the problem size. In the following, the number of variables and constraints of the model presented above will be analyzed. The complexity of the model depends exclusively on the number of nodes, n.

There are two variables in the model, the variables X_{ij}, and Y_{ij}^{od}. All possible links may belong to the solution, so there will be $N(N-1)/2$ variables X_{ij}. Moreover, there are flows between all pairs of nodes, thus $N(N-1)/2$ flows, can be routed through any of the $N(N-1)$ arcs (assuming that each link has two arcs, one in each direction). The number of variables Y_{ij}^{od} is the product of the number of flows by the number of arcs which lead to $(N(N-1))2/2$ variables. Adding the number of variables X_{ij} with Y_{ij}^{od} we obtain the total number of variables in the model,

$$\frac{N(N-1) + (N(N-1))^2}{2} \qquad (11)$$

The number of constraints (9) and (10) is equal to the number of variables. The number of constraints (7) depends on n, and on the number of flows, $n(n-1)/2$, thus is equal to $n2(n-1)/2$. Finally, there are so many constraints of the type (8) as variables x_{ij}, $n(n-1)/2$. Therefore, the total number of constraints of this model can be determined by

$$\frac{2(N(N-1))^2 + N^2(N-1)}{2}. \qquad (12)$$

Figure 9 shows the increase of the number of variables and constraints with the increase of the number of nodes of the network. As can be seen the number of variables and constraints for networks with large number of nodes is huge, making the problem intractable in short time, for large scale networks. As an example, a network with 100 nodes leads to almost 100 million constraints and nearly 50 million variables.

RESULTS

In this section, the computational results obtained using the genetic algorithm and the ILP model are reported. The genetic algorithm is implemented in C++. Using the genetic algorithm, feasible solutions corresponding to upper bounds for the optimal value are obtained. The ILP model is used to obtain lower bounds and is solved using the branch and bound method from the commercial optimization software Xpress IVE 1.18. The results are obtained using a PC Intel Core 2 at 1.83 GHz and 1 GB RAM. The halting criteria used for the ILP model is the obtention of the optimal solution or 10 hours of processing time. In the genetic algorithm we performed 100 iterations, which required less than 4 minutes for the largest network. We only observed marginal improve-

Figure 8. Example of a flow in a network

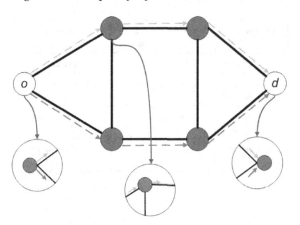

165

Figure 9. Number of variables and constraints of the ILP model

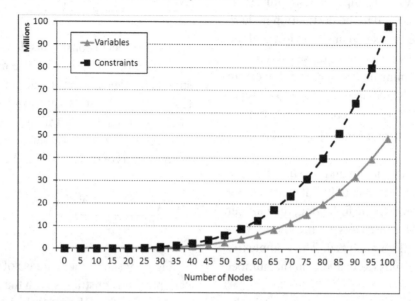

ments in the solutions obtained when increasing this number of iterations.

To evaluate the quality of the obtained solutions the gap between the upper, b_u, and the lower, b_l, bound is calculated as follows:

$$gap = \frac{100\left(b_u - b_l\right)}{b_u},\qquad(13)$$

where b_u is obtained using the genetic algorithm and b_l using the ILP model.

The computational results are obtained for the node location of nine real telecommunications networks. We assume that all links can be implemented and that the cost of deploying a transmission system is independent of the link, i.e., $M_{ij}=M$. For a matter of simplicity we consider $M=0$. The maximum number of optical channels supported by each transmission system is 40, i.e., $K_{ij}=K=40$. We also consider that the maximum distance between optical amplifiers is of 80 km, i.e., $span=80$. The cost with the equipment in normalized monetary units (m.u.) is presented in Table 4.

To assess the impact of the initial population, selection method, crossover operator, and number of individuals in the population, we perform five runs for each combination:

- 100 individuals, roulette wheel selection, single-point crossover.
- 100 individuals, tournament selection, single-point crossover.
- 100 individuals, roulette wheel selection, uniform crossover.

Table 4. Costs with the transmission system (Huelsermann et al., 2008)

Equipment	Notation	Cost (m.u.)	Quantity
Optical Fiber	cf	0.80	per km
Optical Amplifier	coa	1.92	per fiber and per span
WDM Terminal	cterm	8.34	per fiber
Transponder	ct	0.66	per fiber and per channel

- 100 individuals, tournament selection, uniform crossover.
- 500 individuals, roulette wheel selection, single-point crossover.
- 500 individuals, tournament selection, single-point crossover.
- 500 individuals, roulette wheel selection, uniform crossover.
- 500 individuals, tournament selection, uniform crossover.

Impact of the Initial Population

We start by assessing and comparing the quality of the obtained solutions when using different initial population generators. The presented results are obtained using a uniform demand matrix. The initial populations are randomly generated (Labourdette et al., 2005) or following (Pavan et al., 2010). The number of nodes, the number of regions, and the number of nodes placed in each region are presented in Table 5 for all considered networks.

Figure 10 shows the evolution of the gap for the best solution obtained, among all combinations, for initial populations generated using the random topology generator, see Figure 10(a), and using the topology generator presented in (Pavan et al., 2010), see Figure 10(b). As can be seen, for initial populations generated using the random topology generator, the optimal solution is obtained for the three smallest networks. With the increase in the number of nodes the gap also increases reaching almost 15%; see Figure 10(a). For initial populations generated using the topology generator presented in (Pavan et al., 2010), see Figure 10(b), the genetic algorithm also obtains the optimal solution for networks with less than 12 nodes. The exception is the CESNET network, in which the best solution obtained has a gap of 4.1%. Increasing the number of nodes, the gap also increases. However, the solutions obtained

Table 5. Real-world reference networks parameters

Network	Nodes	Regions	Nodes per Region
VIA	9	2	5-4
RNP	10	4	0-8-1-1
vBNS	12	3	3-4-5
CESNET	12	3	4-7-1
ITALY	14	2	12-2
NFSNET	14	2	7-7
AUSTRIA	15	3	3-4-8
GERMANY	17	4	8-2-5-2
SPAIN	17	4	8-2-7-0

within 100 iterations always have gaps smaller than 10%; see Figure 10(b).

Considering the best solution obtained for all networks and combinations, only for the networks in which the optimal solution is obtained, an initial population randomly generated obtains a solution as good as the one obtained using (Pavan et al., 2010). In all the other networks the solutions obtained using the topology generator presented in (Pavan et al., 2010) have smaller cost. The improvements range between 1% and 10%. One reason for this is that in the random topology generator all the links have the same probability to be chosen. Contrariwise, in the topology generator presented in (Pavan et al., 2010) longer links have smaller probability than shorter ones. We also used a ring-based random topology generator in which the ring topology is equal for all initial individuals. However, in this case the links that belong to this ring are maintained at the crossover operation being changed only in the mutation operation, which penalize the obtained results.

Impact of the Combinations

In this section, the eight combinations are compared and analyzed. The presented results are obtained using an initial population generated using

Figure 10. Evolution of the gap for the best solution obtained for the nine reference networks in each iteration for initial populations generated with the (a) random topology generator (Labourdette et al., 2005) and (b) topology generator presented in Pavan et al. (2010)

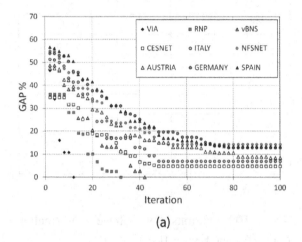

(a)

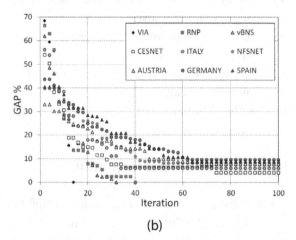

(b)

(Pavan et al., 2010) and a uniform demand model. Figure 11 presents the best solution obtained in each iteration by the genetic algorithm, for each combination. Results for the vBNS network, a network with 12 nodes, are presented in Figure 11(a). In Figure 11(b) are presented the results for the SPAIN network, a network with 17 nodes. The lower bound obtained using the ILP model is also presented as a solid line.

As can be seen in Figure 11(a), for the 12 node network, the convergence to a solution is fast for all combinations. The difference between the best solutions obtained for each combination is not significant. As the number of nodes increases, the convergence to a solution is slower. As can be seen in Figure 11(b), the convergence to a solution is only visible after the 60th iteration. The difference between the quality of the obtained solutions increases as well. To compare the eight combina-

Figure 11. Evolution of the best solution obtained in each iteration using the topology generator presented in Pavan et al. (2010) for the eight considered combinations and lower bound obtained using the ILP model (solid black line) for (a) the vBNS network (12 nodes) and (b) the SPAIN network (17 nodes)

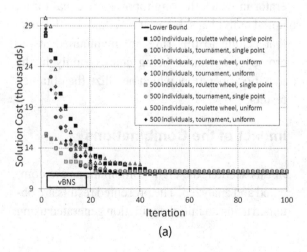

(a)

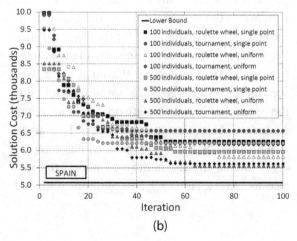

(b)

tions the gap of the best solution obtained for each method, among the five runs, is presented in Table 6. The best solution obtained is bold marked. The genetic algorithm with a population of 500 individuals, roulette wheel selection, and uniform crossover obtains the best solution for eight networks; see Table 6. Moreover, a population of 500 individuals, tournament selection, and uniform crossover equals the best solution obtained in six networks. The second-best solution is also always obtained by one of these combinations. The difference between the solutions obtained by each combination ranges between 0% and 14%, tending to increase with the increase in the number of nodes.

Making a comparison among the combinations, the uniform crossover obtains better solutions than the single-point crossover, independently of the number of individuals and selection method; see Table 6. The uniform crossover does not preserve large blocks of the progenitors' genetic code to the offspring; therefore it increases the population diversity and allows the genetic algorithm to obtain better solutions. On the other hand, fixing the crossover operator, the solutions obtained using the roulette wheel selection method is quite similar to the ones obtained

using the tournament method. Improvements are observed when using the roulette wheel selection method. Comparing the results obtained with the different sizes of population, fixing the selection method and crossover operator, large populations (500 individuals) obtain better solutions than smaller ones (100 individuals). However, runs were also done with populations of 1000 individuals and only residual improvements were obtained, with relation to solutions obtained with 500 individuals.

In spite of the individual generation and the crossover operators being random, the difference between the solutions obtained by each run, among the five, is not significant. Moreover, as the size of the network increases, such difference decreases.

Impact of the Traffic Model

In the following, we analyze the best results obtained using the genetic algorithm and the results obtained using the ILP model, for uniform and non-uniform demand matrices. The non-uniform demand matrices are randomly generated with $0 \geq B_{od} \geq 5$. The gap and the processing time for the solutions obtained using the ILP model and the genetic algorithm (GA) are presented in Table 7.

Table 6. Gap of the best solution obtained with each of the eight considered combinations for initial populations generated using Pavan et al. (2010)

| Network | 100 Individuals | | | | 500 Individuals | | | |
| | Single Point | | Uniform | | Single Point | | Uniform | |
	Roulette Wheel	Tournament	Roulette Wheel	Tournament	Roulette Wheel	Tournament	Roulette Wheel	Tournament
VIA	**0.0**	**0.0**	**0.0**	**0.0**	**0.0**	**0.0**	**0.0**	**0.0**
RNP	2.6	7.9	3.5	2.7	1.9	1.9	**0.0**	**0.0**
vBNS	1.9	2.5	**0.0**	2.7	2.1	2.7	**0.0**	**0.0**
CESNET	6.0	8.9	**4.1**	6.0	7.0	7.3	4.8	**4.1**
ITALY	15.6	16.3	8.5	10.1	21.1	10.4	**6.0**	**6.0**
NFSNET	13.2	22.2	9.7	11.3	10.5	13.1	**8.2**	8.7
AUSTRIA	17.6	14.8	9.8	11.3	13.9	13.7	**7.8**	8.4
GERMANY	19.6	22.4	13.9	13.9	16.8	14.9	**9.5**	**9.5**
SPAIN	18.8	22.7	12.8	17.8	14.9	18.4	**8.8**	9.7

Considering uniform demand matrices, the ILP model obtained the optimal solution for networks with fewer than 12 nodes. Considering the vBNS and CESNET networks, note that in spite of having the same number of nodes, the processing time required using the ILP model to achieve the optimum solution is substantially different; see Table 7. A reason for this may be found in the difference of the geographical area where the networks are implemented. The vBNS network, with 12 nodes, is in the USA and the CESNET network, also with 12 nodes, is in the Czech Republic. Due to the large area that the USA network has to cover, the majority of its links are fixed since the beginning due to the distance. For networks with more than 12 nodes the ILP model obtains a solution with a gap smaller than 8.3% within 10 hours. With the exception of the GERMANY and SPAIN networks, the ILP model obtains a solution with a gap smaller than 10% in less than 3 hours.

The genetic algorithm is much faster than the ILP model and obtains near-optimal solutions. For networks with less than 12 nodes the genetic algorithm obtains either the optimal solution or a solution with a gap of 4% within 1 minute. For networks with more than 12 nodes the genetic algorithm obtains solutions with gaps smaller than 10% within 4 minutes. A solution was obtained in approximately 45 minutes for a network with 100 nodes. In this case, the gap was not calculated as this problem cannot be addressed using the ILP model within a reasonable time and computational effort. The results obtained using the ILP model and the genetic algorithm for the GERMANY network and a uniform demand matrix can be observed in Figure 12(a). The dashed links are the ones that differ in both solutions. The black dashed lines represent the links of the topology obtained using the genetic algorithm. The gray dashed lines represent the links of the topology obtained using the ILP model. The black solid lines represent the common links to both solutions. None of the topologies obtained are optimal; see Table 7. However, the majority of the optimal links are already present in both solutions.

Considering non-uniform demand matrices the complexity of the problem increases. In this case the ILP model only obtained the optimal solution, within the time limit, for networks with

Table 7. Computational results obtained using the ILP model and the genetic algorithm for uniform and non-uniform demand matrices

Network	Nodes	Uniform Demand Model				Non-uniform Demand Model			
		ILP		GA		ILP		GA	
		Time	Gap	Time	Gap	Time	Gap	Time	Gap
VIA	9	1 s	0.0	8 s	0.0	4 s	0.0	8 s	0.0
RNP	10	42 s	0.0	27 s	0.0	24 m	0.0	27 s	3.2
vBNS	12	2 m	0.0	32 s	0.0	10 h	1.8	32 s	4.6
CESNET	12	7 h	0.0	1 m	4.1	10 h	0.3	1 m	5.7
ITALY	14	10 h	4.4	2 m	6.0	10 h	3.2	2 m	9.3
NFSNET	14	10 h	3.0	2 m	8.2	10 h	5.7	2 m	9.6
AUSTRIA	15	10 h	4.4	2 m	7.7	10 h	8.0	2 m	10.8
GERMANY	17	10 h	6.7	4 m	9.5	8 h (OM)	8.6	4 m	12.2
SPAIN	17	10 h	8.3	4 m	8.8	10 h	8.4	4 m	13.0

Figure 12. *Topologies obtained using the ILP model and the genetic algorithm for the node location of (a) the GERMANY network with the uniform demand matrix and (b) the RNP network with the non-uniform demand matrix. The dashed links differ in both solutions and the solid links are common.*

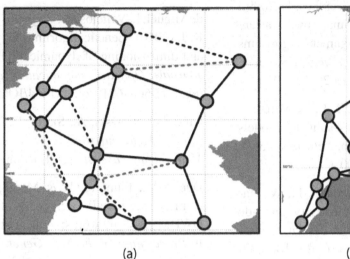

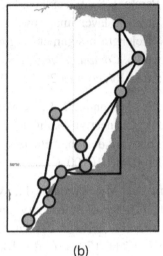

(a) (b)

less than 10 nodes. However, solutions with a gap smaller than 8.6% can still be obtained in 10 hours. We also observe that the ILP model obtains solutions with gaps smaller than 10% within 3 hours of processing time. For the GERMANY network, the computer runs out of memory before the end of the 10 hours of processing time.

The genetic algorithm maintains the processing time, although the results obtained suffered an increase in the gap. We observed that such an increase is due to the routing algorithm. The optimal routing is not always the shortest path; sometimes longer routes can optimize the network available resources. Figure 12(b) depicts the best result obtained with the node location of the RNP network, using the ILP model and the genetic algorithm with a non-uniform demand matrix. As can be seen in Table 7, the genetic algorithm obtained a solution with a gap of 3.2%. Nevertheless, the physical topology obtained is the optimal; see Figure 12(b). The gap is only due to suboptimal routing.

CONCLUSION

We have presented a genetic algorithm for the topological design of minimum capital expenditure survivable optical networks. The results accuracy and the saved processing time encourage the use of this kind of heuristic within the survivable optical network design problem. An integer linear programming model was also presented to evaluate the quality of the genetic algorithm solutions. Two initial population generators, two selection methods, two crossover operators, and two sizes of populations were compared within the genetic algorithm. Computational results obtained using the node location of real telecommunication networks showed that initial populations generated using a method that preserves the main characteristics of real optical networks improves the quality of the obtained solutions. Moreover, crossover operators that do not preserve large blocks of the genetic code increase the diversity of the population and the probability of finding better solutions.

REFERENCES

Azodomilky, S., Klinkowski, M., Marin, E., Careglio, D., Pareta, J. S., & Tomkos, I. (2009). A survey on physical layer impairments aware routing and wavelength assignment algorithms in optical networks. *Computer Networks*, *53*(7), 926–944. doi:10.1016/j.comnet.2008.11.014.

Balakrishnan, A., Magnanti, T. L., & Mirchandani, P. (2004). Connectivity-splitting models for survivable network design. *Networks*, *43*(1), 10–27. doi:10.1002/net.10100.

Balakrishnan, A., Mirchandani, P., & Natarajan, H. P. (2009). Connectivity upgrade models for survivable network design. *Operations Research*, *57*(1), 170–186. doi:10.1287/opre.1080.0579.

Batchellor, R., & Gerstel, O. (2006). Cost effective architectures for core transport networks. In *Proceedings of the Optical Fiber Communication Conference (OFC)*. OFC.

Bouillet, E., Ellinas, G., Labourdette, J. F., & Ramamurthy, R. (2007). *Path routing in mesh optical networks*. Hoboken, NJ: Wiley. doi:10.1002/9780470032985.

Buriol, L. S., Resende, M. G. C., & Thorup, M. (2007). Survivable IP network design with OSPF routing. *Networks*, *49*(1), 51–64. doi:10.1002/net.20141.

Caenegem, B., Parys, W., de Tuck, F., & Demeester, P. (1998). Dimensioning of survivable WDM networks. *IEEE Journal on Selected Areas in Communications*, *16*(7), 1146–1157. doi:10.1109/49.725185.

Chaves, D. A. R., Bastos-Filho, C. J. A., & Martins-Filho, J. F. (2010). Multiobjective physical topology design of all-optical networks considering QoS and Capex. In *Proceedings of the Optical Fiber Communication Conference (OFC)*. OFC.

Cieslik, D. (2009). Network design problems. In *Encyclopedia of Optimization*. London: Springer. doi:10.1007/978-0-387-74759-0_437.

de Miguel, I., Vallejos, R., Beghelli, A., & Durán, R. J. (2010). Genetic algorithm for joint routing and dimensioning of dynamic WDM networks. *Journal of Optical Communications and Networking*, *1*(7), 608–621. doi:10.1364/JOCN.1.000608.

Dréo, J., Pétrowski, A., Siarry, P., & Tailard, E. (2006). *Metaheuristics for hard optimization: Methods and case studies*. London: Springer.

Duelli, M., Pluntke, C., & Menth, M. (2008), Minimizing installation costs of survivable DWDM-mesh networks: A heuristic approach. In *Proceedings of the Next Generation Internet Networks (NGI)*, (pp. 15–22). NGI.

Ford, L. R., & Fulkerson, D. R. (1962). *Flows in networks*. Princeton, NJ: Princeton University Press.

Garey, M. R., & Johnson, D. S. (1979). *Computers and intractability: A guide to the theory of NP-completeness*. New York: W. H. Freeman.

Goldberg, D. E. (1989). *Genetic algorithms in search, optimization and machine learning*. Reading, MA: Addison-Wesley.

Huelsermann, R., Gunkel, M., Meusberger, C., & Schupke, D. A. (2008). Cost modeling and evaluation of capital expenditures in optical multilayer networks. *Journal of Optical Networking*, *7*(9), 814–833. doi:10.1364/JON.7.000814.

Jarray, A., Jaumard, B., & Houle, A. C. (2009). Minimum CAPEX/OPEX design of optical backbone networks. In *Proceedings of the International Conference on Ultra Modern Telecommunications & Workshops (ICUMT)*, (pp. 1–8). ICUMT.

Jungnickel, D. (2008). *Graphs, networks and algorithms: Algorithms and computation in mathematics*. London: Springer. doi:10.1007/978-3-540-72780-4.

Kerivin, H., & Mahjoub, A. R. (2005). Design of survivable networks: A survey. *Networks*, *46*(1), 1–21. doi:10.1002/net.20072.

Klopfenstein, O. (2009). Access network dimensioning with uncertain traffic forecasts. In *Proceedings of the 13th International Telecommunications Network Strategy and Planning Symposium*, (pp. 1–52). IEEE.

Labourdette, J. F., Bouillet, E., Ramamurthy, R., & Akyama, A. A. (2005). Fast approximate dimensioning and performance analysis of mesh optical networks. *IEEE/ACM Transactions on Networking*, *3*(4), 906–917. doi:10.1109/TNET.2005.852880.

Pavan, C., Morais, R. M., Rocha, F., & Pinto, A. N. (2010). Generating realistic optical transport network topologies. *Journal of Optical Communications and Networking*, *2*(1), 80–90. doi:10.1364/JOCN.2.000080.

Pluntke, C., Menth, M., & Duelli, M. (2009). CAPEX-aware design of survivable DWDM mesh networks. In *Proceedings of the IEEE International Conference on Communications (ICC)*, (pp. 2348-2353). IEEE.

Ramamurthy, S., Sahasrabuddhe, L., & Mukherjee, B. (2003). Survivable WDM mesh networks. *IEEE/OSA. Journal of Lightwave Technology*, *21*(4), 870–883. doi:10.1109/JLT.2002.806338.

Ramaswami, R., & Sivarajan, K. N. (2002). *Optical networks: A practical perspective*. San Francisco: Morgan Kaufmann.

Soni, S., Gupta, R., & Pirkul, H. (1999). Survivable network design: the state of the art. *Information Systems Frontiers*, *1*(3), 303–315. doi:10.1023/A:1010058513558.

Soni, S., & Pirkul, H. (2002). Design of survivable networks with connectivity requirements. *Telecommunication Systems*, *20*(1), 133–149. doi:10.1023/A:1015445501694.

Waxman, B. (1988). Routing of multipoint connections. *IEEE Journal on Selected Areas in Communications*, *6*(9), 1617–1622. doi:10.1109/49.12889.

KEY TERMS AND DEFINITIONS

Dedicated Protection: Survivability scheme to protect optical connections against link failures.

Genetic Algorithms: An algorithm based on natural evolution.

Genetic Operators: Functions used in genetic algorithms for the search of better solutions.

Multilayer Networks: Telecommunication networks with an electrical and an optical layer.

Optical Networks: Telecommunication networks that uses optical fibers.

Survivable Topologies: Graphs with at least two disjoint paths between each pair of nodes.

Topologies Generators: Algorithms used to generated survivable topologies.

WDM: Technology used in optical networks to multiplex several wavelengths into a single fiber.

Chapter 8
Artificial Bee Colony Approach for Routing and Wavelength Assignment in Optical WDM Networks

Goran Z. Marković
University of Belgrade, Serbia

ABSTRACT

Routing and Wavelength Assignment (RWA) of lightpaths in optical WDM networks is a challenging task that belongs to a class of complex combinatorial problems. To solve the RWA problem of realistic size, heuristic or meta-heuristic approaches have to be used. In this chapter, an artificial bee colony metaheuristic approach, known as the Bee Colony Optimization (BCO), is used to solve the RWA problem for static lightpath establishment in wavelength routed optical WDM networks. The BCO metaheuristic is tailored here to solve the Max-RWA problem in which the objective is to maximize the number of established lightpaths for a given number of wavelengths. Behind a comprehensive description of the proposed BCO-RWA algorithm, the numerical results obtained by numerous simulations performed over widely used real world European Optical Network (EON) topology are given and compared with some other approaches used to solve the same problem.

INTRODUCTION

Wavelength Routed Optical Networks (WRONs) employing Wavelength Division Multiplexing (WDM) technique are considered as the most promising solution to satisfy the huge amount of traffic that is expected in next generation communication networks. Routing and Wavelength Assignment (RWA) of lightpaths is a central

problem that has to be solved in WRON design and operation. A key matter concerned with routing of lightpaths is that no two lightpaths established over a fiber link can share the same wavelength. Additionally, if there are no wavelength converters in network, a lightpath has to be assigned the same wavelength on all links through which it traverses. Extended review of the RWA problem in optical WDM networks could be found in (Murthy and Gurusamy, 2002).

DOI: 10.4018/978-1-4666-3652-1.ch008

We study here the static case of the RWA problem in which the entire set of lightpath requests that need to be setup over the network is completely known in advance. It is also known as the Static Lightpath Establishing (SLE) problem. SLE is a combinatorial optimization problem that could be formulated as Mixed Integer Linear Program (MILP) and solved in off-line manner. However, it has been shown that static RWA is NP (Nondeterministic-polynomial time) complete problem that could be solved only in the case of small problem dimensionalities. For larger size problems, various heuristics or meta-heuristic algorithms have been proposed. Metaheuristics are general high level procedures that coordinate simple heuristics and rules to find approximate solutions of computationally difficult combinatorial problems. Since approximate algorithms explore only a fraction of the solution space associated to a problem instance, they are able to produce solutions within a reasonable computation time, but without necessarily providing guarantees of solution quality. Therefore, such schemes are suitable in environments where a solution is required in a short time compared to mathematical schemes like ILP or graph colouring. Each heuristic technique has its own advantages and disadvantages and the efficiency of applying a particular technique depends on many factors like the computational complexity, execution time, quality of solution, robustness and so forth. Researchers have developed various global optimization metaheuristic algorithms such as the Simulated Annealing (SA), Tabu Search (TS), and different Evolution Algorithms (EA).

In recent years, a new class of metaheuristics, known as the Swarm Intelligence (SI), have particularly attracted the significant interest of many researchers to solve various complex optimization problems. SI is an emerging optimization approach that takes inspiration from the collective behaviour of social colonies of insects or other animal societies, such as colonies of ants, bees, termites, flocks of birds, schools of fish and oth-

ers in order to develop some artificial algorithms which can mimic insect's problem solution abilities. Inspired by natural behavior of various social colonies, researchers have developed intelligent search algorithms by modelling interactions in natural swarms.

Our focus here is on the bee swarms. Studies on honey bees are in an increasing trend in the literature during the last few years. A number of artificial algorithms inspired by natural bees' activities have been proposed to solve different optimization problems. In this chapter, a novel artificial bee algorithm, based on Bee Colony Optimization (BCO) metaheuristic is proposed to solve the static RWA problem in WRON networks. The BCO is particularly tailored to solve the Max-RWA problem in which the objective is to maximize the number of established lightpaths for a given number of wavelengths in optical WDM networks operating under wavelength continuity constraint (Marković, 2007). To the best of our knowledge, the BCO-RWA is the first artificial bee algorithm proposed in literature to solve the RWA problem in optical WDM networks (Marković et al, 2007). Recently, Rubio-Largo et al. (2011) used the Artificial Bee Colony (ABC) algorithm to solve the static RWA problem as a multi-objective optimization problem. In addition, Rashedi et al. (2011) applied the ABC algorithm to solve dynamic RWA problem for minimizing the blocking probability in optical WDM networks.

A central goal of this chapter is to explain the main features of the BCO-RWA algorithm and explore its efficiency. The chapter is organized as follows. At the beginning, some basic principles of the bee swarm intelligence as well as the BCO metaheuristic concepts are described. After that, a detailed explanation of the proposed BCO-RWA algorithm is given. Later on, numerical results obtained by numerous simulations are presented and compared with some other algorithms proposed in literature. Finally, some conclusions and future directions are given at the end of this chapter.

FROM NATURAL TO ARTIFICIAL BEE SWARM INTELLIGENCE

Colonies of natural bees possess somewhat that is known as the swarm intelligence. A broad definition of this term implies a sophisticated collective insects behavior resulted by primitive interactions amongst members of the group to solve problems beyond the capability of individual members.

Honey-bees are highly organized colonies. Simple interactions between individual bees contribute to the collective intelligence of the bee colony. One of the best examples of such intelligence is the foraging of bees during the collection of nectar. Foraging is the most important task in the hive. This procedure can be explained as follows. In the beginning phase several forager bees leaving the hive in order to search food sources to gather nectar. After that, they return to the hive to unload the nectar and inform other bees about the explored food sources. They do it by performing various form of dancing in the dancing floor area of the hive. Bee dancing represents the interaction between individual bees in the colony. This kind of communication between individual bees contributes to the formation of the "collective intelligence" of the bee colony. By performing dances, bees are able to exchange the information about the direction and distance to patches of flower (food sources) as well as the amount of the available nectar. In this way, bees communicate with each other and exchange the information about the quality of founded food sources. This is a successful mechanism by which some foragers which have found rich nectar sources can recruit more other bees in colony to more promising nectar locations. As more and more bees forage the same source, it becomes the favorite path. In such way, the bee colony is able to adapt its searching pattern according to the quality of nectar sources. Each bee in the hive decides to reach the nectar source by following a hive-mate who has already discovered patch of flowers. Within the dance area, the bee dancers "advertise" dif-ferent food areas. In this way, the bees that have discovered nectar sources are trying to convince their hive-mates to follow them. If a bee decides to leave the hive to get nectar, it follows one of the bee dancers to one of the nectar areas. Upon arrival, the foraging bee takes a load of nectar and returns to the hive unloading the nectar to a food store. After unloading the food, the bee has following options: (*1*) abandon the food source and become again uncommitted follower, (*2*) continue to forage at the food source without recruiting the nest-mates, or (*3*) dance and thus recruit the hive-mates before the return to the food source. The bee opts for one of the above alternatives with a certain probability. The mechanisms by which the bee decides to follow a specific bee dancer are not well understood, but it is considered that the recruitment among bees is always a function of the quality of the food source (Camazine and Sneyd, 1991).

Numerous studies on honey bees behaviour resulted in a several artificial bee algorithms. Lučić and Teodorović (2001, 2002, 2003a) were the first who used the basic principles of collective bee intelligence in solving combinatorial optimization problems. They proposed the Bee System (BS) algorithm and tested it in the case of the Travelling Salesman Problem (TSP). In addition, Lučić and Teodorović (2003b) combined BS and fuzzy logic approach in order to obtain good solutions for stochastic vehicle routing problems. Teodorović and Dell'Orco (2005) proposed a generalization of BS algorithm called the Bee Colony Optimization (BCO), where the proposed BCO algorithm is capable of solving deterministic combinatorial problems, as well as combinatorial problems characterized by uncertainty. Nakrani and Tovey (2003) proposed a honey bee algorithm for dynamic allocation of Internet services. Wedde et al. (2004) introduced the *BeeHive* algorithm for routing in telecommunication networks. Chong et al. (2003) presented a novel approach inspired by Nakrani and Tovey (2003), to solve the job shop scheduling problem. Quijano and Passino (2007) proposed an algorithm, based on the foraging behaviour of honey bees to solve resource allocation problem. Karaboga (2005) proposed the Artificial Bee Colony (ABC) algorithm based on a particular intelligent behaviour of the honey bee swarms. Pham et al. (2006) proposed an optimization algorithm inspired by the natural foraging behaviour of honey bees, called Bees Algorithm. In addition, Karaboga and Bastürk (2007), Yang (2005) and Pham et al (2006) proposed different algorithms for solving continuous optimization problems. A comprehensive survey of various artificial bee algorithms proposed in literature could be found in (Baykasoglu et al., 2007), (Karaboga and Akay, 2009), and (Teodorović, 2009).

Our intention is the BCO metaheuristic algorithm that we have tailored purposely to solve the considered Max-RWA problem in wavelength routed optical WDM networks. It has been shown that BCO has ability to produce promising solutions of complex optimization problems within reasonable amount of computation time (Teodorović, 2009).

THE BEE COLONY OPTIMIZATION: A CENTRAL IDEA

The BCO is a new-born optimization algorithm inspired by the natural behavior of honey bees in food foraging to solve hard combinatorial problems. It is a stochastic random-search technique. The basic idea behind the BCO is to build the multi agent system or colony of artificial bees which behaves to some extent similar with the bees in nature. During the searching process, the artificial bees are able to communicate directly. Using the analogy from natural bee colony, artificial bees are "flying" throughout the particularly created artificial network. Each artificial bee generates one solution to the problem. Every bee performs the so-called forward and backward passes through this network. During a forward

pass, bees create various partial solutions by exploring the search space and using the collective experience from the past. During the backward pass, bees are "flying" back to the hive and exchange the information about the quality of the created partial solutions. In order to find better and better solutions, artificial bees collaborate and exchange information. In the hive, artificial bees compare all generated partial solutions and participate in a decision-making process. Based on the quality of the generated partial solutions (objective function values), some bees abandon from its solutions and some of them continue to expand the same partial solution with or without recruiting other bees. Using collective knowledge and sharing the information among themselves, artificial bees concentrate on more promising areas, and slowly abandon solutions from the less promising areas. This procedure is performed iteratively until some predefined stopping condition is satisfied. The possible stopping condition could be, for example, the maximal total number of forward/backward passes, the maximal total number of passes without the improvement of the objective function etc. At the end, the best found solution (global best) is reported as the final one. A more detailed description of the BCO algorithm could be found in (Teodorović, 2009). However, it will be more explained through our depth description of the proposed BCO-RWA algorithm in afterwards section.

So far, the BCO has been successfully used to solve various complex optimization problems, such as Travelling Salesman Problem (Lučić and Teodorović, 2001), (Lučić and Teodorović, 2003a), the ride matching problem (Teodorović and Dell'Orco, 2005), scheduling of independent tasks (Davidović et al., 2009), the *p*-median problem (Teodorović and Šelmić, 2007) in addition to the routing and wavelength assignment (RWA) problem in optical WDM networks (Marković et al 2007). A comprehensive review of different BCO applications could be found in (Teodorović, 2009).

Statement of the Problem

We consider a WRON network composed of reconfigurable wavelength routing nodes, which are linked by WDM links in a mesh topology. The number of available wavelengths on each link is the same. We suppose that wavelength conversion is not allowed in network nodes and that there is no limit on the number of transmitters and receivers at each node. The traffic mixture of permanent (PLDs) as well as scheduled (SLDs) lightpath demands is considered with the possibility of multiple lightpath demands requested for a given node pair, simultaneously.

By introducing the following notations:

- $G=(N,L)$: Graph that represents physical topology of optical network.
- N: Number of nodes in given network.
- L: Number of physical links.
- W: Number of wavelengths available on each link (same for each link).
- D: Total number of lightpath demands.
- T: Number of time slots.
- R: Number of candidate routes for a lightpath demand.

The considered static RWA problem can be formulated as follows: For the given set of lightpath demands and a given physical optical network topology represented by $G = (N,L)$, the goal is to determine a route and wavelength pairs for lightpaths such that the total number of established lightpaths is maximized for the given number of wavelengths (Max-RWA problem). To establish a lightpath it is necessary to choose an available route from the set of candidates routes (with at least one same wavelength on each link along the selected route) and assign one free wavelength to a lightpath from source node s to destination node d.

The set of traffic demands is composed of PLDs and SLDs, with various percents in total demand D. A PLD i can be represented by a triple (s_i, d_i, q_i), where s_i and d_i are the source the destination nodes of the PLD, respectively and q_i is an integer number representing the number of lightpaths required to be established between nodes s_i and d_i. Note that a demand for which $q_i > 1$ lightpaths may exist if the requested rate is greater than the nominal rate of a lightpath (that is typically 2.5 Gbit/s, 10 Gbit/s or 40 Gbit/s). As well, a SLD i could be represented by a quintuple (s_i, d_i, q_i, t_i^{start}, t_i^{end}), where t_i^{start} and t_i^{end} are starting time and ending time of demand i, respectively. Lightpaths are scheduled to be set up at the beginning of their starting time slots t_i^{start} and be torn-down at the end of their ending time slots t_i^{end}. Note that if we set all SLDs with the same starting and ending times, such problem is reduced to the RWA with PLDs. In other words, a PLD could be considered as a special case of SLD, for which the starting time is zero and ending times is unlimited. In realistic optical networks, it is likely that most of the demands would be initially of PLDs and SLDs type. The reason is that the traffic load in core networks is quite predictable because of its periodic nature (Kuri et al., 2003). Such traffic patterns could be predicted from historical statistics, which repeat every day (or week) with minor variations in timing and volume. Hence, we consider the problem of creating the set of SLDs from periodic traffic, i.e. scheduling the lightpaths. There are various periodic applications, which may be serviced more efficiently by scheduled lightpaths demands. For example, SLDs become highly attractive for service providers, which offer Optical Virtual Private Networks (OVPNs) or Bandwidth on Demand (BoD) services. They have to establish the set of Permanent Lightpaths (PLDs) to provide minimal network connectivity and capacity requirements, but some Scheduled Lightpaths (SLDs) have to be additionally established to increase the required capacities during certain periods of a day or a week.

To make possible lightpath scheduling, the time is slotted. Let T be the total number of time slots for which the traffic is defined. Each time slot t

= 1,2,...,T is assumed to have the same (fixed) length. The wavelength availability in a time slot is independent of its availability in other time slots. As a result, a wavelength can be reused over different links as well as multiple time slots. Since scheduled lightpath demands are not commonly simultaneous, some network resources can be reused by different lightpaths, provided that these lightpaths do not overlap in time. By improving the utilization of network resources, the number of established lightpaths could be increased.

The BCO-RWA Algorithm

The agents that we call artificial bees collaborate in order to solve the considered Max-RWA problem. We create the artificial network shown by Figure 1 throughout the bees are "flying." Each node in such artificial network represents one requested lightpath demand between the given source and given destination in a considered optical WDM network. More precisely, each node

represents a sub-network composed of the set of pre-specified candidate routes for the considered lightpath demand.

We have grouped all requested lightpaths in stages. The first lightpath to be established represents the first stage, the second lightpath to be established represents the second stage, etc. Each stage (one column of the artificial network) contains D nodes, where D represents the total number of requested lightpath demands. In addition, the artificial network is composed of D stages, too. Consequently, there are total of $D \times D$ nodes in a given artificial network.

The BCO-RWA algorithm solves the RWA problem in stages. At the beginning of the search process all artificial bees are located in the hive. The number of bees is specified in advance. Let the total number of bees engaged in the search process be B. Every bee departs from the hive and flies through the artificial network from the left to the right. Bee's tour is performed from stage to stage. At every stage bee chooses to visit one

Figure 1. Artificial network

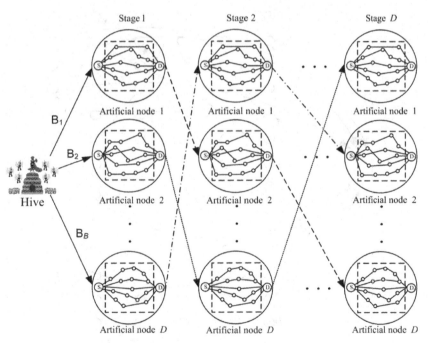

D - total number of requested lightpaths

artificial node. Bee agents' entire flight is collection of explored lightpaths. When flying through the space our bees perform two alternating moves: the forward pass and the backward pass. During a forward pass every bee visits n unvisited artificial nodes (bee tries to establish n new lightpaths). The number of nodes n to be visited during each forward pass is prescribed by the analyst at the beginning of the search process such that $n<<D$. Figure 2 illustrates the first forward pass of the search process, showing the $B=5$ bees which are flying from the hive.

In every stage, a bee chooses randomly one of the artificial nodes not previously visited by that bee. Sequence of the artificial nodes visited by the bee represents one partial solution of the problem. Bee is not always successful in establishing lightpath when visiting artificial node. Bee's success depends on the wavelengths availability on optical WDM links. In this way, generated

partial solutions differ among themselves according to the total number of established lightpaths.

After completing the forward pass, bees perform backward pass, i.e. they return to the hive where they participate in a decision-making process. It is assumed that all bees are able to exchange the information about the quality of the generated partial solutions (i.e. the number of established lightpaths). Based on the quality of the partial solutions (objective function values), every bee decides whether to (*1*) abandon the created partial solution and become uncommitted follower, (*2*) continue to expand the same partial solution without recruiting the hive-mates, or (*3*) dance and thus recruit the hive-mates before returning to the created partial solution. Depending on the quality of the partial solutions generated, every bee possesses certain level of loyalty to the path leading to the previously discovered partial solution. For example, shown

Figure 2. The first forward pass

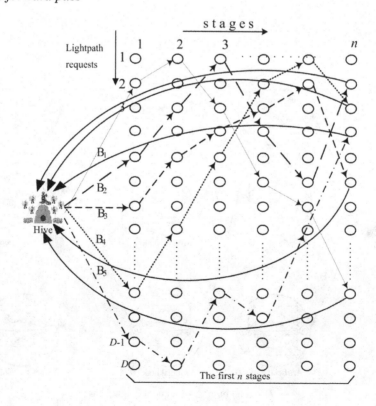

in Figure 3, bees B_2, B_3, and B_4 participate in the decision-making process. By comparing generated partial solutions, these bees decided to abandon already generated paths (partial solutions) and to join bees B_1 and B_5. Figure 3 illustrates possible situation in which the bee B_3 joined the bee B_1, and the bees B_2 and B_4 joined the bee B_5. As a result, during the next (second) forward pass bees B_3 and B_1 fly together along the path generated by the bee B_1, while bees B_2 and B_4 fly together along the path generated by the bee B_5. At the beginning of new forward pass, bees are free to make individual decision about next artificial nodes to be visited. Accordingly, during the second forward pass (see Figure3), bees expand its previously created partial solutions (try to establish additional n lightpaths) and after that perform again the backward pass and return to the hive. In the hive bees again participate in a decision-making process, perform the third forward pass, etc. The total number of forward passes, U in a search process depends on the total number of requested lightpaths D as well as the value of the parameter n, where $U = \lceil D / n \rceil$. Parameter n reflects the granularity of the search process.

When all forward passes are performed, one algorithm iteration is finished. At the end of iteration one or more feasible solutions of the considered problem are created. The best discovered solution during the first iteration is saved, and then the second iteration begins. Within the second iteration, bees again incrementally construct solutions of the problem, etc. The number of algorithm iterations I is specified in advance. The best result found over all algorithm iterations represents the output solution of the considered optimization problem.

Bee's Node Selection Mechanism

A bee is choosing the artificial nodes (lightpath demands) in a random manner, but with the probability proportional to the duration of a demand.

Figure 3. Bees' flights through the artificial network during the first and second passes

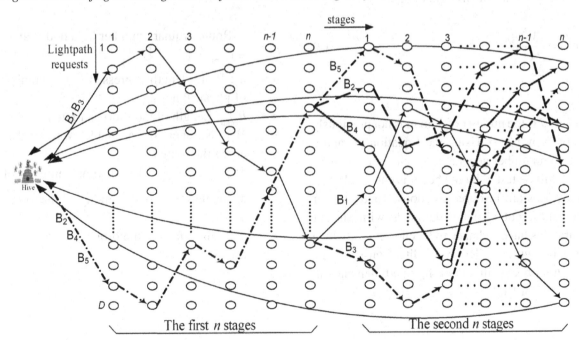

The main idea behind that is to force the bees to choose firstly those demands with longer duration (during more number of continuous time slots) for which it is more difficult to provide free wavelength in a network. In addition, lightpaths with longer durations could be preferable for a service provider because of higher probable revenues they would offer to him. For that reason, all lightpath demands are sorted according to its durations, with the PLDs located on the top of the list.

We define the utility V_i^b that the bee b has to select a SLD i by the following equation:

$$V_i^b = t_i^{end} - t_i^{start} = T_i^{service} \qquad (1)$$

where $T_i^{service}$ is the service time (duration) of a requested demand i. For the PLDs, the same durations $T_i^{service} = T$ are assumed, where T is the total (maximal) number of time slots during the considered period. Longer the duration of a demand, the greater is the utility for a bee to choose it. Based on the bee's utility, we define the probability p_i^b that a bee b will choose a demand i, given by the following equation:

$$p_i^b = \frac{V_i^b}{\sum\limits_{j=1}^{J} V_j^b} \qquad (2)$$

where J is the number of demands not previously chosen by bee b. Using the Equation (2) and a random number generator, a lightpath demand i that will be tested by the bee b is chosen. In this way, bees are favoured to choose firstly longer demands, but also the demands with shorter durations have a chance to be chosen firstly by a bee, but with smaller probability. Consequently, different bees will choose lightpath demands in different order.

Routing and Wavelength Assignment

Let us assume that the specific bee decided to consider the lightpath request between the source node s and the destination node d. In the next step, it is necessary to choose the route and to assign an available wavelength along the route between these two real nodes. We defined for every node pair (s, d), the subset R^{sd} of allowed alternate routes that could be used when establishing the lightpath. We defined these subsets by using the k shortest path algorithm. We calculated for every of the k routes the bee's utility when choosing the considered route. The shorter the chosen route and the higher the number of available wavelengths along the route, the higher is the bee's utilities to choose it. We define the bee's utilities V_r^{sd} when choosing the route r between the node pair (s, d) in the following way:

$$V_r^{s,d} = \left\{ a \frac{1}{h_r - h_{r\min} + 1} + (1-a)\frac{W_r}{W_{\max}} \right. \qquad (3)$$

where:

- r: Route ordinary number for a node pair, $r = 1, 2, ..., k$, $r \in \left\{ R^{sd} \right\}$.
- h_r: Route length expressed in the number of physical hops.
- h_{rmin}: Length of the shortest route r.
- W_r: Number of available wavelengths along the route r.
- $W_{\max} = \max\limits_{r \in R^{sd}} \left\{ W_r \right\}$: Maximal number of available wavelengths among all the routes $r \in R^{sd}$.
- a: Weight factor (importance of the criteria), $0 \leq a \leq 1$.

Bees decide to choose a physical route in a random manner. Inspired by the well-known Logit model (one of the most successful and widely accepted discrete choice model), we have assumed that the probability p_r^{sd} of choosing route r in the case of origin-destination pair (s,d) equals:

$$p_r^{sd} = \begin{cases} \dfrac{e^{V_r^{sd}}}{\sum\limits_{i=1}^{|R^{sd}|} e^{V_i^{sd}}}, & \forall r \in R^{sd} \ \wedge \ W_r > 0 \\ \\ 0, & \forall r \in R^{sd} \ \wedge \ W_r = 0 \end{cases} \quad (4)$$

where $|R^{sd}|$ is the total number of available routes between pair of nodes *(s, d)*. The route r is available if there is at least one available wavelength on all links that belong to the route r. The random number is generated from the interval [0, 1] for every route of the node pair *(s, d)*. Using this random number and the relation (4) bee is assigned to one of the considered routes.

In the next step, using the random strategy, one of the available wavelengths is assigned to the route chosen by the bee. This wavelength has to be available on all links along the route.

Bee's Partial Solutions Comparison

For each bee, we now know the quality of the created partial solution (the number of established lightpaths). It is assumed that every bee in the hive can obtain the information about the partial solution quality created by every other bee. Having all solutions evaluating, every bee makes the decision with a certain probability whether to abandon the created partial solution or to expand it in the next forward pass. The bees with better solution quality (greater number of established lightpaths) have more chances to keep and "advertise" their solutions. The probability p_b^{u+1} that the bee "b" will at beginning of the $u+1$ forward pass use the same partial tour that is defined in forward pass u equals:

$$p_b^{u+1} = e^{-\frac{C_{\max} - C_b}{u}} \quad (5)$$

where:

- C_b: Total number of established lightpaths from the beginning of the search process by the b-th bee.
- C_{max}: Maximal number of established lightpaths from the beginning of the search process by any bee.
- u: Ordinary number of forward pass, $u=1$, 2,...,U.

We can see from Equation (5) that if a bee has discovered the best partial solution in forward pass u ($C_b=C_{max}$), the bee b will continue to fly along the same partial tour in the $u+1$ forward pass with the probability equal to one ($p_b^{u+1} = 1$). The smaller the number of the established lightpaths by the bee, the smaller is the probability that the bee will fly again along the same path. Additionally, the smaller the ordinary number of the forward pass u (at the beginning of the search process) the higher the bees' "freedom of flight." The more forward passes make, the bees have less freedom to explore the solution space. A random number z is generated from the interval [0, 1]. If $z \leq p_b^{u+1}$ the bee "b" will fly along the same partial tour. In the opposite case, i.e. $z > p_b^{u+1}$, the bee will abandon the created partial solution and become uncommitted follower.

Bees Recruitment Process

After making the decision to continue flight along the previously generated path, the bee flies to the dance floor area in the hive and starts dancing. Artificial bees that are loyal to their partial solutions are at the same time recruiters, i.e. their solutions will be considered by other bees. The bee that abandon from its generated partial solution (i.e. does not want to fly further along the same path) become uncommitted follower. Such a bee has to select one of the advertised solutions (follow another dancing bee). In such way, two groups of bees are formed in the dancing area—uncommitted followers ready to join some of the dancing bees, and dancing bees (or recruiters) ready to recruit uncommitted followers.

This decision is taken with a certain probability using the roulette wheel such that better advertised solutions have more chance to be chosen for further exploration. In other words, bees with higher objective function value have greater chance to continue its own partial solution. The probability p_p that the P-th advertised partial solution will be chosen by any of the uncommitted follower equals:

$$p_p = \frac{e^{C_p}}{\sum_{i=1}^{Q} e^{C_i}} \qquad (6)$$

where:

- C_P: Total number of the established lightpaths in the case of the P-th advertised partial solution,
- Q: Total number of advertised partial solutions.

A random number is generated from the interval [0, 1] for every uncommitted follower. Using these random numbers and the relation (6) every uncommitted follower is "assigned" to one of the dancing bees. In such way, the number of recruiters and uncommitted followers is changed before the beginning of each forward pass.

Using the collective knowledge and sharing information among themselves, bees concentrate on more promising search paths, and slowly abandon less promising paths. In other words, as the searching process progress, generated partial solutions converge to optimal. At the end of iteration, each bee generates one feasible solution of the problem. The best one is determined and it is used to update global best solution. At this point,

all B solutions are deleted, and the new iteration can start. The number of iteration is specified in advance.

The pseudo-code for the proposed BCO-RWA algorithm is shown in Table 1. Based on the given pseudo-code, a particular programming code is implemented using the MATLAB program package to carry out the simulation tests. Developed application enables us to find out the solution of the considered Max-RWA problem for various traffic scenarios and different network topologies.

EXPERIMENTAL RESULTS

The proposed BCO-RWA algorithm was tested on a few numerical examples. We present here some computational and comparative results for the BCO-RWA algorithm. The first considered network example is a small optical network topology with $N=8$ and $L=11$, shown in Figure 4. Each edge (link) represents a pair of directed fiber, one for each direction. We assumed that the maximal number of available wavelengths W is same for each fiber link. The total number of bees engaged in discovering the optimal solution equals $B=10$, while the total number of alternative routes between every node pair equals $R_{s,d}=5$.

We compared the obtained BCO-RWA results with the optimal solution for various number of lightpath demands that are to be established and different values of W. The comparison results are shown in the Table 2. Optimal solutions are obtained by solving the ILP formulation of the Max-RWA problem proposed in (Krishnaswamy and Sivarajan, 2001).

It can be seen from the Table 2 that the proposed BCO-RWA algorithm is able to produce the results of a high quality. Namely, the objective function values obtained by the BCO-RWA algorithm are very close to the optimal (ILP) values of the objective function. The relative errors or relative deviations compared to optimal solutions are only few percents (less than 7% in the case of small

Table 1. Pseudo-code of the BCO-RWA algorithm

Initialize B, I, n, D,U, N, L, T, W, R$_{sd}$
begin
X$_0$ – create an initial (empty) solution
set: i=1, u=1, b=1, j=1;
while i <= I
while u <= U
while b <= B
forward pass:
while j <= n
      (1) For each bee b determine the utility to choose an artificial node
      (2) Select the available route r
      (3) Assign a free wavelength w to a lightpath during time slots t.
j = j + 1;
end while;
backward pass:
      (4) each bee b is „flying-back" to the hive;
      (5) update the partial solution quality for every bee b;
b = b + 1;
end while;
      (6) bee's partial solution comparaison,
      (7) bees recruit procedure: every bee decides whether to continue its own partial solution created so far and become a recruiter or to become a follower.
u= u + 1;
end while;
      (8) If the best solution X$_i$ obtained during the i-th iteration is better than the best-known solution found so far, update the best-known solution X:=X$_i$.
i = i + 1;
end while;
      (9) Output the best solution X
end
	• **B:** Number of bees in a hive, b=1,2,...,B
	• **I:** Number of iterations i=1,2,...,I
	• **n:** Number of artificial nodes visited by a bee during one forward pass
	• **D:** Set of lightpath demands, d=1,2,...,D
	U=$\lceil D/n \rceil$: Number of forward passes
	• **N:** Set of network nodes, n=1,2,...,N
	• **L:** Set of network links, l=1,2,...,L
	• **T:** number of time slots, t=1,2,...,T
	• **W:** Set of wavelengths, w=1,2,...W
	• **R$_{sd}$:** Set of routes for (s,d) node pair, r=1,2,...,R$_{sd}$

Figure 4. The considered optical WDM network topology with N=8 routing nodes

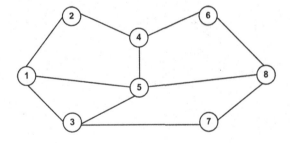

number of available wavelengths). In cases of more complex problems (characterized by the higher number of available wavelengths) the BCO-RWA has produced the optimal solution.

The CPU times required to find the best solutions by the BCO-RWA are very low. In other words, the BCO-RWA is able to produce "very good" solutions in a "reasonable" computation

time. Based on great number of performed tests, it could be shown that the number of bees significantly affects the required computational times, but the solution quality does not change much if the number of bees increases. The results for CPU times, shown in Table 2, are obtained for the case of *I*=10 independent algorithm iterations. All the tests were performed on Intel(R) Pentium(R) computer processor with 1.73GHz and 504MB of RAM.

The second considered example is moderately large realistic network, composed of *N*=20 nodes and *L*=39 links, which represents the backbone European Optical Network (EON). The physical topology of the EON network is shown in Figure 5. We assumed again that each physical link consists of a pair of unidirectional optical fibers, one for each direction, with the same number of wavelengths *W* over each fiber-link and that there

Table 2. The results comparison for the network given in Figure 4

Number of requested lightpaths	Number of wavelengths	Number of established lightpaths		Relative error [%]	CPU time [s]	
		Optimal (ILP) solution	BCO-RWA solution		Optimal (ILP) solution	BCO-RWA solution
28	1	14	14	0	4	4.33
	2	23	23	0	94	4.58
	3	27	27	0	251	4.68
	4	28	28	0	313	4.66
31	1	15	14	6.67	4	4.73
	2	25	25	0	83	5.00
	3	30	30	0	25	5.19
	4	31	31	0	1410	5.21
34	1	15	14	6.67	14	5.19
	2	27	26	3.70	148	5.50
	3	33	33	0	216	5.64
	4	34	34	0	906	5.64
36	1	16	15	6.25	23	5.64
	2	27	26	3.70	325	6.09
	3	34	34	0	788	6.11
	4	36	36	0	1484	6.13
38	1	17	16	5.88	16	5.67
	2	28	27	3.57	247	6.09
	3	35	35	0	261	6.23
	4	38	38	0	1773	6.33
40	1	17	16	5.88	31	6.00
	2	28	27	3.57	491	6.28
	3	35	35	0	429	6.61
	4	40	40	0	1346	6.67

Figure 5. The EON (European optical network) topology (Mahony et al., 1995)

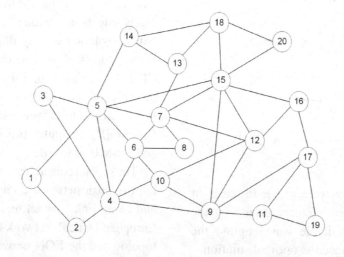

is no wavelength conversion in nodes. The RWA problem for this network topology was also solved in (Krishnaswamy and Sivarajan, 2001). In order to solve the Max-RWA ILP problem the authors of (Krishnaswamy and Sivarajan, 2001) used the LP-relaxation technique. In order to round fractional values of the variables they developed two heuristic algorithms, named the algorithm *A* and the algorithm *B*. We adopted the same traffic matrix as in (Jaumard and Hemarzo), with the aim to provide the fair comparison between the BCO-RWA algorithm and the existing LP-relaxation based approach in (Krishnaswamy and Sivarajan, 2001) as well as the Tabu metaheuristic algorithm proposed in (Dzongang et al., 2005).

The total number of requested demands for this network was *D*=374. The comparison results for various algorithms are illustrated in Figure 6. It can be seen that the BCO-RWA always outperforms the results of the algorithms *A* and *B*, proposed in (Krishnaswamy and Sivarajan, 2001). Also, our BCO-RWA algorithm outperforms the Tabu search metaheuristic algorithm proposed in (Dzongang et al., 2005) for the larger number of available wavelengths. Note that our algorithm gives better performances for more complicated problem. The greater the number of wavelengths the closer the BCO-RWA value to the upper bound.

When the number of available wavelengths is equal to 22, we obtain the maximal possible number of established lightpaths (374).

In all previous experiments, we assumed that lightpath demands are with unlimited (unspecified) durations, i.e. Permanent Lightpath Demands (PLD). However, a more realistic traffic scenario in upcoming WRON is that the lightpaths demands should be established during the predetermined time intervals (for example, few hours, days or weeks) rather than for an indefinite periods. Such demands are also known as Scheduled Lightpath Demands (SLD). Beside the source and destination nodes, each SLD is specified by its starting time and ending time. The SLDs for which set-up and tear-down times are known in advance can take the advantage of the time scheduling property. That is, unless two lightpaths overlap in time, they can be assigned the same wavelength since the paths are disjoint in time.

Figure 6. The result comparison of various algorithms

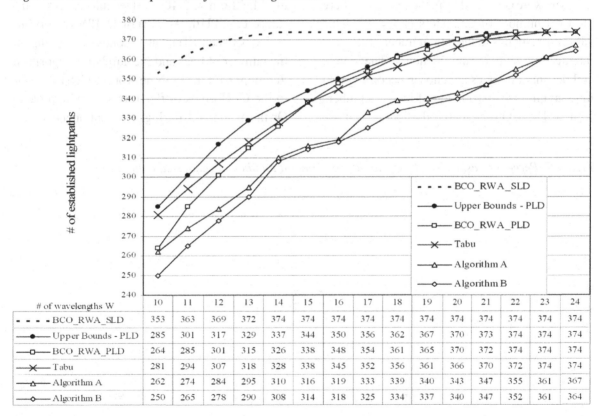

# of wavelengths W	10	11	12	13	14	15	16	17	18	19	20	21	22	23	24
- - - - BCO_RWA_SLD	353	363	369	372	374	374	374	374	374	374	374	374	374	374	374
—●— Upper Bounds - PLD	285	301	317	329	337	344	350	356	362	367	370	373	374	374	374
—□— BCO_RWA_PLD	264	285	301	315	326	338	348	354	361	365	370	372	374	374	374
—✕— Tabu	281	294	307	318	328	338	345	352	356	361	366	370	372	374	374
—△— Algorithm A	262	274	284	295	310	316	319	333	339	340	343	347	355	361	367
—◇— Algorithm B	250	265	278	290	308	314	318	325	334	337	340	347	352	361	364

Our motivation is to demonstrate that by considering the SLDs, the significant improvements in terms of the number of established lightpaths could be achieved compared to PLDs. We have run the simulator for several traffic scenarios. In each case, lightpath demands are generated during a period of 24 hours, with durations that are the multiples of a fixed duration time slot. Note that decreasing the duration of one time slot directly affects the complexity of the problem as well as the efficiency of the algorithm. With a shorter time slot, there are fewer requests per time slot and consequently more lightpaths could be established. The SLDs are generated randomly with the start time and durations following the uniform distribution. If the requested start time of a lightpath is occurred at any time within a time slot, it is assumed that entire slot t is required for that lightpath. In other words, a lightpath can only be scheduled at the beginning of a time slot. Duration (service time) of each SLD is specified as the multiple of one time slot equalled to $\Delta t = 15$ minute. Such integer numbers were generated from the set $[1, T]$, where the total number of time slots is $T = 96$. This value corresponds to the total number of $\Delta t = 15$-minute time slots during 24 hours. The source and destination nodes are chosen according to a random uniform distribution of integer numbers from set $[1, N]$. On any source-destination pair, we

assume that there can be multiple demands. We generated various traffic scenarios for simulation experiments, with the total number of requested lightpath demands, D, ranging from 100 to 1000 and various proportions between PLDs and SLDs (note that PLDs + SLDs = 100%). The obtained results are given by Figure 7 in the cases of $W = 16$ and $W = 32$. It can be seen that considerably more lightpaths could be established if the portion of SLDs in total demand is greater.

Further, the comparison results for a specific traffic pattern with $D = 500$ requested lightpath demands are given by Figure 8. The results are obtained by numerous tests performed for different proportions of PLDs and SLDs in total demand D.

We compared our CPU times with those required for the Tabu search algorithm, proposed in (Dzongang et al., 2005). They reported that "depending on the instance, the computing time of Tabu for each run ranges between 40 and 59 seconds for the EON network". These authors used Pentium 4, 2.4GHz. Depending on the instance, the CPU times of the BCO–RWA algorithm varied between 10 and 40 seconds (depending on the number of bees and the number of algorithm iterations), for the EON network, which is similar to the CPU times of the Tabu search approach. On the other hand, the higher the number of avail-

Figure 7. Percent of established ligthtpaths for different number of requested demands

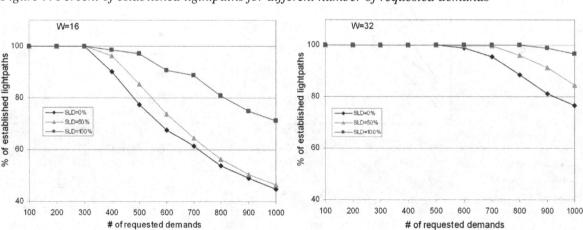

Figure 8. Number of established lightpaths for different proportions of SLDs in total demand D = 500

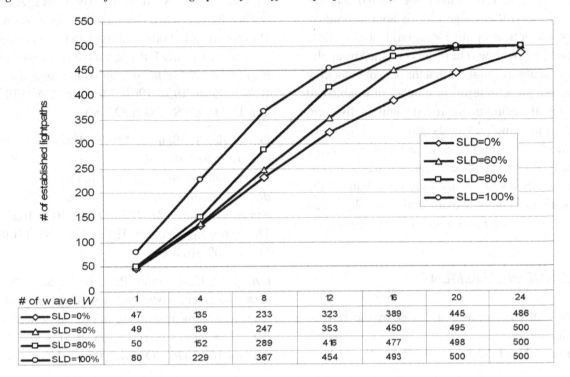

# of wavel. W	1	4	8	12	16	20	24
SLD=0%	47	135	233	323	389	445	486
SLD=60%	49	139	247	353	450	495	500
SLD=80%	50	152	289	416	477	498	500
SLD=100%	80	229	367	454	493	500	500

able wavelengths, the higher is the chance that the BCO–RWA algorithm will outperform the Tabu approach (see Figure 6). The CPU times depend on the problem size, the total number of requested lightpaths, prescribed number of alternative routes for every node pair, prescribed number of algorithm iterations, as well as the total number of bees. In all numerical experiments the total number of bees was set to $B=10$ and the number of algorithms iterations was $I = 10$.

FUTURE RESEARCH DIRECTIONS

Our future studies should possibly include solving the RWA problem in the case of dynamic traffic demands. Additionally, the wavelength conversion could be researched as well as the traffic-grooming problem. Since it has been shown that BCO-RWA is able to produce high-quality performances, it is expected that these problems could be solved in efficient manner, too.

CONCLUSION

In recent years, swarm intelligence becomes more and more attractive for the researchers, who work in the related research field. In this study a relatively new member of swarm intelligence family that is named as Bee Colony Optimization (BCO) is explained in detail. We propose the BCO algorithm tailored for the Routing and Wavelength Assignment (RWA) problem in all-optical WDM networks. The proposed methodology is based on the concepts of collective intelligence. There are no theoretical results at this moment that could support proposed approach. Usually, development of various metaheuristic was based on experimental work in initial stage. Good experimental results usually motivated researchers to try to produce some theoretical results. The concepts proposed here are not exceptions in this sense.

A range of studies have shown that bee inspired algorithms have a very promising potential for modeling and solving complex optimization problems. In this chapter, we proved that the BCO-based RWA algorithm is able to produce optimal or near-optimal solutions in a reasonable computation time. The results obtained by applying our algorithm show that the network blocking performance, in terms of number of established lightpaths could be improved significantly compared to some previously proposed algorithms. The obtained results indicate that the development of new models based on swarm intelligence principles could significantly contribute to the solution of complex optimization problems that arise in telecommunication networks design.

ACKNOWLEDGMENT

This study is partially supported by the Serbian Ministry of Education and Science, Research Projects No. TR-32025 and TR-36021.

REFERENCES

Baykasoglu, A., Özbakýr, L., & Tapkan, P. (2007). Artificial bee colony algorithm and its application to generalized assignment problem. In Chan, F. T. S., & Tiwari, M. K. (Eds.), *Swarm Intelligence: Focus on Ant and Particle Swarm Optimization* (pp. 113–143). Vienna, Austria: I-Tech Education and Publishing. doi:10.5772/5101.

Camazine, S., & Sneyd, J. (1991). A model of collective nectar source by honey bees: Self-organization through simple rules. *Journal of Theoretical Biology*, 149(4), 547–571. doi:10.1016/S0022-5193(05)80098-0.

Chin, T. S. (2005). An ant algorithm for single-hop wavelength assignment in WDM mesh network. In A. Lim (Ed.), *Proceedings of the 17th IEEE International Conference on Tools with Artificial Intelligence ICTAI 2005* (pp. 111–117). Los Alamitos, CA: IEEE Computer Society. doi: 10.1109/ICTAI.2005.33.

Chong, C. S., Low, M. Y. H., Sivakumar, A. I., & Gay, K. Y. (2006). A bee colony optimization algorithm to job shop scheduling. In L.F. Perrone, B. Lawson, J. Liu, & F.P. Wieland (Eds.), *Proceedings of the 37th Conference on Winter Simulation WSC 2006* (pp. 1954–1961). Monterey, CA: IEEE. doi: 10.1109/WSC.2006.322980

Davidović, T., Šelmić, M., & Teodorović, D. (2009). Scheduling of independent tasks – Bee colony optimization approach. In *Proceedings of the 17th Mediterranean Conference on Control and Automation – MED 2009* (pp. 1020-1025). Thessaloniki, Greece: IEEE. doi: 10.1109/MED.2009.5164680

Dzongang, C., Galinier, P., & Piere, S. (2005). A tabu search heuristic for the routing and wavelength assignment problem in optical networks. *IEEE Communications Letters*, 9(5), 426–428. doi: doi:10.1109/LCOMM.2005.05011.

Jaumard, B., & Hemazro, T. D. (2004). Routing and wavelength assignment in single hop all optical networks with minimum blocking. *GERAD -Group for Research in Decision Analysis*. Retrieved from http://www.gerad.ca/fichiers/cahiers/G-2004-12.pdf

Karaboga, D. (2005). *An idea based on honey bee swarm for numerical optimization* (Technical Report TR06). Kayseri, Turkey: Erciyes University. Retrieved from http://www-lia.deis.unibo.it/Courses/SistInt/articoli/bee-colony1.pdf

Karaboga, D., &, B. (2009). A survey: Algorithms simulating bee swarm intelligence. *Artificial Intelligence Review*, 31, 61–85. doi:10.1007/s10462-009-9127-4.

Karaboga, D., & Bastürk, B. (2007). A powerful and efficient algorithm for numerical function optimization: Artificial bee colony (ABC) algorithm. *Journal of Global Optimization*, 39(3), 459–471. doi:10.1007/s10898-007-9149-x.

Krishnaswamy, R. M., & Sivarajan, K. N. (2001). Algorithms for routing and wavelength assignment based on solutions of LP-relaxations. *IEEE Communications Letters*, *5*(10), 435–437. doi:10.1109/4234.957386.

Kuri, J., Puech, N., Gagnaire, M., Dotaro, E., & Douville, R. (2003). Routing and wavelength assignment of scheduled lightpath demands. *IEEE Journal on Selected Areas in Communications*, *21*(8), 1231–1240. doi:10.1109/JSAC.2003.816622.

Lučić, P., & Teodorović, D. (2001). Bee system: modeling combinatorial optimization transportation engineering problems by swarm intelligence. In *Proceedings of the IV Triennial Symposium on Transportation Analysis TRISTAN* (pp. 441-445). Sao Miguel, Portugal: TRISTAN.

Lučić, P., & Teodorović, D. (2002). Transportation modeling: An artificial life approach. In *Proceedings of the 14th IEEE International Conference on Tools with Artificial Intelligence ICTAI 2002* (pp. 216–223). Washington, DC: IEEE Computer Society. doi: 10.1109/TAI.2002.1180807

Lučić, P., & Teodorović, D. (2003a). Computing with bees: Attacking complex transportation engineering problems. *International Journal of Artificial Intelligence Tools*, *12*(3), 375–394. doi:10.1142/S0218213003001289.

Lučić, P., & Teodorović, D. (2003b). Vehicle routing problem with uncertain demand at nodes: The bee system and fuzzy logic approach. In Verdegay, J. L. (Ed.), *Fuzzy Sets Based Heuristics for Optimization* (pp. 67–82). Berlin: Springer-Verlag. doi:10.1007/978-3-540-36461-0_5.

Mahony, M. J., & Simeonidu, D. J., Zhou, & Yu, A. (1995). The design of a European optical network. *IEEE/OSA. Journal of Lightwave Technology*, *3*(5), 817–828. doi:10.1109/50.387798.

Marković, G. (2007). *Optimization of the resource usage in optical wavelength routing networks*. (Ph. D. Thesis). University of Belgrade. Belgrade, Serbia.

Marković, G., & Aćimović-Raspopović, V. (2010). Solving the RWA problem in WDM optical networks using the BCO meta-heuristic. *Telfor Journal*, *2*(1), 43–48.

Marković, G., Teodorović, D., & Aćimović-Raspopović, V. (2007). Routing and wavelength assignment in all-optical networks based on the bee colony optimization. *AI Communications - The European Journal on Artificial Intelligence*, *20*(4), 273-285.

Nakrani, S., & Tovey, C. (2003). On honey bees and dynamic allocation in an Internet server colony. In C. Anderson & T. Balch (Eds.), *Proceedings of the Second International Workshop on the Mathematics and Algorithms of Social Insects* (pp. 115-122). Atlanta, GA: Georgia Institute of Technology.

Navarro-Varela, G., & Sinclair, M. (1999). Ant-colony optimisation for virtual-wavelength-path routing and wavelength allocation. In *Proceedings of the 1999 Congress on Evolutionary Computation CEC'99* (pp. 1809-1816). Washington, DC: IEEE. doi: 10.1109/CEC.1999.785494

Pham, D. T., et al. (2006). The bees algorithm – A novel tool for complex optimization problems. In Pham, Eldukhri, & Soroka (Eds.), *Proceedings of the 2nd International Virtual Conference on Intelligent Production Machines and Systems IPROMS 2006* (pp. 454–459). Oxford, UK: Elsevier.

Quijano, N., & Passino, K. M. (2007). Honey bee social foraging algorithms for resource allocation, part I: Algorithm and theory. In *Proceedings of the 2007 American Control Conference* (pp. 3383-3388). New York, NY: ACC. doi: 10.1109/ACC.2007.4282167

Ram Murthy, C. S., & Gurusamy, M. (2002). *WDM optical networks - Concepts, design and algorithms*. Upper Saddle River, NJ: Prentice Hall PTR.

Rashedi, A., Kavian, Y. S., Ansari-Asl, K., & Ghassemlooy, Z. (2011). Dynamic routing and wavelength assignment: Artificial bee colony optimization. In M. Jaworski, & M. Marciniak (Eds.), *Proceedings of the 13th IEEE International Conference on Transparent Optical Networks ICTON 2011*. Warsaw, Poland: National Institute of Telecommunications - Department of Transmission and Optical Technologies. doi: 10.1109/ICTON.2011.5971015

Teodorović, D., & Dell' Orco, M. (2008). Mitigating traffic congestion: Solving the ride matching problem by bee colony optimization. *Transportation Planning and Technology*, *31*(2), 135–152. doi:10.1080/03081060801948027.

Teodorović, D. (2009). Bee colony optimization (BCO). In Lim, C. P., Jaim, L. C., & Dehuri, S. (Eds.), *Innovations in Swarm Intelligence Studies in Computational Intelligence* (pp. 39–60). Heidelberg, Germany: Springer-Verlag. doi:10.1007/978-3-642-04225-6_3.

Teodorovic, D., & Dell'Orco, M. (2005). Bee colony optimization - A cooperative learning approach to complex transportation problems. In A. Jaszkiewicz et al. (Eds.), *Advanced OR and AI Methods in Transportation - Proceedings of the 16th Mini-EURO Conference and 10th Meeting of Euro Working Group on Transportation (EWGT)* (pp. 51-60). Poznan, Poland: Poznan University of Technology.

Teodorović, D., Lučić, P., Marković, G., & Dell'Orco, M. (2006). Bee colony optimization: Principles and applications. In B. Reljin & S. Stanković (Eds.), *Proceedings of the Eight Seminar on Neural Network Application in Electrical Engineering NEUREL 2006* (pp. 151-156). Belgrade, Serbia: University of Belgrade. doi: 10.1109/NEUREL.2006.341200

Teodorović, D., & Šelmić, M. (2007). The BCO algorithm for the p-median problem. In M. Čangalović & M. Suknović (Eds.), *Proceedings of the XXXIV Serbian Operations Research Conference SYM-OP-IS 2007* (pp. 417-420). Belgrade, Serbia: University of Belgrade.

Wedde, H. F., Farooq, M., & Zhang, Y. (2004). BeeHive: An efficient fault-tolerant routing algorithm inspired by honey bee behavior. *Lecture Notes in Computer Science*, *3172*, 83–94. doi:10.1007/978-3-540-28646-2_8.

Yang, X. S. (2005). Engineering optimizations via nature inspired virtual bee algorithms. *Lecture Notes in Computer Science*, *3562*, 317–323. doi:10.1007/11499305_33.

ADDITIONAL READING

Bitam, S., Batouche, M., & Talbi, E. G. (2010). A survey on bee colony algorithms. In *Proceedings of the International Symposium on Parallel & Distributed Processing, Workshops and PhD Forum IPDPSW 2010* (pp. 420-427). Atlanta, GA: IEEE. doi: 10.1109/IPDPSW.2010.5470701

Bonabeau, E., Dorigo, M., & Theraulaz, G. (1999). *Swarm intelligence: From natural to artificial systems*. New York: Oxford University Press.

Dehuri, S., & Cho, S. B. (Eds.). (2011). *Knowledge mining using intelligent agents - Advances in computing science and engineering: Texts, 6*. London: Imperial College Press.

Pertiwi, A. P., & Suyanto (2011). Globally evolved dynamic bee colony optimization. In A. König et al. (Eds.) *Knowledge-Based and Intelligent Information and Engineering Systems, Part 1* (pp. 52-61). Heidelberg, Germany: Springer Verlag Berlin.

Rubio-Largo, Á., Vega-Rodríguez, M. A., Gómez-Pulido, J. A., & Sánchez-Pérez, J. M. (2011). Tackling the static RWA problem by using a multiobjective artificial bee colony algorithm. In Cabestany, J., Royas, I., & Joya, G. (Eds.), *Advances in Computational Intelligence Part 1* (pp. 364–371). Heidelberg, Germany: Springer Verlag Berlin. doi:10.1007/978-3-642-21498-1_46.

Teodorović, D. (2003). Transport modeling by multi-agent systems: A swarm intelligence approach. *Transportation Planning and Technology*, 26(4), 289–312. doi:10.1080/0308106032000154593.

Teodorović, D. (2008). Swarm intelligence systems for transportation engineering: Principles and applications. *Transportation Research Part C, Emerging Technologies*, 16, 651–782. doi:10.1016/j.trc.2008.03.002.

KEY TERMS AND DEFINITIONS

Bee Colony Optimization (BCO): A new SI metaheuristic approach arisen by modelling the collective behaviour of social bee colonies in order to solve various complex optimization problems.

Lightpath: All-optical communication channel established between the given source and given destination nodes in a Wavelength Routed Optical Network (WRON).

Meta-Heuristic: General optimization procedures that coordinate simple heuristics and rules to find approximate solutions of computationally difficult combinatorial problems.

Routing and Wavelength Assignment (RWA): The procedure which finds an appropriate route and assigns a wavelength to establish a lightpath.

Static Lightpath Establishing: Solving the RWA problem of lightpaths demands which are completely known in advance.

Swarm Intelligence (SI): New optimization approach inspired by the collective intelligence of insects' colonies and other animal societies in nature in order to develop some meta-heuristics which can mimic insect's problem solution abilities. This is the branch of artificial intelligence based on the study of behavior of individual artificial agents in various decentralised systems.

Wavelength Continuity Constraint: A lightpath has to be assigned the same wavelength over all intermediate fiber links between end nodes.

Wavelength Routed Optical Network (WRON): A circuit-switched network that consists of optical cross-connects (OXC) interconnected by WDM fiber links in which the routing of lightpaths is based on their wavelengths.

Chapter 9

Applications of Computational Intelligence to Impairment–Aware Routing and Wavelength Assignment in Optical Networks

Joaquim F. Martins-Filho
Federal University of Pernambuco, Brazil

Daniel A. R. Chaves
Federal University of Pernambuco, Brazil

Carmelo J. A. Bastos-Filho
University of Pernambuco, Brazil

Helder A. Pereira
University of Pernambuco, Brazil

ABSTRACT

Computational intelligence techniques have been used to solve hard problems in optical networks, such as the routing and wavelength assignment problem, the design of the physical and the logical topology of these networks, and the placement of some high cost devices along the network when it is necessary, such as regenerators and wavelength converters. In this chapter, the authors concentrate on the application of computational intelligence to solve the impairment-aware routing and wavelength assignment problem. They present a brief survey on this topic and a detailed description and results for two applications of computational intelligence, one to solve the wavelength assignment problem with an evolutionary strategy approach and the other to tackle the routing problem using ant colony optimization.

INTRODUCTION

The computational intelligence field has experimented an amazing growth in the last years. Beyond the well known techniques, such as Genetic Algorithms (GA) and Multi-Layer Perceptron Artificial Neural Networks (MLP ANN), many novel paradigms have been proposed to tackle different types of problems, such as combinatorial permutation problems in high dimensionality, multimodal optimization and many-objective optimization. In general, these approaches were inspired in nature. Some examples of these novel algorithms are Evolutionary Strategies (ES), Differential Evolution (DE), Particle Swarm Optimization (PSO), Ant Colony Optimization (ACO), Artificial Immune Systems (AIS), Artificial Bee Colony Optimiza-

DOI: 10.4018/978-1-4666-3652-1.ch009

tion (ABC), Fish School Search (FSS), among others (Eberhart, 2007), (Engelbrecht, 2007).

These algorithms have been frequently applied to solve complex problems in many scientific areas since the mid nineties. Furthermore, many researchers have proposed to tackle networking problems with bio-inspired techniques. Dressler (Dressler, 2010A) presented an overview of some key concepts and methodologies of these techniques when applied to solve network problems, addressing some capabilities and their practical relevance. Most of the examples given in (Dressler, 2010A) addresses applications for wireless networks. It shows that these techniques have not been proposed solely to solve problems in optical networks, but in transmission systems and networks in general. A special edition of a renowned journal was dedicated to bio-inspired networking (Dressler, 2010B).

Recently, some efforts have been carried out to demonstrate that these techniques can be useful to tackle tough problems in optical networks, such as to solve the Routing and Wavelength Assignment (RWA) problem, to design the physical and the logical topology of these networks and to properly place some high cost devices along the network when it is necessary, such as regenerators and wavelength converters.

In this chapter we will concentrate on the application of computational intelligence to solve the impairment-aware routing and wavelength assignment problem. We will present a brief survey on this topic and detailed description and results for two applications of computational intelligence, one to solve the wavelength assignment problem with evolutionary strategy and the other to tackle the routing problem using ACO.

BACKGROUND

Wavelength routed optical networks have been considered as the most reliable and economic solution to achieve high transmission capacities

with Quality of Service (QoS). In these networks, the signal remains in the optical domain between the edge nodes, *i.e.* the signal propagates along the core of the optical network without any optical-electrical-optical conversion. One of the main challenges in these optical networks is to define an appropriate RWA algorithm in order to obtain a low blocking probability with an acceptable Quality of Transmission (QoT) for every established lightpath. A suitable impairment-aware RWA algorithm has to find a route and select a wavelength between the source-destination nodes that provides a minimum QoT for every network request, taking into account the impairments imposed by the physical layer. Besides, the RWA algorithm needs to consider the efficient utilization of network resources and the optimization of the network performance (Rahbar, 2011; Azodol-molky, 2009; Martinez, 2006).

In general, the routing problem and the wavelength assignment are treated separately. Several solutions were already proposed for the static problem and for the dynamic problem. Some approaches based on evolutionary computation were proposed for static routing in the past, however we believe the next generation of optical networks will have to deal with dynamic provisioning of resources. Some recent approaches were proposed to tackle the dynamic problem using different computational intelligence paradigms, such as Hopfield Neural Networks (HNN) (Bastos-Filho, 2010), Power Series Routing trained by Particle Swarm Optimization (PSR) (Martins-Filho, 2008, 2012; Chaves, 2011), Ant Colony Optimization (ACO) (Triay, 2010; Pavani, 2010), Evolutionary Strategies (ES) (Bastos-Filho, 2011), among others.

Bastos-Filho *et al.* (Bastos-Filho, 2010) proposed a routing algorithm based on Hopfield Neural Networks for transparent optical networks. The HNN takes into account the matching of available wavelengths between adjacent links along the lightpath and the HNN parameters are selected by a Multi Objective Optimizer in order to both minimize the blocking probability of the optical network and maximize the convergence speed of the HNN algorithm. The HNN algorithm achieved lower blocking probabilities than other well known conventional algorithms. Although the HNN presented good results and can be easily implemented in parallel systems, such as GPUs or FPGAs, it needs a longer time for the offline training, *i.e.* a planning stage is necessary to properly select the HNN parameters according the operational scenario. Bastos-Filho *et al.* (Bastos-Filho, 2011b) implemented the HNN-based routing algorithm and achieved a speed-up of 40 when compared to the CPU version.

Martins-Filho *et al.* (Martins-Filho, 2008) proposed an algorithm to design the link cost function to compose the impairment-aware RWA algorithm, called Power Series Routing (PSR). The algorithm is divided in four steps. At first, one needs to choose the input variables. In the original proposal, the link lengths and the wavelength availability in the links were selected. After that, these inputs must be expanded in terms of a power series. Then, a network performance indicator is selected. Martins-Filho *et al.* proposed to minimize the overall blocking probability. Finally, a reliable computational optimization algorithm has to be used in order to find the series coefficients that optimize the network performance indicator based on offline network simulations. The optimization process is performed by a Particle Swarm Optimizer (PSO). The algorithm can be considered as an adaptive impairment-aware RWA algorithm since the coefficients of the expanded series carry information about the network scenario and impairments. The PSR performance was compared with other algorithms found in the literature by means of computational simulations, and it presented a lower blocking probability with shorter computation time. Furthermore, the authors have demonstrated that the PSR algorithm is capable to adapt itself automatically to topological changes in the network due to both link/node addition/

failure (Chaves, 2011). More recently, the authors demonstrated that the PSR algorithm performs very well in transparent, translucent and opaque network scenarios (Martins-Filho, 2012).

Some approaches based on ACO algorithms were already proposed to solve the RWA algorithm on wavelength continuity constrained optical networks. ACO based algorithms use the idea of pheromone deposition to update the routing tables. The main advantage is its distributed nature, which provides higher survivability to network failures or traffic congestion. Triay *et al.* (Triay, 2010) developed a protocol for optical networks based on the optical switching of bursts. Pavani *et al.* (Pavani, 2010) presented an ACO based algorithm with crankback re-routing extensions to reduce the blocking experienced by the RSVP-TE protocol during lightpath setup or restoration.

To the best of our knowledge, there is just one approach based on computational intelligence to tackle the Wavelength Assignment (WA) problem. Bastos-Filho *et al.* (Bastos-Filho, 2011) presented a wavelength assignment algorithm suitable for optical networks mainly impaired by physical layer effects, named the Intelligent Wavelength Assignment algorithm (iWA). The iWA algorithm determines the wavelength activation order for a first-fit list, which minimizes the impact of the impairments by using a training algorithm based on ES. The authors showed that the iWA algorithm adapts itself to different network scenarios. The iWA algorithm presented better results when compared to other conventional WA algorithms. The authors also demonstrated that the iWA algorithm performs well even when load distribution changes are imposed to the network.

Some recent proposals have been presented to solve simultaneously the routing problem and the wavelength assignment problem. Monoyios and Vlachos (Monoyios, 2011) applied a multi-objective genetic algorithm to jointly solve the static impairment aware routing and wavelength assignment problems. Whereas, Kavian *et al.*

(Kavian, 2008) proposed a genetic algorithm to optimize the network RWA in terms of bandwidth and delay (Kavian, 2008).

SOLUTIONS FOR ROUTING AND WAVELENGTH ASSIGNMENT

The RWA problem is a classic problem in optical networks. It can be divided in two minor problems: the routing process and the wavelength assignment process. A classical approach to solve routing problem is to represent the network topology by a graph, then use some metrics to evaluate the cost of each branch of the graph, and finally, use an algorithm that finds the minimum cost path between two given nodes (Mukherjee, 2000; Zang *et al.* 1999). Classical routing algorithms use some heuristic link cost functions based on a pre-defined metrics, such as, the shortest path (SP), minor delay and load balance (Tanenbaum, 2003). After the routing procedure, the wavelength assignment (WA) algorithm has to decide which available channel should be used to establish the call (Mukherjee 2000; Zhou and Yuan 2002). Again, some heuristics are used in classical RWA to solve the wavelength assignment problem. In the next subsections we present an approach for wavelength assignment using evolutionary computation and a routing algorithm based on ACO trained by Particle Swarm Optimization that takes into account the link lengths and the real-time availability in the links of the candidate lightpath.

Wavelength Assignment with Evolutionary Strategy

There are some well-known WA algorithms for optical networks (Zang *et al.* 1999; Stoica and Sengupta 2000; Alfouzan and Jayasumana 2003). Among them, we can cite: First Fit (FF), Random-Pick (RP), Most Used (MU), Least Used (LU), Max-Sum (MS) and Relative Capacity Loss (RCL) (Zang *et al.* 1999). The FF algorithm chooses the

channel with the lowest index not used in the route. The RP algorithm selects randomly a channel available in the route. The MU algorithm chooses the most used wavelength in the entire network for the route. It presents a similar behavior when compared to the FF algorithm, as it tends to use the wavelengths already used in other links of the network and lets other wavelengths for longer lightpaths. On the other hand, the LU algorithm chooses the least used wavelength in the entire network and spreads the used wavelengths like in the RP algorithm. The max-sum algorithm considers all possible paths in the network and attempts to maximize the remaining path capacities after the lightpath establishment. The relative capacity loss algorithm is based on the MS algorithm by normalizing the evaluation formula used by the MS algorithm.

However, the previous cited WA heuristics were not designed for networks with physical layer limitations. In transparent optical networks, the signal remains in the optical domain between the edge nodes, accumulating noise and other degrading effects, which are not removed. This occurs mainly in transparent networks since there is no signal conversion from optical to electrical in regenerators, such as in opaque networks. Therefore, an improper choice of the wavelength can severely degrade the signal quality and the network performance. Thus, recently, some impairment aware wavelength assignment (IA-WA) algorithms have been proposed to overcome this limitation. He and Brandt-Pearce (He and Brandt-Pearce 2006B) proposed an IA-WA algorithm, called FFwO, which uses the idea of choosing the wavelength according to a list, as in the FF approach, however the order of the list is designed to minimize the occurrence of adjacent channels. The same authors (He and Brandt-Pearce 2006A) proposed other IA-WA algorithm (FFwSS) that tries to find the least physical impaired channel. In the sequence, He *et al.* (He *et al.* 2007) proposed a hybrid algorithm, called AFFwSS, that combines the two previous approaches by switching between them based on a threshold pre-determined in a preliminary calibration simulation. Using a similar approach, Fonseca *et al.* (Fonseca *et al.* 2004) proposed a wavelength assignment algorithm based on the first-fit algorithm using an off-line optimized priority lists. These priority lists are determined using two different classes of heuristics aimed at finding sub-optimal solutions due to a Four Wave Mixing (FWM) noise. Marsden *et al.* (Marsden and Maruta 2008) used a FF scheme in a network impaired by FWM noise, checking the QoS requirements before the connection is set up. In a network impaired by the Residual Dispersion (RD), Zulkifli *et al.* proposed (Zulkifli *et al.* 2007) two heuristics: Best Fit (BF), where wavelengths are indexed according to their end-to-end RD from the lowest to the highest value and Just Enough (JE), that assigns the wavelength that has the closest value of RD below the requested residual dispersion QoS threshold.

All these IA-WA algorithms tend to optimize the network performance for a single impairment, not considering a situation where different impairments have impact on the signal quality and network performance. In a network scenario where impairments that lead to different effects take place, it is difficult to find a first fit list that can balance all impairments together in order to improve the network performance. For example, one must spread the channels to minimize the FWM impairment. On the other hand, one must assign channels as close as possible to the zero residual dispersion wavelength in order to minimize the residual dispersion effect.

In this section we describe an evolutionary strategy based wavelength assignment algorithm for all-optical networks. The main idea is to determine the wavelength activation order in a first fit algorithm taking into account the physical layer impairments by using an optimization algorithm inspired in evolutionary computation concepts, called evolutionary strategies. Our algorithm is, in principle, well suitable for any number of physical impairments, since the first fit list is ob-

tained according to the overall network blocking probability. Thus, it tends to balance all relevant impairments to improve the network performance. The proposed algorithm was designed to satisfy the requirements imposed by our application constraints. The optimization algorithm uses an external archive to store the best solutions obtained by the evolutionary algorithm from previous iterations. The pseudo-code of our algorithm is shown in Table 1.

The external archive is composed by a population with P individuals, where an individual consists of a potential solution for the problem. In this case, each individual is a possible wavelength assignment list with W channels to be used by our WA algorithm. Each channel is labeled with a number from 1 to W according to its position on the wavelength grid. One should note that a channel is not allowed to appear more than once on the same individual.

The fitness is evaluated for all the individuals separately. For each individual, we run a network simulation with the wavelength assignment order

Table 1. Pseudo-code of our evolutionary algorithm used to determine the wave- length assignment order

Pseudo Code	
1	Initialize the external archive with a random population P.
2	Evaluate the fitness of the individuals in the external archive.
3	While the stopping criterion is not reached do.
4	Select an individual from external archive using Roulette wheel (ind 1)
5	Clone this individual.
6	Mutate this individual (Indmutated)
7	Select randomly other individual (ind2)
8	Perform binary tournament between (ind1) and (ind2)
9	If (Indmutated) wins do
10	Replace (Indmutated) in the position of (ind2) in the external archive
11	End

and the fitness of this individual is the blocking probability obtained from this simulation. The lower is the blocking probability, the stronger is the individual.

We perform a predefined number of iterations until there is no significant variation on the network performance. In each iteration, the algorithm selects an individual from the external archive using roulette wheel, *i.e.* individuals with a lower blocking probability have more chance to be selected. It is because the better individuals will need a lower number of modifications to reach the best wavelength assignment order. Because of the constraint imposed by the fact that an individual cannot present repeated wavelengths, the crossover operator is not suitable for this application. Hence, a mutation operator based on swapping positions in the list was used.

After the selection, using the roulette wheel, the selected individual is cloned and a single swap mutation is applied, *i.e.* only one permutation is performed on the clone individual. Then, a binary tournament is performed between this new individual and other individual randomly selected from the external archive. If the modified clone wins, *i.e.* if it presents a lower blocking probability in the network simulation, this individual replaces the individual randomly selected for the tournament in the external archive.

One should observe that this evolutionary process to obtain the optimized first fit list for WA must run offline, *i.e.* prior to the network operation. In the online operation of the network the list is already available. In fact, the optimized first fit list can be frequently updated, to account for any change in network topology or device characteristics, by an offline simulation process that should run in the background to the normal network operation. Because of this reason, we call this offline optimization process as training stage.

The optical network simulation is performed as follows: upon a call request, the route is defined by a routing algorithm using the shortest path cost function. Then, a wavelength is selected by the WA algorithm. After that, the pulse broadening due to residual dispersion is evaluated. If it is above a maximum percentage of pulse broadening $\delta\%_{QoS}$, the call is blocked. Similar checking is performed to Optical Signal to Noise Ratio (OSNR) in the output of the chosen lightpath. If it is above the pre-determined level ($OSNR_{QoS}$) the call is established, otherwise it is blocked. The physical layer models used for the evaluation of the pulse broadening due to residual dispersion and evaluation of OSNR will be described in the next section. The blocked calls are lost. The blocking probability is obtained from the ratio between the number of blocked calls and the total number of call requests. Our algorithm also blocks a call if there is no wavelength available for the respective lightpath.

For each network simulation a set of 10^7 calls are generated by choosing randomly (uniform distribution) the source-destination pair. The call request is characterized as a Poisson process. We assume circuit switched bidirectional connections in two different fibers and no wavelength conversion capabilities. The default parameters used in our simulations are listed in Table 2. Amplifier gains are set to compensate for the link losses. According to equations (10) and (11) in (Bastos-Filho, 2011), the residual dispersion is null at *1541.35* nm.

Figure 1 shows the network topology used in our simulations. It is a large network similar to the NSFNET. We used the physical layer model proposed by Pereira *et al.* (Pereira *et al.*, 2009) to perform the network simulations. This model takes into account the four wave mixing effect in the optical fibers, the spontaneous noise emitted by the optical amplifiers, as well as the gain saturation effect at the output of the optical amplifiers. The broadening of the optical pulses due to the residual dispersion effect is taken into account as in (Bastos-Filho *et al.*, 2011).

All the simulations were carried out in three different scenarios S_1, S_2 and S_3. S_1 scenario takes into account only the FWM impairment, S_2 sce-

Table 2. Default simulation parameters

Parameter	Value	Definition
P_{Laser}	−4 dBm	Output transmission power
P_{sat}	19 dBm	Amplifier output saturation power.
$OSNR_{in}$	30 dB	Input optical signal-to-noise ratio.
$OSNR_{QoS}$	23 dB	Optical signal-to-noise ratio for QoS criterion.
B	40 Gbps	Transmission bit rate.
B_o	100 GHz	Optical filter bandwidth.
W	32	Number of wavelengths in an optical link.
Δf	100 GHz	Channel spacing.
λ_i	1529.56 nm	The lower wavelength of the grid.
λ_0	1557 nm	Zero dispersion wavelength for transmission fiber.
λ_{0DCF}	1550 nm	Zero dispersion wavelength for compensation fiber.
α	0.2 dB/km	Fiber loss coefficient.
L_{Mx}	3 dB	Multiplexer loss.
L_{Dx}	3 dB	Demultiplexer loss.
L_{Sw}	3 dB	Optical switch loss.
$F_0 (NF)$	3.162 (5 dB)	Amplifier noise factor (Noise figure)
$D_{TF}(@1541.35\ nm)$	0.939 ps/km.nm	Dispersion coefficient of the transmission fiber.
$S_{TF}(@1541.35\ nm)$	0.06 ps/km.nm²	Dispersion slope of the transmission fiber.
$D_{DCF}(@1541.35\ nm)$	−1.87 ps/km.nm	Dispersion coefficient of the compensation fiber.
$S_{DCF}(@1541.35\ nm)$	−126.18 ps/km.nm²	Dispersion slope of the compensation fiber.
$\delta_{\%QoS}$	10%	Maximum percentage of pulse broadening

Figure 1. Network topology used in our simulations

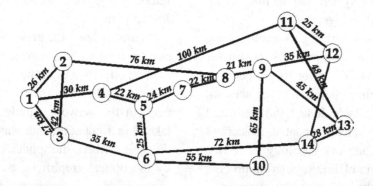

nario considers both FWM effect and residual dispersion effect, whereas S_3 scenario just considers the residual dispersion. Our proposed IA-WA algorithm is compared to others WA algorithms such as First Fit (FF), Best Fit (BF), and Random Pick (RP).

Figure 2 presents the blocking probability distribution for the three scenarios S_1, S_2 and S_3 for a network load of *60* Erlang. For the simulations of Figure 2 we used the BF as WA algorithm. One can note that the calls are blocked in S_1 due to OSNR degradation (FWM), whereas in the scenario S_3

Figure 2. Blocking probability distribution for the three scenarios

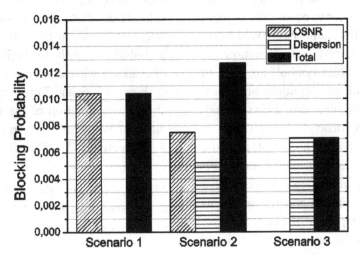

the calls are blocked only by dispersion effects. The causes for blocking in S_2 are balanced.

Figure 3 presents the convergence curves for the training stage for the three different scenarios S_1 (circles), S_2 (triangles) and S_3 (squares). As can be seen from Figure 3, our proposal achieved a stable state after *3000* iterations with a blocking probability around *0.00081* for S_1, after *1000* iterations with a blocking probability around *0.0086* for S_2 and after *1200* iterations with a blocking probability around *0.0065* for S_3. One can observe

that in any case, after about *1000* iterations the blocking probability is reduced by about one order of magnitude. Table 3 presents the wavelength assignment lists for scenarios S_1, S_2 and S_3 found by the evolutionary algorithm in the training stage. The list numbers represent the first to the 32nd wavelength of the grid used in these simulations. For example, for the S_1 scenario the first wavelength to be used is the 5th wavelength in the grid.

Figure 4 shows the number of noise components generated by FWM and relative difference between the number of generated noise components as a function of the number of active channels in the network in scenarios S_1 and S_2. We do not present any result for S_3 since this scenario just considers the residual dispersion. Figure 4

Figure 3. Evolution of the blocking probability as a function of the number of iterations in the training stage, for the three scenarios

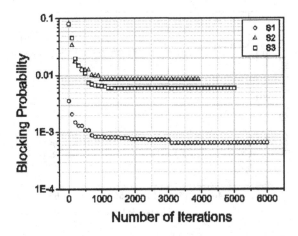

Table 3. Optimized FF lists found after training stage

Scenario	List
S_1	5 30 3 17 26 1 8 24 29 18 9 16 20 22 7 11 15 23 13 6 12 4 10 21 14 2 19 32 25 28 27 31
S_2	21 24 9 22 18 25 11 8 14 7 10 16 23 13 17 20 19 15 12 27 5 6 4 2 3 26 30 28 29 32 1 31
S_3	25 20 17 8 9 19 24 15 16 11 23 22 10 13 14 21 7 12 18 6 26 27 5 4 3 28 2 32 1 29 31 30

was obtained for a single link, rather than for the network, to make it easier to control the number of active channels. The number of FWM noise components was obtained from Equation (3) (Bastos-Filho,2011). Solid symbols are used to present the number of noise components generated for three distinct situations: FF (squares), OpFF in scenario S_1 (triangles) and OpFF in scenario S_2 (circles). The open symbols are used to present the relative difference between the FF and OpFF cases. Figure 4 shows how effective the OpFF algorithm is in reducing the detrimental effect of FWM, compared to the FF algorithm. For example, for *15* active wavelengths in a single link of the network the OpFF leads to the generation of half the number of noise components due to FWM than the FF algorithm, for scenario S_1. For the scenario S_2, the reduction in the number of noise components obtained from the OpFF is *20%*. This is because in S_2 scenario the network is also impaired by residual dispersion. Figure 4 also shows that as the number of active channels increases, towards using *32* out of *32* possible channels, the benefit of using the OpFF decreas-

es. However, one should keep in mind that in this extreme situation, where most of the channels are active at the same time, the network blocking probability would be too high anyhow, due to lack of available wavelengths.

Figures 5, 6, and 7 present the blocking probability as a function of the network load for *4* different WA algorithms in scenarios S_1, S_2 and S_3, respectively. The WA algorithms are first fit

Figure 5. Blocking probability as a function of the network load for 4 different WA algorithms in scenario S_1

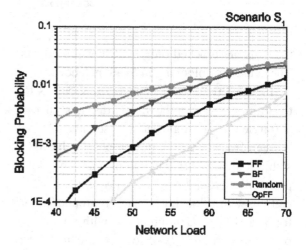

Figure 4. Number of noise components generated by FWM and relative difference between the number of noise components generated by the FF and by the optimized FF, as a function of the number of active channels in the network, in scenarios S1 and S2.

Figure 6. Blocking probability as a function of the network load for 4 different WA algorithms in scenario S2

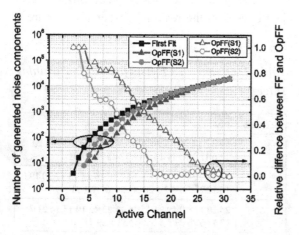

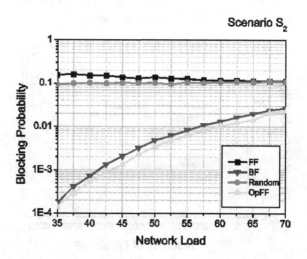

Figure 7. Blocking probability as a function of the network load for 4 different WA algorithms in scenario S_3

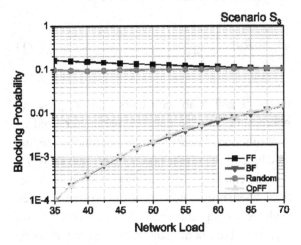

Figure 7. Blocking probability as a function of the network load for 4 different WA algorithms in scenario S_3

(squares), random (circles), best fit (up-triangles) and our proposed optimized first fit (down-triangles).

In all cases, the BF and OpFF WA algorithms outperformed the FF and the random algorithms. In the *S3* scenario BF and OpFF achieved a similar performance since the BF algorithm is designed to avoid dispersion effects. However, the OpFF algorithm obtained a slightly better performance for *S2* scenario. Furthermore, our proposal outperformed all others approaches, including the BF algorithm, for the *S1* scenario. This occurs because the BF algorithm cannot treat other effects such as FWM.

Routing with Ant Colony Optimization

In this subsection of the chapter, we describe and analyze the performance of an adaptive Impairment Aware Routing Algorithm (IA-RWA) for transparent optical networks based on Ant Colony Optimization (ACO). We proposed a novel approach for the cost function, to be considered by the ants in the route calculation based on optical links physical distance and the optical link wavelengths

availability. The algorithm was trained by another optimization technique called Particle Swarm Optimization (PSO). We compare the performance of our proposal to the classical ACO approach applied for routing in communications networks and to other network-layer routing algorithms. We show that our IA-RWA algorithm can learn during the training stage and adapts itself to the network conditions, performing equally or even better than the classical approaches.

Although an ant is a simple creature, collectively ants can present a useful behavior for performing tasks, such as discovering the shortest path between a food source and the nest (Caro and Dorigo, 1998). The colony shares information through Stigmergy, that is a form of indirect communication used by ants in nature by laying a chemical substance called pheromone. The pheromone induces changes in the environment, which can be sensed by other ants. In recent years, a number of models of collective intelligence of ants have been proposed to solve combinatorial optimization problems, such as the asymmetric traveling salesman problem, graph coloring problem, vehicle routing problem and routing in communications networks.

Schoondenwoerd *et al.* (Schoonderwoerd, 1997) proposed an adaptive routing algorithm for telephone networks using the ant-based agents. In Schoonderwoerd's algorithm, the routing tables are refreshed over time. This is caused by the pheromone trail left by the ants. Bonabeau *et al.* (Bonabeau *et al.*, 1998) improved the performance of Schoondenwoerd's algorithm by integrating the principle of dynamic programming, and Ngo *et al.* (2004) adapted the algorithm to WDM optical networks.

Pavani *et al.* (Pavani *et al.*, 2008; Pavani and Waldman, 2008) used ACO for impairment aware routing and wavelength assignment and also for restoration in optical networks. They consider only the optical amplifier noise and optical power budget as physical impairments.

An artificial ant can be implemented as a simple procedure that simulates the laying and sensing of pheromone. Each ant is originated in the source node S and explores the network trying to find the destination node D. Basically, the ants are guided by the pheromone and should have a predefined lifetime (T_{Life}) to find their destination. T_{Life} quantify how long an ant remains moving along the network. An ant needs to be able to find the end of the path until T_{Life} is reached. This preset lifetime helps to avoid loops. When the ant finds the destination node, it returns to the source node in the reverse direction by adding pheromone to the link. The pheromone layered can depend on the total lightpath link. However, in this paper, the pheromone deposited on the routing tables by an ant along the nodes included in the ligthpath is unitary. Furthermore, the colony consists of a data structure that generates ants and records their journey times and the nodes that they pass. In our approach we periodically generate a group of n_{ants} ants with a frequency f and the simulation has a total duration of T_{Total}. After T_{Total} times, the pheromone table state indicates the best route. The ants can be thought as control messages that are sent along the network in order to update the routing tables.

However, this operation alone can lead to a stagnation process. One of the approaches used to mitigate stagnation is to configure ants so that they do not solely rely on sensing pheromone. For this purpose, one can set a mixed probability function for an ant to decide between different links. This can be done using both pheromone concentration and a heuristic function (Sim and Sun 2003). For example, an ant selects a link probabilistically using a composition function of the cost of the link and the pheromone left by previous ants. One common approach to this function is presented in Equation (1), where P_{ij} is the weight used by the ant to choose the next node to visit, Ph_{ij} is the pheromone quantity in the link ij, d_{ij} is the physical length of the link ij and

d'_{ij} is the normalized length of the link ij (Caro and Dorigo 1998). In this case, the ants choose the path that presents the higher P_{ij}.

$$P_{ij} = Rand() \frac{Ph_{ij}^{\alpha}}{d_{ij}'^{\beta}} \qquad (1)$$

where α and β are constants that weights the pheromone and the network parameter used as cost function. $Rand()$ is a random number generated by a uniform distribution in the interval [0,1].

One can also use a technique called evaporation, where in each iteration the pheromone values at all the routing tables are reduced by a predefined factor δ. This parameter describes the ratio of pheromone that evaporates in a link per iteration. δ is used to prevent pheromone concentration in optimal paths from being excessively high. A high concentration of pheromone in some links can excessively polarize the ants. This can affect the ability to explore other routes in the case of network failures.

We propose and evaluate the performance of a new equation to induce the ants choices depicted in Equation (2). We aimed to include physical layer aspect, the link wavelength availability of the network links (λ_{ij}). As can be seen from Equation (2), the percentage of available wavelengths (λ'_{ij}) multiplies the previous equation and is weighted by γ.

$$P_{ij} = Rand() \frac{Ph_{ij}^{\alpha} \Delta \lambda_{ij}'^{\gamma}}{d_{ij}'^{\beta}} \qquad (2)$$

In order to find the best parameters α, β and γ of Equation (1) and Equation (2), we used another optimization technique called Particle Swarm Optimization (PSO). We call this process as the training phase, since the IA-RWA algorithm runs several times for different values of the parameters, to find their best values. This process occurs offline, which means that it occurs before the network operation. The online routing processes occur with the use of ACO and Equations (1) or (2), with the parameters found by PSO. Martins-Filho *et al.* (Martins-Filho *et al.*, 2008) have also used PSO to find the best parameters for a cost function of an IA-RWA algorithm. However, their IA-RWA algorithm does not use ACO to find the routes. Particle Swarm Optimization is a bio-inspired technique proposed by Kennedy and Eberhart in 1995. We used the PSO recommended by Bratton and Kennedy (Bratton and Kennedy, 2007), following the pseudo-code proposed therein. The search space dimensions number was defined according to the used equation. In Equation (1), the optimization problem have two dimensions (α and β), and in Equation 2, three dimensions (α, β and γ). Particles velocities were updated using the constriction factor approach (Clerc and Kennedy, 2002), to avoid overflight across the search space and improve performance. We used k equal to *1*, acceleration constants (c_1 and c_2) equals to *2.05* for both, respecting the constriction factor condition of $\varphi > 4$, for overflight free operation. We used the L_{best} swarm model with ring topology (Bratton and Kennedy 2007) because this is the recommended model for multimodal problems. *21* particles were used in all simulations because we had plans to use clan-based swarm model (Carvalho and Bastos-Filho 2008) on this problem with three clans of seven particles, and compare PSO approaches performance. This swarm size respects the standard defined by Bratton and Kennedy (Bratton and Kennedy 2007).

For our simulations, we observed that *150* iterations are enough for the algorithm to converge. This can be justified by the fact that the se arch space is not too large. Therefore, this number of iterations was established as the training phase period. For each scenario, we repeat five times the training process. The blocking probabilities were calculated as the average of the simulation results.

Each ant have the lifetime configured to $T_{Life} = 2N$, where N is the number of network nodes. Thus, the colony had sufficient time to find optimal solutions with low error rates, and looping ants were quickly destroyed. Colonies have *50* ants and new generations occur in each iteration (*i.e. f=1*) with a maximum of five ants (*i.e. n_{ants}=5*), until the colony is full-filled. After find a route, each ant returns for its origin incrementing pheromone quantity in one unit. The best value for δ found in previous simulations was *0.67*, and we used this in all simulations. We trained and analyzed our algorithm performance in two network topologies with *16* and *32* wavelengths per link. Training network load was defined with the following strategy: we ran RWA simulations with shortest path algorithm, verified load value where this algorithm had calls blocking probability equal to *1%*, and used this network load for our algorithm training. However, sometimes this load value allowed our algorithm to return zero blocking rates quickly. To avoid this type of situation, we increased the network load until it reaches blocking probabilities not equal to zero or not too close to this.

For each network simulation, a set of at least 10^5 calls is generated choosing randomly the source-destination pairs. We used 10^6 calls when the blocking probability is around 10^{-5}. The call request process is characterized as a Poisson process and the time duration for each established call is characterized as an exponential process. Our simulation algorithm works as presented in the last subsection. In this subsection we consider the following effects as physical impairments: amplifier gain saturation, ASE emission, crosstalk in the switch and polarization mode dispersion. Figure 8 shows the network topologies used in our simulations. The first one is a regular and symmetric topology. The second one reproduces the Finland topology for long haul communication. We used this second one to test the routing

Figure 8. Network topology used in our simulations

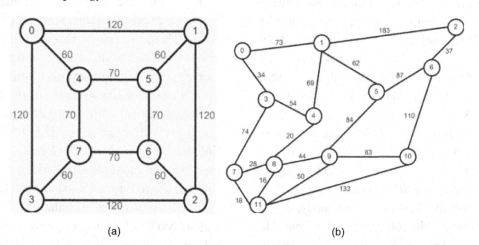

(a)   (b)

algorithm performance on an irregular topology. The amplifier gains are initially set to compensate for the total link losses and the default parameters used in our simulations are shown in Table 4.

We present the results for the training phase of the algorithm for the two network topologies analyzed. Figure 9 presents PSO convergence for

Table 4. Default simulation parameters

Parameter	Value	Definition
P_{Laser}	−3 dBm	Transmitter output power.
P_{sat}	19 dBm	Amplifier output saturation power.
$OSNR_{in}$	40 dB	Optical Signal to Noise Ratio at the transmitter.
$OSNR_{QoS}$	23 dB	Minimum Optical Signal to Noise Ratio at the receiver.
B	40 Gbps	Transmission rate.
α	0.2 dB/km	Fiber loss coefficient.
L_{Mx}	3 dB	Multiplexer insertion loss.
L_{Dx}	3 dB	Demultiplexer insertion loss.
L_{Sw}	3 dB	Switch Loss.
ε	−40 dB	Isolation between ports at the switch.
D_{PMD}	0.01 ps/km$^{1/2}$	PMD coefficient.
F_0 (NF)	3.162 (5 dB)	Amplifier noise factor (Noise figure).

the training phase of the RWA algorithms based on ACO with Regular network. In the scenario of Figure 9(a) and Figure 9(c), ACO Standard and ACO Proposed were trained with *40* Erlangs and *16* wavelengths per link. In the scenario of Figure 9(b) and Figure 9(d), the training was done with *85* Erlangs and *32* wavelengths per link.

In Figure 9(a) scenario, the convergence occurred around the *85th* iteration, with blocking probability of approximately *0.013*. In Figure 9(c) scenario, the PSO converged earlier (around the *30th* iteration), reaching blocking probability around *0.009*. In Figure 9(b) scenario occurred the fastest convergence. In the second iteration of this simulation, the obtained blocking probability was about *0.0026*, and remained with the same value during the following iterations. In Figure 9(d), PSO achieved a blocking probability equal to *0.001* at the *15th* iteration, not reaching any lower value.

Table 5 shows the values of the cost function parameters obtained from the training phase simulations for the RWA based on ACO algorithms with the Regular network. In the scenario with *32* wavelengths, *85* Erlangs and ACO Proposal, three particles with different configurations had the same blocking probability value. Through performance test simulations with *10^6* calls, it

Figure 9. Training phase results for RWA algorithms based on ACO on regular network: training load: (a) standard ACO 40 Erlangs; (b) standard ACO 85 Erlangs; (c) proposed ACO 40 Erlangs; (d) proposed ACO 85 Erlangs

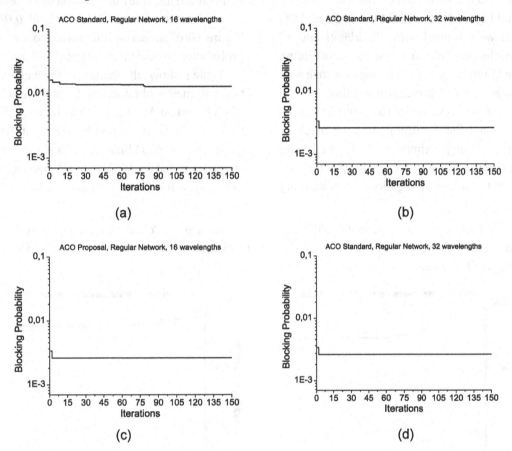

(a)

(b)

(c)

(d)

Table 5. Values of cost function parameters obtained by the training process for RWA based on ACO algorithms with the Regular network

Regular Network Configuration	α	β	γ
16 wavelengths, 40 Erlangs and ACO Standard	1.46175	1.92726	–
16 wavelengths, 40 Erlangs and ACO Proposal	2.08252	2.20869	2.96475
32 wavelengths, 85 Erlangs and ACO Standard	2.67244	3.39465	–
32 wavelengths, 85 Erlangs and ACO Proposal	3.50144	3.01474	3.48118
32 wavelengths, 85 Erlangs and ACO Proposal	1.19588	1.56004	3.98344
32 wavelengths, 85 Erlangs and ACO Proposal	0.110748	1.99878	3.99688

was confirmed that these combinations of weight values really generate similar results. The values $(\alpha=3.50144, \beta=3.01474, \gamma=3.48118)$ were chosen for the ACO Proposal performance evaluation on Regular network with *32* wavelengths per link, because the particle with this configuration was the first to reach the lowest call blocking probability during training phase.

Figure 10 presents PSO convergence for the RWA algorithms based on ACO training phase with Finland network. In the scenario of Figure 10(a) and Figure 10(c), ACO Standard and ACO Proposal were trained with *40* Erlangs and *16* wavelengths per link. In the scenario of Figure 10(b) and Figure 10(d), the training was done with *90* Erlangs and *32* wavelengths per link.

In Figure 10(a) scenario, the convergence occurred around the *75th* iteration, with blocking probability of approximately *0.035*. In Figure 10(c) scenario, the PSO converged earlier (around the *60th* iteration), reaching blocking probability

around *0.028*. In Figure 10(b) scenario occurred the slowest convergence. Only in the *80th* iteration of this simulation the minimum blocking probability was obtained, with value around *0.036*. In Figure 10(d) scenario, PSO achieved a blocking probability around *0.031* at the *75th* iteration.

Table 6 shows the values for the weight function parameters obtained by the training stage for RWA based on ACO algorithms with the Finland network. In both scenarios, the most relevant parameter for ACO Standard was pheromone accumulation, and for ACO Proposal was wavelength availability for *16* wavelengths and pheromone

Figure 10. Training phase results for RWA algorithms based on ACO on Finland network: training load: (a) standard ACO 40 Erlangs; (b) standard ACO 85 Erlangs; (c) proposed ACO 40 Erlangs; (d) proposed ACO 85 Erlangs

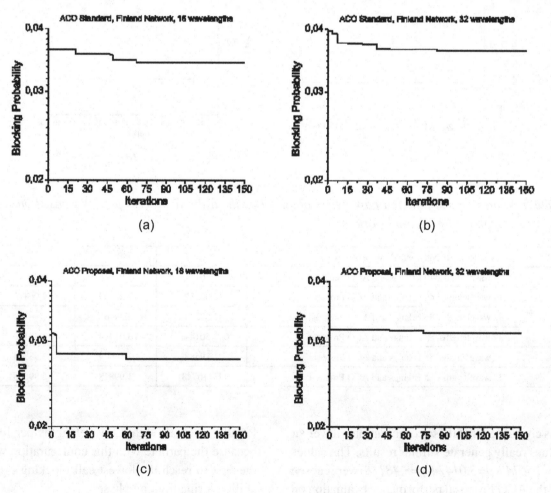

Table 6. Induction equation weight values obtained by the training process for RWA based on ACO algorithms with the Finland network

Regular Network Configuration	α	β	γ
16 wavelengths, 40 Erlangs and ACO Standard	0.398342	0.00283992	–
16 wavelengths, 40 Erlangs and ACO Proposal	0.729141	1.32989	3.33693
32 wavelengths, 90 Erlangs and ACO Standard	3.97025	2.80346	–
32 wavelengths, 90 Erlangs and ACO Proposal	4.46353	0.70601	0.10476

accumulation for *32* wavelengths. One can observe that the importance of the coefficients changed according to network conditions.

We tested and compared the performance of the RWA algorithms in four scenarios, changing network topology, load and wavelength availability per link. Figure 11(a) and Figure 11(b) present the network blocking probability as a function of network load, for five different RWA algorithms, obtained on the Regular topology with *16* wavelengths and *32* wavelengths, respectively. The values shown are the average values of the total blocking probabilities, obtained from five simulation runs.

Figure 11(a) shows that the proposed ACO achieved the best performance for loads of *25* and *30* Erlangs. When the load was increased to *35*

Erlangs and beyond, the RWA algorithms based on hop count, and load balancing presented slightly better performance than the proposed ACO. However, for any network load our proposed ACO algorithm performed better than the standard ACO or the shortest path algorithms. These results show that taking into account the wavelength availability in the weight function leads to an improved performance for the proposed ACO, compared to the standard ACO algorithm.

Figure 11(b) shows similar results to Figure 11(a), however with *32* wavelengths per link. In this scenario there is no call blocking due to lack of available wavelength. Instead, the call blockings are due to the physical impairments. In this scenario the proposed ACO algorithm outperformed by a large margin the other algorithms. This result

Figure 11. Performance comparison of the RWA algorithms: regular network links with (a) 16 wavelengths, and (b) 32 wavelengths

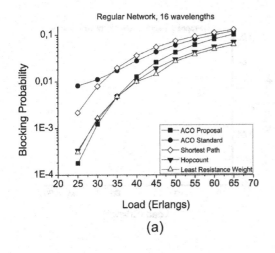
(a)

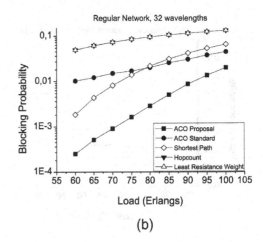
(b)

indicates that it is worth finding the ideal balance between pheromone, link length and wavelength availability in the ACO cost function, through the optimization of the α, β and γ parameters.

Figure 12 shows the boxplot graphics for the standard ACO (a)(b) and the proposed ACO IA-RWA (c)(d) in the regular topology, for *16* (a)(c) and *32* (b)(d) wavelengths. Each box was obtained from five simulations in the same conditions. The higher value of the standard deviation obtained in the simulations was *0.00158*, for *60* Erlangs and *16* wavelengths. The largest percentage change between the lower and upper limits was *23.49%*,

for *25* Erlangs and *16* wavelengths. These variations can be considered negligible when compared to the blocking probability values resulting from increases in network load.

Figure 13(a) and Figure 13(b) shows the blocking probability as a function of network load for different RWA algorithm, obtained from Finland network with *16* wavelengths and *32* wavelengths, respectively. These figures show that the proposed ACO, the standard ACO and the shortest path algorithms presented similar performance, which is considerably better than the hop count and LRW algorithms

Figure 12. Boxplot graphics for the standard ACO (a)(b) and the proposed ACO IA-RWA (c)(d) in the regular topology, for 16 (a)(c) and 32 (b)(d) wavelengths

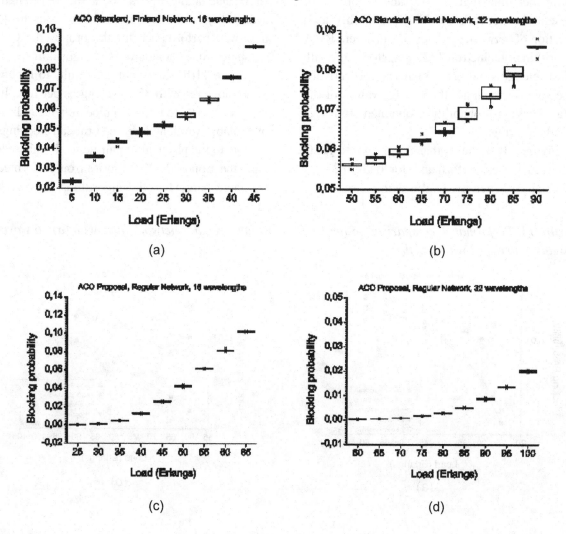

Figure 13. Performance comparison of the RWA algorithms: Finland network links with (a) 16 wave-lengths, and (b) 32 wavelengths

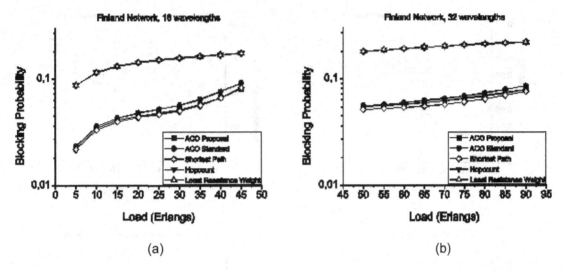

(a)

(b)

Figure 14 shows boxplot graphics for the standard ACO (a)(b) and the proposed ACO IA-RWA (c)(d) in the Finland topology, for *16* (a)(c) and *32* (b)(d) wavelengths. The standard deviation obtained in simulations with ACO Proposal was 0.00187488, to *55* Erlangs and *32* wavelengths. The largest percentage change between the lower and upper limits was 9.54%, to *15* Erlangs and *16* wavelengths for ACO proposed. These variations can be considered negligible when compared to the blocking probability values resulting from increases in network load.

FUTURE RESEARCH DIRECTIONS

An important aspect of the use of computational intelligence in operational processes of optical networks, especially in routing and wavelength assignment, is its response time. Usually the network operation requires fast responses from the algorithms, which may not be achieved by some computational intelligence techniques. One possible way to overcome this limitation is the use of simple transfer functions for the online calculations of the network operation algorithm, whereas the function coefficients are obtained by offline simulations, in a planning phase, prior to the network operation. In this offline simulations the computational intelligence techniques can be applied to obtain the function coefficients that optimize the network operation. Therefore, the time consuming processes involved in the computational intelligence optimization techniques are moved from the online network algorithm to the offline algorithm optimization. This methodology has been successfully demonstrated for impairment-aware routing and wavelength assignment algorithms (Chaves, 2010, 2011). Another possible approach is the use of parallel computing infrastructure to accelerate the computational intelligence processes, reducing the response times. As parallel computers become increasingly powerful, compact, and affordable, we believe this computation time can be greatly reduced for real applications. Bastos-Filho et al. have investigated the use of parallel computing in Graphic Processing Units with CUDA for remote and distributed simulation of optical networks (Bastos-Filho, 2011a, 2011b). A third promising approach is the use of hardware implementations. We believe that Field Programmable Gate

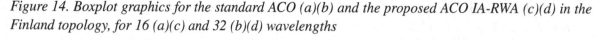

Figure 14. Boxplot graphics for the standard ACO (a)(b) and the proposed ACO IA-RWA (c)(d) in the Finland topology, for 16 (a)(c) and 32 (b)(d) wavelengths

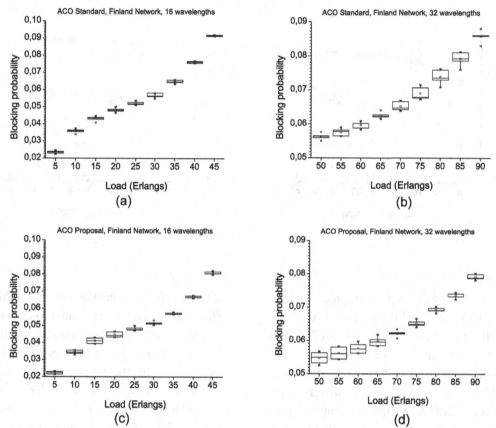

Array (Roebuck, 2011) can be successfully used to implement these algorithms. In some preliminary experiments regarding the implementation of Hopfield Neural Networks for routing in a six-node network, we obtained a speedup of 78, when compared to a desktop computer with an I5 processor and 4 GB RAM.

On the other hand, as the optical transmission technology is evolving to an elastic, gridless architecture, with new modulation formats and new multiplexing schemes, such as O-OFDM (optical orthogonal frequency division multiplexing), new challenges are posed to the optical network operation and planning processes. For example, instead of a routing and wavelength assignment (RWA) algorithm, this new generation of optical networks will require a routing and spectrum assignment (RSA) algorithm, which has different constraints and degrees of freedom to be dealt with. Therefore, these elastic optical networks will require new operation and planning algorithms (Zhang, 2012), which can make use of computational intelligence techniques.

Other efforts have been made to understand certain behaviors in networks. There are some models that have been created to explain emergence effects in networks (Barabasi, 2003). This area is called Network Sciences. Some of these recent approaches make use of interesting metrics, such as natural connectivity, that can be used, for instance, to guide routing and wavelength assignment processes.

CONCLUSION

This chapter reviewed some recent applications of computational intelligence to solve common problems in optical networks, specifically our focus was on the impairment-aware routing and wavelength assignment. These concepts can be extended to be used in problems like regenerator placement and physical topology design problems for transparent and translucent dynamic provisioned wavelength routed optical networks. The number of papers on applications of computational intelligence in optical networks continues to increase, indicating that these novel tools may be very useful to the optical network designers and operators in the near future.

REFERENCES

Alfouzan, I., & Jayasumana, A. (2003). An adaptive wavelength assignment algorithm for WDM networks. *Optical Networks Magazine*, *4*(2), 46–55.

Azodolmolky, S., Klinkowski, M., Marin, E., Careglio, D., Pareta, J., & Tomkos, I. (2009). A survey on physical layer impairments aware routing and wavelength assignment algorithms in optical networks. *Computer Networks*, *53*(7), 926–944. doi:10.1016/j.comnet.2008.11.014.

Barabasi, A.-L. (2003). *Linked – How everything is connected to everything*. New York: Plume.

Bastos-Filho, C. J. A., Chaves, D. A. R., Silva, F. S. F., Pereira, H. A., & Martins-Filho, J. F. (2011). Wavelength assignment for physical-layer-impaired optical networks using evolutionary computation. *Journal of Optical Communications and Networking*, *3*(3), 178–188. doi:10.1364/JOCN.3.000178.

Bastos-Filho, C. J. A., Oliveira Júnior, M. A. C., Silva, D. R. C., & Santana, R. A. (2011a). Optimizing a routing algorithm based on Hopfield neural networks for graphic processing units. In *Proceedings of IEEE Foundations on Computational Intelligence - SSCI 2011* (pp. 88-93). IEEE.

Bastos-Filho, C. J. A., Santana, R. A., Silva, D. R. C., Martins-Filho, J. F., & Chaves, D. A. R. (2010). Hopfield neural networks for routing in all-optical networks. In *Proceedings of the International Conference on Transparent Optical Networks* (pp. 1–4). IEEE.

Bastos-Filho, C. J. A., Santos, A. M., Chaves, D. A. R., & Martins Filho, J. F. (2011b). A model to allow remote and distributed simulation of optical networks using XML. In *Proceedings of the 2011 SBMO/IEEE MTT-S International Microwave and Optoelectronics Conference*, (pp. 430-434). IEEE.

Bonabeau, E., Henaux, F., Gu'erin, S., Snyers, D., Kuntz, P., & Theraulaz, G. (1998). Routing in telecommunications networks with ant-like agents. In Albayrak & Garijo (Eds.), *Intelligent Agents for Telecommunication Applications — Proceedings of the Second International Workshop on Intelligent Agents for Telecommunica-tion (IATA'98)* (LNCS), (vol. 1437). Berlin: Springer-Verlag.

Bratton, D., & Kennedy, J. (2007). Defining a standard for particle swarm optimization. In *Proceedings of the Swarm Intelligence Symposium, 2007*. IEEE.

Caro, G. D., & Dorigo, M. (1998). *Antnet: Distributed stigmergetic control for communications networks*. Academic Press.

Carvalho, D., & Bastos-Filho, C. (2008). Clan particle swarm optimization. In *Proceedings of Evolutionary Computation, 2008*. IEEE.

Chaves, D. A. R., Aguiar, D. O., Bastos-Filho, C. J. A., & Martins-Filho, J. F. (2010). Fast and adaptive impairment aware routing and wavelength assignment algorithm optimized by offline simulations. *Optical Switching and Networking, 7*(3), 127–138. doi:10.1016/j.osn.2010.05.001.

Chaves, D. A. R., Aguiar, D. O., Bastos-Filho, C. J. A., & Martins-Filho, J. F. (2011). A methodology to design the link cost functions for impairment aware routing algorithms in optical networks. *Photonic Network Communications, 22,* 133–150. doi:10.1007/s11107-011-0314-2.

Clerc, M., & Kennedy, J. (2002). The particle swarm - Explosion, stability, and conver-gence in a multidimensional complex space. *IEEE-EC, 6,* 58–73.

Data Tracker. (2005). Impairments and other constraints on optical layer routing - RFC4054. *IETF.* Retrieved from http://datatracker.ietf.org/doc/rfc4054/

Dressler, F., & Akan, O. B. (2010a). Bio-inspired networking: from theory to practice. *IEEE Communications Magazine, 48*(11), 176–183. doi:10.1109/MCOM.2010.5621985.

Dressler, F., Suda, T., Carreras, I., Crowcroft, J., & Murata, M. (2010b). Guest editorial bio-inspired networking. *IEEE Journal on Selected Areas in Communications, 28*(4), 521–523. doi:10.1109/JSAC.2010.100501.

Eberhart, R. C., & Shi, Y. (2007). *Computational intelligence: Concepts to implementations.* San Francisco: Morgan Kaufmann.

Engelbrecht, A. P. (2007). *Computational intelligence.* Hoboken, NJ: John Wiley. doi:10.1002/9780470512517.

Fonseca, I., Almeida, R., Jr., Waldman, H., & Ribeiro, M. (2004). Meeting optical QoS requirements with reduced complexity in dynamic wavelength assignment. In *Proceedings of the First International Conference on Broadband Networks,* (vol. 1, pp. 331–333). IEEE.

He, J., & Brandt-Pearce, M. (2006a). Dynamic wavelength assignment using wavelength spectrum separation for crosstalk limited networks. In *Proceedings of the IEEE International Conference on Broadband Networks – Broadnets,* (pp. 1–9). San Jose, CA: IEEE.

He, J., & Brandt-Pearce, M. (2006b). RWA using wavelength ordering for crosstalk limited networks. In *Proceedings of the IEEE/OSA Optical Fiber Conference – OFC.* Anaheim, CA: IEEE.

He, J., Brandt-Pearce, M., Pointurier, Y., Brown, C., & Subramaniam, S. (2007). Adaptive wavelength assignment using wavelength spectrum separation for distributed optical networks. In *Proceedings of the IEEE International Conference on Communications – ICC,* (pp. 2406–2411). IEEE.

Kavian, Y. S., Rashvand, H. F., Ren, W., Naderi, M., Leeson, M. S., & Hines, E. L. (2008). Genetic algorithm quality of service design in resilient dense wavelength division multiplexing optical networks. *IET Communications, 2*(4), 505–513. doi:10.1049/iet-com:20070312.

Marsden, A., Maruta, A., & Kitayama, K.-I. (2008). Routing and wavelength assignment encompassing FWM in WDM lightpath networks. In *Proceedings of the International Conference on Optical Network Design and Modeling, ONDM,* (vol. 1, pp. 1–6). ONDM.

Martinez, R., Pinart, C., Cugini, F., Andriolli, N., Valcarenghi, L., & Castoldi, P. et al. (2006). Challenges and requirements for introducing impairment-awareness into the management and control planes of ASON/GMPLS WDM networks. *IEEE Communications Magazine*, *44*(12), 76–85. doi:10.1109/MCOM.2006.273103.

Martins-Filho, J. F., Chaves, D. A. R., Aguiar, D. O., & Bastos-Filho, C. J. A. (2008). Intelligent and fast IRWA algorithm based on power series and particle swarm optimization. In *Proceedings of 10th International Conference on Transparent Optical Networks 2008 - ICTON 2008*, (vol. 3, pp. 158–161). ICTON.

Martins-Filho, J. F., Santana, J. L., Pereira, H. A., Chaves, D. A. R., & Bastos-Filho, C. J. A. (2012). Assessment of the power series routing algorithm in translucent, transparent and opaque optical networks. *IEEE Communications Letters*, *16*(6), 941–944. doi:10.1109/LCOMM.2012.032612.120232.

Monoyios, D., & Vlachos, K. (2011). Multi-objective genetic algorithms for solving the impairment-aware routing and wavelength assignment problem. *Journal of Optical Communications and Networking*, *3*(1), 40–47. doi:10.1364/JOCN.3.000040.

Mukherjee, B. (2000). WDM optical communication networks: Progress and challenges. *Journal of Selected Areas in Communications*, *18*, 1810–1824. doi:10.1109/49.887904.

Ngo, S.-H., Jiang, X., & Horiguchi, S. (2004). Adaptive routing and wavelength assignment using ant-based algorithm. (ICON 2004). In *Proceedings of 12th IEEE International Conference on Networks*, (vol. 2, pp. 482–486). IEEE.

Pavani, G. S., & Waldman, H. (2008). Restoration in wavelength-routed optical networks by means of ant colony optimization. *Photonic Network Communications*, *16*(1), 83–91. doi:10.1007/s11107-008-0120-7.

Pavani, G. S., & Waldman, H. (2010). Routing and wavelength assignment with crankback re-routing extensions by means of ant colony optimization. *IEEE Journal on Selected Areas in Communications*, *28*(4), 532–541. doi:10.1109/JSAC.2010.100503.

Pavani, G. S., Zuliani, L. G., Waldman, H., & Magalhaes, M. (2008). Distributed approaches for impairment-aware routing and wavelength assignment algorithms in gm-pls networks. *Computer Networks*, *52*(10), 1905–1915. doi:10.1016/j.comnet.2008.02.010.

Pereira, H. A., Chaves, D. A. R., Bastos-Filho, C. J. A., & Martins-Filho, J. F. (2009). OSNR model to consider physical layer impairments in transparent optical networks. *Photonic Network Communications*, *18*, 137–149. doi:10.1007/s11107-008-0178-2.

Rahbar, A. G. (2011). Review of dynamic impairment-aware routing and wavelength assignment techniques in all-optical wavelength-routed networks. *IEEE Communications Surveys & Tutorials*, 1-25.

Roebuck, K. (2011). *FPGA field programmable gate array*. Lighting Source.

Schoonderwoerd, R., Holland, O., & Bruten, J. (1997). Ant-like agents for load balancing in telecommunications networks. In *Proceedings of the First International Conference on Autonomous Agents*, (pp. 209–216). New York, NY: ACM Press.

Sim, K. M., & Sun, W. H. (2003). Ant colony optimization for routing and load-balancing: Survey and new directions. *IEEE Transactions on Systems, Man, and Cybernetics. Part A, 33*(5), 560–572.

Stoica, A. G., & Sengupta, A. (2000). On a dynamic wavelength assignment algorithm for wavelength routed all-optical networks. In Proceedings of Optical Networking and Communications – OptiComm, (vol. 4233, pp. 211–222). Springer.

Tanenbaum, A. S. (2003). *Computer networks* (4th ed.). Upper Saddle River, NJ: Prentice Hall.

Triay, J., & Cervello-Pastor, C. (2010). An ant-based algorithm for distributed routing and wavelength assignment in dynamic optical networks. *IEEE Journal on Selected Areas in Communications, 28*(4), 542–552. doi:10.1109/JSAC.2010.100504.

Zang, H., Jue, J. P., & Mukherjee, B. (1999). A review of routing and wavelength assignment approaches for wavelength-routed optical WDM networks. *Optical Networks Magazine, 1*(1).

Zhang, G., De Leenheer, M., Morea, A., & Mukherjee, B. (2012). A survey on OFDM-based elastic core optical networking. *IEEE Communications Surveys & Tutorials, PP*(99), 1-23.

Zhou, C. J., & Yuan, X. (2002). A study of dynamic routing and wavelength assignment with imprecise network state information. In *Proceeding of International Conference on Parallel Processing Workshops, 2002,* (pp. 207–213). IEEE.

Zulkifli, N., Almeida, R. C. Jr, & Guild, K. M. (2007). Efficient resource allocation of heterogeneous services in transparent optical networks. *Journal of Optical Networking, 6*(12), 1349–1359. doi:10.1364/JON.6.001349.

Chapter 10
Wavelength and Routing Assignment in All Optical Networks Using Ant Colony Optimization

Ana Maria Sarmiento
Tecnológico de Monterrey, México

Gerardo Castañón
Tecnológico de Monterrey, México

Fernando Lezama
Tecnológico de Monterrey, México

ABSTRACT

Routing and Wavelength Assignment (RWA) in an arbitrary mesh network is an NP-complete problem. So far, this problem has been solved by linear programming for network topologies with a few nodes, and sub-optimally solved for larger networks by heuristic strategies and the application of optimization algorithms such as Genetic Algorithms (GA), Particle Swarm Optimization (PSO), Differential Evolution (DE), etc. In this chapter, the authors present the use of Ant Colony Optimization (ACO) to find near optimal solutions to the routing and wavelength assignment problem in real sized networks with up to 40 nodes and 65 connecting links. They compare their results to the lower bounds obtained by the Nagatsu's method, finding them to be equal or very close (one wavelength over) to them.

INTRODUCTION

Optical networks using Dense Wavelength Division Multiplexing (DWDM) technology are the ideal candidates to handle the problem of the ever-increasing growth of traffic and demand for bandwidth. DWDM systems are popular with telecommunication companies because they allow them to expand their network's capacity without laying out additional fiber. By using DWDM and optical amplifiers, companies can accommodate several generations of technology developments in their optical infrastructure without having to overhaul the backbone network. Worldwide net-

DOI: 10.4018/978-1-4666-3652-1.ch010

working and communication systems and applications use high-speed optical transport networks as appropriate backbones for connecting buildings, cities and countries such as PAN EUROPEAN, NSFNET and COST optical networks (Kavian *et al.*, 2012) and (Ramaswami and Sivarajan, 2009).

To send data from one access node to another in a DWDM network, one needs to establish a connection in the optical layer similar to the one in a circuit-switched network. This can be done determining a path in the network between the two nodes and allocating a free wavelength on all the links on the path. Such an all-optical path is commonly referred to as a lightpath and may span multiple fiber links without any intermediate electronic processing, while using one WDM channel per link. The entire bandwidth on the lightpath is reserved for this connection until it is terminated, at which time the associated wavelengths become available on all the links along the route. It is thus important to provide routes to the lightpath requests and to assign wavelengths on each of the links along this route among all the possible choices so as to optimize a certain performance metric. This is known as the Routing and Wavelength Assignment (RWA) problem. The wavelengths assigned must be such that no two lightpaths that share a physical link use the same wavelength on that link. The RWA problem is critically important in increasing the efficiency of wavelength-routed optical networks. As provisioning of an extra wavelength involves considerable increase in the network's cost, the objective is to minimize the number of wavelengths required, known as the Network Wavelength Requirement (NWR).

The traffic assumptions generally fall into one of two categories: static or dynamic. In static RWA models, it is assumed that the demand is fixed and known, i.e., all the lightpaths that are to be set up in the network are known beforehand. The objective is typically to accommodate the demand while minimizing the number of wavelengths used in all links. By contrast, in a stochastic/dynamic setting, it is assumed that lightpath requests between source-destination pairs arrive one by one at random, and have random terminating times. A typical objective in this case would be to minimize the call blocking probability, or the total (perhaps weighted) number of blocked calls over a given period of time.

The RWA problem is well known to be an NP-complete problem (Chlamtac *et al.*, 1992), and the number of approaches proposed in the literature to obtain sub-optimal solutions can assess its importance. So far this problem has been analyzed by heuristic strategies and the application of optimization algorithms such as Genetic Algorithms (GA), Particle Swarm Optimization (PSO), Ant Colony Optimization (ACO), etc. In (Banerjee and Mukherjee, 1996) a large RWA problem is partitioned into several smaller sub-problems, each of which may be solved independently and efficiently using well-known approximation techniques. In (Navarro and Sinclair, 1999) ACO is used to analyze the RWA problem, considering wavelength conversion. (Somani and Azizoglu, 2000) addresses the wavelength assignment issues in interconnecting optical Local Area Networks (LANs) in which a wavelength cannot be reused for local connections. In (Banerjee and Sharan, 2004) a formulation of the static RWA problem in optical networks as a single objective optimization problem is presented and solved in a novel way using a genetic algorithm. Similar to it, (Rao and Anand, 2006) presents the use of a PSO algorithm to obtain near-optimal solutions to the NP-complete RWA problem in optical networks, without a wavelength conversion capability. In (Hassan and Phillips, 2008) a heuristic approach inspired by PSO is proposed for solving the static RWA problem and a new encoding scheme for members of the swarm population is proposed. The results from (Hassan and Phillips, 2008) are compared to those from (Rao and Anand, 2006) and (Banerjee and Sharan, 2004) showing an improvement both in terms of the number of iterations required and in the Average Path

Length (APL). In (Li, 2008) the authors evaluate the average-case performance of eight heuristic algorithms to solve the routing and wavelength assignment problem and the related throughput maximization problem in wavelength division multiplexing optical networks. (Rubio-Largo *et al.*, 2010) presents a population-based evolutionary algorithm using Differential Evolution (DE) in a multi-objective context to solve the static-RWA problem, under the consideration of wavelength conversion capability. (Zang and Jue, 2000) and (Choi *et al.*, 2000) present surveys on the different approaches to solve the RWA problem. A more recent comprehensive survey on the different solution methods is provided by (Gamst, 2009) in which the importance of the RWA problem is also stressed.

ACO (Dorigo, 1992), (Caro and Dorigo, 1998), (Dorigo *et al.*, 1999) is a class of algorithm, whose first member, called Ant System, was initially proposed by (Dorigo, 1992), (Dorigo *et al.*, 1996), and (Colorni *et al.*, 1991). The main underlying idea, loosely inspired by the behavior of real ants, is that of a parallel search over several constructive computational threads based on local problem data and on a dynamic memory structure containing information on the quality of previously obtained result. The collective behavior emerging from the interaction of the different search threads has proved effective in solving Combinatorial Optimization (CO) problems. Given the nature of the RWA problem, the ACO algorithm has proven to be a good implementation in obtaining near optimal solutions. (Arnous *et al.*, 2007) propose a modification of the AntNet (Caro and Dorigo, 1998) algorithm, which solves the problem of routing packets in communication networks. They consider a small network, with 8 nodes and 9 bidirectional links with equal cost, and propose two improvements to the routing AntNet algorithm, to change the rate of creation of ants that are launched into the network for analysis, and also to include load balancing to the routing problem. (Tekiner *et al.*, 2004) also presents a modifica-

tion of the AntNet algorithm for the NSFNet, which has 14 nodes and 21 links. (Ducatelle *et al.*, 2010) presents an excellent overview of the fundamentals of the algorithms that use swarm intelligence as bottom-up design of distributed systems, specifically applied to the telecommunications area, for both, wired and wireless networks. Other reviews of the use of swarm intelligence are presented in (Horst and Farooq, 2006) and (Sim and Sun, 2003). (Bean and Costa, 2005) presents an analytical framework for the ant based routing algorithms, in view of encouraging the advancement of theoretical research in the area. (Tekiner *et al.*, 2004) use multiple ant colonies as a means to avoid stagnation and compare results with the AntNet evaporation method. They showed an increase in throughput. One major disadvantage of using multiple ant colonies is the resources used in every node. More colonies would be required (thus routing tables), when applying multiple ant colonies to larger sized networks in order to exploit more paths. (Ngo *et al.*, 2006) proposes an algorithm for the RWA dynamic problem and presents results for networks with 6, 14, and 21 nodes and up to 26 links. (Navarro and Sinclair, 1999) reported on the use of an ACO algorithm for the *NWR* problem on networks with 4, 9 and 15 nodes from which they equal (Nagatsu *et al.*, 1995) lower bound for the 4 node network only (they were one and two wavelengths above the lower bound for the 9 and 15 node networks, respectively). Our work presents results for real sized networks with up to 40 nodes and 65 links. Showing that for the majority of the networks analyzed, we obtain Nagatsu's lower bound, or are only one wavelength above it. We were not able to find, in the available literature, applications of an ACO algorithm on networks the size of Europe (19 nodes), USA (40 nodes) and Japan (40 nodes) to compare our results with.

In this chapter we present the application of an ACO algorithm to the RWA problem in networks with static traffic and with wavelength conversion capability., The ACO-RWA algorithm has an implicit advantage, due to the nature of the algorithm, the ants are discourage from making too many hops to reach their destination, while they continue to look for ways to reach them without saturating (or equalizing traffic load of) specific links. This advantage means that the ants minimize the *NWR* while they are trying to minimize the *APL* as well. The ACO-RWA algorithm could be improved and extended in further work to include other features, such as impairment aware, energy efficient, survivability, optical spectrum allocation, among other in optical networks.

The chapter is structured as follows, second section presents a brief review of the general ACO algorithm and its motivation, third section presents the description and mathematical formulation of the RWA problem, forth section presents the lower bound and lower bound information strategy in order to compare our ACO algorithm's performance. Fifth section presents the specifics of the ACO algorithm we developed for the RWA problem, sixth section presents results and the last section contains the conclusions and proposed further work.

ACO ALGORITHM

Ant colonies, and more generally social insect societies, are distributed systems that, in spite of the simplicity of their individuals, present a highly structured social organization. As a result of this organization, ant colonies can accomplish complex tasks that in some cases far exceed the individual capabilities of a single ant. The field of "ant algorithms" studies models derived from the observation of real ants' behavior, and uses these models as a source of inspiration for the design of novel algorithms for the solution of optimization and distributed control problems (Dorigo *et al.*, 1999).

The main idea is that the self-organizing principles, which allow the highly coordinated behavior of real ants, can be exploited to coordinate populations of artificial agents that collaborate to solve computational problems. Several different aspects of the behavior of ant colonies have inspired different kinds of ant algorithms. Examples are foraging, division of labor, brood sorting, and cooperative transport. In all these examples, ants coordinate their activities via stigmergy, a form of indirect communication mediated by modifications of the environment. For example, a foraging ant deposits a chemical on the ground, which increases the probability that other ants will follow the same path. Biologists have shown that many colony-level behaviors observed in social insects can be explained through rather simple models in which only stigmergic communication is present. In other words, biologists have shown that it is often sufficient to consider stigmergic, indirect communication to explain how social insects can achieve self-organization (i.e. without any central planning or control).

An excellent experiment designed by (Deneubourg *et al.*, 1990), exposes the basic principles behind stigmermic communication. This experiment shows the way in which ants are able to find the shortest path from their nest to a food source by collectively exploiting pheromones they deposit on the ground while moving in order to mark the path they follow.

The experiment is described next. A nest of a colony of Argentine ants is connected to a food source by two bridges of the same length as shown in Figure 1.

Figure 1. Branches have equal lengths

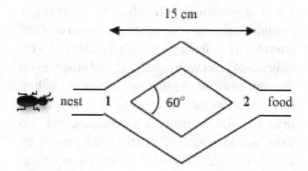

Ants can reach the food source and get back to the nest using any of the two bridges. The goal of the experiment is to observe the resulting behavior of the colony. What is observed is that if the two bridges have the same length, ants tend to converge towards the use of one of the two bridges. If the experiment is repeated a number of times, it is observed that each of the two bridges is used in about 50% of the cases. These results can be explained by the fact that, while moving, ants deposit pheromone on the ground; and whenever they must choose which path to follow, their choice is biased by pheromone: the higher the pheromone concentration found on a particular path, the higher is the probability to follow that path.

When both bridges have the same length, the following happens: at the start of the experiment, ants explore the surroundings of the nest. When they arrive at the decision point 1 (refer to Figure 1) in which they have to choose which of the two bridges to use, they choose probabilistically, with a probability biased by the pheromone they sense on the two bridges. Initially, each ant chooses one of the two bridges with 50% probability, as there is no pheromone on the branches yet. However, after some time, because of random fluctuations one of the two bridges presents a higher concentration of pheromone than the other and, therefore, attracts more ants. This in turn increases the pheromone level on that bridge, making it more attractive. It is this autocatalytic mechanism that makes the whole colony converges towards the use of the same bridge.

The experiment went on to vary the length of one of the bridges as shown in Figure 2.

The ratio r between lengths of the two branches defined as, $r = L_l / L_s$ was varied, this is the length of the longer branch (dashed line in Figure 2) divided by length of the shorter one (dotted line in Figure 2). When this ratio was around 2 (the longer branch is twice as long as the shorter) the observed result was that after a short period of time, the majority of the ants would use the

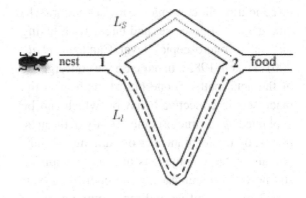

Figure 2. Branches have different lengths

shorter bridge. This is explained as follows: assume two ants leaving from decision point 1 (see Figure 2), call them ant 1 and ant 2, assume also that ant 1 takes the shorter bridge, while ant 2 takes the longer one. When ant 1 reaches the food source, ant 2 is only half way to it since the length ratio r is equal to 2. When ant 1, while moving back to the nest, encounters the decision point 2, it senses a higher pheromone level on the shorter bridge (since ant 2 is still on the move), which is chosen with higher probability and once again receives additional pheromone. When ant 1 reaches the nest on its way back, ant 2 is only reaching the food source. Consider now a third ant that stands at decision point 1, there exists a high probability that it will take the shorter branch, since it senses double the amount of pheromone (left by ant 1 on its way to the food source and back) than that laid down by ant 2 (that has not reached the nest back yet). Ant 3 will further increase the amount of pheromone that is laid down in the shorter branch when it moves to the food source, which increases the probability that further ants select the shorter path rather than the long one. Then a larger number of ants on a branch results in a larger amount of pheromone on that branch; this larger amount of pheromone in turn stimulates more ants to choose that branch again, and so on until finally the ants converge to one single path. This autocatalytic or positive feedback process is, in fact, an example of a self-organizing behavior of the ants: a macroscopic pattern (corresponding to the convergence toward one branch) emerges out of processes and interactions taking place at a "microscopic" level (Camazine *et al.*, 2001; Haken, 1983). In our case the convergence of the ants' paths to one branch represents the macroscopic collective behavior, which can be explained by the microscopic activity of the ants, that is, by the local interactions among the individuals of the colony. It is also an example of stigmergic communication: ants coordinate their activities, exploiting indirect communication mediated by modifications of the environment in which they move.

When compared to the experiment with the two branches of equal length, the influence of initial random fluctuations is much reduced, and stigmergy, autocatalysis, and differential path length are the main mechanisms at work. Interestingly, it can be observed that, even when the long branch is twice as long as the short one, not all the ants use the short branch, but a small percentage may take the longer one. This may be interpreted as a type of "path exploration."

Based on the findings for real ants and overcoming all impairments that may exist in the real ant's colonies, the idea behind ant algorithms is then to use a form of artificial stigmergy to coordinate societies of artificial agents. Ant Colony Optimization (ACO) is, in general, a model for designing metaheuristic algorithms for combinatorial optimization problems. The first algorithm which can be classified within this framework was presented in 1991 (Dorigo *et al.*, 1991) and (Colorni *et al.*, 1991) and, since then, many diverse variants of the basic principle have been reported in the literature. The essential distinction of ACO algorithms is the combination of a priori information about the structure of a promising solution with a posteriori information about the structure of previously obtained good solutions.

Metaheuristic algorithms are algorithms which, in order to escape from local optima, drive some basic heuristic: either a constructive heuristic starting from a null solution and adding elements to build a good complete one, or a local search heuristic starting from a complete solution and iteratively modifying some of its elements in order to achieve a better one. The metaheuristic part permits the low level heuristic to obtain solutions better than those it could have achieved alone, even if iterated.

The ACO algorithm that we use in this work is a metaheuristic that evolved from an algorithm called Ant System presented by (Dorigo, 1992), and (Dorigo *et al.*, 1991, 1996). The basic idea is to use a set of artificial agents called "ants" to work in a cooperative way, to build a solution to the problem by exchanging information via pheromone deposited on the edges of a graph. While moving, they build solutions and modify the problem representation by adding collected information to the graph (Dorigo and Gambardella, 1997). Paths that ants take are influenced by the concentration of their own pheromone on the links of the graph as well as by the amount of the pheromone from other ants. Thus, emulating real ants that make a stimulus response to their environment; now, while ACO is inspired by real ants, there are important differences. Artificial ants have memory for storing actions they have performed or to record places they have been, in order to avoid loops; they are not completely blind (as is the case for some real ants that are guided by stigmergy), but have sight based on distance, pheromone levels, traffic flow, congestion, cut-set links information, etc.; and their environment operates on discrete time. There are several requirements that a problem must comply with in order for ACO to be successfully applied to it: the problem should be suitable to be represented as a search on a graph by simple agents; a positive feedback mechanism must be identified, equivalent to pheromone; a greedy heuristic must be incorporated to allow a constructive definition of the solutions and appropriate constraints must be provided through the memories of the individual ants.

RWA PROBLEM

The demand for bandwidth has been increasing significantly during the last few years and will most probably continue to increase in the near future. The main drivers for the increased demand are: Very high resolution video applications as high definition (HD) video download, (HD) video telephony, and (HD) teleconferencing systems, IP telephony, multimedia applications and employees working from home instead of in the office.

DWDM optical network systems promise many benefits because of their high capacity for telecommunications. This capacity is obtained through the use of optical technologies with components that provide routing and restoration at the wavelength level. The origin of the optical networking technology is linked to WDM, which provides additional capacity on existing optical fibers. In a DWDM network a connection in the optical layer is done when data needs to be sent from a source to a destination node. This is accomplished by establishing a path between two nodes, which is referred to as a lightpath. However, in the absence of wavelength conversion, these lightpaths must be chosen without violating any of the following two constraints (Gagnaire *et al.*, 2007):

- **Wavelength Capacity Constraint:** States that a wavelength may be used only once per fiber at any given point in time.
- **Wavelength Continuity Constraint:** States that the lightpath uses the same wavelength on all links it traverses from source to destination.

In our work, the second constraint is the most restrictive one since it directly relates to the number of wavelengths used in the network. The RWA problem can be formally stated as follows: given a set of traffic demands between any given pair of nodes in a network, establish paths and assign wavelengths to each of those paths, so that all demand is met and the net wavelength requirement is minimized, subject to the wave-length capacity and continuity constraints. As previously mentioned, the RWA problem can be generally categorized into two cases: RWA with static off-line traffic and RWA with incremental dynamic on-line traffic (Gagnaire *et al.*, 2007). In our approach we are considering static traffic, because most backbone networks usually have a predetermined traffic demand.

As previously mentioned, the objective is to reduce the NWR since this has an economic implication: the lower the number of wavelengths required, the lower the cost of the network. At the same time it is also expected that the paths established will have the shortest path length in order to minimize the average path length (APL) of the network, which is defined as the average number of links used by all selected routes. The reduction of the APL has a primary impact on the delays and transmission impairments of the signal; it also helps to reduce network resource wastage.

Furthermore, the NWR can be analyzed in two ways: 1) considering the wavelength continuity constraint, which means the network has not a wavelength conversion capability, which in turn reduces its cost significantly, and 2) considering it does not have the wavelength continuity constraint, which means the network has a wavelength conversion capability in some nodes which is a less restrictive approach. The calculation of the NWR is explained in the following two subsections.

NWR Meeting the Wavelength Continuity Constraint

As stated before, the main goal of the RWA problem is to meet all traffic demand while minimizing both, the number of wavelengths (NWR) and the *APL*. The physical network is modeled as an undirected graph $G = (V, E)$, where V is the set of physical nodes numbered 1, 2, ..., $|V|$, and E is the set of physical links.

The RWA problem, also known as the static lightpath establishment (SLE) problem, with the wavelength-continuity constraint, can be formulated as an integer linear program (ILP) in which the objective function is to minimize the number of wavelengths or flow on each link, which in turn, corresponds to minimizing the number of lightpaths passing through a particular link.

Let λ_{sdw} denote the traffic (number of connection requests) from any source s to any destination d on any wavelength w. We assume that two or more lightpaths may be set up between the same source-destination node pairs, if necessary, but each one of them must employ a distinct wavelength; hence, $\lambda_{sdw} \leq 1$. Let F_{ij}^{sdw} denote the traffic (number of connection requests) from source s to destination d on link $i\,j$ and wavelength w. $F_{ij}^{sdw} \leq 1$ since a wavelength on a link can be assigned to only one path. Given a network physical topology, a set of wavelengths, and the traffic matrix Λ in which Λ_{sd} denotes the number of connections needed between source s and destination d, the problem can be formulated as follows (Zang and Jue, 2000):

$$Min\ F_{\max} = \max \sum_{sdw} F_{ij}^{sdw} \qquad \forall ij \in E$$

s. t.

$$F_{\max} \geq \sum_{sdw} F_{ij}^{sdw}$$

$$\sum_{i} F_{ij}^{sdw} - \sum_{k} F_{jk}^{sdw} = \begin{cases} \lambda_{sdw} & if \quad s = j \\ -\lambda_{sdw} & if \quad d = j \\ 0 & otherwise \end{cases} \quad (1)$$

$$\sum \lambda_{sdw} = \Lambda_{sd}$$

$$F_{ij}^{sdw} = 0, 1$$

$$\sum_{sd} F_{ij}^{sdw} \leq 1$$

The static RWA problem formulated by ILP using multi-commodity flow results in a rapid increase in the number of equations and variables depending on the size of the network. Even after apply some reduction techniques, solving the static RWA using ILP is computationally extensive and typically requires a huge execution time. Hence, different heuristic-based algorithms have been used to solve the problem. It is important to emphasize that each algorithm has its own advantages and disadvantages and the efficiency of applying a particular technique depends on factors like execution time, quality of solution, and so forth.

NWR without the Wavelength Continuity Constraint

Without the wavelength continuity constraint, the static RWA problem can be formulated as a multicommodity problem with integer flows along each link. The objective function in this case is to minimize the flows on each link, which in turn, corresponds to minimize the number of lightpaths passing through a particular link.

Let λ_{sd} = Traffic (i.e. ligthpaths) from source s to destination d; $\lambda_{sd} = 1$ if there is a lightpath from source s to destination d, considering at most one lightpath at a time, otherwise $\lambda_{sd} = 0$; $F_{ij}^{sd} = Traffic$ (in terms of number of lightpaths) that is flowing from source s to destination d on the physical link $i\,j$. The Integer Linear Problem formulation can be written as (Banerjee and Mukherjee, 1996):

$$Min\ F_{\max} = \max \sum_{sd} F_{ij}^{sd} \qquad \forall ij \in E$$

s. t.

$$F_{\max} \geq \sum_{sd} F_{ij}^{sd}$$

$$\sum_i F_{ij}^{sd} - \sum_k F_{jk}^{sd} = \begin{cases} \lambda_{sd} \ if \quad s = j \\ -\lambda_{sd} \ if \quad d = j \\ 0 \quad otherwise \end{cases} \quad (2)$$

$$\lambda_{sd} = 0,1$$

$$F_{ij}^{sd} = 0,1$$

In many cases, full wavelength conversion capability is not recommended or not even necessary, due to its high cost or the possibility of an acceptable performance of the network without it. Note that the main difference between the formulation in (2) and that of (1) is that in (2) the restriction $\sum_{sd} F_{ij}^{sdw} \leq 1$ is not considered. In fact, the formulation in (2) does not involve the variable w, because the problem is to minimize the number of lightpaths that traverse a particular link without considering a wavelength assignment.

LOWER BOUNDS

The minimum number of wavelengths required equals the evaluated numbers of paths with the maximum link load. The lower bound, which is equal to or less than the true minimum can be obtained without optimizing the path routes using (Nagatsu *et al.*, 1995) and (Wischik, 1996) algorithms. The lower bound is useful for judging the degree of routing optimality. When the obtained value equals the lower bound, the obtained value is assured to be the near optimum. To illustrate how to obtain the lower bounds and the cut-set links information we use Figure 3 where the NSFnet network is shown. We can obtain the lower bound for the network using the cut-set links shown in Figure 3a. The solid bold line in Figure 3a passes over the cut-set links. Cut-set links were found using uniform traffic and the algorithm given in (Wischik, 1996). First we divide the network into

two sub-graphs Figure 3b and Figure 3c by removing the cut-set links. We then count the cut-set paths m that are the paths that cross through the cut-set links and then we divide by the number of cut-set links c. The lower bound NWR (Nagatsu *et al.*, 1995) is given by

$$NWR = \left\lceil \frac{m}{c} \right\rceil \quad (3)$$

where $\lceil \ \rceil$ is the ceil function. In case of assuming uniform traffic the number of paths crossing through the cut-set links is given by $m = n_1 \times n_2$ where n_1 and n_2 are the number of nodes of the two sub graphs G1 and G2 respectively shown in Figure 3.

ACO FOR THE RWA PROBLEM

Classically, most approximate algorithms are either *construction* algorithms or *local search* algorithms. These two types of methods are significantly different, because construction algorithms work on partial solutions trying to extend these in the best possible way to complete problem solutions, while local search methods move in the search space of complete solutions.

Therefore, construction algorithms build solutions to a problem under consideration in an incremental way starting with an empty initial solution and iteratively adding opportunely defined solution components without backtracking until a complete solution is obtained. Our application of the ACO algorithm, which is a construction algorithm, begins by creating ants to cover all possible node-to-node pairs in the network. In this way a network with 19 nodes will require 342 ants and a network with 40 nodes 1,560 ants, therefore, the number of ants is fixed for a particular network. At each iteration of the algorithm all ants are launched from their node of origin to search paths to reach their node destinations, a discrete event

Figure 3. NSF network and Subnets result after removing the main cut-set links: (a) NSFnet topology and its main cut-set links: 14 nodes, 21 links; (b) Subnet G1; (c) Subnet G2 after removing the cut-set links

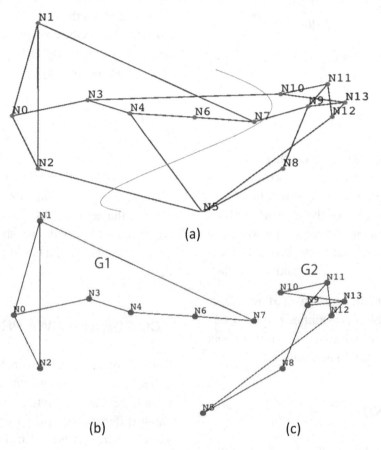

(a)

(b)   (c)

simulation implements the algorithm, each step within an iteration will advance all ants one link over the network. Because of this, the number of steps it takes for all ants to reach their destination is not the same for all ants and for all iterations. At each step of the algorithm, ants need to decide which link to take next, each individual ant makes this decision based on a probability measure that is obtained from the weight of attraction and repulsion the specific ant sees for all allowed links coming out from the node it is currently at. It is important to note that not all links coming out from a node might be allowed for a specific ant, this is because ants have memory of the links they have already visited, and this memory capability assures that no loops are created and that all ants

will reach their destinations in a finite number of steps. The action of marking a link as not allowed is called backtracking (Navarro and Sinclair, 1999).

In the simplest case of the construction algorithms the solution components on which the complete solution is constructed, are added randomly. Often better results are obtained if a heuristic estimate of the myopic benefit of adding solution components is taken into account. Our implementation takes into consideration the lower bounds obtained from Nagatsu to update the amount of pheromone left and evaporated by all ants in their ways through the networks. At certain point of the algorithm a fixed amount of pheromone is placed on the links ants have traversed. This action can be done locally, this is at each step within iterations of the algorithm as ants are creating their paths, or globally at the end of each iteration, after all ants have reached their destination. We performed tests for both cases and found that a global updating of the pheromone levels yields better results. At the end of each iteration, pheromone levels are evaporated as well from all links by a certain factor. In the following subsections we present the specifics of our algorithm; such as the rule by which each ant decides which link to take next, how to update pheromone levels on the links of the graph and all specific additional restrictions we implemented, along with their motivation.

RULE FOR DECIDING WHICH LINK TO TAKE NEXT

The decision of the link an ant is to take next from the set of those allowed from the current node is done based on a probability measure. The *weight of attraction* ant j has for link k, α_{jk}, is obtained by normalizing the amount of the ant's own pheromone type on the link, p_{jk}, by the sum of its pheromone over all allowed links in set A_j (from which it must choose) from (Navarro and Sinclair 1999).

$$\alpha_{jk} = \frac{p_{jk}}{\sum_{i \in A_j} P_{ji}} \qquad (4)$$

The weight of repulsion an ant has for link k, β_{jk}, is a normalization of the utilization, u_k of the link. The utilization is calculated as the number of ants that have traversed the link (Navarro and Sinclair, 1999).

$$\beta_{jk} = \frac{u_{jk}}{\sum_{\vec{i} \in A_j} u_{ji}} \qquad (5)$$

The two weights are combined to obtain the probability that ant j will take link k, γ_{jk}, as (Navarro and Sinclair, 1999):

$$\gamma_{jk} = \frac{\alpha_{jk} / \beta_{jk}^{\varepsilon}}{\sum_{i \in A_j} \alpha_{jk} / \beta_{jk}^{\varepsilon}} \qquad (6)$$

ε is used to vary the relative dependence of probability on the two weights. At the next step of the algorithm, ants will traverse the link with the highest probability according to (6).

Pheromone Updating Rule

At the beginning of the algorithm a fixed amount Q_j, of pheromone type j (for ant j) is laid down on each link, this is done for all ants and the amount is the same for all of them. After each iteration, the pheromone for an ant over the links in its route is updated depending on the number of hops the ant took to reach its destination, according to (Navarro and Sinclair, 1999):

$$p_{jk}^{t+1} = p_{jk}^{t} + Q_j / H_j \quad \forall \ k \in R_j \qquad (7)$$

where ant j used link k in its route R_j (which has H_j of hops), at iteration t of the simulation.

ACO algorithms can consider that some pheromone is evaporated or not from the paths ants have taken, in this case from the links ants have traversed. It has been observed that the inclusion of some degree of pheromone's evaporation helps algorithms to avoid stagnation in local optima (Deneubourg *et al.*, 1990). If evaporation is used, the evaporation rate should be chosen carefully, since a high evaporation rate will make information from all previous solutions to vanish, diminishing the construction of the optimal solution. If, on the other hand, the pheromone's evaporation rate is too low, the search for alternative solutions that might lead to the global optimum is seriously restricted.

In our work, the amount of pheromone that is evaporated from the links depends on the number of hops an ant takes to reach its destination; we use a limit on the number of hops, *AverageHops*, to decide whether to evaporate more or less pheromone, the motivation is to *discourage* ants from making too many hops to reach their destination, minimizing as consequence the *APL*, while we ensure that they continue to look for ways to reach them without saturating specific links. Therefore, if the number of hops, H_j, ant j makes to reach its destination is greater than *AverageHops*, the factor of evaporation is ρ^+, otherwise, the factor is ρ. Thus, the amount of pheromone of ant j on link k on its route R_j, after evaporation at iteration t will be

$$p_{jk}^{t+1} = \begin{cases} p^+ \cdot p_{jk}^t, & H_j \geq AverageHops \\ p \cdot p_{jk}^t, & o.w. \end{cases} \quad (8)$$

This evaporation procedure is done for links in the routes taken by all ants. An additional evaporation is done for those links that, after each iteration, have a *NWR* higher than the lower bound of the network (this lower bound is obtained from (Nagatsu *et al.*, 1995)). The motivation is to *encourage* ants to prefer those links that have not been used as much as those with a higher *NWR*. We use a factor τ to perform this additional evaporation on the links. Thus,

$$p_{jk}^{t+1} = \tau \cdot p_{jk}^t \, \forall k \in A_{higher}$$
for all pheremone types

where A_{Higher} is the set of links that have a *NWR* higher than the lower bound.

Utilization Updating Rule

Load balancing in telecommunication networks is essentially the construction of routing schemes which distribute the network's traffic over the network in such a way that links are rarely fully occupied and failures in node to node communication occur only infrequently. When designing the network's capacity required, i.e. its *NWR*, this balancing takes the form of the most leveled distribution of wavelengths in the links of the network.

As mentioned before, the link's utilization, u_k, is proportional to the number of ants that have traversed link k. After each iteration, the utilization is evaporated by a factor ϕ for those links that have a *NWR* that is lower than the lower bound of the network (remember that the lower bound of the network is the highest *NWR* for all links). This is to further encourage ants to use those less utilized links and balance the load in the network. Thus, the utilization of link k after evaporation at iteration t will be

$$u_k^{t+1 \rightarrow} = \phi \cdot u_k^t \quad (10)$$

RESULTS AND DISCUSSION

We tested our algorithm on four real sized networks, NSF, Europe, USA and Japan; their respective topologies are presented in Figures 3a to 6. Table 1 summarizes results for *NWR* of the four networks on which we applied our ACO algorithm.

The average number of iterations run on each network to find the results presented in Table 1, were as follows: NSF, 50 iterations (less than 1 second in a laptop computer with one microprocessor working at 2 GHz, *NWR* =13), Europe,

Table 1. NWR for Nagatsu and our ACO algorithm

Network	Number of nodes	Number of links	Nagatsu	ACO
NSF	14	21	13	13
Europe	19	39	17	17
USA	40	58	107	108
Japan	40	65	134	135

220 iterations (13 seconds, *NWR* = 17), USA, 840 iterations (167 seconds, *NWR* = 108) and Japan, 1140 iterations (270 seconds, *NWR* = 135). Figure 7 shows the *NWR* for each of the networks against the number of iterations.

We performed a parametric analysis of the four networks; the parameters used to obtain the results presented in Table 1 are reported in Table 2.

After some preliminary trials it can be noticed that the Japan topology presents some particularities that were affecting the final results. In order to reduce the topology effects on the obtained results, we have developed some special restrictions, which lead to better quality of solutions. The two restrictions and their motivations are described below.

Table 2. Parameters used in the ACO algorithm to obtain the results of Table 1

Network	AverageHops	$\rho+$	ρ	ϕ	τ	ε
NSF	6	0.6	0.9	0.9	1	1
Europe	6	0.6	0.9	0.9	1	1
USA	6	0.6	0.9	0.7	0.78	2
Japan	8	0.6	0.9	0.9	0.85	1

Figure 4. Europe network topology and its main cut-set, 19 nodes, 39 links

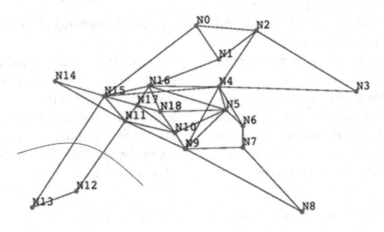

Figure 5. USA network topology and its main cut-set, 40 nodes, 58 links

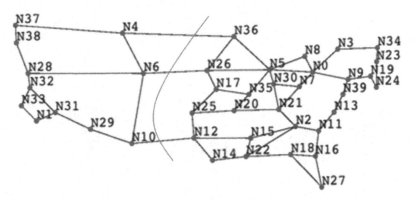

Triangle Restriction

According to (Nagatsu *et al.*, 1995), there are three cut set links in the Japanese network (refer to Figure 6), links (17,18), (21,22), and (15,24) where the pairs of numbers indicate the node numbers those links connect. Observe in the Japanese network topology that there are two triangles (made by nodes 18, 19 and 20 and nodes 22, 24 and 25) that have one of their vertices connected to a cut set link. We noticed that, in some cases, ants going from nodes in the cut set on the left to the one on the right using those triangles were forced to take the cut set links even when those links had a very high utilization. This is because ants could not form loops, which would be formed if they were to avoid using the highly utilized cut set links. In other words, they did not have the opportunity to look for alternative routes with less utilized links; therefore, sometimes even though the utilization of a certain cut set link was very high, ants did not have other option than to take it because they were avoiding creating a loop in the triangle. To overcome this effect, we identified the four specific cases in which ants were forced to take highly utilized cut set links of the triangles and made those ants to backtrack one step, in order to give them the opportunity to look for alternative routes with less utilized links. This is equivalent to allow them to have a vision of their future route and to backtrack in order for them to avoid the highly utilized cut set links. With this measure we were able to obtain a lower *NWR* on those cut set links, since there are always alternative and less utilized routes ants can follow. Note that although nodes 20, 22 and 27 also create a triangle that has a vertex connected to a cut set link, ants going into that triangle do have the option of looking for alternative routes if the cut set link (connecting nodes 21 and 22) has a high utilization. For this reason, this triangle was not included in the restrictions. Notice that the triangle restriction was only imposed for the two triangles mentioned above, and not for all triangles in the network because links connected to all other triangles are not in the cut set (not critical), and due to the nature of the ants algorithm those triangles do not cause the *NWR* to be higher.

Double-Crossing Restriction

This restriction was also included for the Japanese network only and is simply to keep ants coming from a node in one of the cut set and having their destination nodes in the other, to cross cut set links twice; this means, to keep ants from trying to look for routes that take them back to the node set they are coming from.

Figure 6. Japan network topology and its main cut-set, 40 nodes, 65 links

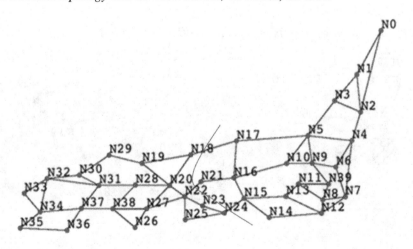

Figure 7. NWR value against number of iterations for the (a) NSF network (b) European network, (c) USA network, and (d) Japanese network

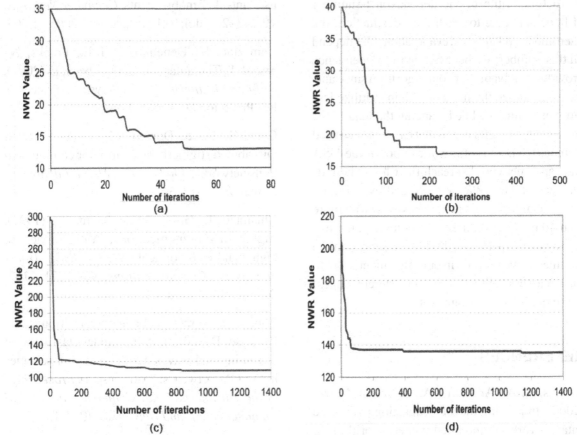

The two restrictions presented above were included only for the Japanese network and resulted in a decrease of the *NWR* from 144 to 135, it is interesting to note that the 135 *NWR* is required only in two of the 65 links in the network, the rest of the links have a *NWR* of 134 or lower. The two links that have a 135 *NWR* are links in the cut set, the one connecting nodes 17 and 18 and the one connecting nodes 15 and 24.

CONCLUSION AND FURTHER WORK

We implemented an ACO algorithm, via a discrete event simulation, to obtain optimal and near optimal solutions for the *NWR* problem on

WDM networks. We tested our algorithm on four real-sized network configurations, the NSF (14 nodes), Europe (19 nodes), USA (40 nodes) and Japan (40 nodes) and compared our results with the lower bounds reported by Nagatsu. We were not able to find applications of an ACO algorithm on networks the size of Europe, USA and Japan to compare our results with. (Navarro and Sinclair, 1999) reported on the use of an ACO algorithm for the *NWR* problem on networks with 4, 9 and 15 nodes from which they found Nagatsu's lower bound for the 4 node network only (they were one and two wavelengths above the lower bound for the 9 and 15 node networks, respectively). We found a *NWR* equal to the lower bound for the NSF and Europe networks and a *NWR* that is one wavelength higher than the lower bound for the USA and Japan networks. Our implementation of the ACO algorithm heavily depends on the number of hops ants take to reach their destination, the pheromone updating and evaporation rules depend on this number; we believe that this dependence provides an advantage to our algorithm since ants try to minimize the number of hops (utilize less number of links) while balancing the load in the network (looking for routes that have not been used as much). There is still work to do on the USA and Japan networks to reach their lower bounds (decrease their *NWR* by one), and even implement our algorithm in larger networks (with more than 40 nodes and different topologies), there is also a need to perform additional research on the parameters we propose in our implementation, to further assess their influence (in different ranges) in the quality of the solutions.

REFERENCES

Arnous, R. A., Arafat, H. A., & Salem, M. M. (2007). Improving the load balancing within the data network via modified antnet algorithm. In *Proceedings of the 5th International Conference on Information and Communications Technology*, (vol. 5, pp. 189 – 195). IEEE.

Banerjee, D., & Mukherjee, B. A. (1996). A practical approach for routing and wavelength assignment in large wavelength-routed optical networks. *IEEE Journal on Selected Areas in Communications*, *14*, 903–908. doi:10.1109/49.510913.

Banerjee, N., & Sharan, S. (2004). A evolutionary algorithm for solving the single objective static routing and wavelength assignment problem in WDM networks. In *Proceedings of International Conference on Intelligent Sensing and Information Processing*, (pp. 13 – 18). IEEE.

Bean, N., & Costa, A. (2005). An analytic modeling approach for network routing algorithms that use "ant-like" mobil agents. *Computer Networks*, *49*, 243–268. doi:10.1016/j.comnet.2005.01.008.

Camazine, S., Deneubourg, J.-L., Franks, N., Sneyd, J., Theraulaz, G., & Bonabeau, E. (2001). *Self-organization in biological systems*. Princeton, NJ: Princeton University Press.

Caro, G. D., & Dorigo, M. (1998). AntNet: Distributed stigmergetic control for communications networks. *Journal of Artificial Intelligence Research*, *9*, 317–365.

Chlamtac, I., Ganz, A., & Karmi, G. (1992). Lightpath communications: An approach to high bandwidth optical WAN's. *IEEE Transactions on Communications*, *40*, 1171–1182. doi:10.1109/26.153361.

Choi, J. S., Golmie, N., Lapeyrere, F., Mouveaux, F., & Su, D. (2000). A functional classification of routing and wavelength assignment schemes in DWDM networks: Static case. In *Proceedings of the 7th International Conference on Optical Communication and Networks*. OPNET.

Colorni, A., Dorigo, M., & Maniezzo, V. (1991). Distributed optimization by ant colonies. In *Proceedings of European Conference on Artificial Life*, (pp. 134-142). IEEE.

Deneubourg, Aron, Goss, & Pasteels, (1990). The self-organizing exploratory pattern of the Argentine ant. *Journal of Insect Behavior*, *3*, 159-168.

Dorigo, M. (1992). *Optimization, learning and natural algorithms*. (Ph.D. Thesis). Politecnico di Milano, Milano, Italy.

Dorigo, M., Caro, G. D., & Gambardella, L. (1999). Ant algorithms for discrete optimization. *Artificial Life*, *5*, 137–172. doi:10.1162/106454699568728 PMID:10633574.

Dorigo, M., & Gambardella, L. (1997). Ant colony system: A cooperative learning approach to the travelling salesman problem. *IEEE Transactions on Evolutionary Computation, 1*, 53–66. doi:10.1109/4235.585892.

Dorigo, M., Maniezzo, V., & Colorni, A. (1991). *The ant system: An autocatalytic optimizing process* (Technical Report TR91-016). Milan, Italy: Politecnico di Milano.

Dorigo, M., Maniezzo, V., & Colorni, A. (1996). The ant system: Optimization by a colony of cooperating agents. *IEEE Transactions on Systems, Man, and Cybernetics Part B, 26*, 1–13. doi:10.1109/3477.484436.

Ducatelle, F., Caro, G. A., & Gambardella, L. M. (2010). *Principles and applications of swarm intelligence for adaptive routing in telecommunications networks*. New York: Springer. doi:10.1007/s11721-010-0040-x.

Gagnaire, M., Koubaa, M., & Puech, N. (2007). Network dimensioning under scheduled and random lightpath demands in all-optical WDM networks. *IEEE Journal on Selected Areas in Communications, 25*, 58–67. doi:10.1109/JSAC-OCN.2007.027506.

Gamst, M. (2009). *A survey of the routing and wavelength assignment problem (Technical Report)*. Copenhagen, Denmark: Technical University of Denmark.

Haken, H. (1983). *Advanced synergetics: Instability hierarchies of self-organizing systems and devices*. Berlin: Springer-Verlag.

Hassan, A., & Phillips, C. (2008). Static routing and wavelength assignment inspired by particle swarm optimization. In *Proceedings of 3rd International Conference on Information and Communication Technologies: From Theory to Applications, ICTTA*, (pp. 1 –6). ICTTA.

Horst, W., & Farooq, M. (2006). A comprehensive review of nature inspired routing algorithms for fixed telecommunication networks. *Journal of Systems Architecture, 52*, 461–484. doi:10.1016/j.sysarc.2006.02.005.

Kavian, Y.S., Rashedi, Mahani, & Ghassemlooy. (2012). Routing and wavelength assignment in optical networks using artificial bee colony algorithm. *Optik - International Journal for Light and Electron Optics*.

Li, K. (2008). Heuristic algorithms for routing and wavelength assignment in WDM optical networks. In *Proceedings of IEEE International Symposium on Parallel and Distributed Processing, IPDPS 2008*, (pp. 1–8). IEEE.

Nagatsu, N., Hamazumi, Y., & Sato, K. (1995). Optical path accommodation designs applicable to large scale networks. *IEICE Transactions on Communications. E (Norwalk, Conn.), 78-B*, 597–607.

Navarro, G., & Sinclair, M. (1999). Ant colony optimization for virtual wavelength path routing and wavelength allocation. In *Proceedings of the Congress on Evolutionary Computation, CEC 99*, (vol. 3, pp. 1809–1816). CEC.

Ngo, S. H., Jiang, X., & Horiguchi, S. (2006). An ant-based approach for dynamic RWA in optical WDM networks. *Photonic Network Communications, 11*, 39–48. doi:10.1007/s11107-006-5322-2.

Ramaswami, R., & Sivarajan, K. (2009). *Optical networks: A practical perspective*. San Francisco: Morgan Kaufmann.

Rao, T., & Anand, V. (2006). Particle swarm optimization for routing and wavelength assignment in optical networks. In *Proceedings of the IEEE Sarnoff Symposium*, (pp. 1 –4). IEEE.

Rubio-Largo, A., Vega-Rodriguez, M. A., Gomez-Pulido, J. A., & Sanchez-Perez, J. M. (2010). A differential evolution with pareto tournaments for solving the routing and wavelength assignment problem in WDM networks. In *Proceedings of IEEE Congress on Evolutionary Computation (CEC)*, (pp. 1–8). CEC.

Sim, K. M., & Sun, W. H. (2003). Ant colony optimization for routing and load-balancing: Survey and new directions. *IEEE Transactions on Systems, Man, and Cybernetics. Part A, Systems and Humans*, *33*, 560–572. doi:10.1109/TSMCA.2003.817391.

Somani, A., & Azizoglu, M. (2000). Wavelength assignment algorithms for wavelength routed interconnection of LANs. *Journal of Lightwave Technology*, *18*, 1807–1817. doi:10.1109/50.908738.

Tekiner, F., Ghassemlooy, F., & Alkhayatt, S. (2004). Investigation of antnetrouting algorithm by employing multiple ant colonies for packet switched networks to overcome the stagnation problem. [LCS.]. *Proceedings of, LCS04*, 185–188.

Wischik, D. (1996). *Routing and wavelength assignment in optical networks (Technical Report)*. Cambridge, UK: University of Cambridge.

Zang, H., & Jue, J. P. (2000). A review of routing and wavelength assignment approaches for wavelength-routed optical WDM networks. *Optical Networks Magazine*, *1*, 47–60.

Chapter 11
Hopfield Neural Networks for Routing in Communication Networks

Carmelo José Albanez Bastos-Filho
University of Pernambuco, Brazil

Dennis Rodrigo da Cunha Silva
University of Pernambuco, Brazil

Marcos Antonio da Cunha Oliveira Junior
University of Pernambuco, Brazil

Jheymesson Apolinário Cavalcanti
University of Pernambuco, Brazil

Victor Vilmarques Capistrano Pedrosa
University of Pernambuco, Brazil

ABSTRACT

Although some interesting routing algorithms based on HNN were already proposed, they are slower when compared to other routing algorithms. Since HNN are inherently parallel, they are suitable for parallel implementations on parallel platforms, such as Field Programmable Gate Arrays (FPGA) and Graphic Processing Units (GPU). In this chapter, the authors show parallel implementations of a routing algorithm based on Hopfield Neural Networks (HNN) for GPU and for FPGAs, considering some implementation issues. They analyze the hardware limitation on the devices, the memory bottlenecks, the complexity of the HNN, and, in the case of GPU implementation, how the kernel functions should be implemented, as well as, in the case of the FPGA implementation, the accuracy of the number representation and memory storage on the device. The authors perform simulations for one variation of the routing algorithm for three communication network topologies with increasing number of nodes. They achieved speed-ups up to 78 when compared the FPGA model simulated to the CPU sequential version and the GPU version is 55 times faster than the sequential one. These new results suggest that it is possible to use the HNN to implement routers for real networks, including optical networks.

DOI: 10.4018/978-1-4666-3652-1.ch011

INTRODUCTION

Routing algorithms have been intensively discussed in the scientific community, mainly because the routing process impacts drastically on the performance of communication networks. An ideal routing algorithm comprises finding the best path between the source and the destination nodes, enabling high quality transmission, avoiding penalties caused by physical layer impairments and reserving resources for future requests. There are different ways to determine a route. Some algorithms determine the routes based on the shortest path (SP) (Dijkstra, 1959), the minor delay (Ali & Kamoun, 1993), the higher Signal to Noise Ratio (Pereira, Chaves, Bastos-Filho, & Martins-Filho, 2008), the better load distribution (N. Kojic, Reljin, & Reljin, 2004), among others.

Computational Intelligence is a set of techniques with an ability to learn and to deal with new situations (Engelbrecht, 2007). Among these techniques, Neural Networks are inspired by the brain and by the biological neurons. They have the ability of learning and decision-making.

Hopfield Neural Network (HNN) is a class of Neural Networks with feedback that may be used for routing computer networks (Hopfield, 1982). Once they are adaptive, they are an interesting option to be used as routing algorithm in order to handle the dynamic behavior presented in computer networks. Moreover, it is also possible to be used in optical networks (N. Kojic, Reljin, & Reljin, 2004; N. S. Kojic, Reljin, & Reljin, 2006, 2007, 2009; Bastos-Filho, Santana, Silva, Martins-Filho, & Chaves, 2010).

However, although they work well to solve the routing problem, they are still slower than the other approaches used nowadays (Dijkstra, 1959). On the other hand, the neural networks are inherently parallel, once the neurons perform their operations individually. Therefore, they are suitable to be implemented on parallel platforms in order to improve their performance.

In the recent years, the use of Graphic Processing Units (GPUs) has been proposed for many scientific applications (Bastos-Filho, Oliveira Junior, Silva & Santana, 2011). The GPU parallel floating point processing capacity allows one to obtain high speed-ups. Nevertheless, there are some aspects that should be considered to adapt an application to run on these platforms, such as memory allocation and communication between blocks. Furthermore, hardware limitations of the GPUs bound the use of this technology for general purposes.

Field Programmable Gate Arrays (FPGA) are programmable logic devices organized in a bi-dimensional matrix of logic cells (Pedroni, 2004). The architecture presented in the FPGAs allows them to process data in parallel manner, thus they may be used to implement parallel algorithms.

Therefore, due to the parallel behavior of the neural networks and the parallel architecture of the FPGA and the GPUs, it is possible to have an routing algorithm based on Hopfield Networks running on these parallel platforms and have a similar performance to the standard algorithms used nowadays (Bastos-Filho, Oliveira Junior, Silva & Santana, 2011; Oliveira Junior & Bastos-Filho, 2011).

Furthermore, the adaptive capability of the neural networks may be used in real networks. In this chapter, we propose a Hopfield Neural Networks model for FPGA. We validate the model and show that it is possible to have the routing algorithm running on FPGAs. Moreover, we also show that the approximation on the activation function does not harm the model performance mitigation. Since Bastos-Filho (2011) demonstrated that it is possible to use HNN for routing in optical networks, we believe that one can extend the results presented in this paper to optical networks in order to develop a fast router for these networks.

This chapter is organized as follows: in the next section we review the Hopfield Neural Networks model to solve the routing problem. In Section III, we introduce some basic concepts of the NVIDIA CUDA architecture and GPU computing, as well as the GPU-Based HNN model. In the Section IV, a brief introduction of the FPGAs is given and we also propose the HNN parallel model. In Section V the results are presented and the conclusions are given in Section VI.

BACKGROUND

Hopfield Neural Networks

Hopfield Neural Networks (HNN) are recurrent artificial neural networks (ANN) proposed by John Hopfield in 1982 (Hopfield, 1982). In this type of ANN, the processing elements are the neurons and every output of each neuron is connected to the input of all other neurons via synaptic weights. The HNN block diagram is depicted in the Figure 1.

HNNs may be used as an associative memory, where the neural network stores information based on some of its internal states (Haykin, 1994). Moreover, it can also solve combinatory optimization problems. In this case, the HNN has an energy function which provides a performance measurement for the optimization problem that has a huge set of possible solutions (Santana, 2010).

The Hopfield model consists of a set of neurons and a corresponding set of unit-time delays, forming a multiple-loop feedback system. The number of feedback loops is equal to the number of neurons. The output of each neuron is fed back, via a unit-time delay element, to each of the other neurons in the network. In other words, there is no self-feedback in the model (Haykin, 1994).

The Hopfield Neural Networks are based on McCulloch-Pitts neurons (Mcculloch & Pitts, 1943). They are the processing elements and every output of each one is connected to the input of all the other neurons via synaptic weights. The neurons output can be calculated using the Equation (1):

Figure 1. Hopfield neural network topology

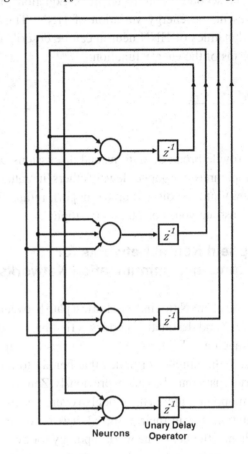

Neurons   Unary Delay Operator

$$V_i = g(U_i) = \frac{1}{1 + e^{-\lambda U_i}}, \tag{1}$$

The HNN updating dynamics for an input neuron is described by Equation (2):

$$\frac{dU_i}{dt} = -\frac{U_i}{\tau} + \sum_{j=1}^{n} T_{ij}V_j + I_i, \tag{2}$$

where is the time constant (Hopfield, 1984). The energy (Lyapunov) function of the Hopfield network is defined as follows (Haykin, 1994; Hopfield, 1984; Cohen & Grossberg, 1988):

$$E = -\frac{1}{2}\sum_{i=1}^{N}\sum_{j=1}^{N}T_{ij}V_iV_j - \sum_{i=1}^{N}I_iV_i, \tag{3}$$

The second and third terms of Equation (3) represent the energy variation of HNN. Thus, the dynamics of HNN neuron can be described in terms of the energy function:

$$\frac{dU_i}{dt} = -\frac{U_i}{\tau} - \frac{\partial E}{\partial V_i}.$$ (4)

Provide broad definitions and discussions of the topic and incorporate views of others (literature review) into the discussion to support, refute or demonstrate your position on the topic.[1]

Hopfield Neural Networks for Routing in Communication Networks

The use of HNNs to find the shortest path between a source and destination node was first proposed by Rauch and Winarske (1988). In this first approach, the number of nodes that belong to the shortest path must be known previously. Zang and Thomopoulos altered the model to overcome this limitation, but in their proposal, it is necessary to change the neural network topology for every request between each source-destination pair (Thomopoulos, Zhang, & Wann, 1991). Later on, Ali and Kamoun proposed a new adaptive algorithm, in which the weight matrix just carries convergence information, and the link costs and the topology are informed by bias inputs of the neurons (Ali & Kamoun, 1993).

Each link in the communication network between two adjacent nodes is associated to one neuron (Ali & Kamoun, 1993). For instance, a link from node x to node i refers to the neuron xi. The output of a neuron V_{xi} depends on the input U_{xi} and is evaluated by the Equation (1). The input of each neuron corresponds to the sum of all the outputs of the other neurons yj weighted by a synaptic weights $T_{xi,yj}$ plus the bias I_{xi}. The parameter λ determines the computation time to convergence and the correctness of the algorithm. The higher the parameter λ is, more the logistic function tends to a step function.

$$V_{xi} = \frac{1}{1 + e^{-\lambda U_{xi}}},$$ (5)

$$\forall (x, i) \in \bar{N} x \bar{N} \mid x \neq i$$

If every link in the network has a non-negative associated cost C_{ij}, the goal of the HNN is to find the path that minimizes the cost from a source node s to a destination node d. Thus, the HNN should indicate a directed path as an ordered sequence of nodes connecting s to d. The path that provides the minimum cost is defined as L_{SD}.

In most cases, the cost matrix is symmetric ($C_{xi} = C_{ix}$) and the elements C_{ii} are nulls because no node cannot be connected to itself.

The matrix ρ_{xi} defines if the link xi exists in the communication network topology. ρ_{xi} is defined as:

$$\rho_{xi} = \begin{cases} 1, & \textit{if the link } xi \textit{ does not exists;} \\ 0, & \textit{otherwise.} \end{cases}$$ (6)

The HNN converges when the variation of every output values between consecutive iterations (ΔV_{xi}) are below a threshold, e.g., $\Delta V_{th} < 10^{-5}$. After that, a new matrix (Y_{xi}) is evaluated. If the output has a value greater than 0.5, Y_{xi} is adjusted to "1", otherwise Y_{xi} is set to "0". If $Y_{xi} = 1$, the the link xi belongs to the shortest path L_{SD}, otherwise it does not.

Each neuron is externally excited by input bias I_{xi}. It is used in order to include the information of the link costs and the network topology in the neural network. I_{xi} is evaluated as follows:

$$I_{xi} = -\frac{\mu_1}{2} C_{xi} \left(1 - \delta_{xd}\delta_{is}\right)$$
$$-\frac{\mu_2}{2} \rho_{xi} \left(1 - \delta_{xd}\delta_{is}\right) - \frac{\mu_4}{2} + \frac{\mu_5}{2} \delta_{xd}\delta_{is},$$ (7)

$$\forall (x \neq i), \forall (y \neq i),$$

in which δ is the Kronecker function and μ_1, μ_2, μ_3 and μ_5 are HNN parameters. μ_1 minimizes the total cost, μ_2 prevents nonexistent links from being included in the chosen path, μ_4 avoids the convergence to a unstable state and μ_5 is introduced to ensure that the source and the destination nodes belong to the solution.

The HNN synaptic matrix $T_{xi,yj}$ is described as (Ali & Kamoun, 1993):

$$T_{xi,yj} = \mu_4 \delta_{xy}\delta_{ij} + \mu_3 \delta_{xy} + \mu_3 \delta_{ij} + \mu_3 \delta_{jx} + \mu_3 \delta_{iy} \tag{8}$$

in which μ_3 is a parameter used to guarantee HNN convergence.

The energy of the HNN is evaluated as follows:

$$E = E_1 + E_2 + E_3 + E_4 + E_5 \tag{9}$$

where:

$$E_1 = \frac{\mu_1}{2} \sum_{\substack{x=1 \\ (x,i)\neq(d,s)\, i\neq x}}^{n} \sum_{i=1}^{n} C_{xi} V_{xi},$$

$$E_2 = \frac{\mu_2}{2} \sum_{\substack{x=1 \\ (x,i)(\neq d,s)\, i\neq x}}^{n} \sum_{i=1}^{n} \rho_{xi} V_{xi},$$

$$E_3 = \frac{\mu_3}{2} \sum_{x=1}^{n} \left\{ \sum_{\substack{i=1 \\ i\neq x}}^{n} V_{xi} - \sum_{\substack{i=1 \\ i\neq x}}^{n} V_{ix} \right\},$$

$$E_4 = \frac{\mu_4}{2} \sum_{x=1}^{n} \sum_{\substack{i=1 \\ i\neq x}}^{n} V_{xi}(1 - V_{xi}),$$

$$E_5 = \frac{\mu_5}{2}\left(1 - V_{ds}\right),$$

where μ_1, μ_2, μ_3, μ_4 and μ_5 are constants.

Therefore, if the system is stable in the Lyapunov sense, then a smaller output changes is expected over the iterations. As a consequence, after a sufficient number of iterations, the HNN do converge.

Thus, the Equations (2) and (4) of the HNN dynamics considering the neuron representation applied for routing problem can be redefined:

$$\frac{dU_{xi}}{dt} = -\frac{U_{xi}}{\tau} + \sum_{y=1}^{n} \sum_{\substack{j=1 \\ y\neq j}}^{n} T_{xi,yj} V_{yj} + I_{xi}, \tag{10}$$

$$\frac{dU_{xi}}{dt} = -\frac{U_{xi}}{\ddot{A}} - \frac{\partial E}{\partial V_{xi}}, \tag{11}$$

Several researchers improved Ali and Kamoun approach. Smeda and Hawary simplified the energy equation (Smeda & El-Hawary, 1999); Park and Choi (1998) showed that Ali and Kamoun model does not converge for networks composed by more than 20 nodes and proposed a new approach suitable for bigger networks. Ahn *et al.* presented an algorithm with faster convergence than the older approaches (Ahn, Ramakrishna, Kang, & Choi, 2001). Bastos-Filho *et al.* proposed a simple discrete and finite difference equation in order to substitute the differential equation proposed by Ali and Kamoun (Bastos-Filho, Santana, & Oliveira, 2007):

$$U_{xi}[n+1] = U_{xi}[n] - AU_{xi}[n-1] - BU_{xi}[n-2] + C\left\{ \sum_{y=1}^{n} \sum_{\substack{j=1 \\ y\neq j}}^{n} T_{xi,yj} V_{yj}[n] + CI_{xi} \right\}, \tag{12}$$

where $U_{xi}[n+1]$ is the next neuron xi input calculated taking into account its own input in the past $U_{xi}[n]$, $U_{xi}[n-1]$ and $U_{xi}[n-2]$, the output of every neurons of the network $V_{yj}[n]$, the synaptic weights matrix $T_{xi,yj}$ and the polarization bias matrix $I_{xi}[n]$.

A simpler version of the Equation (12) was proposed by Schuler *et al* (Schuler, Bastos-Filho, & Oliveira, 2007). The difference and finite equation described in the Equation (13) is used to update the neurons.

$$U_{xi}[n+1] = U_{xi}[n] + A U_{xi}[n-1]$$
$$+B\sum_{y=1}^{n}\sum_{\substack{j=1\\y\neq j}}^{n}T_{xi,yj}V_{yj}[n] + CI_{xi}. \qquad (13)$$

By using this equation, Schuler *et al.* obtained a lower number of iterations needed to reach the convergence and a lower number of errors finding the paths. It also made the technique suitable for implementations, where the computing units have few resources with high parallelizing capability.

The pseudo-code for the HNN-based routing algorithm is shown in the Algorithm 1. U_{xi} is initialized with low and Frandom values ($-0,0002 < U_{xi} < 0,0002$) in order to speed-up the convergence faster.

GPU Computing and CUDA Architecture

GPUs were traditionally designed for image and graphic processing on computers. The use of GPU for general purpose computing was inspired by its ability to process thousands of threads simultaneously. GPUs became popular in recent years through a NVIDIA technology called CUDA (Compute Unified Device Architecture). CUDA allows programmers to develop software to solve complex computational problems by automatically distributing these threads to many-core simple processors.

Algorithm 1. Pseudo-code of the routing algorithm using Hopfield neural networks

```
Receive parameters (including C_ij)
Determine T_xi,yj
Evaluate ρ_xi
Receive source and destination
Evaluate I_xi
Insert initial noise in U_xi
Evaluate V_xi (Threshold of U_xi)
while ΔV_xi < ΔV_th < 10^-5 do
      U_xi and V_xi;
      Upgrade the neurons inputs
using Equation 5
      Upgrade the neurons outputs
using Equation 13
Evaluate ΔV_xi
Determine Y_xi (binarization of V_xi)
Get path from Y_xi
```

The CUDA GPUs follows an architecture called SIMT, which stands for single-instruction multiple-thread architecture (SIMT) (NVIDIA, 2009). In this architecture, the same instruction set is executed on different processors at the same time. This approach presents less overhead in parallel computing, which is suitable to intensive and repetitive computation.

The CUDA parallel programming model allows one to split the main problem in many sub-problems that can be executed independently in parallel. Each one can be decomposed in many other modules that may have their operations performed cooperatively in parallel. Actually, each sub-problem is equivalent to a block of threads and each thread is a module. The function that is performed to solve a sub-problem is called kernel function.

When a kernel function is invoked, it will run on each thread in parallel within the corresponding block. Each thread executing a kernel function is identified by its thread identifier. One can access it within the kernel through built-in variables provided by the CUDA API (NVIDIA, 2010).

Threads within a block can cooperate by sharing data through a dedicated memory, but they need to synchronize the memory access in order to avoid data dependence errors. A barrier placed on the code allows a thread to wait for the other cooperative threads. They guarantee the correctness of the algorithm running on the GPU, but influence on the implementation performance.

Each thread has a private local memory and each block of threads has a shared memory that can be accessed by all threads inside the block. Moreover, all threads can access the same global memory. These memories follow a memory hierarchy: the fastest one is the local memory and the slowest is the global memory; the smallest one is the local memory and the largest is the global memory.

Random number generators are widely used in computational intelligence techniques. They are naturally sequential, since they are based on states. GPU-based random numbers generators are discussed by (Nguyen, 2007) and (Thomas, Howes, & Luk, 2009). An approach that is CPU-free for generating random numbers on demand is presented by (Bastos-Filho, Oliveira Junior, Silva & Santana, 2011). They showed that a medium quality random generator is enough to provide good results in some computational intelligence techniques.

GPU-Based HNN Model

The HNN-based routing algorithm has an embarrassingly parallel behavior since all operations can be executed individually because each one has an independent input. The first step to adapt the algorithm to a parallel platform is to identify the bottlenecks. The main bottleneck is the update process of the neurons described from the 9th to the 12th line of the algorithm 1. This process only ends when a predefined threshold is reached. In the following subsections, we present how we

adapted the algorithm to the parallel platform. First we show how we call the GPU functions from the host and then we describe the GPU functions themselves.

The Host Code

The host code has the duty to call all the kernel functions. It is the slowest part of the implementation, since it does not run in the GPU and cannot be implemented in parallel. Thus, one should avoid intensive operations at this point and move as much operations as possible to the kernel functions. In our first implementation, we developed the naive model described in the Algorithm 2. In each kernel function call (shown in italic), the parameters inside the operands <<>> describe how many threads will run inside a block.

Once the hardware limits the maximum number of threads running on a block, the evaluations of the inputs and the outputs of the neurons must be split in blocks. A consequence, the convergence test must be performed in the host. Obviously, this approach harms the performance, since the blocks cannot be executed in parallel and the host and the device must establish a communication during the process. Actually, there is no correct way to get rid of this issue. However, we may assume that there will not be needed more than an exactly number of threads

Algorithm 2. Pseudo-code of the first version of the host code for the HNN-routing algorithm

```
set-weights <<nodes*nodes>>
initialize <<nodes*nodes>>
converged = false;
while (!convergedHost)
        iteration <<nodes*nodes>>;
        copy-from-device (con-
verged);
        iterations
Determine Yₓᵢ <<nodes*nodes>>;
```

Algorithm 3. Pseudo-code of the second version of the Host Code for the HNN-routing algorithm for GPU

```
initialize <<nodes*nodes>>
iteration <<nodes*nodes>>
Determine Y_xi <<nodes*nodes>>
```

running inside the block. Thus, there will be only one block of threads in the GPU. Assuming this, we could improve the implementation performance. This second version is shown in Algorithm 3. The kernel function iterations run in the GPU until the threshold is reached. By doing this, no communication between host and device is required during this process. Thus, it is probably the best approach for the host code.

The Device Code

The functions called by the host code to run in the GPU are known as kernel functions. These functions run in each thread in parallel. The main functions of the algorithm are the ones used to execute all the iterative process until the convergence. They are: the *iteration()* and *iterations()* functions. Both of them call a device function named *calculate-sum()* to evaluate the sum used to update the input of the neurons as shown in the Equation (13).

In the following subsections, the kernel functions and the device function *calculate-sum* are presented. Moreover, we present how we reduced the complexity of the update process and how we avoid some memory bottleneck issues.

- **The Kernel Functions:** The initial version of the host code calls the *iteration* function described in the Algorithm 4. It uses a global variable called *converged* that it is copied by the host code from the device to know whether the threshold is reached.

Algorithm 4. The first version of the kernel function iterations

```
sum = calculate-sum
update-input-and-output(sum)
synchronization-barrier
if (threshold is reached) then
        converged = false
```

The second version of the host code calls the function *iterations* and it is described in Algorithm 5. It runs all iterations of the algorithm until the threshold is reached. It also has a variable *converged*, but it is in the shared memory space. This variable can be viewed and modified by all threads inside the block.

- **Reduction of the Complexity of the Update Equation:** The function *calculate-sum* is described in the Algorithm 6. The *ty* and *tx* variables are the thread identifiers. This description is the simplest way to implement the Equation (13). It has complexity $O(n^2)$ and as it is used by each neuron, the full algorithm has complexity $O(n^3)$.

Nevertheless, if the weights are analyzed as they are generated, the algorithm may be described as in Algorithm 7.

Algorithm 5. The second version of the kernel function iterations

```
converged = false;
while (!converged) do
        sum = calculate-sum;
        update-input-and-
output(sum);
        converged = true;
        synchronization-barrier;
        if (threshold is reached)
then
        converged = false;
```

Algorithm 6. The first version of the device function calculate-sum

```
for (k = 0 to number-of-nodes)
    for (l = 0 to number-of-nodes)
        if (k != l)
            sum += weights[ty][tx][k][l] * outputOld[k][l];
```

Algorithm 7. The optimized version of the device function calculate-sum

```
for (l = 0 to number-of-nodes) do
    if (l != ty) then
        sum += weights[ty][tx][ty][l] * output[ty][l];
        if (l != tx) then
        sum += weights[ty][tx][l][tx] * output[l,tx];
            sum += weights[ty][tx][l][ty] * output[l][ty];
    if (l != tx) then
        sum += weights[ty][tx][tx][l] * output[tx][l];
```

This approach is $O(n)$ and it might be implemented in a CPU sequential version as well.

- **The Memory Bottleneck:** There is a memory hierarchy in the GPU. The closer to the GPU is the memory, the faster the memory access is. Therefore, closer memories should be used when it is possible.

In *iteration* and *iterations* kernel functions, the global memory is accessed constantly. Higher performance can be achieved if a faster shared memory is used. It is possible to store some in-formation in the block shared memory, such as the input and output matrices. Unfortunately, the shared memory is limited and it is not possible to store the synaptic weights matrix, once it is a 4-dimensional matrix. However, the weights may be generated on demand instead generating all of them for after-accessing through the global memory. The code is very similar, the only difference is that a device function named *weight* is called for each time it is necessary to use a synaptic weight. One should notice that it generates more floating-point operations, but reduces the number of access to the memory.

Algorithm 8. Pseudo-code of the second version of the Host Code for the HNN-routing algorithm for GPU

```
for (l = 0 to number-of-nodes)
    if (l != ty)
        sum += weight(ty,tx,ty,l) * output[ty][l];
        if (l != tx)
            sum += weight(ty,tx,l,tx) * output[l][tx];
            sum += weight(ty,tx,l,ty) * output[l][ty];
    if (l != tx)
        sum += weight(ty,tx,tx,l) * output[tx][l];
```

In a previous work (Oliveira Junior & Bastos-Filho, 2011) we analyzed five different GPU versions for the HNN-based routing algorithm. In this chapter, only the most optimized GPU HNN-based version is considered.

FPGA

A Field Programmable Gate Array (FPGA) is a logical device organized by a bi-dimensional matrix of logical cells and configurable connections created by the Xilinx Company in 1985 (Brown, Francis, Rose, & Vranesic, 1992). The conceptual structure of a FPGA is shown in the Figure 2.

FPGAs have programmable logic components called Configurable Logic Blocks (CLBs). Each CLB can be configured in order to perform a specific function (Chu, 2008). The connections can be also defined to create interconnection between the blocks. Therefore, logical circuits are implemented in FPGA by splitting the logic in small blocks, and then interconnecting them. This parallel architecture where each CLB may work individually makes the platform inherently parallel.

A common FPGA may have hundreds of thousands of different types of CLBs in a single device

Figure 2. FPGA basic architecture

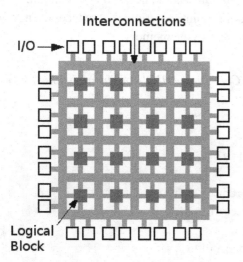

allowing complex devices are implemented on a single chip and configured easily. Modern FPGAs are capable of synthesizing 32-bit processors in a single device (Wilson, 2007).

Once the configuration of blocks and connection are made in the field, there is no need to send any design to an Integrated Circuit foundry in order to manufacture a chip (ASIC – Application Specified Integrated Circuit). Thus, FPGAs allow faster time production when compared to the ASIC and then meet the needs of fields that have short time-to-market. Moreover, by using programmable devices, it is more comfortable to prototype new logics, and to test them in real environments as well.

A Hardware Description Language (HDL) is a class of programming language that makes easier to document, to project and to create digital systems (Xiu, 2007; Dubey, 2008). A HDL allows FPGAs to be programmed quickly as it describes how the digital system is split and how it is connected (Rafiquzzaman, 2000). VHDL (Very High-speed integrated circuit Hardware Description Language) was used in all the experiments presented in this present work.

VHDL was originally sponsored by the Department of Defense United States and later transferred to the IEEE (Institute of Electrical and Electronics Engineers). It was the first standardized language for IEEE, more precisely with the IEEE 1076 (Chu, 2008). The pattern is rectified in 1987 (known as VHDL-87) and has been reviewed several times (93-VHDL, VHDL-2002, etc.).

Due to the VHDL standardization, it can be used to implement a circuit in a programmable device of various types and brands. Moreover, it can be sent to a factory for creating an ASIC (Pedroni, 2004).

VHDL has a behavior different from other programming languages. While declarations in the other are normally sequential, in VHDL they are parallel. Actually, this is one of the reasons that it is generally referred to as code, rather than program (Pedroni, 2004). Also, the major advantage of VHDL is the ability to use various levels of templates for different architectures (Wilson, 2007).

FPGA-Based HNN Model

In the proposed FPGA-based HNN model, the behavior of each neuron is ruled by a state machine, as shown in Figure 3. The values inside each one are the binary representations of the states used in the VHDL model. Moreover, these states are shared by the others neurons. Thus, it is possible to each neuron be aware of the state of the others. This information may be used as a synchronization barrier between the states.

When a neuron is in the state *S0*, it updates its input, as shown in the Equation (13). The main bottleneck of the whole routing algorithm using HNN is on this state, it is on evaluating this equation.

After a neuron has its input updated, it changes its state to the state *S1*. When all the neurons are in the state *S1*, the output of each one is updated. There is an implicit synchronization barrier here in order to evaluate correctly the neuron updates, once the sum present in the initial state *S0* uses all the current neurons outputs.

The threshold test of each neuron also happens in the state *S1*, as mentioned in the Algorithm 1.

In the case of the threshold is reached, the neurons changes its state to the state *S2*, otherwise, it goes to the state *S0*. Once the system reaches the state *S2*, the binary output is evaluated.

The possible states of the neurons are summarized in Table 1. However, it must be emphasized that each neuron only evaluates its operation in a specific state solely if all the neurons are in the same state. For instance, the output of a neuron is only updated if all the other neurons are in the same update state.

Actually, it is possible to say that the neural network has also states and they are based on the neurons states. The diagram of this finite state machine, in the case of a HNN with two neurons, is shown in Figure 4. The values inside the rectangles are the neuron states concatenated.

Once all the neurons must agree in state with each other, it may happen a stagnation state in the

Table 1. The possible states of a neuron in the Hopfield neural network for routing in FPGA

State	Action
S 0	Neuron input update.
S 1	Neuron output update and threshold test.
S 2	Binary output evaluation

Figure 4. State machine of the neural network modeled in FPGA

Figure 3. State machine of a neuron modeled in FGPA

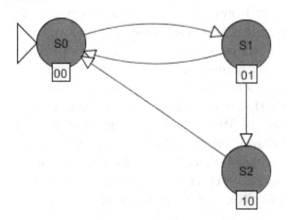

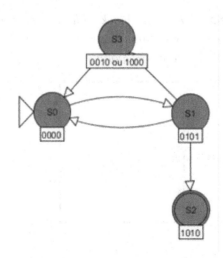

neural network when a neuron reaches the threshold and the other does not (it is depicted as state *S3* in Figure 4). Therefore, if a neuron reaches the threshold and the others do not, the first one changes its state to the initial state.

Figure 5 shows the proposed block of a neuron of the Hopfield Neural Network for routing. This neuron is from a neural network with twelve neurons in a case to route a communication network with four nodes.

The logical block has as input: the output of each neuron in the neural network; the pair source/destination of a routing requisition; the pair of indexes that means which link the neuron does represent; the state of the other neurons; the clock signal and the reset signal. The input and output are defined in the VHDL code described in the Algorithm 9.

Matrices Storage and Algorithm Optimization

The synaptic matrix $T_{xi,yj}$, defined by the Equation (8), is a 4-dimensional matrix. The storage of this matrix in hardware is impracticable. In order to get rid of this, the weights are generated on demand.

The external bias matrix of the neurons I_{xi}, defined by the Equation (7), has as input the link costs C_{xi} of the network communication. In order

Figure 5. Conceptual block with the inputs and outputs of a HNN neuron for solve routing problem of a 4-nodes network topology

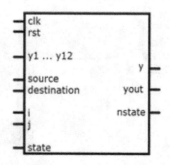

to let the model more dynamic, the bias value is evaluated also on demand and it is not stored in the device.

The input update of each neuron, given by the third them of the Equation (13), is the main bottleneck of the algorithm and may have a complexity $O(n^2)$. However, an approach described in (Bastos-Filho, Oliveira Junior, Silva & Santana, 2011) can be used in order to have a complexity $O(n)$. Still, this optimization process presents some other constraints. Therefore, the two approaches were aiming to analyze if this optimization is worthwhile in this platform.

Number Representation

One of the most important issues on implementing a neural network in a FPGA is concerned with the relation between the accuracy of the number representation and the device resource usage (Oliveira Junior & Bastos-Filho, 2011). The benefit of using single or double floating point is that there are fewer errors in the operations made by the neurons and, thus, less error in the neural network. However, more hardware resources are needed to implement this approach, and sometimes it is impractical to have this representation level.

On the other hand, the fixed point representation uses less hardware resources. However, there are more precision errors in the operations. Thus, it may introduce significant errors in the neural network.

Holt and Banker have shown that a 16-bit fixed point representation is the minimum accuracy requirement in order to use a MLP network with the back-propagation algorithm, in which they have used a normalized output [0,1] with a sigmoidal logistic function (Rafiquzzaman, 2000). Although the HNN is not mentioned in this work, the HNN and the MLP network probably have the same behavior, once they have the same MCP neuron and they both use the sigmoid function (Holt & Baker, 1991). Therefore, in this work, it is used 16-bit fixed point representation.

Algorithm 9. The input and output of a neuron in the FPGA model coded with VHDL

```
COMPONENT Neuron IS
GENERIC (  bits:              INTEGER:= 16;
                nodes:            INTEGER:= 4;
                neurons:          INTEGER:= 4 * (4 - 1) );
PORT (
         state:              INOUT          bit_vector (2 * neurons - 1
DOWNTO 0);
         yout:               OUT                sfixed (bits DOWNTO
-bits);
         y1:                 IN                 sfixed (bits DOWNTO -bits);
         y2:                 IN                 sfixed (bits DOWNTO -bits);
         y3:                 IN                 sfixed (bits DOWNTO -bits);
         y4:                 IN                 sfixed (bits DOWNTO -bits);
         y5:                 IN                 sfixed (bits DOWNTO -bits);
         y6:                 IN                 sfixed (bits DOWNTO -bits);
         y7:                 IN                 sfixed (bits DOWNTO -bits);
         y8:                 IN                 sfixed (bits DOWNTO -bits);
         y9:                 IN                 sfixed (bits DOWNTO -bits);
         y10:                IN                 sfixed (bits DOWNTO
-bits);
         y11:                IN                 sfixed (bits DOWNTO
-bits);
         y12:                IN                 sfixed (bits DOWNTO
-bits);
         clk:              IN             STD_LOGIC;
         rst:              IN             STD_LOGIC;
         y:                OUT            bit;
         source:        IN               INTEGER;
         destination:     IN             INTEGER;
         tx:              IN             INTEGER;
         ty:              IN             INTEGER;
         nstate:            INOUT         bit_vector (1 DOWNTO 0)
);
END Neuron;
```

The "fixed_pkg_c" library is used in order to have this representation in the implementation (Mcculloch & Pitts, 1943). It is hardware synthesizable and also VHDL-93 compatible.

Besides the number representation, there is other important issue on the neural network imple-mentation related to the activation function present in the MCP neurons, as shown in the Equation 5. Although many linear functions may be used, the sigmoid function, shown in the Figure 6, is the most used one. However, the cost to implement this function is impracticable in hardware. Actu-

Figure 6. Sigmoid logistic function with $\lambda = 1.0$

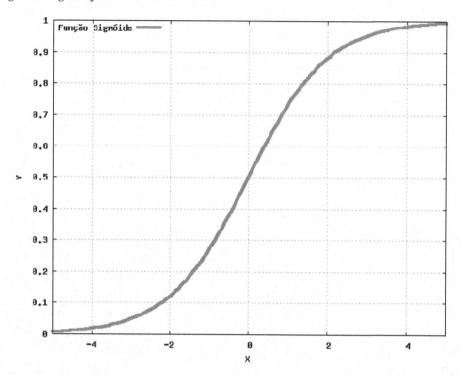

ally, some other alternatives can be used taking into account the performance, the accuracy and the hardware cost.

However, these simplifications usually lead to errors on the function evaluation. It should be highlighted that this function has an important role in the neuron activation and its quality must be guaranteed in order not to have undesired states in the neural network. The main alternatives for the evaluation of the sigmoid function are the Look-Up Table and the Interpolation.

The Look-Up Table is a table stored in the hardware memory where each interval is associated to a specific value. The error of this quantization is related to the size of each interval. Figure 7 shows the sigmoid function and the value for each range of the Look-Up Table. In this chapter, a Look-Up Table with 17 intervals is used. The intervals are generated in the interval [-4, 4] with a difference $\Delta = 0.5$ (Bishop, 2009).

On the other hand, the interpolation can be used with approximation of parts of the sigmoid function. In this approach, the intervals are as-

sociated to an equation with specific coefficients stored in the device memory. Figure 8 depicts the approximation of the sigmoid function.

A higher interval number in the two approaches means a better approximation to the sigmoid function but more memory space is used in the device. In the particular case of the interpolation, it needs evaluation of the equation and, in the case of the Look-Up Table, it needs more conditionals. Therefore, the two approaches are analyzed in order to show which one is better to be implemented in the FPGA.

EXPERIMENTS

Benchmark Networks

The simulations were performed for three networks. They have increasing number of nodes in order to understand the algorithm scalability. The networks topologies have four, five and six node, as depicted, respectively, in the Figures 9, 10, and

Figure 7. Sigmoid function approximation using look-up table

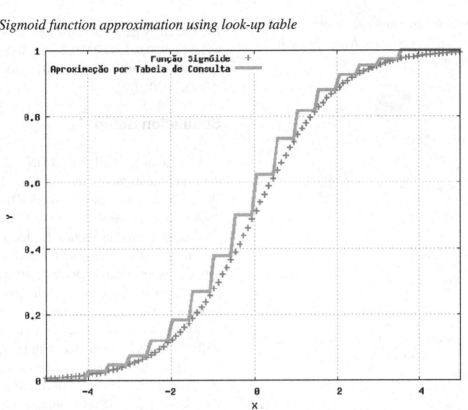

Figure 8. Sigmoid function approximation using interpolation

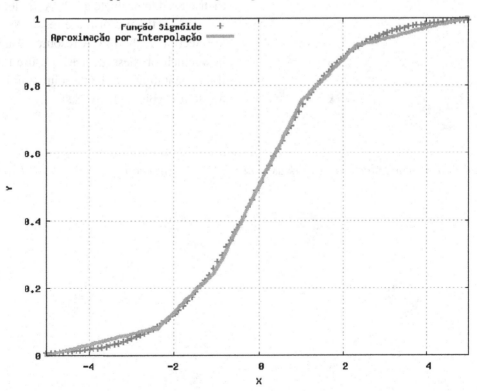

Figure 9. 4-nodes communication network used in the HNN architecture modeling for solving routing problems

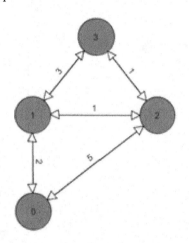

11. The HNN parameters used for all simulation were: $Ì_1$=950.0, $Ì_2$=2500.0, $Ì_3$=2500.0, $Ì_4$=475.0, $Ì_5$=2500.0, A=0.001, B=0.001 and C=0.001 (Santana, 2010)

Simulation Setup

In the case of the GPU-based HNN for routing, the experiments were executed on an Intel Core Quad 2.40 GHz computer with a NVIDIA GeForce 9800 GTX+. Moreover, since GPU E algorithm version, discussed in Section III, has previously shown the highest speed-up for finding shortest path in a communication topology when compared to the other GPU-based algorithm versions, it will be the one discussed in this work.

The FPGA version of the HNN was coded with VHDL and it was simulated with the Quartus II 9.1 Web Edition. The target device set was the model EP3SE50F780I4L, from the Stratix family. This device has 38,000 Combinational ALUT's, 19,000 Memory ALUT's, 38,000 Dedicated Logic Register, 488 I/O Pins, and 48 DSP Blocks. The metric used to evaluate a FPGA implementation is based on the use of these resources. Thus, in the Section 7, the FPGA resource usage means how much of these devices are used. Once an implementation uses few resources, it is possible to use it for bigger networks.

Figure 10. 5-nodes communication network used in the HNN architecture modeling for solving routing problems

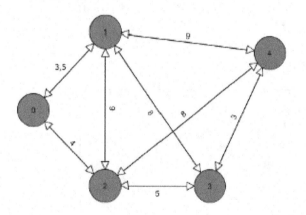

Figure 11. 6-nodes communication network used in the HNN architecture modeling for solving routing problems

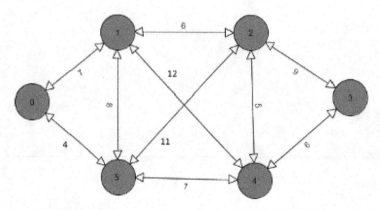

The sizes of the benchmark networks are far less than the size of the ones that may have problems of convergence and non-optimal routing results (Park & Choi, 1998). Therefore, there are no errors on these networks and thus this analysis is not made in this chapter.

In both cases, the stop criterion is when $\Delta V_{xi} < 0.001$.

RESULTS

The FPGA Resource Usage

The FPGA resources usage of the HNN for the three networks is shown in the Table 2 and Table 3. The resources usage for the two approaches of the neuron update is described in the Table 2.

One can observe that the neuron update optimization is not scalable. In the case of the 4-nodes network, this approach uses less FPGA resource. However, as the networks increase, this optimization is not worthwhile, once it uses more FPGA resource.

Table 2. The FPGA resource usage for the two optimizations of the input update neuron with different networks

	O ()	O ()
4 - nodes	18%	21%
5 - nodes	41%	40%
6 - nodes	78%	70%

Table 3. The FPGA resources usage for two cases of the sigmoidal function approximation with different networks

	Look - up Table	Interpolation
4 - nodes	18%	25%
5 - nodes	41%	55%
6 - nodes	78%	96%

On the other hand, the FPGA resource usage for the two approximation approaches, described in the Section 4, is shown in the Table 3. In this results, the neuron updated used is the one with complexity order $O(n)$.

Analyzing Table 3, it is noteworthy that the Look-Up Table clearly makes use of fewer FPGA resources. For instance, it uses 23% fewer resources than the Interpolation approach in the case of the 6-nodes network.

The Average Time

The average HNN convergence time in order to answer a routing requisition is shown in the Table 4. The average time and the standard deviation for each benchmark network and for both CUDA Model and FPGA Model are presented.

One can observe high speed-ups obtained through the HNN implementation versions in each network, when compared to the GPU and FGPA Model. The GPU Model implementation has reached a 5.44 speed-up in the 6-nodes network topology, a 2.77 speed-up in the 5-nodes network topology and a 1.51 speed-up in the 4-nodes network topology when compared to the Sequential Model. It can be noticed that higher the number of nodes in the communication network is, higher is the speed-up achieved using the GPU Model.

The FPGA implementation is 14.44 times faster than the GPU implementation in the 6-nodes

Table 4. The average converge time of the HNN for routing communication networks with different platforms and networks

	4 - nodes	5 - nodes	6 - nodes
Sequential Model (µs)	463.0 (2.10145)	1239.0 (3.29484)	2593.0 (4.38272)
GPU Model (µs)	309.939 (9.3564)	429.567 (22.7308)	476.454 (34.9075)
FPGA Model (µs)	30.1042 (9.28512)	29.2370 (5.44445)	33.2107 (7.94997)

network. Moreover, while the GPU implementation increases its average time as the network size increase, the FPGA implementation keeps the convergence time statistically the same for these network sizes.

CONCLUSION

Although the algorithm for routing networks using Hopfield Neural Networks implemented on CPUs is slower than the usual approaches for routing, Hopfield Neural Networks have a parallel scheme that allows faster implementations on parallel platforms.

We presented in this chapter two models for the HNN implementation on two parallel platforms: FPGA and GPU. We also analyzed different approaches and possible optimizations on the implementation, as well as their scalability with different networks.

In the FPGA implementation, all the simplification approaches of the activation function did not bring significant errors to the routing algorithm. Moreover, the Look-Up Table approach – besides its worse approximation when compared to Interpolation approach – makes use of fewer FPGA resources.

Furthermore, the neuron update optimization is not scalable on FPGA. Although this approach is faster in the GPU platform, it uses more hardware resources of the FPGA.

Finally, the FPGA model simulated is 78 faster than a sequential version of the Hopfield Neural Networks in a personal computer for a network communication with six nodes. Moreover, the speed-up reached when compared to the GPU version is almost 15.

The high speed-ups shows that HNN for routing are suitable to be implemented in FPGA, whereas the average time to find routes suggests that it is possible to use this approach in real scenarios. However, there is still a big room for the HNN

optimization in order to use few FPGA resources and, thus, to allow bigger networks to be routed by the HNN in this parallel platform.

Since some previous works have demonstrated that it is possible to apply HNN-based model for routing in optical networks, we intend to extend the model presented and analyzed in this paper to build router for optical networks. We believe we can produce fast, reliable and adaptive routers for these networks.

REFERENCES

Ahn, C. W., Ramakrishna, R. S., Kang, C. G., & Choi, I. C. (2001). Shortest path routing algorithm using Hopfield neural network. *Electronics Letters*, *37*(19), 1176–1178. doi:10.1049/el:20010800.

Ali, M. K. M., & Kamoun, F. (1993). Neural networks for shortest path computation and routing in computer networks. *IEEE Transactions on Neural Networks*, *4*(6), 941–954. doi:10.1109/72.286889 PMID:18276524.

Bastos-Filho, C. J. A., Oliveira Junior, M. A. C., Silva, D. R. C., & Santana, R. A. (2011). Optimizing a routing algorithm based on hopfield neural networks for graphic processing units. [IEEE.]. *Proceedings of Foundations of Computational Intelligence*, *2011*, 88–93.

Bastos-Filho, C. J. A., Santana, R. A., & Oliveira, A. L. I. (2007). A novel approach for a routing algorithm based on a discrete time Hopfield neural network. [IEEE.]. *Proceedings of the Foundations of Computational Intelligence*, *2007*, 363–369.

Bastos-Filho, C. J. A., Santana, R. A., Silva, D. R. C., Martins-Filho, J. F., & Chaves, D. A. R. (2010). Hopfield neural networks for routing in optical networks. In *Proceedings of the 12th International Conference on Transparent Optical Networks*, *2010*. IEEE.

Bishop, D. (2009). *Fixed point package user's guide.*

Brown, S., Francis, R., Rose, J., & Vranesic, Z. (1992). *Field-programmable gate arrays* (4th ed.). Secaucus, NJ: Springer-Verlag. doi:10.1007/978-1-4615-3572-0.

Chu, P. P. (2008). *FPGA prototyping by vhdl examples: Xilinx spartan-3 version.* London: Elsevier.

Cohen, M. A., & Grossberg, S. (1988). *Absolute stability of global pattern formation and parallel memory storage by competitive neural networks.* Academic Press.

Dijkstra, E. (1959). A note on two problems in connection with graphs. *Numerische Mathematik, 1,* 269–271. doi:10.1007/BF01386390.

Dubey, R. (2008). *Introduction to embedded system design using field programmable gate arrays.* London: Springer.

Engelbrecht, A. P. (2007). *Computational intelligence: An introduction.* New York: Wiley Publishing. doi:10.1002/9780470512517.

Haykin, S. (1994). *Neural networks: A comprehensive foundation. New York.* Macmillan.

Holt, J., & Baker, T. (1991). Back propagation simulations using limited precision calculations. In *Proceedings of Neural Networks, 1991* (*Vol. 2,* pp. 121–126). IEEE. doi:10.1109/IJCNN.1991.155324.

Hopfield, J. J. (1982). Neural networks and physical systems with emergent collective computational abilities. *Proceedings of the National Academy of Sciences of the United States of America, 79*(8), 2554–2558. doi:10.1073/pnas.79.8.2554 PMID:6953413.

Hopfield, J. J. (1984). Neurons with graded response have collective computational properties like those of two-state neurons. *Proceedings of the National Academy of Sciences of the United States of America, 81*(10), 3088–3092. doi:10.1073/pnas.81.10.3088 PMID:6587342.

Kojic, N., Reljin, I., & Reljin, B. (2004). Neural network for finding optimal path in packet-switched network. [IEEE.]. *Proceedings of Neural Network Applications in Electrical Engineering, 2004,* 91–96.

Kojic, N. S., Reljin, I. S., & Reljin, B. D. (2006). Routing in optical networks by using neural network. [IEEE.]. *Proceedings of Neural Network Applications in Electrical Engineering, 2006,* 65–68.

Kojic, N. S., Reljin, I. S., & Reljin, B. D. (2007). Different wavelength assignment techniques in all-optical networks controlled by neural network. In Proceedings of Telecommunications in Modern Satellite, Cable and Broadcasting Services, 2007, (pp. 401-404). IEEE.

Kojic, N. S., Reljin, I. S., & Reljin, B. D. (2009). All-optical network with simultaneous in-node routing and wavelength assignment. *Telfor Journal, 1.*

Mcculloch, W., & Pitts, W. (1943). A logical calculus of the ideas immanent in nervous activity. *Bulletin of Mathematical Biology, 5*(4), 115–133. PMID:2185863.

Nguyen, H. (2007). *Gpu gems 3.* Reading, MA: Addison-Wesley Professional.

NVIDIA. (2009). *Nvidia cuda programming guide 2.3.*

NVIDIA. (2010). *Cuda c best practices guide 3.2.* NVIDIA Corporation.

Oliveira Junior, M. A. C., & Bastos-Filho, C. J. A. (2011). Uma implementação em FPGA de redes neurais de hopfield para roteamento em redes de comunicação. *Anais do X Congresso Brasileiro de Inteligência Computacional.*

Omondi, A. R., & Rajapakse, J. C. (2006). *Fpga implementations of neural networks.* Secaucus, NJ: Springer-Verlag. doi:10.1007/0-387-28487-7.

Park, D. C., & Choi, S. E. (1998). A neural network based multi-destination routing algorithm for communication network. []. IEEE.]. *Proceedings of Neural Networks, 2,* 1673–1678.

Pedroni, V. A. (2004). *Circuit design with VHDL.* Cambridge, MA: MIT Press.

Pereira, H., Chaves, D., Bastos-Filho, C. J. A., & Martins-Filho, J. (2008). Osnr model to consider physical layer impairments in transparent optical networks. *Photonic Network Communications, 18*(2), 137–149. doi:10.1007/s11107-008-0178-2.

Pyetro, A. F. (2008). *Implementação de uma arquitetura de redes neurais mlp utilizando fpga. Trabalho de Graduaçao. CIn.* UFPE.

Rafiquzzaman, M. (2000). *Fundamentals of digital logic and microcomputer design* (3rd ed.). Rafi Systems, Incorporated.

Rauch, H. E., & Winarske, T. (1988). Neural networks for routing communication traffic. *IEEE Control Systems Magazine, 8*(2), 26–31. doi:10.1109/37.1870.

Santana, R. A. (2010). *Roteamento em redes ópticas transparentes utilizando redes neurais de hopfield. (Dissertação de Mestrado).* UPE.

Schuler, W. H., Bastos-Filho, C. J. A., & Oliveira, A. L. I. (2007). A hybrid Hopfield network-simulated annealing approach to optimize routing processes in telecommunications networks. In *Proceedings of Intelligent Systems Design and Applications, 2007.* ISDA. doi:10.1109/ISDA.2007.8.

Smeda, A. A., & El-Hawary, M. E. (1999). Application of Hopfield neural network in routing for computer networks. In *Proceedings of Electrical and Computer Engineering, 1999* (Vol. 1, pp. 145–149). IEEE. doi:10.1109/CCECE.1999.807186.

Thomas, D. B., Howes, L., & Luk, W. (2009). *A comparison of cpus, gpus, fpgas, and massively parallel processor arrays for random number generation.* New York, NY: ACM. Retrieved from http://doi.acm.org/10.1145/1508128.1508139

Thomopoulos, S. C. A., Zhang, L., & Wann, C. D. (1991). Neural network implementation of the shortest path algorithm for traffic routing in communication networks. In *Proceedings of Neural Networks, 1991* (Vol. 3, pp. 2693–2702). IEEE. doi:10.1109/IJCNN.1991.170276.

Wilson, P. (2007). *Design recipes for fpgas: Using verilog and vhdl.* London: Elsevier.

Xiu, L. (2007). *Vlsi circuit design methodology demystified: A conceptual taxonomy.* New York: Wiley - IEEE Press. doi:10.1002/9780470199114.

Chapter 12
Antnet Routing Algorithm with Link Evaporation and Multiple Ant Colonies to Overcome Stagnation Problem

Firat Tekiner
University of Manchester, UK

Zabih Ghassemlooy
Northumbria University, UK

ABSTRACT

Antnet is a software agent-based routing algorithm that is influenced by the unsophisticated and individual ant's emergent behaviour. The aim of this chapter is twofold, firstly to introduce improvements to the antnet routing algorithm and then to critically review the work that is done around antnet and reinforcement learning in routing applications. In this chapter a modified antnet algorithm for packet-based networks has been proposed, which offers improvement in the throughput and the average delay by detecting and dropping packets routed through the non-optimal routes. The effect of traffic fluctuations has been limited by applying boundaries to the reinforcement parameter. The round trip feedback information supplied by the software agents is reinforced by updated probability entries in the distance vector table. In addition, link usage information is also used to prevent stagnation problems. Also discussed is antnet with multiple ant colonies applied to packet switched networks. Simulation results show that the average delay experienced by data packets is reduced for evaporation for all cases when non-uniform traffic model traffic is used. However, there is no performance gain on the uniform traffic models. In addition, multiple ant colonies are applied to the packet switched networks, and results are compared with the other approaches. Results show that the throughput could be increased when compared to other schemes, but with no gain in the average packet delay time.

DOI: 10.4018/978-1-4666-3652-1.ch012

INTRODUCTION

In today's fast growing Internet traffic conditions changes and link failures occasionally occurs at some parts of the network in an unpredictable manner. Therefore, there is a need for an algorithm to manage traffic flows and deliver packets from the source to the destination in a realistic time period. The routing algorithm is the key element in networks performance and reliability, and can be seen as the "brain" of the network, which manages the traffic flow through the network. An ideal routing algorithm should be node and link independent, and be able to deliver packets to their destination with the minimum amount of delay, regardless of the network size and the traffic load. The only way to achieve this would be by employing intelligent and distributed routing algorithms. The routing algorithms currently in use lack intelligence, and need human assistance and interpretation in order to adapt themselves to failures and changes within the network. Routing is considered to be an NP-Hard optimization problem, therefore widely used optimisation problems have been applied in the literature: to name a few, Genetic Algorithms, Neural Networks, Simulated Annealing, Software Agents and the Reinforcement Learning.

In recent years, agent based systems and reinforcement learning have attracted researchers' interest. This is because these methods do not need any supervision and are distributed in nature. Swarm intelligence particularly ant based systems (Dorigo et al., 2002), Q-learning (Boyan & Littman, 1994) methods and hybrid agent based Distance Vector algorithms (Amin & Mikler, 2004) have shown promising and encouraging results. The ant-based approach applied to the routing problem was first reported in (Schoonderwoerd, 1996), which itself was influenced by the work done in (Appleby & Steward, 1994) on the software agents used for control in telecommunication networks. An improved version of the algorithm in (Schoonderwoerd, 1996) was applied to the connection-oriented systems (Bonabeau et al., 1998). In (Subramanian et al., 1997) for the first time the ant based routing was applied to the packet based connection-less systems. In (Di Caro & Dorigo, 1997) the idea was applied to the application of mobile agents in adaptive routing, namely antnet, which is also used as the basis in this work. In real life scenario, ants deposit some kind of chemical substance called the pheromone to mark the path that they use to find food. Having found the food source ants choose the path with the most pheromones back to their colony, which is of course, is always the shortest path. Ants (nothing but software agents) in antnet are used to collect traffic information and to update the probabilistic distance vector routing table entries. Recently research has been focused on improving antnet's performance. In (Park & Kim, 2007) performance analysis of the antnet were carried out and compared to the Open Shortest Path First (OSPF) routing algorithm. It is shown that in low traffic loads the antnet end-to-end packet delay is larger than OSPF whereas it is the opposite in heavy traffic loads. In (Strobbe et al., 2005) a simple network is implemented and compared to OSPF, where a self-tuning number of variables for the optimum performance is proposed.

Although ant based routing algorithms have shown some interesting results, they are still far away from being the ideal. Tests carried out have shown that by detecting and dropping a few of the packets, routed through the non-optimal routes, the average delay per packet is decreased and the network throughput is increased. In addition, one of the major problems with the antnet approach is the stagnation, in which the network freezes and consequently the routing algorithm gets trapped in the local optima and therefore is unable to find new improved paths (Sim & Sun, 2003). A number of methods have been used to overcome this problem, such as: evaporation, ageing, pheromone control and hybrid algorithms (Dorigo & Stutzle, 2004). However, most of these methods, except for evaporation, are rather complex or not efficient requiring other heuristics such as genetic algorithms (White et al., 1998). Evaporation links is a simple method and adding a negligible overhead to the node itself. In this chapter the focus is on the antnet routing algorithm. In the original antnet algorithm, the only feedback provided to the system by the software agents is the trip time observed on their way from source to destination. This feedback signal is reinforced by updating the related probability entry in the distance vector table. In this work the link usage information is used as the second feedback to the system in order to prevent stagnation problems. For every link the usage information is held at every node based on a predefined time window. Routing table entries then are reinforced with a negative signal based on the calculated evaporation information based on the link usage statistics. In addition multiple colonies are used in antnet for packet switched networks, which also improves the performance of the algorithm compared to the original approach. However, this improved node and algorithm complexity as separate data variables are kept for each colony. The chapter is organised as follows: In section two the behaviour ants in real life will be given. This will be followed by the description of the antnet routing algorithm. Section four describes the test environment and outlines the assumptions made. The proposed improvements together with evaporation and multiple ant colonies are given in section 5. Results and discussion are given in sections 6 and 7, critical discussion on antnet improvements and other nature inspired algorithms are given in section 8, which is followed by the concluding remarks.

BACKGROUND

Ants in Real Life

Individual ants are unsophisticated and simple insects, but when they act in a collective and collaborative manner they are capable of performing a variety of complex tasks (Beckers et al., 1992). The real ant behaviour has been observed by many researches and as a result a set of collective behaviour of several species has been agreed (Dorigo et al., 2002; Schoonderwoerd, 1996; Beckers et al., 1992). Ants in real life carry out the following tasks.

- Explore particular areas for food.
- Build and protect nests.
- Sort brood and food items.
- Cooperate in carrying large items.
- Immigrate as a colony.
- Leave pheromones on return path (the shortest path) to their colony.
- Preferentially exploit the richest available food source.
- Store information on the nature (uses world as a memory).
- Make decision on a stochastic way.
- Find the shortest paths to their nests or food source.
- Are blind, cannot foresee the future.
- Have very limited memory.

It is believed that these behaviours emerge from interactions within a large colony and the environment. A notion of stigmergy, which is a form of indirect communication through the environment, is used by ants (Dorigo et al., 2002) (Schoonderwoerd, 1996). They lay pheromone, some kind of chemical, to mark the path used to find the food source, which evaporates over a certain time. For example, in Figure 1(a) initially ants have no idea which direction to go. Path is chosen purely randomly. It is expected that on average, half of the ants will choose the shorter path and the other half will choose the longer path, since they have no information or knowledge of paths ahead. It can be observed from Figure 1(b) that ants choosing the shorter path will reach the food source and return to their nest well before the others. Following the footsteps of these ants, more

Figure 1. Ants food searching path where pheromones are laid

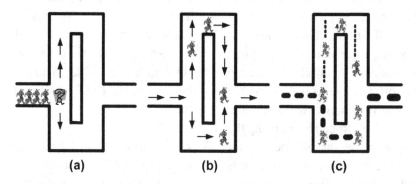

(a)   (b)   (c)

ants will choose the shortest path by sensingthe laid pheromones to research the food source and back to the colony, see Figure 1(c).

Antnet routing algorithm

Antnet (Di Caro & Dorigo, 1998) is an agent based routing algorithm, influenced by the real ants behaviour, where ants (nothing but software agents) explores the network to find the optimal paths from the randomly selected source destination pairs. Moreover, while exploring the network ants update the probabilistic routing tables and build a statistical model of the nodes local traffic and uses these information to communicate with each other. To collect network statistics and to update the routing table, the algorithm uses two types of agents namely; forward and backward agents. In each node there are two types of queues; low priority queues that are used by data packets and the forward ants and high priority queues which are used by the backward ants. In (Di Caro & Dorigo, 1998) forward ants also use the high priority queues and employ some heuristics in order to predict the observed trip time *T* rather than carrying this information (Di Caro & Dorigo, 1998).

Agents communicate via two data structures that are stored in every node (see Figure 2) as outlined below (Di Caro & Dorigo, 1998):

Figure 2. Probabilistic routing table and traffic statistic

Network Nodes (N)

P_{11}	P_{12}	.....	P_{1N}
P_2			P_{2N}
			P_{L-1N}
P_{L1}	...	$P_{L N-1}$	P_{LN}

Outgoing Links (L)

Network Nodes (N)

Statistic(1)	Statistic(2)	....	Statistic(N)

1. A distance vector routing table T_k with a distance metric is defined with probabilistic entries where for each possible destination *d* and a neighbouring node *n* there is a probability value P_{nd}, which reflects the goodness of the link (path), which is given as:

$$\sum_{n \mu N_k} P_{nd} = 1, d \; \varepsilon \; [1, N],$$

(1)

$$N_k = \{\text{Neighbours}(k)\}$$

2. An array M_k (μ_d, σ_d^2, W_d) defines a simple statistical traffic model experienced by the node k over the network. Where W_d is the observation window used to compute the estimated mean μ_d and variance $\sigma_d^{2,1}$ given as, respectively:

$$\mu_d = \mu_d + \eta(o_{k \to d} - \mu_d) \qquad (2)$$

$$\sigma_d^2 = \sigma_d^2 + \eta((o_{k \to d} - \mu_d)^2 - \sigma_d^2) \qquad (3)$$

where $o_{k \to d}$ is the new observed trip time experienced by the agent while travelling from the node k to the destination d.

The antnet behaviour is summarised as (Di Caro & Dorigo, 1998):

1. At regular intervals (defined by the user) from every node an agent A is sent out to a randomly selected destination node d.

2. Each agent first defines the possible neighbour nodes (unvisited neighbour nodes) at the current node by using its routing table. Then, an agent chooses the next node n within the identified possible (unvisited) nodes by using the probabilistic values in the table, taking into account the state of the associated queue as follows[2]:

$$P'_{nd} = \frac{P_{nd} + \alpha\, l_n}{1 + \alpha(|N_k| - 1)} \qquad (4)$$

where l_n is the heuristic correction value with respect to the probability values stored in the routing table that gives a quantitative measure of the queue waiting time, defined as:

$$l_n = 1 - \frac{q_n}{\displaystyle\sum_{n'=1}^{|N_k|} q_{n'}} \qquad (5)$$

where q_n is the bit length (or number of packets if packet size is fixed) waiting to be sent to the queue on the output port of node n.

3. If the selected port is full, then an agent is stored in the first-in-first-out output buffer for a time being until the availability of a port. It is assumed that the buffer size is infinitely large.

4. Information on every node visited and the time elapsed since the agent is despatched from the source are stored in the stack memory $S(k)$ carried by the agent.

5. If an agent is forced to visit previously visited node, i.e. if cycle exists, then it deletes all the entries for the nodes associated with the cycle.

6. On reaching the destination, the agent changes its type to a backward agent and uses the same path to return back to its source node. On the return journey, the agent pops every visited node from its stack and updates the associated routing table entries (probabilities) for all the nodes along the path by using the following rules:

    a. M_k (μ_d, σ_d^2, W_d) is updated with values stored in $S(k)$. The time elapsed to arrive (for the forward ant) at the destination ($o_{k \to d}$) is used to update the estimated mean μ'_d, variance σ'^2_d and the best trip value over the observation window W'_d.

    b. T_k is updated by incrementing the probability of selecting neighbour f when the destination is d' given as:

$$P_{fd'} = P_{fd'} + r(1 - P_{fd'}) \qquad (6)$$

Probabilities $P_{nd'}$ for rest of the neighbour nodes are updated as:

$$P_{nd'} = P_{nd'} - rP_{nd'}, n\varepsilon N_k, \qquad n \neq f \qquad (7)$$

The goodness of the path taken by the ant, and is used as the only feedback (reinforcement) information used in the original antnet routing algorithm to update the routing tables (Equation 8).

$$r = c_1 \left(\frac{W_{best}}{T} \right) + c_2 \left(\frac{I_{sup} - I_{inf}}{(I_{sup} - I_{inf}) + (T - I_{inf})} \right) \quad (8)$$

where c_1 and c_2[3] are the constants used to control the effect of last T, W_{best} is the ant's best trip time for a given destination and the last observation period. $I_{inf} = W_{best}$ and $I_{sup} = \mu * z * (\sigma/\sqrt{|w|})$[4] are the lower and upper limits for the confidence interval μ, respectively.

More details and discussion about the variables and parameters used can be found in (Di Caro & Dorigo, 1998).

ANTNET SIMULATION ENVIRONMENT

In this chapter, 36-node irregular grid and 29-node randomly created networks will be used for carrying out the tests. Evaporation criteria are applied to the modified antnet routing algorithm (Tekiner et al., 2004) and are implemented in the following environment.

- Algorithms are implemented in the C language and mapped onto a parallel environment using a Parallel Virtual Machine (PVM) model.
- Inter-process behaviour is simulated by assigning processes to different nodes both on the same or different machines.
- A poisson traffic distribution is used on non-uniform data traffic where 33% of the traffic is forwarded to nodes 1 and 21 with the 29-node random network (see Figure 3).
- A non-uniform data traffic is used with the 36-node irregular grid where nodes 0-5 generate traffic for nodes 30-35 and vice versa (see dark coloured nodes in Figure 4).
- There are only two paths available from left of the grid to the right of the grid, and vice versa.
- No packet creation is destined to the immediate neighbours.
- Paths discovery and initialisation of the probabilistic routing table entries are completed in 10 seconds.

Figure 3. 29-Node random network

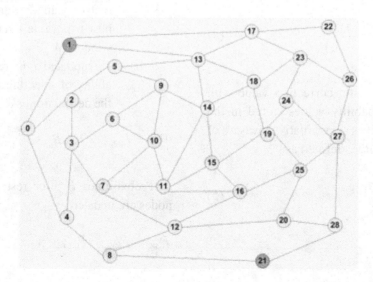

Figure 4. 36-Node irregular grid

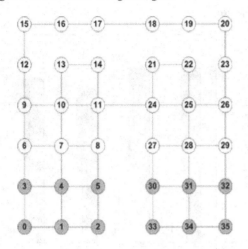

- The ant creation rate is set to 10 seconds per node
- For each simulation, packet generation is stopped after creation of 2500 packets per node and simulation is stopped after all packets are arrived at their destinations or are detected and deleted from the network.
- Every simulation is run 10 times and the average of the results is used for accuracy. It is assumed that the packet size is fixed and there are no packet losses.
- All experiments are implemented for varying link evaporation rates, since it has a significant effect on the performance of the algorithm.

The average packet delay is used for evaluating the performance of the algorithm, which is the average delay experienced by the packet while it is being routed from source to the destination.

ANTNET IMPROVEMENTS

Based on the original antnet routing algorithm, initially two modifications has been proposed and tested. In addition, in (Arnous et al., 2007) it is shown that the number of ants in the network

has to be limited for the optimum performance. Therefore have suggested to control the ant rate between 0.40 - 0.70 per packet after a series of test. In this work, we have also limited the number of ants in system simulation.

Deleting Aged Packets

During the simulations of the original antnet routing algorithm it was discovered that some packets travel via a number of hops until they reach their destination. This problem occurs because of probabilistic nature of the routing tables, where few packets are directed to non-optimal routes and cycles. As explained earlier there is a mechanism that deletes the memory associated with the cycles previously visited by the forward ants. A simple rule is defined to detect and drop these packets from the network as follows:

$$if\ Packket\ age\ >\ 2\ x\ No\_of\_nodes \\ Drop\ packet \qquad (9)$$

This rule is based on the information gained from experimental results. It was observed that only 1% and 1.2% of the packets experience this problem for 29-node and 36-node configurations, respectively. Further details regarding packet loss information can be found in (Tekiner et al., 2004).

Limiting the Effect of r Due to Traffic Fluctuations

The reinforcement *r* applied to the routing table entries is limited by the lower and upper bounds defined as follows:

$$if\left(No\_of\_nodes\ <=\ 5\right) \\ 0.1\ <\ r\ <\ \left(1-0.1\ *\ No\_of\_nodes\right) \\ else \\ 0.05\ <\ r\ <\ \left(1-0.05\ *\ Np\_of\_nodes\right) \\ (10)$$

The values used are based on experimental datas and it is intended to limit the effect of traffic fluctuations in the network at a given time. A similar method to control the effect of *r* has also been reported in (Baran, 2001). However, if *r* does not satisfy these values for three consecutive times and is less than 0.95, then reinforcement is applied to the routing table entry. It is believed that by limiting the impact of *r* on routing table entries the algorithm would not freeze as easily as it would on the originally proposed algorithm.

Figures 5 and 6 shows the performance comparison of the original and the modified antnets in terms of the average packet delay experienced per packet for different ant creation rates for 29-node and 36-node networks, respectively. The modified antnet illustrates improved average packet delay compared to the original antnet routing algorithm for all cases. For example, for the ant creation rate of 1 ant/10 second ~4% and ~22.5% improvement for a 29-node random network and for a 36-node irregular grid are observed, respectively. With different ant creation rates improvements between 3.5 – 5% for 29-node and 21.5 - 27.5% for 36-node configurations are achieved. The significant

Figure 6. Avgerage delay vs. ant creation rate 36-node

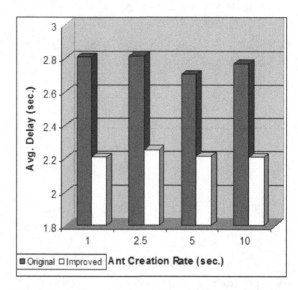

gain achieved with the irregular grid is due to its architectural characteristics. Only two paths are available for packets to travel from left-hand side of the grid to its right-hand side and vice versa. Therefore, packets rerouting themselves in order to fully utilise less congested nodes as often as possible.

ANTNET STAGNATION PROBLEM

Although the modifications proposed improve the performance of the algorithm, but it does not avert stagnation problems. Stagnation occurs when a network reaches its equilibrium state. This is an undesirable property of the routing algorithm where ants recursively chooses the same path to reach their destination. Therefore, routing optimisation may get stranded in the local optima and as a result may not be able to discover new paths that became optimal due to the changes in network traffic and topology (i.e. due to link/node failures or deleting/adding new nodes). Moreover, finding the shortest path by the ants is a statistical process (Bonabeau et al., 2000). It is highly probable that

Figure 5. Average delay vs. ant creation rate for 29-node

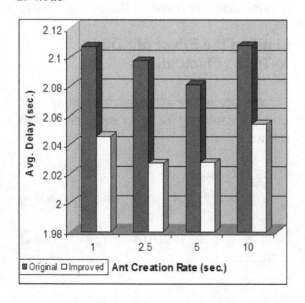

other ants will use the non-optimal path chosen by leading ants at the start of the exploration. Several methods such as the noise function, evaporation, multiple ant colonies and other heuristics beside the ant colony optimisation have been used and studied in the literature to overcome the stagnation problem (Kim & Sun, 2003). However, the most widely used method is the noise function where predefined percentages of the ants are forwarded to random destinations. But this is only a primitive method and does not provide a solution (see Figures 5 and 6).

Solutions to Stagnation: Evaporation

In this work link usage information is used as the second feedback to the system in order to prevent stagnation problem. For every link the usage information is held at the node that they are connected and for a predefined time window (period). Then, routing table entries are reinforced based on the evaporation information based on the link usage statistics periodically (in the rate of the time window). The real life scenario influences this where chemical substances deposited by the ants evaporate over time. The link usage ratio $L(x)$ defined as in (11) is used in calculating the evaporation rate $E(x)$ defined in (12) (Tekiner et al., 2004) [5].

$$L(x) = \frac{ant\_send(x)}{\sum_{i=0}^{N} ant\_send(i)} \qquad (11)$$

$$E(x) = \left[1 - \left(ax\frac{(N-R)}{N} + bxL(x)\right)\right]xP(x) \qquad (12)$$

, where $a + b = 1$

Equation 12 is divided into two parts; the recent usage ranking parameter R and the link usage ratio[6] $L(x)$. The effect of each part is controlled by a constant variable a and b, respectively. If $a = 0$ and $b = 1$, then evaporation is only based on

recent usage ranking, whereas and if $a = 1$ and $b = 0$[7] then evaporation is based on the link usage ratio. For example, in the real life scenario let's consider that there are N-path from current the node y to the destination node d. Then, if the last ant is forwarded through the neighbour node x, one would expect that the chemical substance laid on the path to x to evaporate the least. The major difference between the real life scenario and antnet based scenario is in the simulation environment. Where in the latter we deal with discrete values, therefore probabilities associated with the links cannot be evaporated continuously, and are evaporated at the end of each timing window. Therefore, (12) measures the proportion of ants sent via node x to the total of ants send within that timing window. On the other hand, the so called ranking parameter represents the node where an ant has laid its pheromone on the last link among N number of links. For example, $R = 0$ suggests that a particular link is the last to be used, thus indicating a pheromone has just been laid down. Therefore, the least amount of pheromone is expected to be evaporated from that node (x).

Evaporation $E(x)$ for the neighbour x calculated is subtracted from the probability associated with node x, see (13). The amount of probability evaporated from node x is then distributed equally to the other neighbouring nodes (since, sum of all probabilities for the neighbours is 1), see (14). Variables that keep track of the number of ants forwarded to the neighbours are reset after a specific time window and new information is collected within the next timing window.

$$P(i) = P(i) - E(x), \quad i = x \qquad (13)$$

Since, for all N, the sum of all probabilities is equal to 1, then the probability of evaporation from node x distributed equally to the other neighbours is given by:

$$P(i) = P(i) + \frac{E(x)}{N-1}, i \neq x \qquad (14)$$

Results for the average delay against the evaporation rate are presented in Figures 7 and 8 for different values of *a* and *b* and are compared to the case with no evaporation. It can be seen from the figures that for all cases the algorithm with evaporation has performed better than the non-evaporation version (evap(0.0, 0.0), *a* and *b* are both 0, thus $E(x)$ is 0). Results also show that, with the evaporation algorithm the lowest average delay is achieved when the evaporation window is set to 1 second. Thus, showing ~7% and ~16% improvement for 29-node random network and 36-nod irregular grid, respectively when compared to the non-evaporating algorithm. However, while conducting tests it was observed that the evaporation algorithm was not as stable as the non-evaporation algorithm. Not much difference was observed on 10 set of tests conducted by the non-evaporation configuration, whereas there was around 0.2 to 0.5 seconds difference

among the best and worst cases observed with the evaporation case for 29 and 36 node configurations, respectively. It is believed that this is due to the two main reasons. Firstly, the non-uniform traffic model used in tests, and secondly for the algorithm capturing the wrong timing window as that is the only factor in choosing the time to evaporate.

Solutions to Stagnation: Multiple Ant Colonies

The idea of using multiple ant colonies was first applied to the wavelength routing in optical wavelength division multiplexing based networks (Varela & Sinclair, 1999). In this work, more than one ant colony is used to distribute different wavelengths over the network in order to accomplish increased availability of wavelengths routing. In the original antnet, ants are only attracted by the

Figure 7. Average delay vs. evaporation rate for 29-node

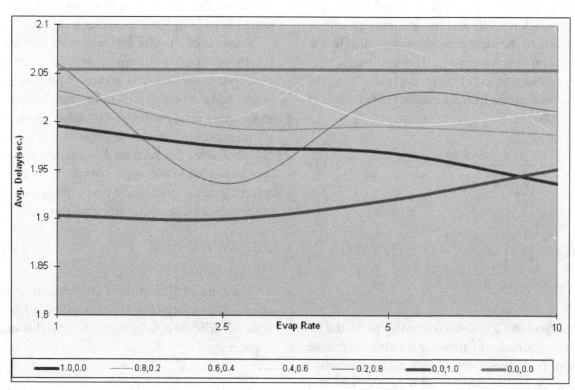

Figure 8. Average delay vs. evaporation rate for 36-node

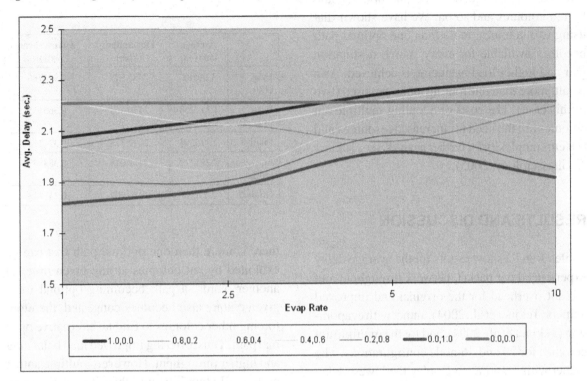

pheromone trails laid by ants from their own species (as there is only one colony considered at any given time). Also introduced in this work is the concept of ants being repelled by the pheromone laid by other species, in addition ants being attracted to the pheromone trails laid by their own species. Three variants of the algorithms have been proposed namely: local update, global update/distance and the global update/occupancy (Varela & Sinclair, 1999). In the local update and the global update table entries are updated every hop and at the end of each cycle[8], respectively. In the global update two variants (i.e. different repulsion

techniques) are used to distribute wavelengths within the network based on the distance or the link occupancy.

Multiple ant colonies have also been applied in the circuit switched networks, assuming that there exists more than one ant colony and no information are given on ant colonies repelling or attracting each other as reported in (Kim & Sun, 2002). Here, the application of multiple ant colony algorithms in packet-switched networks has been reported. Here we investigate two ant colonies as illustrated in Figure 9, where red and blue ants each use different pheromone tables.

Figure 9. Ant path showing the interaction of multiple ant colonies

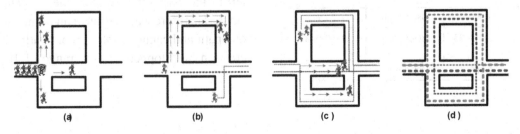

The red ants only update the pheromones laid by red colonies and so on. We have shown that using two colonies, more than one optimal path becomes available for every source destination pair and higher load balancing is achieved. As a result, more than one routing tables are used (two in this case). The costs of adopting multiple ant colonies are the need for increased resources and system complexity for further analysis see (Tekiner & Ghassemlooy, 2005).

RESULTS AND DISCUSSION

Tables 1 and 2 show results for the average delay experienced per packet, network throughput and the ant overhead for the original and improved antnets (Tekiner et al., 2004), antnet with evaporation (Tekiner et al., 2004), and for the multiple ant colonies for 29 and 36-node configurations. The antnet with evaporation display the lowest delay experienced by data packets for both configurations, but at marginally higher agent overhead and lower throughput compared to the multiple ant colonies and improved antnet. Packets are delivered 34.5% faster when evap(0,1) is used in 36-node irregular grid compared to the original antnet algorithm. Higher throughput is achieved with the multiple ant colonies. This is because

Table 1. Comparison of various antnets for 29-node

	Average delay(s)	Throughput (kb/s)	Ant overhead (%)
Evap (1,0)	1.99588	1864.592557	0.700888
Evap (0,1)	1.903141	1813.605429	0.713602
Multi	1.990436	1986.881114	0.632666
Im-proved	2.054038	1869.882673	0.698548
Original	2.108055	1590.898421	0.728073

Table 2. Comparison of various antnets for 36-node

	Average delay (s)	Throughput (kb/s)	Ant overhead (%)
Evap (1,0)	1.99588	2485.927	0.391786
Evap (0,1)	1.817258	2470.463	0.365155
Multi	2.316294	2692.178	0.321153
Im-proved	2.211272	2412.018	0.388868
Original	2.77031	1946.902	0.353448

there is more than one optimal path that can be exploited by ant colonies at any given time. In another words, a path becoming optimal for a given colony also becomes congested, therefore forcing other colonies to find an alternative optimal path. Thus, offering improved load balancing and higher throughput. However, multiple antnet performed slightly worse than improved antnet algorithm with 36-node configuration in terms of the average packet delay. This is because; in 36 node irregular grid there are only two paths that exist from left of the grid to the right of the grid and vice versa. Thus, each colony could only select the other congested path as the alternative.

Figures 10 and 11 shows the network throughput for the improved antnet, the antnet with evaporation and the antnet with multiple ant colonies for 29 and 36 node configurations. For 29-node configuration, the performance is similar for all cases, except for multiple ant colonies, where the throughput is marginally higher and lower over time range of 10-110 seconds for 29 and 36-node configurations, respectively. This is because there are only two paths available from left of the grid to the right of the grid and vice versa. Therefore, each colony can dominate only one path and cannot explore more paths. Packet creation has stopped at time range of 100-200

Figure 10. Throughput characteristics for the improved antnet, antnet with evaporation and antnet with multiple ant colonies for 29-node

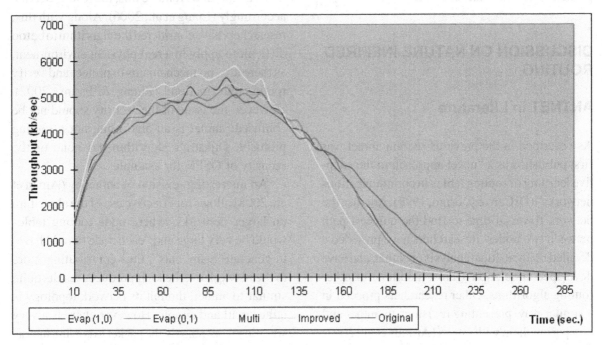

Figure 11. Throughput characteristics for the improved antnet, antnet with evaporation, and antnet with multiple ant colonies for 36-node

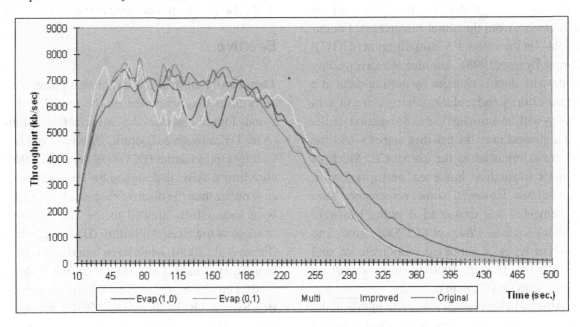

second (every node in the network stops creating packets after 2500 packet creation).

DISCUSSION ON NATURE-INSPIRED ROUTING

ANTNET in Literature

As described in the previous section antnet was first published as a "novel approach to the adaptive learning of routing tables in communications networks" (Di Caro & Dorigo, 1998). Ants use the network traversal time to find the quickest path between two nodes. Researchers have provided a detailed mathematical analysis of antnet, and have developed simulation against a number of other routing algorithms. Other researchers proceed in a similar way, presenting revisions to antnet and comparing them with others (Arnous et al., 2007; Baran & Sosa, 2000; Dhillon & Van Mieghem, 2007), see Table 3.

As such antnet has under gone a number of revisions from a wider community, as well as refinements from the initial researchers. For example—in the antnet-FA, initially antnet-CO (Di Caro & Dorigo, 1998)—the idea of ants travelling along with data is changes by putting them at a higher priority and replacing the measure of path latency with an estimated vlaue. Simulation results are improved over the existing antnet – and the system is renamed as the antnet-CL. Much of antnet's evaluation has been performed with simulations. However, some researchers have implemented and examined it in the hardware domain, such as (Yang et al., 2002) analysing different types of ant-based reinforcement, and (Di Caro & Dorigo, 1998) where comparison results with OSPF are measured.

Although the research is quick to highlight the benefits of antnet it is worth highlighting the trivial case; "when the traffic load is low, almost all the algorithms perform similarly" (Di Caro & Dorigo, 1998). The performance of antnet relies heavily on the availability of "global information," and when adaptations remove this, the results decline accordingly (Liang et al., 2006). Along with this, researchers have considered the algorithm to be too difficult to apply in a real physical environment, as there are "no mechanisms to protect and verify routing information" (Zhong & Evans, 2002). However, the issue of the security should not be confused; antnet is an algorithm, not a routing protocol. Dijkstra's algorithm has none of the security of OSPF, for example.

An interesting revision of antnet by (Aman et al., 2008) allows for effective use of the algorithm on larger networks, where node routing tables would be very large and "each node (would have) to generate many ants", thus contributing more to the network overhead. It produces results quite similar to antnet, though its network topology is quite small and simple. However, there is a very significant decrease in the packet loss using hierarchical routing between groups of local and "super" ants. This has similarities to the short and long distance agents of the BeeHive algorithm (Wedde et al., 2004), which is covered in the next section.

Beehive

There are a number of different optimisation algorithms that are based on the model of bee colony foraging, such as the Artificial Bee Colony (ABC) (Karaboga & Basturk, 2008) and the Bee Colony Optimisation (BCO) (Wong et al., 2008) algorithms. ABC is designed for the continuous case rather than the discrete case, while BCO has been successfully applied to the TSP. Another of these is the Bees Algorithm (BA) as given in (Pham et al., 2006); while it has found application in industry (Pham et al., 2006) it has not yet been used for combinatorial problems. Furthermore, the Bee System (BS) (Teodorovic, 2003), has been developed and refined for the transportation modelling. However, there is a bee-inspired algorithm specifically for network routing, called BeeHive.

Table 3. Antnet algorithm revisions, comparisons, or implementations

Authors	Algorithm / Implementation	Topologies	Year published
Brief explanation of paper			
(Di Caro & Dorigo, 1998)	antnet	**SimpleNet, NSFNET, NTTnet**	1998
Discussion of routing problem, initial presentation of antnet, and comparison with 6 other algorithms (OSPF, SPF, Bellman-Ford, Q-Routing, Predictive Q-Routing, and 'ideal') in various different traffic modes; (Poisson, fixed, temporary high; uniform, random, 'hot spots').			
(Di Caro & Dorigo, 1998)	antnet-FA	**NTTnet**	1998
antnet-FA is introduced (as antnet-CO) – all ants are now high priority. It is compared with the original antnet and the 6 algorithms above, using random and uniform Poisson distribution traffic modes. It produces better results than the original antnet.			
(Baran & Sosa, 2000)	**antnet1.1**	**NTTnet**	**2000**
antnet1.1 adds initial knowledge of neighbour nodes, retention of information about lost links, more exploration and determinism, a limit to ants within a network, and conditions for ant self-destruction. Results show it to perform similar to, or better than, antnet.			
(Liang et al., 2002)	**LocalAnt**	**NTTnet**	**2002**
Presents the Distributed Genetic Algorithm (DGA), and discusses GAs. LocalAnt is the same as antnet, but nodes **only** hold routing tables for neighbouring nodes. Results indicate LocalAnt performs worse than DGA, which itself performs worse than the (global) antnet.			
(Yang et al., 2002)	**antnet over LAN**	**Own design**	**2002**
Physical implementation of antnet. Uses constant and dynamic reinforcement methods of antnet discussed in (Di Caro & Dorigo, 1998), on a small (5 node) LAN. Results show dynamic method improves network performance under heavy load.			
(Cheng & Hou, 2002)	**GAs and ant routing**	**Own design (mesh)**	**2003**
The original antnet algorithm is used by this algorithm, to generate a number of paths. These paths are combined using the GA principle of crossover, and the reinforcement values are altered based on the result. When compared to "antnet-like" algorithms, performance is slightly better under moderate network load.			
(Wedde et al., 2004)	**antnet (CO/CL?)**	**NTTnet**	**2004**
Presents BeeHive. BeeHive is a similar agent-based algorithm to antnet though using the honey bee foraging model. It uses smaller routing tables, only uses forward agents, and eliminates the need for clock sync. It is compared to antnet – although it is unclear which method is used – and displays similar results.			
(Strobbe et al.,2005)	**Adapted antnet over LAN**	**Own design**	**2005**
Another physical implementation of antnet. It uses some statistical adaptations from (Baran, 2001) (Baran & Sosa, 2000) and avoids needing clock sync between routers by using abstracted time values – also helping avoid the effects of routing loops. It then compares antnet to OSPF, showing improved throughput but a diminished response to link failures.			
(Tekiner et al., 2004) (Tekiner & Ghassemlooy, 2005)	**'Improved' antnet(s)** **Multi-colony antnet**	**Random grid** **Own (irregular) design**	**2004-2009**
This revision of antnet deletes old ants and limits routing table reinforcement values for small node numbers. Further revisions use gradual 'evaporation' of reinforcement values, and a multi-colony approach. Compared with original antnet, changes show improvement under different types of load on both tested topologies.			
(Arnous et al., 2007)	**Modified antnet**	**SimpleNet**	**2007**
This adds a limit to ant number and a load balancing technique to the standard antnet. It is compared to the original antnet within a simulation. The results show similar throughput, and a reduction of packet delay.			
(Dhillon & Van Mieghem, 2007)	**antnet (with assumptions)**	**Random graphs**	**2007**
Provides a more in-depth look at other ant routing methods, with more focus on mathematics and complexity. A number of random graphs and node lattices are tested with the antnet algorithm. antnet is found to produce better performance than Dijkstra's in many situations, and is quite robust, with natural load balancing.			
(Aman et al., 2008)	**Super-antnet**	**Own design**	**2008**
This revision proposes a hierarchical algorithm using two types of ants, "local" and "super" ants, to improve scalability. It is compared to antnet, and results show lower overhead and jitter, as well as a lower ant loss. It is also compared to 'DV' and 'LS' algorithms, showing slight improvements but more overhead than DV.			

BeeHive, proposed by (Wedde et al., 2004), is independent of the other bee colony models and is immediately compared to antnet, listing some improvements; the bee agents "need not be equipped with a stack", each node can have a "smaller routing table", BeeHive "requires only forward moving agents," etc. (Wedde et al., 2004). It uses two kinds of agents, short and long distance, and nominally divides a given network into 'foraging regions', creating a hierarchical routing situation. Unlike the antnet definition, the researchers make explicit reference to TCP/IP and packet sizes with a view to implementation, and (Farooq, 2006) describes a practical experiment using BeeHive. Like other bee-inspired algorithms, published materials for BeeHive are quite few in number and largely attributable to members of the same research group (Wedde et al., 2004; Farooq, 2006; Wedde & Farooq, 2005). The foremost paper compares BeeHive to antnet, DGA, and OSPF. It makes use of the NTTnet topology, as is also found through many of the papers in Figure 1. Wedde et al. (2004) demonstrates that "BeeHive achieves a better or similar performance as compared to antnet" (Wedde et al., 2004), but does not specify whether the experiment used the original specification, or antnet-FA.

Some of BeeHive's results do not show much difference to antnet, although it has a low throughput jitter and a very low packet delay during a particular 'hot spot' simulation. Conversely, during simulated node failures, the throughput does not significantly differ. Additionally, BeeHive's packet delay results are quite excessive, surpassing even DGA, which did comparatively worse than the swarm intelligence algorithms.

Others

Based on Di Caro and Dorigo's work, the paper (Liang et al., 2002) has questioned antnet's use of 'global information', and has noted that "as forward ants propagate across the network, the amount of information they need to 'carry' also increases" (Liang et al., 2002). To address this, the distributed genetic algorithm (DGA) has been developed, making use of Genetic Algorithms (GA) (Mitchell, 1998), another method of searching inspired by natural systems. GA makes use of models of genetic processes—selection, crossover, and random mutation. Important mechanisms of DGA are that "best case solutions are allowed to periodically migrate between neighbouring nodes" (Liang et al., 2006), and routing tables contain 'link offsets', pointers to links between nodes. DGA does not store full routes, merely the next best 'hop'. While DGA do not perform as well as antnet as originally defined, it produces improved results compared to 'LocalAnt', an adaptation where nodes could only route directly to neighbouring nodes.

Another GA approach reported in (Munetomo, 1999) is known as the Genetic Adaptive Routing Algorithm (GARA). It inspired from the Liang's work, though unlike DGA's 'link offsets' the routing table entries for GARA specify nodes absolutely. (Munetomo et al., 2002) have modelled a network and simulated GARA upon it, comparing it to the SPF algorithm—they have shown that it performs better than SPF on "heavily-loaded networks". Initial performance is similar to SPF, as before routing tables are refined, GARA uses Dijkstra's algorithm (Dijkstra, 1959) to route packets. Results show that GARA does outperform in certain cases, but a full comparison of network packets was not shown in the results.

A novel idea on genetic ant routing algorithm was published in (Cheng & Hou, 2002), which is also called GARA. This combined both antnet and GA principles. It uses ants to generate paths, as per ACO, and introduces an element of crossover, where paths are refined against one another. The paper produced a proof of concept, comparing an antnet-like interpretation with their crossover idea, and results suggested an improvement – but no follow-up work has yet appeared.

An in-depth review of a number of routing algorithms, nature-inspired and mathematical can be found in (Wedde & Farooq, 2006). This paper is a very detailed survey explaining the research and theory behind many different algorithms, with some outside the scope of this work. One such method not otherwise covered is Q-Routing, proposed by (Boyan & Littman, 1993), and it is an example of an algorithm with a similar learning approach to the swarm intelligence. When a node x sends some data a to node y, x receives the estimated time of delivery for a. Based on this, its own estimation of the delivery changes – not to the value produced by y, but in a way affected by it – i.e., x is learning about the state of y. Q-Routing was compared to OSPF over the NSFNET topology and the results show with very little difference (Tekiner, Ghassemlooy & Srikanth, 2004).

CONCLUSION

It has been shown that by detection and dropping of packets that travel continuously within the network the antnet's performance, in terms of network throughput and the average packet delay, can be improved. The effect of traffic fluctuations on the network performance has been limited by the introduction of boundaries. To overcome the problem of stagnation and adaptability, a new antnet algorithm was proposed which used link usage statistics as a feedback signal and reinforced the solution by evaporation parameter to improve the performance of the algorithm. Evaporation parameter was calculated based on the link usage statistics held by every node. Simulation results showed that under non-uniform traffic conditions the algorithm with evaporation displayed a reduced average delay per packet compared with algorithm with no evaporation, without adding a significant overhead to the network and to the node. The only disadvantage being the difference observed in the best and the worst case performance of the algorithm. We have shown that evaporating path probabilities have no effect on uniform and non-problematic traffic conditions. Multiple ant colonies was applied to the packet switched networks and results were compared with the other approaches. Results showed that the throughput could be increased when compared with other schemes, but with no gain in average packet delay. However, for larger size networks more ant colonies would be required (thus large number of routing tables).

REFERENCES

Aman, Akbarzadeh-T, & Naghibzadeh. (2008). A novel approach to distributed routing by super-AntNet. In *Proceedings of CEC 2008*, (pp. 2151-2157). CEC.

Amin, & Mikler. (2003). Agent-based distance vector routing: a resource efficient and scalable approach to routing in large communication networks. *Journal of Systems and Software, 71*(3), 215-227.

Appleby, & Steward. (1994). Mobile software agents for control in telecommunication networks. *British Telecom Technical Journal, 12*, 104-113.

Arnous, A. (2007). Improving the load balancing within the data network via modified antnet algorithm. In *Proceeding of ICICT 2007* (pp. 189–195). Salem: ICICT. doi:10.1109/ITICT.2007.4475646.

Barán, & Sosa. (2000). A new approach for antnet routing. In *Proceedings of the 9th International Conference on Computer Communications and Networks*, (pp. 303-308). IEEE.

Baran. (2001). Improved AntNet routing. *ACM SIGCOMM, 31*(2), 42-48.

Beckers, Deneubourg, & Goss. (1992). Trails and u-turns in the selection of a path by the ant Lasius Niger. *Journal of Theoretical Biology, 159*, 397–415. doi:10.1016/S0022-5193(05)80686-1.

Bonabeau, Dorigo, & Theraulaz. (2000). Inspiration for optimization from social insect behavior. *Nature, 406*, 39–42. doi:10.1038/35017500 PMID:10894532.

Bonabeau, H´enaux, Gu´erin, Snyers, Kuntz, & Theraulaz. (1998). Routing in telecommunications networks with smart ant-like agents. In *Proceedings of IATA '98, 2nd Int. Workshop on Intelligent Agents for Tele. Applns* (LNAI), (vol. 1437, pp. 60-71). Berlin: Springer-Verlag.

Boyan, & Littman. (1994). Packet routing in dynamically changing networks: A reinforcement learning approach. In *Proceedings of Advances in Neural Information Processing Systems*, (pp. 671-671). IEEE.

Caro, D. & Dorigo. (1997). *AntNet: A mobile agents approach to adaptive routing* (In Tech. Report 97-12). Universit´e Libre de Bruxelles, IRIDIA.

Di Caro, & Dorigo. (1998). Two ant colony algorithms for best-effort routing in datagram networks. In *Proceedings of 10th Intern. Conf. on Parallel and Distributed Computing and Systems*. Las Vegas, NV: IEEE.

Caro, Di, & Dorigo. (1998). AntNet: Distributed stigmergetic control for communications networks. *Journal of Artificial Intelligence Research, 9*, 317–365.

Cheng, & Hou. (2002). A study of genetic ant routing algorithm. In *Proceedings of the 2nd International Conference on Machine Learning and Cybernetics*, (Vol. 4, pp. 2041-2045). IEEE.

Dhillon, & Van Mieghem. (2007). Performance analysis of the antnet algorithm. *Computer Networks, 51*(8), 2104-2125.

Dijkstra. (1959). A note on two problems in connexion with graphs. *Numerische Mathematik, 1*, 269-271.

Dorigo, Di Caro, & Sampels. (2002). Ant algorithms. In *Proceedings of ANTS 2002*. Brussels, Belgium: Springer-Verlag. ISBN: 3540441468 Boyan, & Littman. (1994). Packet routing in dynamically changing networks: A reinforcement learning approach. In *Advances in NIPS 6*. San Francisco: Morgan Kauffman.

Dorigo & Stutzle. (2004). *Ant colony optimization*. Bradford Book.

Farooq. (2006). *From the wisdom of the hive to intelligent routing in telecommunication networks: A step towards intelligent network management through natural engineering*. (PhD Thesis). Technische Universität Dortmund, Dortmund, Germany.

Karaboga, & Basturk. (2008). On the performance of artificial bee colony (ABC) algorithm. *Applied Soft Computing, 8*(1), 687-697.

Liang, Zincir-Heywood, & Heywood. (2002). Intelligent packets for dynamic network routing using distributed genetic algorithm. In *Proceedings of the Genetic and Evolutionary Computation Conference (GECCO)*, (pp. 88-96). GECCO.

Liang, Zincir-Heywood, & Heywood. (2006). Adding more intelligence to the network routing problem: AntNet and Ga-agents. *Applied Soft Computing, 6*(3), 244–257. doi:10.1016/j.asoc.2005.01.005.

Mitchell. (1998). *An introduction to genetic algorithms*. Cambridge, MA: MIT Press.

Munetomo, Y. Akama, & Sato. (2002). Empirical investigations on the genetic adaptive routing algorithm in the internet. In *Proceedings of CEC 2002*, (pp. 1236-1243). CEC.

Munetomo. (1999). Designing genetic algorithms for adaptive routing algorithms in the internet. In *Proceedings of the GECCO 1999, Workshop on Evolutionary Telecommunications: Past, Present and Future*. GECCO.

Park, & Kim. (2007). Performance analysis of AntNet routing scheme with queuing approach. In *Proceedings of the Asia-Pacific Conference on Communications*, (pp. 317-320). IEEE.

Pham, G., & Koc, O. Rahim, & Zaidi. (2006). The bees algorithm – A novel tool for complex optimisation problems. In *Proceedings of the Innovative Production Machines and Systems Conference (IPROMS)*, (pp. 454-461). IPROMS.

Pham, S., & Ghanbarzadeh, K. Otri, & Packianather. (2006). Optimising neural networks for identification of wood defects using the bees algorithm. In *Proceedings of INDIN 2006*, (pp. 1346-1351). INDIN.

Schoonderwoerd. (1996). *Collective intelligence for network control*. (M.S.c Thesis). Delft University of Technology, Delft, The Netherlands.

Sim & Sun. (2003). Ant colony optimization for routing and load-balancing: Survey and new directions. *IEEE Transactions on Man and Cybernetics Systems Part A, 33*(5), 560–572. doi:10.1109/TSMCA.2003.817391.

Sim, & Sun. (2002). Multiple ant-colony optimization for network routing. In *Proceedings of 1st Int. Symp. Cyberworld*, (pp. 277-281). IEEE.

Sim, & Sun. (2003). Ant colony optimization for routing and load-balancing: survey and new directions. *IEEE Transactions on Man and Cybernetics n Systems, Part A, 33*(5), 560-572.

Strobbe, V., & Van Breusegem, C. Pickavet & Demeester. (2005). Implementation and evaluation of AntNet, a distributed shortest-path algorithm. In *Proceedings of the Advanced Industrial Conference on Telecommunications/Service Assurance with Partial and Intermittent Resources Conference/E-Learning on Telecommunications Workshop (AICT/SAPIR/ELETE 2005)*, (pp. 320-325). AICT.

Subramanian, Druschel, & Chen. (1997). Ants and reinforcement learning: A case study in routing in dynamic networks. [San Francisco: Morgan Kauffman.]. *Proceedings of, IJCAI-97*, 832–838.

Tekiner, G. S. & Al-khayatt. (2004). Antnet routing algorithm-improved version. In *Proceedings of CSNDSP04*, (pp. 416-419). CSNDSP.

Tekiner, Ghassemlooy, & Al-khayatt. (2004). Improved antnet routing algorithm with link probability evaporation over the given time window. [SOFTCOM.]. *Proceedings of, SOFTCOM04*, 502–505.

Tekiner, Ghassemlooy, & Srikanth. (2004). Comparison of the Q-routing and shortest path routing algorithms. In *Proceedings of the PGNET*, (pp. 428-432). PGNET.

Tekiner, & Ghassemlooy. (2005). Improved antnet routing algorithm for packet switching. *Mediterranean Journal of Computer Networks, 1*(2), 69-76.

Teodorović. (2003). Transport modelling by multi-agent systems: A swarm intelligence approach. *Transportation Planning and Technology, 26*(4), 289–312. doi:10.1080/0308106032000154593.

Varela, & Sinclair. (1999). Ant colony optimization for virtual-wavelength-path routing and wavelength allocation. In *Proceedings of Congress Evolutionary Computation*, (pp. 1809-1816). IEEE.

Wedde, Farooq, & Zhang. (2004). BeeHive: An efficient fault-tolerant routing algorithm inspired by honey bee behaviour. In *Proceedings of the 4th International Workshop on Ant Colony Optimization and Swarm Intelligence (ANTS) 2004*, (pp. 83-94). ANTS.

Wedde, & Farooq. (2005). A performance evaluation framework for nature inspired routing algorithms. In F. Rothlauf et al. (Eds.), *Applications of Evolutionary Computing*, (pp. 136-146). Berlin: Springer.

Wedde, & Farooq. (2005). Beehive: New ideas for developing routing algorithms inspired by honey bee behavior. In S. Olariu & A. Y. Zomaya (Eds.), *Handbook of Bioinspired Algorithms and Applications*, (pp. 321-339). London: Chapman and Hall/CRC.

Wedde, & Farooq. (2006). A comprehensive review of nature inspired routing algorithms for fixed telecommunications networks. *Journal of Systems Architecture, 52*(8-9), 461-484.

White, Pagurek, & Oppacher. (1998). ASGA: Improving the ant system by integration with genetic algorithms. In *Proceedings of 3rd Conference on Genetic Programming (GP/SGA'98)*, (pp. 610-617). GP/SGA.

Wong, Low, & Chong. (2008). Bee colony optimization with local search for travelling salesman problem. In *Proceedings of the 6th IEEE International Conference on Industrial Informatics (INDIN)*, (pp. 1019-1025). INDIN.

Yang, Z.-H. Heywood, & Srinivas. (2002). Agent-based routing algorithms on a LAN. In *Proceedings of the IEEE Canadian Conference on Electrical and Computer Engineering 2002*, (pp. 1442-1447). IEEE.

Zhong, & Evans. (2002). *When ants attack: security issues for stigmergic systems* (Technical Report CS-2002-23). Blacksburg, VA: University of Virginia.

ENDNOTES

[1] η weights is the number of samples that affect the average and set to 0.05 (Di Caro et al., 1998).

[2] α weights l_n with respect to routing table entries and set to 0.3 (Di Caro et al., 1998).

[3] c_1 and c_2 are chosen experimentally to be 0.3 and 0.7 respectively.

[4] $z = 1/\sqrt{(1-\gamma)}$, γ lies is the confidence, $\gamma \in [0.75, 0.8]$.

[5] In [17] $a = 0$, $b = 1$.

[6] In our previous work evaporation is defined as link usage ratio only, where $a = 0$ and $b = 1$ (Tekiner et al., 2004).

[7] When $a = 1.0$ and $b = 0.0$ it is represented as evap (1.0,0.0).

[8] An ant is said to complete its cycle when it completes its journey from source node to the destination node.

Compilation of References

Ahn, C. W., Ramakrishna, R. S., Kang, C. G., & Choi, I. C. (2001). Shortest path routing algorithm using Hopfield neural network. *Electronics Letters*, *37*(19), 1176–1178. doi:10.1049/el:20010800.

Akyildiz, I. F., Wang, X., & Wang, W. (2005). Wireless mesh networks: A survey. *Computer Networks*, *47*(4), 31–42. doi:10.1016/j.comnet.2004.12.001.

Alfouzan, I., & Jayasumana, A. (2003). An adaptive wavelength assignment algorithm for WDM networks. *Optical Networks Magazine*, *4*(2), 46–55.

Alharbi, F., & Ansari, N. (2005). Distributed bandwidth allocation for resilient packet ring networks. *Computer Networks*, *49*(2), 161–171. doi:10.1016/j.comnet.2004.12.004.

Alharbi, F., & Ansari, N. (2006). SSA: Simple scheduling algorithm for resilient packet ring networks. *IEE Proceedings. Communications*, *153*(2), 183–188. doi:10.1049/ip-com:20045232.

Ali, M. K. M., & Kamoun, F. (1993). Neural networks for shortest path computation and routing in computer networks. *IEEE Transactions on Neural Networks*, *4*(6), 941–954. doi:10.1109/72.286889 PMID:18276524.

Aman, Akbarzadeh-T, & Naghibzadeh. (2008). A novel approach to distributed routing by super-AntNet. In *Proceedings of CEC 2008*, (pp. 2151-2157). CEC.

Amin, & Mikler. (2003). Agent-based distance vector routing: a resource efficient and scalable approach to routing in large communication networks. *Journal of Systems and Software, 71*(3), 215-227.

Anderson, D. Z., Mizrahi, V., Erdogan, T., & White, A. E. (1993). Production of in-fiber gratings using a diffractive element. *Electronics Letters*, *29*(6), 566–568. doi:10.1049/el:19930379.

Anderson, T., Peterson, L., Shenker, S., & Turner, J. (2005). Overcoming the internet impasse through virtualization. *Computer*, *38*(4), 34–41. doi:10.1109/MC.2005.136.

Antonakopoulos, S., & Zhang, L. (2009). Approximation algorithms for grooming in optical network design. In *Proceedings of IEEE INFOCOM*. IEEE.

Appleby, & Steward. (1994). Mobile software agents for control in telecommunication networks. *British Telecom Technical Journal, 12*, 104-113.

Arnous, R. A., Arafat, H. A., & Salem, M. M. (2007). Improving the load balancing within the data network via modified antnet algorithm. In *Proceedings of the 5th International Conference on Information and Communications Technology*, (vol. 5, pp. 189 – 195). IEEE.

Arnous, A. (2007). Improving the load balancing within the data network via modified antnet algorithm. In *Proceeding of ICICT 2007* (pp. 189–195). Salem: ICICT. doi:10.1109/ITICT.2007.4475646.

Assi, C., Ye, Y., Dixit, S., & Ali, M. (2003). Dynamic bandwidth allocation for quality-of-service over ethernet PONs. *IEEE Journal on Selected Areas in Communications*, *21*, 1467–1477. doi:10.1109/JSAC.2003.818837.

Azodolmolky, S. et al. (2011). Experimental demonstration of an impairment aware network planning and operation tool for transparent/translucent optical networks. *Journal of Lightwave Technology*, *29*, 439–448. doi:10.1109/JLT.2010.2091622.

Azodolmolky, S., Klinkowski, M., Marin, E., Careglio, D., Pareta, J., & Tomkos, I. (2009). A survey on physical layer impairments aware routing and wavelength assignment algorithms in optical networks. *Computer Networks*, *53*(7), 926–944. doi:10.1016/j.comnet.2008.11.014.

Balakrishnan, A., Magnanti, T. L., & Mirchandani, P. (2004). Connectivity-splitting models for survivable network design. *Networks*, *43*(1), 10–27. doi:10.1002/net.10100.

Balakrishnan, A., Mirchandani, P., & Natarajan, H. P. (2009). Connectivity upgrade models for survivable network design. *Operations Research*, *57*(1), 170–186. doi:10.1287/opre.1080.0579.

Baliga, J., Ayre, R., Hinton, K., Sorin, W. V., & Tucker, S. (2009). Energy consumption in optical IP networks. *Journal of Lightwave Technology*, *27*(13), 2391–2403. doi:10.1109/JLT.2008.2010142.

Banerjee, N., & Sharan, S. (2004). A evolutionary algorithm for solving the single objective static routing and wavelength assignment problem in WDM networks. In *Proceedings of International Conference on Intelligent Sensing and Information Processing*, (pp. 13 – 18). IEEE.

Banerjee, D., & Mukherjee, B. A. (1996). A practical approach for routing and wavelength assignment in large wavelength-routed optical networks. *IEEE Journal on Selected Areas in Communications*, *14*, 903–908. doi:10.1109/49.510913.

Barabasi, A.-L. (2003). *Linked – How everything is connected to everything*. New York: Plume.

Barán, & Sosa. (2000). A new approach for antnet routing. In *Proceedings of the 9th International Conference on Computer Communications and Networks*, (pp. 303-308). IEEE.

Baran. (2001). Improved AntNet routing. *ACM SIGCOMM, 31*(2), 42-48.

Bastos-Filho, C. J. A., Oliveira Júnior, M. A. C., Silva, D. R. C., & Santana, R. A. (2011). Optimizing a routing algorithm based on Hopfield neural networks for graphic processing units. In *Proceedings of IEEE Foundations on Computational Intelligence - SSCI 2011* (pp. 88-93). IEEE.

Bastos-Filho, C. J. A., Santana, R. A., Silva, D. R. C., Martins-Filho, J. F., & Chaves, D. A. R. (2010). Hopfield neural networks for routing in all-optical networks. In *Proceedings of the International Conference on Transparent Optical Networks* (pp. 1–4). IEEE.

Bastos-Filho, C. J. A., Santos, A. M., Chaves, D. A. R., & Martins Filho, J. F. (2011). A model to allow remote and distributed simulation of optical networks using XML. In *Proceedings of the 2011 SBMO/IEEE MTT-S International Microwave and Optoelectronics Conference*, (pp. 430-434). IEEE.

Bastos-Filho, C. J. A., Chaves, D. A. R., Silva, F. S. F., Pereira, H. A., & Martins-Filho, J. F. (2011). Wavelength assignment for physical-layer-impaired optical networks using evolutionary computation. *Journal of Optical Communications and Networking*, *3*(3), 178–188. doi:10.1364/JOCN.3.000178.

Bastos-Filho, C. J. A., Oliveira Junior, M. A. C., Silva, D. R. C., & Santana, R. A. (2011). Optimizing a routing algorithm based on hopfield neural networks for graphic processing units.[IEEE.]. *Proceedings of Foundations of Computational Intelligence, 2011*, 88–93.

Bastos-Filho, C. J. A., Santana, R. A., & Oliveira, A. L. I. (2007). A novel approach for a routing algorithm based on a discrete time Hopfield neural network.[IEEE.]. *Proceedings of the Foundations of Computational Intelligence, 2007*, 363–369.

Batchellor, R., & Gerstel, O. (2006). Cost effective architectures for core transport networks. In *Proceedings of the Optical Fiber Communication Conference (OFC)*. OFC.

Baykasoglu, A., Özbakýr, L., & Tapkan, P. (2007). Artificial bee colony algorithm and its application to generalized assignment problem. In Chan, F. T. S., & Tiwari, M. K. (Eds.), *Swarm Intelligence: Focus on Ant and Particle Swarm Optimization* (pp. 113–143). Vienna, Austria: I-Tech Education and Publishing. doi:10.5772/5101.

Bean, N., & Costa, A. (2005). An analytic modeling approach for network routing algorithms that use "ant-like" mobil agents. *Computer Networks*, *49*, 243–268. doi:10.1016/j.comnet.2005.01.008.

Beckers, Deneubourg, & Goss. (1992). Trails and u-turns in the selection of a path by the ant Lasius Niger. *Journal of Theoretical Biology, 159*, 397–415. doi:10.1016/S0022-5193(05)80686-1.

Becouarn, L., et al. (2004). *42 x 42.7 Gb/s RZ-DPSK transmission over a 4820 km long NZDSF deployed line using C-band-only EDFAs*. Paper presented at the OFC'04. Los Angeles, CA.

Bendilli, G. (2000). *Optical performance monitoring techniques*. Paper presented at 26th European Conference on Optical Communication (ECOC'00). Munich, Germany.

Bhandari, S., & Park, E. K. (2006). Hybrid optical wireless networks. In *Proceedings of the International Conference on Networking, International Conference on Systems, and International Conference on Mobile Communications and Learning Technologies*, (pp. 113–117). IEEE.

Bishop, D. (2009). *Fixed point package user's guide*.

Blumenthal, D. J., Olsson, B. E., Rossi, G., Dimmick, T. E., Rau, L., & Masanovic, M. et al. (2000). All-optical label swapping networks and technologies. *IEEE/OSA. Journal of Lightwave Technology, 18*(12), 2058–2075. doi:10.1109/50.908817.

Bo, X., Zuqing, Z., Haijun, Y., Wei, J., Harris, D. L., & Ikezawa, K. ... Yoo, S.J.B. (2007). *First field trial of OLS network testbed with all-optical contention resolution of asynchronous, variable-length optical packets*. Paper presented at OFC/NFOEC 2007. Anaheim, CA.

Bonabeau, E., Henaux, F., Gu´erin, S., Snyers, D., Kuntz, P., & Theraulaz, G. (1998). Routing in telecommunications networks with ant-like agents. In Albayrak & Garijo (Eds.), *Intelligent Agents for Telecommunication Applications — Proceedings of the Second International Workshop on Intelligent Agents for Telecommunica-tion (IATA'98)* (LNCS), (vol. 1437). Berlin: Springer-Verlag.

Bonabeau, H´enaux, Gu´erin, Snyers, Kuntz, & Theraulaz. (1998). Routing in telecommunications networks with smart ant-like agents. In *Proceedings of IATA '98, 2nd Int. Workshop on Intelligent Agents for Tele. Applns* (LNAI), (vol. 1437, pp. 60-71). Berlin: Springer-Verlag.

Bonabeau, Dorigo, & Theraulaz. (2000). Inspiration for optimization from social insect behavior. *Nature, 406*, 39–42. doi:10.1038/35017500 PMID:10894532.

Borne, D., et al. (2006). *1.6-b/s/Hz spectrally efficient 40 x 85.6-Gb/s transmission over 1,700 km of SSMF using POLMUX-RZ-DQPSK*. Paper presented at the OFC'06. Los Angeles, CA.

Boudriga, N., Lazzez, A., Khlifi, Y., & Zghal, M. (2008). *All optical network switching: A new scheme for QoS provision and virtual memory control*. Paper presented at 10th International Conference on Transparent Optical Networks (ICTON'08). Athens, Greece.

Bouillet, E., Ellinas, G., Labourdette, J. F., & Ramamurthy, R. (2007). *Path routing in mesh optical networks*. Hoboken, NJ: Wiley. doi:10.1002/9780470032985.

Boyan, & Littman. (1994). Packet routing in dynamically changing networks: A reinforcement learning approach. In *Proceedings of Advances in Neural Information Processing Systems*, (pp. 671-671). IEEE.

Bratton, D., & Kennedy, J. (2007). Defining a standard for particle swarm optimization. In *Proceedings of the Swarm Intelligence Symposium, 2007*. IEEE.

Brown, S., Francis, R., Rose, J., & Vranesic, Z. (1992). *Field-programmable gate arrays* (4th ed.). Secaucus, NJ: Springer-Verlag. doi:10.1007/978-1-4615-3572-0.

Bruno, R., Conti, M., & Gregori, E. (2005). Mesh networks: Commodity multihop ad hoc networks. *IEEE Communications Magazine, 43*(3), 123–131. doi:10.1109/MCOM.2005.1404606.

Buriol, L. S., Resende, M. G. C., & Thorup, M. (2007). Survivable IP network design with OSPF routing. *Networks, 49*(1), 51–64. doi:10.1002/net.20141.

Caenegem, B., Parys, W., de Tuck, F., & Demeester, P. (1998). Dimensioning of survivable WDM networks. *IEEE Journal on Selected Areas in Communications, 16*(7), 1146–1157. doi:10.1109/49.725185.

Calabretta, N., Jung, H. D., Herrera Llorente, J., Tangdiongga, E., Koonen, A. M. J., & Dorren, H. J. S. (2008). *1 x 4 all-optical packet switch at 160 Gb/s employing optical processing of scalable in-band address labels*. Paper presented at OFC 2008. San Diego, CA.

Calabretta, N., Contestabile, G., d'Errico, A., & Ciaramella, E. (2005). All-optical label processor/erasure for label swapping of 12.5 Gbit/s spectrally separated bit-serial DPSK label and payload. *Electronics Letters*, *41*, 541–543. doi:10.1049/el:20050449.

Calabretta, N., Contestabile, G., Kim, S. H., Lee, S. K., & Ciaramella, E. (2006). Exploiting time-to-wavelength conversion for all-optical label processing. *IEEE Photonics Technology Letters*, *18*, 436–438. doi:10.1109/LPT.2005.863207.

Calabretta, N., de Waardt, H., Khoe, G. D., & Dorren, H. J. S. (2004). Ultrafast asynchronous multi-output all-optical header processor. *IEEE Photonics Technology Letters*, *16*, 1182–1184. doi:10.1109/LPT.2004.824993.

Calabretta, N., Presi, M., Contestabile, A., & Ciaramella, E. (2007). All-optical asynchronous serial-to-parallel converter circuit for DPSK optical packets. *IEEE Photonics Technology Letters*, *19*, 783–785. doi:10.1109/LPT.2007.895895.

Calabretta, N., Wang, W., Ditewig, T., Raz, O., Agis, F. G., de Waardt, S. Z. H., & Dorren, H. J. S. (2010). Scalable optical packet switches for multiple data formats and data rates packets. *IEEE Photonics Technology Letters*, *22*(7), 483–485. doi:10.1109/LPT.2010.2040993.

Camazine, S., Deneubourg, J.-L., Franks, N., Sneyd, J., Theraulaz, G., & Bonabeau, E. (2001). *Self-organization in biological systems*. Princeton, NJ: Princeton University Press.

Camazine, S., & Sneyd, J. (1991). A model of collective nectar source by honey bees: Self-organization through simple rules. *Journal of Theoretical Biology*, *149*(4), 547–571. doi:10.1016/S0022-5193(05)80098-0.

Caro, D. & Dorigo. (1997). *AntNet: A mobile agents approach to adaptive routing* (In Tech. Report 97-12). Universit´e Libre de Bruxelles, IRIDIA.

Caro, Di, & Dorigo. (1998). AntNet: Distributed stigmergetic control for communications networks. *Journal of Artificial Intelligence Research*, *9*, 317–365.

Carvalho, D., & Bastos-Filho, C. (2008). Clan particle swarm optimization. In *Proceedings of Evolutionary Computation, 2008*. IEEE.

Chabarek, J., Sommers, J., Barford, P., Estan, C., Tsang, D., & Wright, S. (2008). Power awareness in network design and routing. In *Proceedings of IEEE INFOCOM* (pp. 457–465). IEEE. doi:10.1109/INFOCOM.2008.93.

Chang, C. T., Cassaboom, J. A., & Taylor, H. F. (1977). Fibre-optic delay-line devices for R. F. signal processing. *Electronics Letters*, *13*(22), 678–680. doi:10.1049/el:19770481.

Chao, H.-L., & Liao, W. (2003). Credit-based slot allocation formultimedia mobile ad hoc networks. *IEEE Journal on Selected Areas in Communications*, *21*(10), 1642–1651. doi:10.1109/JSAC.2003.815232.

Charbonneau, N., & Vokkarane, V. M. (2010). Routing and wavelength assignment of static manycast demands over all-optical wavelength-routed WDM networks. *IEEE/OSA Journal of Optical Communication and Networking*, *2*(7), 427-440.

Chaves, D. A. R., Bastos-Filho, C. J. A., & Martins-Filho, J. F. (2010). Multiobjective physical topology design of all-optical networks considering QoS and Capex. In *Proceedings of the Optical Fiber Communication Conference (OFC)*. OFC.

Chaves, D. A. R., Aguiar, D. O., Bastos-Filho, C. J. A., & Martins-Filho, J. F. (2010). Fast and adaptive impairment aware routing and wavelength assignment algorithm optimized by offline simulations. *Optical Switching and Networking*, *7*(3), 127–138. doi:10.1016/j.osn.2010.05.001.

Chaves, D. A. R., Aguiar, D. O., Bastos-Filho, C. J. A., & Martins-Filho, J. F. (2011). A methodology to design the link cost functions for impairment aware routing algorithms in optical networks. *Photonic Network Communications*, *22*, 133–150. doi:10.1007/s11107-011-0314-2.

Cheng, & Hou. (2002). A study of genetic ant routing algorithm. In *Proceedings of the 2nd International Conference on Machine Learning and Cybernetics*, (Vol. 4, pp. 2041-2045). IEEE.

Chen, W., Tucker, R. S., Yi, X., Shieh, W., & Evans, J. S. (2005). Optical signal-to-noise ratio monitoring using uncorrelated beat noise. *IEEE Photonics Technology Letters*, *17*(11), 2484–2486. doi:10.1109/LPT.2005.858100.

Chen, W., Zhong, S., Zhu, Z., Chen, W., & Chen, Y. J. (2003). Adding OSNR and wavelength monitoring functionalities on a double resolution AWG-based power monitoring circuit. *IEEE Photonics Technology Letters*, *15*(6), 858–860. doi:10.1109/LPT.2003.811138.

Chin, T. S. (2005). An ant algorithm for single-hop wavelength assignment in WDM mesh network. In A. Lim (Ed.), *Proceedings of the 17th IEEE International Conference on Tools with Artificial Intelligence ICTAI 2005* (pp. 111–117). Los Alamitos, CA: IEEE Computer Society. doi: 10.1109/ICTAI.2005.33.

Chi, N., Zhang, J., & Jeppesen, P. (2003). All-optical subcarrier labeling based on the carrier suppression of the payload. *IEEE Photonics Technology Letters*, *15*, 781–783. doi:10.1109/LPT.2003.810260.

Chlamtac, I., Ganz, A., & Karmi, G. (1992). Lightpath communications: An approach to high bandwidth optical WAN's. *IEEE Transactions on Communications*, *40*, 1171–1182. doi:10.1109/26.153361.

Choi, J. S., Golmie, N., Lapeyrere, F., Mouveaux, F., & Su, D. (2000). A functional classification of routing and wavelength assignment schemes in DWDM networks: Static case. In *Proceedings of the 7th International Conference on Optical Communication and Networks*. OPNET.

Chong, C. S., Low, M. Y. H., Sivakumar, A. I., & Gay, K. Y. (2006). A bee colony optimization algorithm to job shop scheduling. In L.F. Perrone, B. Lawson, J. Liu, & F.P. Wieland (Eds.), *Proceedings of the 37th Conference on Winter Simulation WSC 2006* (pp. 1954–1961). Monterey, CA: IEEE. doi: 10.1109/WSC.2006.322980

Chowdhury, P. (2011). *Energy-efficient next-generation networks (NGN)*. (Doctoral Dissertation). University of California Davis, Davis, CA.

Chowdhury, P., Tornatore, M., & Mukherjee, B. (2010). On the energy efficiency of mixed-line-rate networks. In *Proceedings of Optical Fiber Communication Conference*, (pp. 1-3). IEEE.

Chowdhury, N., & Boutaba, R. (2009). Network virtualization: state of the art and research challenges. *IEEE Communications Magazine*, *47*, 20–26. doi:10.1109/MCOM.2009.5183468.

Chowdhury, N., Rahman, M., & Boutaba, R. (2009). Virtual network embedding with coordinated node and link mapping. In *Proceedings of IEEE INFOCOM* (pp. 783–791). IEEE. doi:10.1109/INFCOM.2009.5061987.

Chowdhury, P., Mukherjee, B., Sarkar, S., Kramer, G., & Dixit, S. (2009). Hybrid wireless-optical broadband access network (WOBAN), prototype development and research challenges. *IEEE Network*, *23*(3), 41–48. doi:10.1109/MNET.2009.4939262.

Chowdhury, P., Mukherjee, B., Sarkar, S., & Mukherjee, B. (2010). Building a green wireless-optical broadband access network (WOBAN). *IEEE/OSA. Journal of Lightwave Technology*, *28*(16), 2219–2229. doi:10.1109/JLT.2010.2044369.

Chow, P. S., Cioffi, J. M., & Bingham, J. A. C. (1995). A practical discrete multitone transceiver loading algorithm for data transmission over spectrally shaped channels. *IEEE Transactions on Communications*, *43*, 773–775. doi:10.1109/26.380108.

Chung, Y. C. (2000). *Optical monitoring technique for WDM networks*. Paper presented at IEEE/LEOS Summer Topical Meetings 2000. New York, NY.

Chung-Li, L., Sabido, D. J., Poggiolini, P., Hofmeister, R. T., & Kazovsky, L. G. (1995). CORD-a WDMA optical network: Subcarrier-based signaling and control scheme. *IEEE Photonics Technology Letters*, *7*, 555–557. doi:10.1109/68.384542.

Chu, P. P. (2008). *FPGA prototyping by vhdl examples: Xilinx spartan-3 version*. London: Elsevier.

Chu, X., Li, B., & Zhang, Z. (2003). A dynamic RWA algorithm in a wavelength-routed all-optical network with wavelength converters. In *Proceedings of IEEE INFOCOM* (pp. 1795–1802). IEEE.

Cieslik, D. (2009). Network design problems. In *Encyclopedia of Optimization*. London: Springer. doi:10.1007/978-0-387-74759-0_437.

Cisco. (2003). *Internetworking technologies handbook*. Indianapolis, IN: Cisco Systems, Inc.

Cisco. (n.d.). *Data sheet: OC-192/STM-64 line card portfolio for the Cisco ONS 15454 SONET/SDH multiservice provisioning platforms*. Indianapolis, IN: Cisco.

Clerc, M., & Kennedy, J. (2002). The particle swarm - Explosion, stability, and conver-gence in a multidimensional complex space. *IEEE-EC*, *6*, 58–73.

Cohen, M. A., & Grossberg, S. (1988). *Absolute stability of global pattern formation and parallel memory storage by competitive neural networks*. Academic Press.

Colorni, A., Dorigo, M., & Maniezzo, V. (1991). Distributed optimization by ant colonies. In *Proceedings of European Conference on Artificial Life*, (pp. 134-142). IEEE.

Data Tracker. (2005). Impairments and other constraints on optical layer routing - RFC4054. *IETF*. Retrieved from http://datatracker.ietf.org/doc/rfc4054/

Davidović, T., Šelmić, M., & Teodorović, D. (2009). Scheduling of independent tasks – Bee colony optimization approach. In *Proceedings of the 17th Mediterranean Conference on Control and Automation – MED 2009* (pp. 1020-1025). Thessaloniki, Greece: IEEE. doi: 10.1109/MED.2009.5164680

Davik, F., Yilmaz, M., Gjessing, S., & Uzun, N. (2004). IEEE 802.17 resilient packet ring tutorial. *IEEE Communications Magazine*, *42*, 112–118. doi:10.1109/MCOM.2004.1273782.

de Miguel, I., Vallejos, R., Beghelli, A., & Durán, R. J. (2010). Genetic algorithm for joint routing and dimensioning of dynamic WDM networks. *Journal of Optical Communications and Networking*, *1*(7), 608–621. doi:10.1364/JOCN.1.000608.

Deneubourg, Aron, Goss, & Pasteels, (1990). The self-organizing exploratory pattern of the Argentine ant. *Journal of Insect Behavior, 3*, 159-168.

Desurvire, E. (1994). *Erbium-doped fiber amplifiers, principles and applications*. New York: John Wiley & Sons, Inc..

Dhillon, & Van Mieghem. (2007). Performance analysis of the antnet algorithm. *Computer Networks, 51*(8), 2104-2125.

Di Caro, & Dorigo. (1998). Two ant colony algorithms for best-effort routing in datagram networks. In *Proceedings of 10th Intern. Conf. on Parallel and Distributed Computing and Systems*. Las Vegas, NV: IEEE.

Dijkstra. (1959). A note on two problems in connexion with graphs. *Numerische Mathematik, 1*, 269-271.

Ding, L., Zhong, W. D., Lu, C., & Wang, Y. (2004). A new bit error rate monitoring method based on histograms and curve fitting. *Optics Express*, *12*(11), 2507–2511. doi:10.1364/OPEX.12.002507 PMID:19475088.

Dorigo & Stutzle. (2004). *Ant colony optimization*. Bradford Book.

Dorigo, Di Caro, & Sampels. (2002). Ant algorithms. In *Proceedings of ANTS 2002*. Brussels, Belgium: Springer-Verlag. ISBN: 3540441468 Boyan, & Littman. (1994). Packet routing in dynamically changing networks: A reinforcement learning approach. In *Advances in NIPS 6*. San Francisco: Morgan Kauffman.

Dorigo, M. (1992). *Optimization, learning and natural algorithms*. (Ph.D. Thesis). Politecnico di Milano, Milano, Italy.

Dorigo, M., Maniezzo, V., & Colorni, A. (1991). *The ant system: An autocatalytic optimizing process* (Technical Report TR91-016). Milan, Italy: Politecnico di Milano.

Dorigo, M., Caro, G. D., & Gambardella, L. (1999). Ant algorithms for discrete optimization. *Artificial Life*, *5*, 137–172. doi:10.1162/106454699568728 PMID:10633574.

Dorigo, M., & Gambardella, L. (1997). Ant colony system: A cooperative learning approach to the travelling salesman problem. *IEEE Transactions on Evolutionary Computation*, *1*, 53–66. doi:10.1109/4235.585892.

Dorigo, M., Maniezzo, V., & Colorni, A. (1996). The ant system: Optimization by a colony of cooperating agents. *IEEE Transactions on Systems, Man, and Cybernetics Part B*, *26*, 1–13. doi:10.1109/3477.484436.

Dréo, J., Pétrowski, A., Siarry, P., & Tailard, E. (2006). *Metaheuristics for hard optimization: Methods and case studies*. London: Springer.

Dressler, F., & Akan, O. B. (2010). Bio-inspired networking: from theory to practice. *IEEE Communications Magazine*, *48*(11), 176–183. doi:10.1109/MCOM.2010.5621985.

Dressler, F., Suda, T., Carreras, I., Crowcroft, J., & Murata, M. (2010). Guest editorial bio-inspired networking. *IEEE Journal on Selected Areas in Communications, 28*(4), 521–523. doi:10.1109/JSAC.2010.100501.

Dubey, R. (2008). *Introduction to embedded system design using field programmable gate arrays.* London: Springer.

Ducatelle, F., Caro, G. A., & Gambardella, L. M. (2010). *Principles and applications of swarm intelligence for adaptive routing in telecommunications networks.* New York: Springer. doi:10.1007/s11721-010-0040-x.

Duelli, M., Pluntke, C., & Menth, M. (2008), Minimizing installation costs of survivable DWDM-mesh networks: A heuristic approach. In *Proceedings of the Next Generation Internet Networks (NGI),* (pp. 15–22). NGI.

Dupas, A. et al. (1998). 2R all-optical regenerator assessment at 2.5 Gbit/s over 3600 km using only standard fibre. *Electronics Letters, 34*(25), 2424–2425. doi:10.1049/el:19981621.

Durhuus, T. et al. (1996). All-optical wavelength conversion by semiconductor optical amplifiers. *Journal of Lightwave Technology, 14*(6), 942–954. doi:10.1109/50.511594.

Dutta, R., Kamal, A. E., & Rouskas, G. N. (2008). *Traffic grooming for optical networks: Foundations, techniques and frontiers.* New York: Springer. doi:10.1007/978-0-387-74518-3.

Dutta, R., & Rouskas, G. N. (2000). A survey of virtual topology design algorithms for wavelength routed optical networks. *Optical Networks, 1*(1), 73–89.

Dutta, R., & Rouskas, G. N. (2002). On optimal traffic grooming in WDM rings. *IEEE Journal on Selected Areas in Communications, 20*(1), 110–121. doi:10.1109/49.974666.

Dutta, R., & Rouskas, G. N. (2002). Traffic grooming in WDM networks: Past and future. *IEEE Network, 16*(6), 46–56. doi:10.1109/MNET.2002.1081765.

Dzongang, C., Galinier, P., & Piere, S. (2005). A tabu search heuristic for the routing and wavelength assignment problem in optical networks. *IEEE Communications Letters, 9*(5), 426–428. doi: doi:10.1109/LCOMM.2005.05011.

Eberhart, R. C., & Shi, Y. (2007). *Computational intelligence: Concepts to implementations.* San Francisco: Morgan Kaufmann.

Effenberger, F., Cleary, D., Haran, O., Kramer, G., Li, R. D., Oron, M., & Pfeiffer, T. (2007). An introduction to PON technologies. *IEEE Communications Magazine, 45*(3), S17–S25. doi:10.1109/MCOM.2007.344582.

Engelbrecht, A. P. (2007). *Computational intelligence: An introduction.* New York: Wiley Publishing. doi:10.1002/9780470512517.

Euliss, G. W., & Athale, R. A. (1994). Time-integrating correlator based on fiber-optic delay lines. *Optics Letters, 19*, 649–651. doi:10.1364/OL.19.000649 PMID:19844401.

Farooq. (2006). *From the wisdom of the hive to intelligent routing in telecommunication networks: A step towards intelligent network management through natural engineering.* (PhD Thesis). Technische Universität Dortmund, Dortmund, Germany.

Fisher, R. A. (1956). *Statistical methods and scientific inference.* Edinburgh, UK: Oliver and Boyd.

Fonseca, I., Almeida, R., Jr., Waldman, H., & Ribeiro, M. (2004). Meeting optical QoS requirements with reduced complexity in dynamic wavelength assignment. In *Proceedings of the First International Conference on Broadband Networks,* (vol. 1, pp. 331–333). IEEE.

Ford, L. R., & Fulkerson, D. R. (1962). *Flows in networks.* Princeton, NJ: Princeton University Press.

Fsaifes, I., Lepers, C., Lourdiane, M., Gabet, R., & Gallion, P. (2006). *Pulsed laser source coherence time impairments in a direct detection DS-OCDMA system.* Paper presented at Conference on Lasers Electro-Optics (CLEO'06). Long Beach, CA.

Fsaifes, I., Lepers, C., Obaton, A., & Gallion, P. (2006). DS-OCDMA encoder/ decoder performance analysis using optical low-coherence reflectometry. *IEEE/OSA Journal of Lightwave Technology, 24*(8), 3121–3126. doi:10.1109/JLT.2006.878039.

Fukuchi, K., et al. (2001). *10.92-Tb/s (273*40-Gb/s) triple-band/ultra-dense WDM optical repeatered transmission experiment.* Paper presented at the OFC 2001. Los Angeles, CA.

Funabashi, M. et al. (2006). Optical clock recovery and 3R regeneration for 10-Gb/s NRZ signal to achieve 10,000-hop cascadability and 1,000,000-km transmission. *IEEE Photonics Technology Letters, 18*(20), 2078–2080. doi:10.1109/LPT.2006.883247.

Gagnaire, M., Koubaa, M., & Puech, N. (2007). Network dimensioning under scheduled and random lightpath demands in all-optical WDM networks. *IEEE Journal on Selected Areas in Communications, 25*, 58–67. doi:10.1109/JSAC-OCN.2007.027506.

Gamst, M. (2009). *A survey of the routing and wavelength assignment problem (Technical Report)*. Copenhagen, Denmark: Technical University of Denmark.

Gao, J., & Li, D. (2008). *BoD service with VCAT/LCAS and GMPLS signaling*. Paper presented at NOMS Workshops 2008. Salvador da Bahia, Brazil.

Garey, M. R., & Johnson, D. S. (1979). *Computers and intractability: A guide to the theory of NP-completeness*. New York: W. H. Freeman.

Geary, N., Antonopoulos, A., Drakospoulos, E., & O'Reilly, J. (2001). Analysis of optimization issues in multi-period DWDM network planning. In *Proceedings of IEEE INFOCOM*. IEEE.

Ghazisaidi, N., & Maier, M. (2010). Advanced aggregation techniques for integrated next-generation WLAN and EPON networks. In *Proceedings of the IEEE Consumer Communications & Networking Conference (CCNC)*, (pp. 1-5). IEEE.

Ghazisaidi, N., & Maier, M. (2011). Fiber-wireless (FiWi) access networks: Challenges and opportunities. *IEEE Network, 25*(1), 36–42. doi:10.1109/MNET.2011.5687951.

Ghazisaidi, N., Paolucci, F., & Maier, M. (2009). Super-MAN: Optical-wireless integration of RPR and WiMAX. *OSA Journal of Optical Networking, 8*, 249–271. doi:10.1364/JON.8.000249.

Goldberg, D. E. (1989). *Genetic algorithms in search, optimization and machine learning*. Reading, MA: Addison-Wesley.

Gomez-Agis, F., Calabretta, N., Albores-Mejia, A., & Dorren, H. J. S. (2010). Clock-distribution with instantaneous synchronization for 160 Gbit/s optical time domain multiplexed systems packet transmission. *Optics Letters, 35*(19), 3255–3257. doi:10.1364/OL.35.003255 PMID:20890351.

Gordon, J. P., & Kogelnik, H. (2000). *PMD fundamentals: Polarization-mode dispersion in optical fibers*. Washington, DC: National Academy of Sciences. doi:10.1073/pnas.97.9.4541.

Green, P. E. et al. (1996). WDM protocol-transparent distance extension using R2 remodulation. *IEEE Journal on Selected Areas in Communications, 14*(5), 962–967. doi:10.1109/49.510920.

Grover, W. D. (2003). *Mesh-based survivable transport networks*. Upper Saddle River, NJ: Prentice Hall.

Guerber, P., et al. (2000). *Chirp optimised operation of an optical 3R regenerator*. Paper presented at the ECOC'00. New York, NY. Retrieved from http://www.cisco.com/en/US/products/ps5763/prod_models_comparison.html

Guillemot, C., Renaud, M., Gambini, P., Janz, C., Andonovic, I., & Bauknecht, R. (1998). Transparent optical packet switching: the European ACTS KEOPS project approach. *Journal of Lightwave Technology, 16*, 2117–2134. doi:10.1109/50.736580.

Gupta, M., & Singh, S. (2003). Greening of the internet. In *Proceedings of SIGCOMM*, (pp. 19-26). ACM.

Habib, I., & Song, Q. (2006). Deployment of the GMPLS control plane for grid applications in experimental high-performance networks. *IEEE Communications Magazine, 44*(3), 65–73. doi:10.1109/MCOM.2006.1607868.

Haken, H. (1983). *Advanced synergetics: Instability hierarchies of self-organizing systems and devices*. Berlin: Springer-Verlag.

Hamilton, S. A., & Robinson, B. S. (2002). 40-Gb/s all-optical packet synchronization and address comparison for OTDM networks. *IEEE Photonics Technology Letters, 14*(2), 209–211. doi:10.1109/68.980524.

Hassan, A., & Phillips, C. (2008). Static routing and wavelength assignment inspired by particle swarm optimization. In *Proceedings of 3rd International Conference on Information and Communication Technologies: From Theory to Applications, ICTTA*, (pp. 1 –6). ICTTA.

Hauer, M. C., McGeehan, J. E., Kumar, S., Touch, J. D., Bannister, J., & Lyons, E. R. et al. (2003). Optically assisted Internet routing using arrays of novel dynamically reconfigurable FBG-based correlators. *IEEE/OSA. Journal of Lightwave Technology, 21*(11), 2765–2778. doi:10.1109/JLT.2003.819144.

Haykin, S. (1994). *Neural networks: A comprehensive foundation. New York*. Macmillan.

He, J., & Brandt-Pearce, M. (2006). Dynamic wavelength assignment using wavelength spectrum separation for crosstalk limited networks. In *Proceedings of the IEEE International Conference on Broadband Networks – Broadnets*, (pp. 1–9). San Jose, CA: IEEE.

He, J., & Brandt-Pearce, M. (2006). RWA using wavelength ordering for crosstalk limited networks. In *Proceedings of the IEEE/OSA Optical Fiber Conference – OFC*. Anaheim, CA: IEEE.

He, J., Brandt-Pearce, M., Pointurier, Y., Brown, C., & Subramaniam, S. (2007). Adaptive wavelength assignment using wavelength spectrum separation for distributed optical networks. In *Proceedings of the IEEE International Conference on Communications – ICC*, (pp. 2406–2411). IEEE.

Herrera, J., Raz, O., Tangdiongga, E., Liu, Y., Mulvad, H. C. H., & Ramos, F. et al. (2008). 160-Gb/s all-optical packet switching over a 110-km field installed optical link. *Journal of Lightwave Technology, 26*, 176–182. doi:10.1109/JLT.2007.913068.

Hill, K., & Meltz, G. (1997). Fiber Bragg grating technology fundamentals and overview. *IEEE/OSA. Journal of Lightwave Technology, 15*(8), 1263–1276. doi:10.1109/50.618320.

Holt, J., & Baker, T. (1991). Back propagation simulations using limited precision calculations. In *Proceedings of Neural Networks, 1991* (Vol. 2, pp. 121–126). IEEE. doi:10.1109/IJCNN.1991.155324.

Hopfield, J. J. (1982). Neural networks and physical systems with emergent collective computational abilities. *Proceedings of the National Academy of Sciences of the United States of America, 79*(8), 2554–2558. doi:10.1073/pnas.79.8.2554 PMID:6953413.

Hopfield, J. J. (1984). Neurons with graded response have collective computational properties like those of two-state neurons. *Proceedings of the National Academy of Sciences of the United States of America, 81*(10), 3088–3092. doi:10.1073/pnas.81.10.3088 PMID:6587342.

Horst, W., & Farooq, M. (2006). A comprehensive review of nature inspired routing algorithms for fixed telecommunication networks. *Journal of Systems Architecture, 52*, 461–484. doi:10.1016/j.sysarc.2006.02.005.

Huang, S., Dutta, R., & Rouskas, G. N. (2006). Traffic grooming in path, star, and tree networks: Complexity, bounds, and algorithms. *IEEE Journal on Selected Areas in Communications, 24*(4), 66–82. doi:10.1109/JSAC.2006.1613773.

Huelsermann, R., Gunkel, M., Meusberger, C., & Schupke, D. A. (2008). Cost modeling and evaluation of capital expenditures in optical multilayer networks. *Journal of Optical Networking, 7*(9), 814–833. doi:10.1364/JON.7.000814.

Hu, H., Yu, J., Zhang, L., Zhang, A., Li, Y., Jiang, Y., & Yang, E. (2007). Pulse source based on directly modulated laser and phase modulator. *Optics Express, 15*(14), 8931–8937. doi:10.1364/OE.15.008931 PMID:19547231.

Hutcheson, L. (2008). FTTx: Current status and the future. *IEEE Communications Magazine, 46*(7), 90–95. doi:10.1109/MCOM.2008.4557048.

Idzikowski, F., Orlowski, S., Raack, C., Woesner, H., & Wolisz, A. (2010). Saving energy in IP-over-WDM networks by switching off line cards in low-demand scenarios. In Proceedings of Optical Network Design and Modeling (ONDM), (pp. 1-6). ONDM.

Jackson, K. P., Newton, S. A., Moslehi, B., Tur, M., Cutler, C. C., Goodman, J. W., & Shaw, H. J. (1985). Optical fiber delay-line signal processing. *IEEE Transactions on Microwave Theory and Techniques, 33*, 193–209. doi:10.1109/TMTT.1985.1132981.

Jaekel, A. (2006). Lightpath scheduling and allocation under a flexible schedule traffic model. In *Proceedings of IEEE Globecom*. IEEE.

Jaekel, A., & Chen, Y. (2006). Routing and wavelength assignment for prioritized demand under a scheduled traffic model. In *Proceedings of Broadnets Workshop on Guaranteed Optical Service Provisioning*. IEEE.

Jaekel, A., & Chen, Y. (2007). Demand allocation without wavelength conversion under a sliding scheduled traffic model. In *Proceedings of IEEE Broadnets*. IEEE.

Jarray, A., Jaumard, B., & Houle, A. C. (2009). Minimum CAPEX/OPEX design of optical backbone networks. In *Proceedings of the International Conference on Ultra Modern Telecommunications & Workshops (ICUMT)*, (pp. 1–8). ICUMT.

Jaumard, B., & Hemazro, T. D. (2004). Routing and wavelength assignment in single hop all optical networks with minimum blocking. *GERAD -Group for Research in Decision Analysis*. Retrieved from http://www.gerad.ca/fichiers/cahiers/G-2004-12.pdf

Jaumard, B., Meyer, C., & Thiongane, B. (2009). On column generation formulations for the RWA problem. *Discrete Applied Mathematics*, *157*(6), 1291–1308. doi:10.1016/j.dam.2008.08.033.

Jinno, M., Takara, H., & Kozicki, B. (2009). Filtering characteristics of highly-spectrum efficient spectrum-sliced elastic optical path (SLICE) network. In *Proceedings of OFC*. OFC.

Jinno, M., Kozicki, B., Takara, H., Watanabe, A., Sone, Y., Tanaka, T., & Hirano, A. (2010). Distance-adaptive spectrum resource allocation in spectrum-sliced elastic optical path network. *IEEE Communications Magazine*, *48*, 138–145. doi:10.1109/MCOM.2010.5534599.

Jinno, M., Takara, H., Kozicki, B., Tsukishima, Y., & Sone, Y. (2009). Spectrum-efficient and scalable elastic optical path network: Architecture, benefits, and enabling technologies. *IEEE Communications Magazine*, *47*, 66–73. doi:10.1109/MCOM.2009.5307468.

Joergensen, C. et al. (1997). All-optical wavelength conversion at bit rates above 10 Gb/s using semiconductor optical amplifiers. *IEEE Journal on Selected Topics in Quantum Electronics*, *3*(5), 1168–1180. doi:10.1109/2944.658592.

Jourdan, A., Chiaroni, D., Dotaro, E., Elienberger, G. J., Masetti, F., & Renaud, M. (2001). The perspective of the optical packet switching in IP-dominant backbone and metropolitan networks. *IEEE Communications Magazine*, *39*(3), 137–141. doi:10.1109/35.910601.

Jungnickel, D. (2008). *Graphs, networks and algorithms: Algorithms and computation in mathematics*. London: Springer. doi:10.1007/978-3-540-72780-4.

Kang, K. I. et al. (1996). Comparison of Sagnac and Mach-Zehnder ultrafast all-optical interferometric switches based on a semiconductor resonant optical nonlinearity. *Applied Optics*, *35*(3), 417–426. doi:10.1364/AO.35.000417 PMID:21069026.

Karaboga, & Basturk. (2008). On the performance of artificial bee colony (ABC) algorithm. *Applied Soft Computing*, *8*(1), 687-697.

Karaboga, D. (2005). *An idea based on honey bee swarm for numerical optimization* (Technical Report TR06). Kayseri, Turkey: Erciyes University. Retrieved from http://www-lia.deis.unibo.it/Courses/SistInt/articoli/bee-colony1.pdf

Karaboga, D., &, B. (2009). A survey: Algorithms simulating bee swarm intelligence. *Artificial Intelligence Review*, *31*, 61–85. doi:10.1007/s10462-009-9127-4.

Karaboga, D., & Bastürk, B. (2007). A powerful and efficient algorithm for numerical function optimization: Artificial bee colony (ABC) algorithm. *Journal of Global Optimization*, *39*(3), 459–471. doi:10.1007/s10898-007-9149-x.

Karlsson, M., et al. (2004). *PMD compensation using 2R and 3R regenerators*. Paper presented at the ECOC'04. New York, NY.

Kashyap, R. (n.d.). *Fiber Braggs gratings*. San Diego, CA: Academic Press.

Kavian, Y.S., Rashedi, Mahani, & Ghassemlooy. (2012). Routing and wavelength assignment in optical networks using artificial bee colony algorithm. *Optik - International Journal for Light and Electron Optics.*

Kavian, Y. S., Rashvand, H. F., Ren, W., Naderi, M., Leeson, M. S., & Hines, E. L. (2008). Genetic algorithm quality of service design in resilient dense wavelength division multiplexing optical networks. *IET Communications, 2*(4), 505–513. doi:10.1049/iet-com:20070312.

Kerivin, H., & Mahjoub, A. R. (2005). Design of survivable networks: A survey. *Networks, 46*(1), 1–21. doi:10.1002/net.20072.

Kilper, D. C. (2005). *Optical performance monitoring applications in transparent networks.* Paper presented at International Conference on Wireless and Optical Communications (WOCC'05). New York, NY.

Kilper, D. C. (2002). Optical performance monitoring. *IEEE/OSA. Journal of Lightwave Technology, 22*(1), 294–304. doi:10.1109/JLT.2003.822154.

Kilper, D. C., Bach, R., Blumenthal, D. J., Einstein, D., Landolsi, T., & Ostar, L. et al. (2004). Optical performance monitoring. *IEEE/OSA. Journal of Lightwave Technology, 22*(1), 294–304. doi:10.1109/JLT.2003.822154.

Klonidis, D., Politi, C. T., Nejabati, R., O'Mahony, M. J., & Simeonidou, D. (2005). OPSnet: Design and demonstration of an asynchronous high-speed optical packet switch. *Journal of Lightwave Technology, 23*(10), 2914–2925. doi:10.1109/JLT.2005.856167.

Klopfenstein, O. (2009). Access network dimensioning with uncertain traffic forecasts. In *Proceedings of the 13th International Telecommunications Network Strategy and Planning Symposium,* (pp. 1–52). IEEE.

Koch, B. R., Hu, Z., Bowers, J. E., & Blumenthal, D. J. (2006). Payload-envelope detection and label-detection integrated photonic circuit for asynchronous variable-length optical packet switching with 40-Gb/s RZ payloads and 10-Gb/s NRZ labels. *Journal of Lightwave Technology, 24*, 3409–3417. doi:10.1109/JLT.2006.879221.

Kodialam, M. (2003). Dynamic routing of restorable bandwidth-guaranteed tunnels using aggregated network resource usage information. *IEEE/ACM Transactions on Networking, 11*, 399–410. doi:10.1109/TNET.2003.813044.

Kogelnik, H. (1976). Filter response of nonuniform almost-periodic structures. *The Bell System Technical Journal, 55*, 109–126.

Kojic, N. S., Reljin, I. S., & Reljin, B. D. (2007). Different wavelength assignment techniques in all-optical networks controlled by neural network. In Proceedings of Telecommunications in Modern Satellite, Cable and Broadcasting Services, 2007, (pp. 401-404). IEEE.

Kojic, N. S., Reljin, I. S., & Reljin, B. D. (2009). All-optical network with simultaneous in-node routing and wavelength assignment. *Telfor Journal, 1.*

Kojic, N. S., Reljin, I. S., & Reljin, B. D. (2006). Routing in optical networks by using neural network.[IEEE.]. *Proceedings of Neural Network Applications in Electrical Engineering, 2006*, 65–68.

Kojic, N., Reljin, I., & Reljin, B. (2004). Neural network for finding optimal path in packet-switched network. [IEEE.]. *Proceedings of Neural Network Applications in Electrical Engineering, 2004*, 91–96.

Koyama, K., Hashimoto, J. I., Tsuji, Y., Ishizuka, T., & Katsuyama, T. (2007). Optical label encoder/correlator on GaAs-based photonic integrated circuit for photonic networks. *SEI Technical Review, 65*, 11–14.

Koza, J. (1992). *Genetic programming: On the programming of computers by means of natural selection.* Cambridge, MA: MIT Press.

Kramer, G. (2005). *Ethernet passive optical networks.* New York: McGraw-Hill, Inc..

Kramer, G., Mukherjee, B., Dixit, S., Ye, Y., & Hirth, R. (2002). Supporting differentiated classes of service in ethernetpasrive optical networks. *Journal on Optical Networks, 1*(8), 280–298.

Krishnaswamy, R. M., & Sivarajan, K. N. (2001). Algorithms for routing and wavelength assignment based on solutions of LP-relaxations. *IEEE Communications Letters*, 5(10), 435–437. doi:10.1109/4234.957386.

Kuran, M. S., & Tugcu, T. (2007). A survey on emerging broadband wireless access technologies. *Computer Networks*, 51, 3013–3046. doi:10.1016/j.comnet.2006.12.009.

Kuri, J. (2003). *Optimization problems in WDM optical transport networks with scheduled lightpath demands.* (Unpublished Doctoral Dissertation). ENST Paris, Paris, France.

Kuri, J., Puech, N., Gagnaire, M., Dotaro, E., & Douville, R. (2003). Diverse routing of scheduled lightpath demands in an optical transport network. In *Proceedings of Fourth International Workshop on the Design of Reliable Communication Networks*. IEEE.

Kuri, J., & Puech, N. (2003). Routing and wavelength assignment of scheduled lightpath demands. *IEEE Journal on Selected Areas in Communications*, 21(8), 1231–1240. doi:10.1109/JSAC.2003.816622.

Kuri, J., Puech, N., Gagnaire, M., Dotaro, E., & Douville, R. (2003). Routing and wavelength assignment of scheduled lightpath demands. *IEEE Journal on Selected Areas in Communications*, 21(8), 1231–1240. doi:10.1109/JSAC.2003.816622.

Labourdette, J. F., Bouillet, E., Ramamurthy, R., & Akyama, A. A. (2005). Fast approximate dimensioning and performance analysis of mesh optical networks. *IEEE/ACM Transactions on Networking*, 3(4), 906–917. doi:10.1109/TNET.2005.852880.

Le Minh, H., Ghassemlooy, Z., & Ng, W. P. (2006). OPN06-3: Multiple-hop routing based on the pulse-position modulation header processing scheme in all-optical ultrafast packet switching network. In *Proceedings of IEEE Global Telecommunications Conference 2006 (GLOBECOM '06)*, (pp. 1 – 5). IEEE.

Leclerc, O. et al. (2003). Optical regeneration at 40 Gb/s and beyond. *Journal of Lightwave Technology*, 21(11), 2779–2790. doi:10.1109/JLT.2003.819148.

Leguizamon, G. P., Ortega, B., & Capmany, J. (2009). Advanced subcarrier multiplexed label swapping in optical packet switching nodes for next generation internet networks. *Journal of Lightwave Technology*, 27, 655–669. doi:10.1109/JLT.2008.926951.

Lemaire, P. J., Atkins, R. M., Mizrahi, V., & Reed, W. A. (1993). High pressure H2 loading as a technique for achieving ultrahigh UV photosensitivity and thermal sensitivity in GeO2 doped optical fibres. *Electronics Letters*, 29(13), 1191–1193. doi:10.1049/el:19930796.

Lenhman, T., & Sobieski, J. (2006). DRAGON: A framework for service provisioning in heterogeneous grid networks. *IEEE Communications Magazine*, 44(3), 84–90. doi:10.1109/MCOM.2006.1607870.

Leuthold, J. (2002). *Signal regeneration and all-optical wavelength conversion.* Paper presented at the LEOS'02. New York, NY.

Li, K. (2008). Heuristic algorithms for routing and wavelength assignment in WDM optical networks. In *Proceedings of IEEE International Symposium on Parallel and Distributed Processing, IPDPS 2008*, (pp. 1–8). IEEE.

Li, T., & Wang, B. (2005). On optimal survivability design in WDM optical networks under a scheduled traffic model. In *Proceedings of DRCN*. DRCN.

Li, T., Wang, B., Xin, C., & Zhang, X. (2005). On survivable service provisioning in WDM optical networks under a scheduled traffic model. In *Proceedings of IEEE Globecom*. IEEE.

Liang, Zincir-Heywood, & Heywood. (2002). Intelligent packets for dynamic network routing using distributed genetic algorithm. In *Proceedings of the Genetic and Evolutionary Computation Conference (GECCO)*, (pp. 88-96). GECCO.

Liang, Zincir-Heywood, & Heywood. (2006). Adding more intelligence to the network routing problem: AntNet and Ga-agents. *Applied Soft Computing*, 6(3), 244–257. doi:10.1016/j.asoc.2005.01.005.

Lin, W.-P., Kao, M.-S., & Chi, S. (2003). A reliable architecture for broadband fiber-wireless access networks. *IEEE Photonics Technology Letters*, 15(2), 344–346. doi:10.1109/LPT.2002.806890.

Li, X., Chakravarthy, V., Wang, B., & Wu, Z. (2011). *Spreading code design of adaptive non-contiguous SOFDM for cognitive radio and dynamic spectrum access.* IEEE Journal of Selected Topics in Signal Processing.

Lučić, P., & Teodorović, D. (2001). Bee system: modeling combinatorial optimization transportation engineering problems by swarm intelligence. In *Proceedings of the IV Triennial Symposium on Transportation Analysis TRISTAN* (pp. 441-445). Sao Miguel, Portugal: TRISTAN.

Lučić, P., & Teodorović, D. (2002). Transportation modeling: An artificial life approach. In *Proceedings of the 14th IEEE International Conference on Tools with Artificial Intelligence ICTAI 2002* (pp. 216–223). Washington, DC: IEEE Computer Society. doi: 10.1109/TAI.2002.1180807

Lučić, P., & Teodorović, D. (2003). Computing with bees: Attacking complex transportation engineering problems. *International Journal of Artificial Intelligence Tools*, *12*(3), 375–394. doi:10.1142/S0218213003001289.

Lučić, P., & Teodorović, D. (2003). Vehicle routing problem with uncertain demand at nodes: The bee system and fuzzy logic approach. In Verdegay, J. L. (Ed.), *Fuzzy Sets Based Heuristics for Optimization* (pp. 67–82). Berlin: Springer-Verlag. doi:10.1007/978-3-540-36461-0_5.

Luo, Y., & Ansari, N. (2005). Bandwidth allocation for multi-service access on EPONs. *IEEE (Optical). Communications Magazine*, *43*(2), S16–S21. doi:10.1109/MCOM.2005.1391498.

Luo, Y., & Ansari, N. (2005). LSTP for dynamic bandwidth allocation and QoS provisioning over EPONs. *OSA Journal of Optical Networking*, *4*(9), 561–572. doi:10.1364/JON.4.000561.

Mahony, M. J., & Simeonidu, D. J., Zhou, & Yu, A. (1995). The design of a European optical network. *IEEE/OSA. Journal of Lightwave Technology*, *3*(5), 817–828. doi:10.1109/50.387798.

Maier, M., Ghazisaidi, N., & Reisslein, M. (2008). The audacity of fiber-wireless (FiWi) networks. In *Proceedings of the ICST ACCESSNETS*, (pp. 1-10). ICST.

Mambretti, J., & Lillethun, D. (2006). Optical dynamic intelligent network services (ODIN), an experimental control-plane architecture for high-performance distributed environments based on dynamic lightpath provisioning. *IEEE Communications Magazine*, *44*(3), 92–99. doi:10.1109/MCOM.2006.1607871.

Manousakis, K. et al. (2009). Offline impairment-aware routing and wavelength assignment algorithms in translucent WDM optical networks. *Journal of Lightwave Technology*, *27*, 1866–1877. doi:10.1109/JLT.2009.2021534.

Manousakis, K. et al. (2010). Joint online routing, wavelength assignment and regenerator allocation in translucent optical networks. *Journal of Lightwave Technology*, *28*, 1152–1163. doi:10.1109/JLT.2010.2041527.

Marcuse, D. (1990). Derivation of analytical expression for the bit-error probability in lightwave systems with optical amplifiers. *Journal of Lightwave Technology*, *8*, 1816–1823. doi:10.1109/50.62876.

Maric, S. V. (1993). New family of algebraically designed optical orthogonal codes for use in CDMA fibre-optic networks. *Electronics Letters*, *29*(6), 538–539. doi:10.1049/el:19930359.

Marković, G. (2007). *Optimization of the resource usage in optical wavelength routing networks.* (Ph. D. Thesis). University of Belgrade. Belgrade, Serbia.

Marković, G., Teodorović, D., & Aćimović-Raspopović, V. (2007). Routing and wavelength assignment in all-optical networks based on the bee colony optimization. *AI Communications - The European Journal on Artificial Intelligence, 20*(4), 273-285.

Marković, G., & Aćimović-Raspopović, V. (2010). Solving the RWA problem in WDM optical networks using the BCO meta-heuristic. *Telfor Journal*, *2*(1), 43–48.

Marsden, A., Maruta, A., & Kitayama, K.-I. (2008). Routing and wavelength assignment encompassing FWM in WDM lightpath networks. In *Proceedings of the International Conference on Optical Network Design and Modeling, ONDM*, (vol. 1, pp. 1–6). ONDM.

Martinez, R. et al. (2010). Experimental translucent-oriented routing for dynamic lightpath provisioning in GMPLS-enabled wavelength switched optical networks. *Journal of Lightwave Technology*, *28*(8), 1241–1255. doi:10.1109/JLT.2010.2043335.

Martinez, R., Pinart, C., Cugini, F., Andriolli, N., Valcarenghi, L., & Castoldi, P. et al. (2006). Challenges and requirements for introducing impairment-awareness into the management and control planes of ASON/GMPLS WDM networks. *IEEE Communications Magazine*, *44*(12), 76–85. doi:10.1109/MCOM.2006.273103.

Martins-Filho, J. F., Chaves, D. A. R., Aguiar, D. O., & Bastos-Filho, C. J. A. (2008). Intelligent and fast IRWA algorithm based on power series and particle swarm optimization. In *Proceedings of 10th International Conference on Transparent Optical Networks 2008 - ICTON 2008*, (vol. 3, pp. 158–161). ICTON.

Martins-Filho, J. F., Santana, J. L., Pereira, H. A., Chaves, D. A. R., & Bastos-Filho, C. J. A. (2012). Assessment of the power series routing algorithm in translucent, transparent and opaque optical networks. *IEEE Communications Letters*, *16*(6), 941–944. doi:10.1109/LCOMM.2012.032612.120232.

Maxwell, G. (2008). *Hybrid integration technology for high functionality devices in optical communications*. Paper presented at the OFC 2008. Los Angeles, CA.

Mcculloch, W., & Pitts, W. (1943). A logical calculus of the ideas immanent in nervous activity. *Bulletin of Mathematical Biology*, *5*(4), 115–133. PMID:2185863.

McGarry, M. P., Maier, M., & Reisslein, M. (2006). WDM ethernet passive optical networks. *IEEE Communications Magazine*, *44*, S18–S25. doi:10.1109/MCOM.2006.1593545.

McGeehan, J., Kumar, S., Gurkan, D., Motaghian Nezam, S. M. R., Willner, A. E., & Fejer, M. M. et al. (2003). All-optical decrementing of a packet's time-to-live (TTL) field and subsequent dropping of a zero-TTL packet. *IEEE/OSA. Journal of Lightwave Technology*, *21*, 2746–2751. doi:10.1109/JLT.2003.819131.

Meflah, L., Thomsen, B., Savory, S., Mitchell, J., & Bayvel, P. (2006). *Single technique for simultaneous monitoring of OSNR and chromatic dispersion at 40Gbit/s*. Paper presented at 32nd European Conference on Optical Communication (ECOC'06). Cannes, France.

Mehrotra, A., & Trick, M. A. (1996). A column generation approach for graph coloring. *INFORMS Journal on Computing*, *8*(4), 344–354. doi:10.1287/ijoc.8.4.344.

Meltz, G., Morey, W. W., & Glenn, W. H. (1989). Formation of Bragg gratings in optical fibers by a transverse holographic method. *Optics Letters*, *14*(15), 823–825. doi:10.1364/OL.14.000823 PMID:19752980.

Mikkelsen, B. et al. (1996). All-optical noise reduction capability of interferometric wavelength converters. *Electronics Letters*, *32*(6), 566–567. doi:10.1049/el:19960343.

Miller, C. M. (1994). High-speed digital transmitter characterization using eye diagram analysis. *Hewlett-Packard Journal*, *45*(4), 29–37.

Mishra, A. K., Ellis, A. D., Cotter, D., Smyth, F., Connolly, E., & Barry, L. P. (2006). Spectrally compact optical subcarrier multiplexing with 42.6 Gbit/s AM-PSK payload and 2.5 Gbit/s NRZ labels. *Electronics Letters*, *42*, 1303–1304. doi:10.1049/el:20062414.

Mitchell. (1998). *An introduction to genetic algorithms*. Cambridge, MA: MIT Press.

Mohan, G., & Murthy, C. S. R. (2000). Light-path restoration in WDM optical networks. *IEEE Network*, *14*(6), 24–32. doi:10.1109/65.885667.

Monoyios, D., & Vlachos, K. (2011). Multiobjective genetic algorithms for solving the impairment-aware routing and wavelength assignment problem. *Journal of Optical Communications and Networking*, *3*(1), 40–47. doi:10.1364/JOCN.3.000040.

Morais, R. et al. (2011). Genetic algorithm for the topological design of survivable optical transport networks. *Journal of Optical Communications and Networking*, *3*, 17–26. doi:10.1364/JOCN.3.000017.

Mork, J. et al. (2003). Analytical expression for the bit error rate of cascaded all-optical regenerators. *IEEE Photonics Technology Letters, 15*(10), 1479–1481. doi:10.1109/LPT.2003.818059.

Mukherjee, B. (2000). WDM optical communication networks: Progress and challenges. *Journal of Selected Areas in Communications, 18,* 1810–1824. doi:10.1109/49.887904.

Munetomo, Y. Akama, & Sato. (2002). Empirical investigations on the genetic adaptive routing algorithm in the internet. In *Proceedings of CEC 2002,* (pp. 1236-1243). CEC.

Munetomo. (1999). Designing genetic algorithms for adaptive routing algorithms in the internet. In *Proceedings of the GECCO 1999, Workshop on Evolutionary Telecommunications: Past, Present and Future.* GECCO.

Murakami, M., et al. (2009). *Power consumption analysis of optical cross-connect equipment for future large capacity optical networks.* Paper presented at the ICTON'09. New York, NY.

Nag, A. et al. (2010). Optical network design with mixed line rates and multiple modulation formats. *Journal of Lightwave Technology, 28,* 466–475. doi:10.1109/JLT.2009.2034396.

Nagatsu, N., Hamazumi, Y., & Sato, K. (1995). Optical path accommodation designs applicable to large scale networks. *IEICE Transactions on Communications. E (Norwalk, Conn.), 78-B,* 597–607.

Nakrani, S., & Tovey, C. (2003). On honey bees and dynamic allocation in an Internet server colony. In C. Anderson & T. Balch (Eds.), *Proceedings of the Second International Workshop on the Mathematics and Algorithms of Social Insects* (pp. 115-122). Atlanta, GA: Georgia Institute of Technology.

Navarro-Varela, G., & Sinclair, M. (1999). Ant-colony optimisation for virtual-wavelength-path routing and wavelength allocation. In *Proceedings of the 1999 Congress on Evolutionary Computation CEC'99* (pp. 1809-1816). Washington, DC: IEEE. doi: 10.1109/CEC.1999.785494

Nayebi, K., Barnwell, T. P. III, & Smith, M. J. T. (1994). Low delay FIR filter banks: Design and evaluation. *IEEE Transactions on Signal Processing, 42*(1), 24–31. doi:10.1109/78.258118.

Ngo, S.-H., Jiang, X., & Horiguchi, S. (2004). Adaptive routing and wavelength assignment using ant-based algorithm. (ICON 2004). In *Proceedings of 12th IEEE International Conference on Networks,* (vol. 2, pp. 482–486). IEEE.

Ngo, S. H., Jiang, X., & Horiguchi, S. (2006). An ant-based approach for dynamic RWA in optical WDM networks. *Photonic Network Communications, 11,* 39–48. doi:10.1007/s11107-006-5322-2.

Nguyen, H. (2007). *Gpu gems 3.* Reading, MA: Addison-Wesley Professional.

Noirie, L., Cerou, F., Moustakides, G., Audouin, O., & Peloso, P. (2002). *New transparent optical monitoring of the eye and BER using asynchronous undersampling of the signal.* Paper presented at 28th European Conference on Optical Communication (ECOC'02). Copenhagen, Denmark.

NVIDIA. (2009). *Nvidia cuda programming guide 2.3.*

NVIDIA. (2010). *Cuda c best practices guide 3.2.* NVIDIA Corporation.

O'Mahony, M. J., Simeonidou, D., Hunter, D. K., & Tzanakaki, A. (2001). The application of optical packet switching in future communication networks. *IEEE Communications Magazine, 39*(3), 128–135. doi:10.1109/35.910600.

Odlyzko, A. M. (2003). Internet traffic growth: sources and implications. *Proceedings of the Society for Photo-Instrumentation Engineers, 5247,* 1–15. doi:10.1117/12.512942.

Ohlen, P. et al. (1997). Noise accumulation and BER estimates in concatenated nonlinear optoelectronic repeaters. *IEEE Photonics Technology Letters, 9*(7), 1011–1013. doi:10.1109/68.593383.

Ohlen, P. et al. (1998). BER caused by jitter and amplitude noise in limiting optoelectronic repeaters with excess bandwidth. *IEE Proceedings. Optoelectronics, 145*(3), 147–150. doi:10.1049/ip-opt:19981963.

Ohlen, P. et al. (2000). Measurements and modeling of pattern-dependent BER and jitter in reshaping opto-electronic repeaters. *IEE Proceedings. Optoelectronics, 147*(2), 97–103. doi:10.1049/ip-opt:20000289.

Oliveira Junior, M. A. C., & Bastos-Filho, C. J. A. (2011). Uma implementação em FPGA de redes neurais de hopfield para roteamento em redes de comunicação. *Anais do X Congresso Brasileiro de Inteligência Computacional.*

Omondi, A. R., & Rajapakse, J. C. (2006). *Fpga implementations of neural networks.* Secaucus, NJ: Springer-Verlag. doi:10.1007/0-387-28487-7.

Pachnicke, S., et al. (2008). *Physical impairment based regenerator placement and routing in translucent optical networks.* Paper presented at the OFC 2008. Los Angeles, CA.

Papneja, R., & Vapiwala, S. (2011). *Methodology for benchmarking MPLS protection mechanisms. Internet draft, draft-ietf-bmwg-protection-meth-09.txt, work in progress.* IETF.

Park, & Kim. (2007). Performance analysis of AntNet routing scheme with queuing approach. In *Proceedings of the Asia-Pacific Conference on Communications,* (pp. 317-320). IEEE.

Park, D. C., & Choi, S. E. (1998). A neural network based multi-destination routing algorithm for communication network.[). IEEE.]. *Proceedings of Neural Networks, 2,* 1673–1678.

Pavan, C., Morais, R. M., Rocha, F., & Pinto, A. N. (2010). Generating realistic optical transport network topologies. *Journal of Optical Communications and Networking, 2*(1), 80–90. doi:10.1364/JOCN.2.000080.

Pavani, G. S., & Waldman, H. (2008). Restoration in wavelength-routed optical networks by means of ant colony optimization. *Photonic Network Communications, 16*(1), 83–91. doi:10.1007/s11107-008-0120-7.

Pavani, G. S., & Waldman, H. (2010). Routing and wavelength assignment with crankback re-routing extensions by means of ant colony optimization. *IEEE Journal on Selected Areas in Communications, 28*(4), 532–541. doi:10.1109/JSAC.2010.100503.

Pavani, G. S., Zuliani, L. G., Waldman, H., & Magalhaes, M. (2008). Distributed approaches for impairment-aware routing and wavelength assignment algorithms in gmpls networks. *Computer Networks, 52*(10), 1905–1915. doi:10.1016/j.comnet.2008.02.010.

Pedroni, V. A. (2004). *Circuit design with VHDL.* Cambridge, MA: MIT Press.

Pereira, H. A., Chaves, D. A. R., Bastos-Filho, C. J. A., & Martins-Filho, J. F. (2009). OSNR model to consider physical layer impairments in transparent optical networks. *Photonic Network Communications, 18,* 137–149. doi:10.1007/s11107-008-0178-2.

Pereira, H., Chaves, D., Bastos-Filho, C. J. A., & Martins-Filho, J. (2008). Osnr model to consider physical layer impairments in transparent optical networks. *Photonic Network Communications, 18*(2), 137–149. doi:10.1007/s11107-008-0178-2.

Petropoulos, P., Wada, N., The, P. C., Ibsen, M., Chojo, W., Kitayama, K. I., & Richardson, D. J. (2001). Demonstration of a 64-chip OCDMA system using super-structured fiber gratings and time-gating detection. *IEEE Photonics Technology Letters, 13*(11), 1239–1241. doi:10.1109/68.959376.

Pham, G., & Koc, O. Rahim, & Zaidi. (2006). The bees algorithm – A novel tool for complex optimisation problems. In *Proceedings of the Innovative Production Machines and Systems Conference (IPROMS),* (pp. 454-461). IPROMS.

Pham, S., & Ghanbarzadeh, K. Otri, & Packianather. (2006). Optimising neural networks for identification of wood defects using the bees algorithm. In *Proceedings of INDIN 2006,* (pp. 1346-1351). INDIN.

Pluntke, C., Menth, M., & Duelli, M. (2009). CAPEX-aware design of survivable DWDM mesh networks. In *Proceedings of the IEEE International Conference on Communications (ICC),* (pp. 2348-2353). IEEE.

Poretsky, S., & Papneja, R. (2011). *Benchmarking terminology for protection performance.* RFC 6414.

Poulsen, H. N., et al. (1997). *Transmission enhancement by deployment of interferometric wavelength converters within all-optical cross connects.* Paper presented at the OFC'97. Los Angeles, CA.

Pyetro, A. F. (2008). *Implementação de uma arquitetura de redes neurais mlp utilizando fpga. Trabalho de Graduaçao. CIn.* UFPE.

Quijano, N., & Passino, K. M. (2007). Honey bee social foraging algorithms for resource allocation, part I: Algorithm and theory. In *Proceedings of the 2007 American Control Conference* (pp. 3383-3388). New York, NY: ACC. doi: 10.1109/ACC.2007.4282167

Rafiquzzaman, M. (2000). *Fundamentals of digital logic and microcomputer design* (3rd ed.). Rafi Systems, Incorporated.

Rahbar, A. G. (2011). Review of dynamic impairment-aware routing and wavelength assignment techniques in all-optical wavelength-routed networks. *IEEE Communications Surveys & Tutorials*, 1-25.

Ram Murthy, C. S., & Gurusamy, M. (2002). *WDM optical networks - Concepts, design and algorithms.* Upper Saddle River, NJ: Prentice Hall PTR.

Ramamurthy, B., et al. (2001). *Translucent optical WDM networks for the next-generation backbone networks.* Paper presented at the GLOBECOM 2001. New York, NY.

Ramamurthy, S., Sahasrabuddhe, L., & Mukherjee, B. (2003). Survivable WDM mesh networks. *IEEE/OSA. Journal of Lightwave Technology*, *21*(4), 870–883. doi:10.1109/JLT.2002.806338.

Ramaswami, R. et al. (2002). *Optical networks a practical perspective* (2nd ed.). San Diego, CA: Academic Press.

Ramaswami, R., & Sivarajan, K. (2009). *Optical networks: A practical perspective.* San Francisco: Morgan Kaufmann.

Ramaswami, R., & Sivarajan, K. N. (1995). Routing and wavelength assignment in all-optical networks. *IEEE/ACM Transactions on Networking*, *3*(5), 489–500. doi:10.1109/90.469957.

Ramaswami, R., & Sivarajan, K. N. (2002). *Optical networks - A practical perspective.* San Francisco: Morgan Kaufmann Publishers.

Ramos, F., Kehayas, E., Martinez, J. M., Clavero, R., Marti, J., & Stampoulidis, L. (2005). IST-LASAGNE: Towards all-optical label swapping employing optical logic gates and optical flip-flops. *Journal of Lightwave Technology*, *23*, 2993–3011. doi:10.1109/JLT.2005.855714.

Rao, T., & Anand, V. (2006). Particle swarm optimization for routing and wavelength assignment in optical networks. In *Proceedings of the IEEE Sarnoff Symposium*, (pp. 1 –4). IEEE.

Rao, N. S. V., & Wing, W. R. (2005). Ultrascience net: network testbed for large-scale science applications. *IEEE Communications Magazine*, *43*(11), s12–s17. doi:10.1109/MCOM.2005.1541694.

Rashedi, A., Kavian, Y. S., Ansari-Asl, K., & Ghassemlooy, Z. (2011). Dynamic routing and wavelength assignment: Artificial bee colony optimization. In M. Jaworski, & M. Marciniak (Eds.), *Proceedings of the 13th IEEE International Conference on Transparent Optical Networks ICTON 2011.* Warsaw, Poland: National Institute of Telecommunications - Department of Transmission and Optical Technologies. doi: 10.1109/ICTON.2011.5971015

Rauch, H. E., & Winarske, T. (1988). Neural networks for routing communication traffic. *IEEE Control Systems Magazine*, *8*(2), 26–31. doi:10.1109/37.1870.

Raybon, G., et al. (2002). *40 Gbit/s pseudo-linear transmission over one million kilometers.* Paper presented at the OFC'02. Los Angeles, CA.

Richter, A. (2002). Optical performance monitoring in transparent and configurable dwdm networks. *IEEE Proceedings*, *149*(1), 1–5.

Roebuck, K. (2011). *FPGA field programmable gate array.* Lighting Source.

Rouskas, G. N. (2003, January/February). Optical layer multicast: Rationale, building blocks, and challenges. *IEEE Network*, 60–65. doi:10.1109/MNET.2003.1174179.

Rubio-Largo, A., Vega-Rodriguez, M. A., Gomez-Pulido, J. A., & Sanchez-Perez, J. M. (2010). A differential evolution with pareto tournaments for solving the routing and wavelength assignment problem in WDM networks. In *Proceedings of IEEE Congress on Evolutionary Computation (CEC)*, (pp. 1–8). CEC.

Santana, R. A. (2010). *Roteamento em redes ópticas transparentes utilizando redes neurais de hopfield. (Dissertação de Mestrado).* UPE.

Saradhi, C. V., & Gurusamy, M. (2007). Scheduling and routing of sliding scheduled lightpath demands in WDM optical networks. In *Proceedings of OFC*. OFC.

Saradhi, C., et al. (2010). *Practical and deployment issues to be considered in regenerator placement and operation of translucent optical networks*. Paper presented at the ICTON 2010. New York, NY.

Saradhi, C. V., Wei, L. K., & Gurusamy, M. (2004). Provisioning fault-tolerant scheduled lightpath demands in WDM mesh networks. In *Proceedings of Broadnets* (pp. 150–159). IEEE. doi:10.1109/BROADNETS.2004.70.

Sarkar, S., Dixit, S., & Mukherjee, B. (2007). Hybrid-Wireless-optical broadband-access network (WOBAN): A review of relevant challenges. *IEEE/OSA. Journal of Lightwave Technology, 25*, 3329–3340. doi:10.1109/JLT.2007.906804.

Scaffardi, M., Lazzeri, E., Furukawa, H., Wada, N., Miyazaki, T., Potì, L., & Bogoni, A. (2010). 160 Gb/s/port 2x2 OPS node test-bed performing 50 Gchip/s all-optical active label processing with contention detection. *IEEE/OSA. Journal of Lightwave Technology, 28*, 922–930. doi:10.1109/JLT.2009.2035524.

Schoonderwoerd, R., Holland, O., & Bruten, J. (1997). Ant-like agents for load balancing in telecommunications networks. In *Proceedings of the First International Conference on Autonomous Agents*, (pp. 209–216). New York, NY: ACM Press.

Schoonderwoerd. (1996). *Collective intelligence for network control*. (M.S.c Thesis). Delft University of Technology, Delft, The Netherlands.

Schuler, W. H., Bastos-Filho, C. J. A., & Oliveira, A. L. I. (2007). A hybrid Hopfield network-simulated annealing approach to optimize routing processes in telecommunications networks. In *Proceedings of Intelligent Systems Design and Applications, 2007*. ISDA. doi:10.1109/ISDA.2007.8.

Seddighian, P., Baby, V., Habib, C., Chen, L. R., Rusch, L. A., & LaRochelle, S. (2007). *All-optical swapping of spectral amplitude code labels for packet switching*. Paper presented at Photonics in Switching. San Francisco, CA.

Shake, I., Takara, H., Kawanishi, S., & Yamabayashi, Y. (1998). Optical signal quality monitoring method based on optical sampling. *Electronics Letters, 34*(22), 2152–2154. doi:10.1049/el:19981465.

Shaw, W. T., Wong, S. W., Cheng, N., Balasubramanian, K., Qiao, C., Yen, S. H., & Azovsky, L. G. (2008). Reconfigurable optical backhaul and integrated routing algorithm for load balancing in hybrid optical-wireless access networks. In *Proceedings of the IEEE International Conference on Communications (ICC)*, (pp. 5697-5701). IEEE.

Shaw, W.-T., Wong, S.-W., Cheng, N., Balasubramanian, K., Zhu, X., Maier, M., & Kazovsky, L. (2007). Hybrid architecture and integrated routing in a scalable optical–wireless access network. *Journal of Lightwave Technology, 25*(11), 3329–3340. doi:10.1109/JLT.2007.909202.

Shen, G., & Tucker, R. S. (2009). Energy-minimized design for IP over WDM networks. *Journal of Optical Communications and Networking, 1*(1), 176–186. doi:10.1364/JOCN.1.000176.

Shen, G., Tucker, R. S., & Chae, C.-J. (2007). Fixed mobile convergence architectures for broadband access: Integration of EPON and WiMAX. *IEEE Communications Magazine, 45*, 44–50. doi:10.1109/MCOM.2007.4290313.

Shinomiya, N. et al. (2007). Hybrid link/path-based design for translucent photonic network dimensioning. *Journal of Lightwave Technology, 25*, 2931–2941. doi:10.1109/JLT.2007.905224.

Shiomoto, K., & Farrel, A. (2011). *Advice on when it is safe to start sending data on label switched paths established using RSVP-TE*. RFC 6383.

Sim & Sun. (2003). Ant colony optimization for routing and load-balancing: Survey and new directions. *IEEE Transactions on Man and Cybernetics Systems Part A, 33*(5), 560–572. doi:10.1109/TSMCA.2003.817391.

Sim, & Sun. (2002). Multiple ant-colony optimization for network routing. In *Proceedings of 1st Int. Symp. Cyberworld*, (pp. 277-281). IEEE.

Sim, K. M., & Sun, W. H. (2003). Ant colony optimization for routing and load-balancing: Survey and new directions. *IEEE Transactions on Systems, Man, and Cybernetics. Part A, 33*(5), 560–572.

Smeda, A. A., & El-Hawary, M. E. (1999). Application of Hopfield neural network in routing for computer networks. In *Proceedings of Electrical and Computer Engineering, 1999 (Vol. 1*, pp. 145–149). IEEE. doi:10.1109/CCECE.1999.807186.

Somani, A., & Azizoglu, M. (2000). Wavelength assignment algorithms for wavelength routed interconnection of LANs. *Journal of Lightwave Technology, 18*, 1807–1817. doi:10.1109/50.908738.

Sone, Y., Watanabe, A., Imajuku, W., Tsukishima, Y., Kozicki, B., Takara, H., & Jinno, M. (2009). Highly survivable restoration scheme employing optical bandwidth squeezing in spectrum-sliced elastic optical path (SLICE) network. In *Proceedings of OFC*. OFC.

Soni, S., Gupta, R., & Pirkul, H. (1999). Survivable network design: the state of the art. *Information Systems Frontiers, 1*(3), 303–315. doi:10.1023/A:1010058513558.

Soni, S., & Pirkul, H. (2002). Design of survivable networks with connectivity requirements. *Telecommunication Systems, 20*(1), 133–149. doi:10.1023/A:1015445501694.

St Arnaud, B., & Bjerring, A. (2004). Web services architecture for user control and management of optical Internet networks. *Proceedings of the IEEE, 92*(9), 1490–1500. doi:10.1109/JPROC.2004.832948.

Stampoulidis, L., Kehayas, E., Avramopoulos, H., Liu, Y., Tangdiongga, E., & Dorren, H. J. S. (2005). *40 Gbit/s fast-locking all-optical packet clock recovery*. Paper presented at Optical Fiber Communication Conference (OFC'05). Anaheim, CA.

Stephens, R. (2004). Analyzing jitter at high data rates. *IEEE Communications Magazine, 42*, 6–10. doi:10.1109/MCOM.2003.1267095.

Stern, T. E., Ellinas, G., & Bala, K. (2009). *Multiwavelength optical networks: Architectures, design, and control*. Cambridge, UK: Cambridge University Press. doi:10.1017/CBO9780511811708.

Stoica, A. G., & Sengupta, A. (2000). On a dynamic wavelength assignment algorithm for wavelength routed all-optical networks. In Proceedings of Optical Networking and Communications – OptiComm, (vol. 4233, pp. 211–222). Springer.

Strobbe, V., & Van Breusegem, C. Pickavet & Demeester. (2005). Implementation and evaluation of AntNet, a distributed shortest-path algorithm. In *Proceedings of the Advanced Industrial Conference on Telecommunications/Service Assurance with Partial and Intermittent Resources Conference/E-Learning on Telecommunications Workshop (AICT/SAPIR/ELETE 2005)*, (pp. 320-325). AICT.

Subramanian, Druschel, & Chen. (1997). Ants and reinforcement learning: A case study in routing in dynamic networks.[San Francisco: Morgan Kauffman.]. *Proceedings of, IJCAI-97*, 832–838.

Sun, W., & Hu, W. (2011). *Distributing digital TV over a hybrid packet- and circuit-switched network*. Retrieved January 5, 2011, from http://spie.org/x17175.xml?ArticleID=x17175

Sun, W., & Zhang, G. (2010). *Label switched path (LSP) dynamic provisioning performance metrics in generalized MPLS networks*. RFC 5814.

Sun, W., & Xie, G. (2008). A cross-layer optical circuit provisioning framework for data intensive IP end hosts. *IEEE Communications Magazine, 46*(2), S30–S37. doi:10.1109/MCOM.2008.4473084.

Sun, W., & Zhang, G. (2012). *Label switched path (LSP) data path delay metric in generalized MPLS/MPLS-TE networks*. draft-ietf-ccamp-dpm-06.txt, Internet draft, work in progress. IETF.

Sun, Z., & Guo, W. (2008). Scheduling algorithm for workflow-based applications in optical grid. *Journal of Lightwave Technology, 26*(17), 3011–3020. doi:10.1109/JLT.2008.923935.

Swallow, G., &, Drake, J. (2008). *Generalized multiprotocol label switching (GMPLS) user-network interface (UNI), resource reservation protocol-traffic engineering (RSVP-TE) support for the overlay model*. RFC 4208. IETF.

Swanson, B., & Gilder, G. (2008). *Estimating the exaflood*. Seattle, WA: Discovery Institute. Retrieved from http://www.scribd.com/doc/6483200/Estimating_the_Exaflood_012808_by_Bret_

Taesombot, N., & Uyeda, F. (2006). The OptIPuter: High-performance, QoS-guaranteed network service for emerging E-science applications. *IEEE Communications Magazine, 44*(5), 38–45. doi:10.1109/MCOM.2006.1637945.

Tafur Monroy, I., Vegas Olmos, J., Koonen, A. M. J., Huijskens, F. M., de Waardt, H., & Khoe, G. D. (2004). Optical label switching by using differential phase shift keying and in-band subcarrier multiplexing modulation format. *Optical Engineering (Redondo Beach, Calif.)*, *43*, 1476. doi:10.1117/1.1760086.

Takara, H., Kozicki, B., Sone, Y., Tanaka, T., Watanabe, A., Hirano, A., et al. (2010). Distance-adaptive super-wavelength routing in elastic optical path network (SLICE) with optical OFDM. In *Proceedings of ECOC*. ECOC.

Takasaki, Y. (1991). *Digital transmission design and jitter analysis*. Norwood, MA: Artech Housen.

Takenaka, M., Raburn, M., Takeda, K., & Nakano, Y. (2006). *All-optical packet switching by MMI-BLD optical flip-flop*. Paper presented at: OFC 2006. Anaheim, CA.

Takiguchi, K., Shibata, T., & Itoh, M. (2002). Encoder/decoder on planar lightwave circuit for time-spreading/wavelength-hoping optical CDMA. *Electronics Letters*, *38*(10), 469–470. doi:10.1049/el:20020314.

Tanenbaum, A. S. (2003). *Computer networks* (4th ed.). Upper Saddle River, NJ: Prentice Hall.

Teixeira, A., Costa, L., Franzl, G., Azodolmolky, S., Tomkos, I., & Vlachos, K. et al. (2009). An integrated view on monitoring and compensation for dynamic optical networks: From management to physical layer. *Photonic Network Communications*, *18*, 191–210. doi:10.1007/s11107-008-0183-5.

Tekiner, & Ghassemlooy. (2005). Improved antnet routing algorithm for packet switching. *Mediterranean Journal of Computer Networks, 1*(2), 69-76.

Tekiner, G. S. & Al-khayatt. (2004). Antnet routing algorithm-improved version. In *Proceedings of CSNDSP04*, (pp. 416-419). CSNDSP.

Tekiner, Ghassemlooy, & Srikanth. (2004). Comparison of the Q-routing and shortest path routing algorithms. In *Proceedings of the PGNET*, (pp. 428-432). PGNET.

Tekiner, F., Ghassemlooy, F., & Alkhayatt, S. (2004). Investigation of antnetrouting algorithm by employing multiple ant colonies for packet switched networks to overcome the stagnation problem.[LCS.]. *Proceedings of, LCS04*, 185–188.

Tekiner, Ghassemlooy, & Al-khayatt. (2004). Improved antnet routing algorithm with link probability evaporation over the given time window.[SOFTCOM.]. *Proceedings of, SOFTCOM04*, 502–505.

Teodorovic, D., & Dell'Orco, M. (2005). Bee colony optimization - A cooperative learning approach to complex transportation problems. In A. Jaszkiewicz et al. (Eds.), *Advanced OR and AI Methods in Transportation - Proceedings of the 16th Mini-EURO Conference and 10th Meeting of Euro Working Group on Transportation (EWGT)* (pp. 51-60). Poznan, Poland: Poznan University of Technology.

Teodorović, D., & Šelmić, M. (2007). The BCO algorithm for the p-median problem. In M. Čangalović & M. Suknović (Eds.), *Proceedings of the XXXIV Serbian Operations Research Conference SYM-OP-IS 2007* (pp. 417-420). Belgrade, Serbia: University of Belgrade.

Teodorović, D., Lučić, P., Marković, G., & Dell'Orco, M. (2006). Bee colony optimization: Principles and applications. In B. Reljin & S. Stanković (Eds.), *Proceedings of the Eight Seminar on Neural Network Application in Electrical Engineering NEUREL 2006* (pp. 151-156). Belgrade, Serbia: University of Belgrade. doi: 10.1109/NEUREL.2006.341200

Teodorović. (2003). Transport modelling by multi-agent systems: A swarm intelligence approach. *Transportation Planning and Technology*, *26*(4), 289–312. doi:10.1080/03081060320001545 93.

Teodorović, D. (2009). Bee colony optimization (BCO). In Lim, C. P., Jaim, L. C., & Dehuri, S. (Eds.), *Innovations in Swarm Intelligence Studies in Computational Intelligence* (pp. 39–60). Heidelberg, Germany: Springer-Verlag. doi:10.1007/978-3-642-04225-6_3.

Teodorović, D., & Dell' Orco, M. (2008). Mitigating traffic congestion: Solving the ride matching problem by bee colony optimization. *Transportation Planning and Technology*, *31*(2), 135–152. doi:10.1080/03081060801948027.

Thomas, D. B., Howes, L., & Luk, W. (2009). *A comparison of cpus, gpus, fpgas, and massively parallel processor arrays for random number generation*. New York, NY: ACM. Retrieved from http://doi.acm.org/10.1145/1508128.1508139

Thomopoulos, S. C. A., Zhang, L., & Wann, C. D. (1991). Neural network implementation of the shortest path algorithm for traffic routing in communication networks. In *Proceedings of Neural Networks, 1991 (Vol. 3*, pp. 2693–2702). IEEE. doi:10.1109/IJCNN.1991.170276.

Tornatore, M., Baruffaldi, A., Zhu, H., Mukherjee, B., & Pattavina, A. (2007). Dynamic traffic grooming of sub-wavelength connectios with known duration. In *Proceedings of OFC*. OFC.

Tornatore, M., Pattavina, A., Zhang, J., Mukherjee, B., & Ou, C. (2005). Efficient shared-path protection exploiting the knowledge of connection-holding time. In *Proceedings of OFC*. OFC.

Triay, J., & Cervello-Pastor, C. (2010). An ant-based algorithm for distributed routing and wavelength assignment in dynamic optical networks. *IEEE Journal on Selected Areas in Communications*, *28*(4), 542–552. doi:10.1109/JSAC.2010.100504.

Trischitta, P. R. et al. (1989). *Jitter in digital transmission systems*. Norwood, MA: Artech House.

Vapiwala, S., & Ratnam, K. (2008). *Motivation for benchmarking MPLS TE scalability and performance*. Internet Draft, draft-bmwg-rsvpte-convergece-motivation-01.txt, work in progress.

Varela, & Sinclair. (1999). Ant colony optimization for virtual-wavelength-path routing and wavelength allocation. In *Proceedings of Congress Evolutionary Computation*, (pp. 1809-1816). IEEE.

Veeraraghavan, M., & Zheng, X. (2006). On the use of connection-oriented networks to support grid computing. *IEEE Communications Magazine*, *44*(3), 118–123. doi:10.1109/MCOM.2006.1607874.

Vegas Olmos, J. J., Zhang, J., Holm-Nielsen, P. V., Monroy, I. T., Polo, V., & Koonen, A. M. J. et al. (2004). Simultaneous optical label erasure and insertion in a single wavelength conversion stage of combined FSK/IM modulated signals. *Photonics Technology Letters*, *16*, 2144–2146. doi:10.1109/LPT.2004.833084.

Vilar, R., Ramos, F., & Marti, J. (2007). *Optical signal quality monitoring using fibre-Bragg-grating-based correlators in optical packet-switched networks*. Paper presented at 33rd European Conference on Optical Communication (ECOC'07). Berlin, Germany.

Vilar, R., Garcia, J., Tremblay, G., Kim, Y., LaRochelle, S., Ramos, F., & Marti, J. (2009). Monitoring the quality of signal in packet-switched networks using optical correlators. *IEEE/OSA. Journal of Lightwave Technology*, *27*(23), 5417–5425. doi:10.1109/JLT.2009.2028034.

Wada, N., Furukawa, H., & Miyazaki, T. (2007). Prototype 160Gbit/s/port optical packet switch based on optical code label processing. *Journal of Selected Topics in Quantum Electronics*, *13*, 1551–1559. doi:10.1109/JSTQE.2007.897602.

Wai, P. K. A., Chan, L. Y., Lui, L. F. K., Hwa-Yaw, T., & Demokan, M. S. (2005). 1 x 4 All-optical packet switch at 10 Gb/s. *Photonics Technology Letters*, *17*, 1289–1291. doi:10.1109/LPT.2005.846492.

Wang, B., & Li, T. (2006). Approximating optimal survivable scheduled service provisioning in WDM optical network with iterative survivable routing. In *Proceedings of IEEE Broadnets*. IEEE.

Wang, B., Li, T., Luo, X., & Fan, Y. (2004). Traffic grooming under a sliding scheduled traffic model in WDM optical networks. In *Proceedings of IEEE Workshop on Traffic Grooming*. IEEE.

Wang, B., Li, T., Luo, X., Fan, Y., & Xin, C. (2005). On service provisioning under a scheduled traffic model in reconfigurable WDM optical networks. In *Proceedings of IEEE Broadnets*, (pp. 15-24). IEEE.

Wang, H., Garg, A. S., Bergman, K., & Glick, M. (2010). *Design and demonstration of an all-optical hybrid packet and circuit switched network platform for next generation data centers*. Paper presented at OFC 2010. Los Angeles, CA.

Wang, Y., Cao, X., & Pan, Y. (2011). A study on the routing and spectrum allocation in SLICE networks. In *Proceedings of IEEE INFOCOM*. IEEE.

Wang, J. P., Robinson, B. S., Hamilton, S. A., & Ippen, E. P. (2006). Demonstration of 40-Gb/s packet routing using all-optical header processing. *Photonics Technology Letters, 18*, 2275–2277. doi:10.1109/LPT.2006.884727.

Wang, Y., & Jin, Y. (2007). Joint scheduling for optical grid applications. *Journal of Optical Networking, 6*(3), 304–318. doi:10.1364/JON.6.000304.

Waxman, B. (1988). Routing of multipoint connections. *IEEE Journal on Selected Areas in Communications, 6*(9), 1617–1622. doi:10.1109/49.12889.

Wedde, & Farooq. (2005). A performance evaluation framework for nature inspired routing algorithms. In F. Rothlauf et al. (Eds.), *Applications of Evolutionary Computing*, (pp. 136-146). Berlin: Springer.

Wedde, & Farooq. (2005). Beehive: New ideas for developing routing algorithms inspired by honey bee behavior. In S. Olariu & A. Y. Zomaya (Eds.), *Handbook of Bioinspired Algorithms and Applications*, (pp. 321-339). London: Chapman and Hall/CRC.

Wedde, & Farooq. (2006). A comprehensive review of nature inspired routing algorithms for fixed telecommunications networks. *Journal of Systems Architecture, 52*(8-9), 461-484.

Wedde, H. F., Farooq, M., & Zhang, Y. (2004). BeeHive: An efficient fault-tolerant routing algorithm inspired by honey bee behavior. *Lecture Notes in Computer Science, 3172*, 83–94. doi:10.1007/978-3-540-28646-2_8.

Weinert, C. M. et al. (1999). Measurement and modeling of timing jitter in optoelectronic repeaters and frequency converters. *IEEE Photonics Technology Letters, 11*(2), 278–280. doi:10.1109/68.740729.

Wen, Y. G., & Chan, V. W. S. (2005). Ultra-reliable communication over vulnerable all-optical networks via lightpath diversity. *IEEE Journal on Selected Areas in Communications, 23*(8), 1572–1587. doi:10.1109/JSAC.2005.851763.

White, Pagurek, & Oppacher. (1998). ASGA: Improving the ant system by integration with genetic algorithms. In *Proceedings of 3rd Conference on Genetic Programming (GP/SGA'98)*, (pp. 610-617). GP/SGA.

Wilson, P. (2007). *Design recipes for fpgas: Using verilog and vhdl*. London: Elsevier.

Wischik, D. (1996). *Routing and wavelength assignment in optical networks (Technical Report)*. Cambridge, UK: University of Cambridge.

Wong, Low, & Chong. (2008). Bee colony optimization with local search for travelling salesman problem. In *Proceedings of the 6th IEEE International Conference on Industrial Informatics (INDIN)*, (pp. 1019-1025). INDIN.

Wu, Y., Chiaraviglio, L., Mellia, M., & Neri, F. (2009). Power-aware routing and wavelength assignment in optical networks. In *Proceedings of the 35th European Conference on Optical Communication*, (pp. 1-2). IEEE.

Wu, Z., Ratazzi, P., Chakravarthy, V., & Hong, L. (2008). Performance evaluation of adaptive non-contiguous MC-CDMA and non-contiguous CI/MC-CDMA for dynamic spectrum access. In *Proceedings of 3rd International Conference on Cognitive Radio Oriented Wireless Networks and Communications*. IEEE.

Xin, C., Wang, B., Cao, X., & Li, J. (2006). Logical topology design for dynamic traffic grooming in mesh WDM optical networks. *IEEE/OSA. Journal of Lightwave Technology, 24*(6), 2267–2275. doi:10.1109/JLT.2006.874562.

Xiu, L. (2007). *Vlsi circuit design methodology demystified: A conceptual taxonomy*. New York: Wiley - IEEE Press. doi:10.1002/9780470199114.

Yamada, M., & Sakuda, K. (1987). Analysis of almost-periodic distributed feed-back slab waveguide via a fundamental matrix approach. *Applied Optics, 26*(16), 3474–3478. doi:10.1364/AO.26.003474 PMID:20490085.

Yang, H., Lee, S. C. J., Tangdiongga, E., Breyer, F., Randel, S., & Koonen, A. M. J. (2009). *40-Gb/s transmission over 100m graded-index plastic optical fiber based on discrete multitone modulation*. Paper presented at OFC 2009. San Diego, CA.

Yang, J., Jeon, M. Y., Pan, J. C. Z., & Yoo, S. J. B. (2003). *Performance monitoring by sub-carrier multiplexing in optical label switching network*. Paper presented at Optical Fiber Communication Conference (OFC'03). Atlanta, GA.

Yang, J., Zhu, Z., Yang, H., Pan, Z., & Yoo, S. J. B. (2004). *All-optical time-to-live using error-checking labels in optical label switching networks*. Paper presented at 30th European Conference on Optical Communication (ECOC'04). Stokholm, Sweden.

Yang, Z.-H. Heywood, & Srinivas. (2002). Agent-based routing algorithms on a LAN. In *Proceedings of the IEEE Canadian Conference on Electrical and Computer Engineering 2002*, (pp. 1442-1447). IEEE.

Yang, K., Ou, S., Guild, K., & Chen, H.-H. (2009). Convergence of ethernet PON and IEEE 802.16 broadband access networks and its QoS-aware dynamic bandwidth allocation scheme. *IEEE Journal on Selected Areas in Communications*, *27*, 101–116. doi:10.1109/JSAC.2009.090202.

Yang, X. S. (2005). Engineering optimizations via nature inspired virtual bee algorithms. *Lecture Notes in Computer Science*, *3562*, 317–323. doi:10.1007/11499305_33.

Ye, D., & Zhong, W. D. (2007). Improved BER monitoring based on amplitude histogram and multi-Gaussian curve fitting. *Journal of Optical Networking*, *6*, 584–598. doi:10.1364/JON.6.000584.

Yetginer, E., Liu, Z., & Rouskas, G. N. (2010). RWA in WDM rings: An efficient formulation based on maximal independent set decomposition. In *Proceedings of IEEE LANMAN*. IEEE.

Yetginer, E., Liu, Z., & Rouskas, G. N. (2011). Fast exact ILP decompositions for ring RWA. *Journal of Optical Communications and Networking*, *3*(7). doi:10.1364/JOCN.3.000577.

Yi, X., Chen, W., & Shieh, W. (2006). An OSNR monitor for optical packet switched networks. *IEEE Photonics Technology Letters*, *18*(13), 1448–1450. doi:10.1109/LPT.2006.877571.

Yoshikane, N., et al. (2004). *1.14 b/s/Hz spectrally-efficient 50 x 85.4 Gb/s transmission over 300 km using copolarized CS-RZ DQPSK signals*. Paper presented at the OFC'04. Los Angeles, CA.

Yu, H., Anand, V., Qiao, C., & Sun, G. (2011). Enhancing virtual infrastructure to survive facility node failures. In *Proceedings of OFC*, (pp. 1-3). OFC.

Yu, H., Qiao, C., Anand, V., Liu, X., Di, H., & Sun, G. (2010). Survivable virtual infrastructure mapping in a federated computing and networking system under single regional failures. In *Proceedings of IEEE Globecom*, (pp. 1-6). IEEE.

Zang, H., Jue, J. P., & Mukherjee, B. (1999). A review of routing and wavelength assignment approaches for wavelength-routed optical WDM networks. *Optical Networks Magazine*, *1*(1).

Zang, H., & Jue, J. P. (2000). A review of routing and wavelength assignment approaches for wavelength-routed optical WDM networks. *Optical Networks Magazine*, *1*, 47–60.

Zang, H., Jue, J. P., & Mukherjee, B. (2000). A review of routing and wavelength assignment approaches for wavelength-routed optical WDM networks. *Optical Networks*, *1*(1), 47–60.

Zhang, G., De Leenheer, M., Morea, A., & Mukherjee, B. (2012). A survey on OFDM-based elastic core optical networking. *IEEE Communications Surveys & Tutorials*, *PP*(99), 1-23.

Zhang, Y., Chowdhury, P., Tornatore, M., & Mukherjee, B. (2010, July). Energy efficiency in telecom optical networks. *IEEE Communications Surveys and Tutorials*.

Zhang, J., & Ansari, N. (2010). An application-oriented fair resource allocation scheme for EPON. *IEEE Systems Journal*, *4*(4), 424–431. doi:10.1109/JSYST.2010.2082210.

Zhang, J., & Ansari, N. (2011). Toward energy-efficient 1GEPON and 10G-EPON with sleep-aware MAC control and scheduling. *IEEE Communications Magazine*, *49*(2), S33–S38. doi:10.1109/MCOM.2011.5706311.

Zhang, J., Ansari, N., Luo, Y., Effenberger, F., & Ye, F. (2009). Next-generation PONs: A performance investigation of candidate architectures for next-generation access stage 1. *IEEE Communications Magazine*, *47*(8), 49–57. doi:10.1109/MCOM.2009.5181892.

Zheng, J., & Mouftah, H. T. (2005). Media access control for ethernet passive optical networks: An overview. *IEEE Communications Magazine*, *43*, 145–150. doi:10.1109/MCOM.2005.1391515.

Zheng, X., & Veeraraghavan, M. (2005). CHEETAH: Circuit-switched high-speed end-to-end transport architecture testbed. *IEEE Communications Magazine, 43*(8), s11–s17. doi:10.1109/MCOM.2005.1497551.

Zhong, & Evans. (2002). *When ants attack: security issues for stigmergic systems* (Technical Report CS-2002-23). Blacksburg, VA: University of Virginia.

Zhou, C. J., & Yuan, X. (2002). A study of dynamic routing and wavelength assignment with imprecise network state information. In *Proceeding of International Conference on Parallel Processing Workshops, 2002*, (pp. 207–213). IEEE.

Zhou, R., Li, X., Wu, Z., Chakravarthy, V., & Li, H. (2010). The demonstration of SMSE based cognitive radio in mobile environment via software defined radio. In *Proceedings of IEEE Globecom Demo Session*. IEEE.

Zhou, D., & Subrammaniam, S. (2000). Survivability in optical networks. *IEEE Network, 14*(6), 16–23. doi:10.1109/65.885666.

Zhu, Z. (2011). *Design green and cost-effective translucent optical networks*. Paper presented at the OFC 2011. Los Angeles, CA.

Zhu, Z., et al. (2005). *43 Gb/s 264 km field fiber transmission using 2R regeneration in a tunable all-optical signal regenerator*. Paper presented at the CLEO 2005. New York, NY.

Zhu, Z. (2011). Mixed placement of 1R/2R/3R regenerators in translucent optical networks to achieve green and cost-effective design. *IEEE Communications Letters, 15*(7), 752–754. doi:10.1109/LCOMM.2011.051011.110519.

Zulkifli, N., Almeida, R. C. Jr, & Guild, K. M. (2007). Efficient resource allocation of heterogeneous services in transparent optical networks. *Journal of Optical Networking, 6*(12), 1349–1359. doi:10.1364/JON.6.001349.

About the Contributors

Yousef S. Kavian received the B.Sc. (Hons) degree in Electronic Engineering from the Shahid Beheshti University, Tehran, Iran, in 2001, the M.Sc. degree in Control Engineering from the Amkabir University, Tehran, Iran, in 2003, and the Ph.D. degree in Electronic Engineering from the Iran University of Science and Technology, Tehran, Iran, in 2007. After a one-year appointment at Shahid Beheshti University, in 2008 he joined the Shahid Chamran University as an Assistant Professor for both research and teaching. He worked as a postdoctoral research fellow at Esslingen University and IAER, Germany, in 2010. His research interests include digital circuits and systems design, optical and wireless networking. Dr. Kavian has over 50 technical publications including journal and conference papers and book chapters in these fields. He is a senior industrial engineer and trainer with more than 10 years industrial collaborations and experiences.

Zabih Ghassemlooy, CEng, Fellow of IET, Senior Member of IEEE, received his BSc (Hons) degree in Electrical and Electronics Engineering from the Manchester Metropolitan University in 1981, and his MSc and PhD in Optical Communications from the University of Manchester Institute of Science and Technology (UMIST), in 1984 and 1987, respectively, with scholarships from the Engineering and Physical Science Research Council, UK. From 1986-87 worked in UMIST and from 1987 to 1988 was a Post-Doctoral Research Fellow at the City University, London. In 1988, he joined Sheffield Hallam University as a Lecturer, becoming a Reader in 1995 and a Professor in Optical Communications in 1997. From 2004 until 2012 was an Associate Dean for Research in the School of Computing and Engineering, and in 2012 he became Associate Dean for Research and Innovation in the Faculty of Engineering and Environment at Northumbria University at Newcastle, UK. He also heads the Northumbria Communications Research Laboratories within the Faculty. In 2001, he was a recipient of the Tan Chin Tuan Fellowship in Engineering from the Nanyang Technological University in Singapore to work on the photonic technology. He is the Editor-in-Chief of the *International Journal of Optics and Applications* and *The Mediterranean Journal of Electronics and Communications*. He currently serves on the Editorial Committees of number international journals. He is the founder and the Chairman of the IEEE, IET International Symposium on Communication Systems, Network, and Digital Signal Processing. His research interests are on photonics switching, optical wireless and wired communications, visible light communications, and mobile communications. He has supervised a large number of PhD students (more than 40) and has published over 440 papers (154 in journals + 11 book chapters) and presented several keynote and invited talks. He is a co-author of a CRC book on *Optical Wireless Communications – Systems and Channel Modelling with Matlab* (2012); a co-editor of an IET book on *Analogue Optical Fibre Communications*. From 2004-06 he was the IEEE UK/IR Communications Chapter Secretary, the Vice-Chairman (2004-2008), the Chairman (2008-2011), and Chairman of the IET Northumbria Network (Oct 2011-). His personal Website is http://soe.northumbria.ac.uk/ocr/people/ghassemlooy/.

* * *

Nirwan Ansari is Professor of Electrical and Computer Engineering at NJIT. His current research focuses on various aspects of broadband networks and multimedia communications. He has served on the Editorial/Advisory Board of eight journals. He is an IEEE Fellow and some of his recent recognitions include the 2008 NJIT Excellence in Teaching Award in Outstanding Professional Development, a 2008 IEEE MGA Leadership Award, the 2009 NCE Excellence in Teaching Award, a couple of best paper awards, a 2010 Thomas Alva Edison Patent Award, 2012 NJIHOF Inventor of the Year Award and designation as an IEEE Communications Society Distinguished Lecturer. He was also granted over twenty US patents.

Carmelo J. A. Bastos-Filho was born in Recife, Brazil, in 1978. He received the B.Sc. in Electronics Engineering and the M.Sc. and Ph.D. degrees in Electrical Engineering from Federal University of Pernambuco (UFPE) in 2000, 2003, and 2005, respectively. In 2006, he received the best Brazilian thesis award in electrical engineering. His interests are related to optical networks, swarm intelligence, evolutionary computation, multiobjective optimization, and biomedical applications. He is currently an Associate Professor at the Polytechnic School of the University of Pernambuco. He is the head of the research division of the Polytechnic School of Pernambuco and coordinates the Masters course on Systems Engineering. He is an IEEE senior member and a Research fellow of the National Research Council of Brazil (CNPq). More information at http://scholar.google.com/citations?user=t3A96agAAAAJ&hl=en.

Nicola Calabretta received the M.Sc. degree in Telecommunications Engineering from Politecnico di Torino, Turin, Italy, in 1999. In 2004, he received the Ph.D. degree from the Eindhoven University of Technology, Eindhoven, The Netherlands. From 2004 to 2007, he was with Scuola Superiore Sant'Anna University, Pisa, Italy. In 2007, he visited the Technical University of Denmark, Denmark. He is currently with COBRA Research Institute, the Eindhoven University of Technology. He co-authored over 180 journal papers and conference proceedings and holds 3 international patents. His fields of interest are all-optical signal processing and optical packet switching for optical interconnected networks.

Gerardo Castañón, Associate professor, member of the national research system in Mexico. Dr. Castañón received the Bachelor of Science in Physics Engineering from the Monterrey Institute of Technology and Higher Education (ITESM), México, in 1987. He received the Master of Science degree in Physics (Optics) from the Ensenada Research Centre and Higher Education, México, in 1989. He also received the Master and Ph.D. degrees in Electrical and Computer Engineering from the State University of New York (SUNY) at Buffalo in 1995 and 1997, respectively. He was supported by the Fulbright scholarship through his Ph.D. studies. From January of 1998 to November of 2000, he was a Research Scientist working with Alcatel USA Corporate Research Center in Richardson, TX, where he was doing research on IP over WDM, dimensioning and routing strategies for next generation optical networks and the design of all-optical routers. From December of 2000 to August of 2002, he was a Senior Researcher with Fujitsu Network Communications doing research on ultra high speed transmission systems. He is now working in the Center of Electronics and Telecommunications at ITESM since September of 2002. Dr. Castañón has over 50 publications in journals and conferences and 2 international patents. He frequently acts as a reviewer for IEEE journals. He is a Senior member of the IEEE Communications and Photonics societies. He is a member the Academy of Science in Mexico.

Jheymesson Cavalcanti was born in Recife, Brazil, in 1989. He is currently a B.Sc. candidate in Computer Engineering at the University of Pernambuco. His primary research interests include robotics and programmable hardware.

Daniel A. R. Chaves was born in Recife, Brazil, in 1981. He received the B.Sc. degree in Electronics Engineering from Federal University of Pernambuco (UFPE) in 2006. He received the M.Sc. and Ph.D degrees in Electrical Engineering from Federal University of Pernambuco (UFPE), in 2008 and 2012, respectively. He is Professor of Computer Engineering Group (E-Comp) in the Polytechnic School of University of Pernambuco (UPE). Dr. Chaves currently is working with Research Group on Networks and Communications (UPE) and with Laboratory of Optical Networks (UFPE). His interests are related to lightwave communication systems, including high capacity WDM transmission, optical networking, impairment aware routing and wavelength assignment algorithms, design of all-optical and translucent networks and applications of computational intelligence in optical networks optimization.

Fernando Lezama Cruzvillasante was born in Córdoba, Veracruz, México, on Jun 30th, 1986. He received the B.S. degree in Electronic Engineering from the Minatitlán Institute of Technology (ITM), Veracruz, México, in 2009. He obtained the degree of Master of Science in Electronic Engineering (Telecommunications) from the Monterrey Institute of Technology and Higher Education (ITESM), México, in May 2011. Currently, he is pursuing a Ph.D degree at the ITESM, México. He is a member of the research chair of Optical Communications in the Center of Electronics and Telecommunications at ITESM since August of 2009. His research interests include optical networks optimization and evolutionary computation.

Wei Guo got her BS, MS, and Ph.D degree in Computer Science from Wuhan University in 1985, 1990, and 1998, respectively. She is a professor of state key lab of advanced optical communication system and network in Shanghai Jiao Tong University. Before she entered in Shanghai Jiao Tong University, she was a senior engineer and a project manager of the Fiberhome Telecommunication Technologies Co., Ltd. from 2001-2003. Before 2001, she worked as an Associate Professor in Wuhan University from 1997-2001 and worked as a Research Assistant in Hong Kong Polytechnic University from 1998-2000. She has over 50 publications in technical journals and conferences. Her research interests include optical grid, architecture of automatically switched optical network, network management system, network planning, optimization algorithm.

Weisheng Hu received BS (86), MS (89), and PhD (94) from Tsinghua, BUST, and Nanjing University. He joined WUST as Assistant Professor in 1989-94, SJTU as Post-Doctorate Fellow in 1997-99, and as Professor in 1999. He was Director of SKL of advanced optical communication systems and networks (2003-07). He serves TPC for OFC, APOC, Optics East, LEOS/PS, CLEO/PS, ICICS, and editorial board for JLT, COL, and FOC. He published 78 peer journal papers, 26 OFC and ECOC conference papers. He gave 16 invited talks. He holds 38 patents.

Yaohui Jin received BS degree in Applied Physics from Anhui University in 1992, MS degree in Condensed Matter Physics from in University of Science and Technology of China in 1995, and Ph.D degree in Electromagnetic Field and Microwave Technology from Shanghai Jiao Tong University in 2000. His research focuses on triple play convergence, future Internet evolution, data center network, and network data mining. He published more than 100 technical papers in leading conferences and journals. He holds seven Chinese patents.

Marcos Oliveira Júnior received the BS Degree in Computer Engineering from the University of Pernambuco, in 2011. He is currently a M.Sc. candidate at the University of Pernambuco and he is an active member of the CIRG@UPE (Computational Intelligence Research Group at UPE). His primary research interests include computational intelligence, network science, swarm intelligence, neural networks, parallel platforms, and GPU computing.

Goran Marković received his B.Sc., M.Sc., and Ph.D degrees, all in Telecommunication Traffic Engineering from the University of Belgrade, Serbia, in 1996, 2002, and 2007, respectively. Since 1997, he has been with the Department of Telecommunication Traffic and Networks at the Faculty of Transport and Traffic Engineering, University of Belgrade. He is currently an Assistant Professor. His research interests include traffic routing in communication networks, optical networking, and application of swarm intelligence for solving various optimization problems in telecommunication network design and operation.

Joaquim F. Martins Filho was born in Recife, Brazil, in 1966. He received the B.Sc. degree in Electronics Engineering from the Federal University of Pernambuco (UFPE), in Recife, in 1989, and the M.Sc. degree in Physics from the same institution in 1991. He received his PhD degree in Electronics Engineering from the University of Glasgow, Scotland, in 1995. Between 1995 and 1998, he was a Visiting Professor at the Physics Department of UFPE. In 1998, he joined the Photonics Group, Department of Electronics and Systems of UFPE, in Recife, where he currently is an Associate Professor. His research interests are in devices, subsystems, transmission systems, and networking for optical communications and optical sensors. In 2005, he received a prize from the Brazilian Ministry of Education and the Ministry of Science for the supervision of the best PhD thesis of Brazil in Electrical Engineering. He has coordinated several research projects financed by state and federal agencies as well as by industries like SIEMENS-Brazil, PARKS, and PADTEC. He also took part in other research projects sponsored by ERICSSON-Brazil and CHESF. He has authored more than 100 papers and 1 international patent. Along his career he has given contributions on non-linear short pulse propagation in optical fibers, ultrafast optical pulse generation from mode-locked semiconductor quantum well lasers, erbium doped fiber amplifiers, thulium doped fiber amplifiers, in physical impairments aware routing, and wavelength assignment algorithms for optical networks, in the use of computational intelligence techniques for the optimization of optical networks, and in the development of fiber-optic sensor systems for the monitoring of: corrosion, leakage current in insulator strings of high power transmission lines, and dissolved gases in transformer oil. Prof. Joaquim Martins-Filho is a Senior Member of the IEEE (Institute of Electrical and Electronics Engineers), Senior Member of OSA (Optical Society of America), Member of SBMO (Brazilian Microwave and Optoelectronics Society), SBrT (Brazilian Telecommunication Society), and SBF (Brazilian Physics Society), as well as a Research Fellow of the National Research Council of Brazil

(CNPq). He was the coordinator of the Post-Graduate Program (MSc and PhD) in Electrical Engineering of UFPE from 2003 to 2007. He is a member of the Editorial Board of the journal *ISRN Communications and Networking*. Since 2009, he is a member of the Engineering, Science, and Technology Board of FACEPE (Foundation for Science and Technology Development of the State of Pernambuco, Brazil).

Rui Manuel Morais was born in Gouveia, Portugal. He graduated in Applied Mathematics and Computation and obtained the M.Sc. degree in Mathematics and Applications, both from the University of Aveiro, Aveiro, Portugal, in 2006 and 2008, respectively. In 2007, he joined Instituto de Telecomunicações working on the dimensioning of optical networks. He is currently working toward his Ph.D. degree at the Department of Electronics, Telecommunications and Informatics, University of Aveiro, Portugal, and Nokia Siemens Networks Portugal, S.A.. His main research interest is the planning and optimization of multilayer optical transport networks.

Victor Vilmarques Capistrano Pedrosa was born in Recife, Brazil, in 1990. He is currently a B.Sc. candidate in Computer Engineering at the University of Pernambuco. His primary research interests include software engineering and programmable hardware.

Helder A. Pereira was born in Paulista, Brazil, in 1980. He received the B.Sc. degree in electronics Engineering from University of Pernambuco (UPE), Recife, Brazil, in 2000, the M.Sc. degree at Telecommunication National Institute (Inatel), Santa Rita do Sapucaí, Brazil, in 2002, and the PhD degree in Electrical Engineering at the Federal University of Pernambuco (UFPE), Recife, Brazil, in 2007. He is a professor at the Electrical Engineering Department of University of Pernambuco (DEE-UPE).

Armando Nolasco Pinto received the Ph.D. degree in Electrical Engineering from the University of Aveiro, in 1999. In 1994, he joined the Instituto de Telecomunicações as a Researcher, and in 2000, he became Assistant Professor at the Electrical, Telecommunications, and Informatics Department of the University of Aveiro. During 2006 and 2007, he was a Visiting Professor at the Institute of Optics, University of Rochester. At present, he leads a research group dedicated to the design and optimization of high-speed optical communication systems and networks. He has published more than 150 scientific papers in international journals and conferences. He is an Associate Editor of several scientific journals, including the *The International Journal of Optics*, the *Advances in Applied Physics*, and the *International Journal on Advances in Networks and Services*. Dr. Pinto is a Senior Member of the IEEE and a member of the Optical Society of America.

Francisco Ramos received the M.Sc. and Ph.D. degrees in Telecommunication Engineering from the Polytechnic University of Valencia in 1997 and 2000, respectively. Since 1998, he has been with the Department of Communications at the same university, where he is now Professor. He has participated in several national and European research projects on areas such as optical access networks, and broadband wireless systems. Prof. Ramos has co-authored more than 100 papers in international journals and conferences and he has acted as reviewer for the IEE, IEEE, Elsevier, and OSA Publishers. He is also the recipient of the Prize of the Telecommunication Engineering Association of Spain for his thesis dissertation. His current research interests include nonlinear photonics and chaos.

Ana Maria Sarmiento received the Bachelor of Science in Physics Engineering from the Monterrey Institute of Technology and Higher Education (ITESM), México, in 1989. She received the Master and Ph.D. degrees in Industrial Engineering from the State University of New York (SUNY) at Buffalo in 1995 and 2001, respectively. Her dissertation research was on the integrated production-logistics network optimization for the partner-chain design in agile manufacturing. Her dissertation topic received the 1998 Doctoral Dissertation Award presented by the International Society of Logistics. She worked at i2 Technologies from 1999 to 2001 in Irving, TX. She is teaching as a Lecturer Professor in the Department of Industrial Engineering at ITESM in Monterrey since January of 2007. Her current research activities include the application of optimization methods of operations research to telecommunication networks.

Dennis Silva was born in Recife, Brazil, in 1989. He is currently a B.Sc. candidate in Computer Engineering at UPE. He started working with Computational Intelligence (CI) algorithms in 2009, and since then, he has worked with several approaches for dealing with real-world problems.

Weiqiang Sun received his BS (1999) and Ph. D (2004) degree both from the University of Science and Technology of China, and is now an Associate Professor in Shanghai Jiao Tong University. Dr. Sun is actively involved in the research of high-speed networks, network control and management, and network applications. He has about 60 publications in peer reviewed journals and conferences. He led the standardization of Generalized MPLS performance measurement in IETF and is the co-editor of RFC 5814 and one other working group document. He has served as an invited speaker on several international conferences including AOE 2005, COIN 2006/2009, ANTS 2007, ACCESS 2009, IWOO 2010, ACP 2009/2010, ICP 2012, and ICTON 2012. He was invited to BoD 2010 as a panelist. Dr. Sun is member of Technical Program Committee of COIN 2008 (Tokyo, Japan) and organizer of the Sino-Korea Workshop on IPTV and NGN (2007-2010).

Mina Taheri received the B.Sc degree in Electrical Engineering with focus on Electronics and the M.Sc degree in Electrical Engineering with specialization on Communications (Networks) from Isfahan University of Technology (IUT) in 2007 and 2010, respectively. Currently, she is working toward her Ph.D degree in Electrical Engineering at the New Jersey Institute of Technology (NJIT), Newark. Her research interests includes energy consumption, optical network architectures, and cloud computing.

Firat Tekiner received an MBA for Engineering and IT Managers from the University of Manchester, a PhD in Communications Engineering from Northumbria University, Newcastle UK, an MSc in Information Systems Engineering from UMIST, Manchester, UK, and a BSc in Computer Engineering from the Eastern Mediterranean University, Cyprus. He is an honorary Research Fellow at the University of Manchester. His career spanning from a PostDoc to a Senior Academic to Business Consultant gives him insight in Research and Industrial Applications. He is a Data Scientist and Big Data Architect focusing in large networks, big data, Large Information Systems, and Analytics applications.

Ruth Vilar received the B.S. and Ph.D. degrees in Telecommunications from the Universitat Politecnica de Valencia, Valencia, Spain, in 2004 and 2010, respectively. She is currently with the Nanophotonics Technology Center as a research professional. She has participated in several national and European research projects on areas such as optical networks and optical networking. Her current research activities are focused on advanced modulated formats. Other research interests include photonic integrated devices, optical networking, optical signal processing, and optical security.

Bin Wang received the Ph.D. degree in Electrical Engineering from the Ohio State University. He is a Full Professor of Computer Science and Engineering, Department of Computer and Engineering, Wright State University. Dr. Wang has led numerous research projects funded by DoD, NSF, DoE, AFOSR, AFRL, ODOD, and other sources. He is a recipient of US Department of Energy CAREER Award. Dr. Wang's research interests include cyber security, network security visualization, user behavior modeling, trust management, security and information assurance, game theory, layered sensing, wireless communication, wireless and mobile computing, wireless sensor networks, pervasive/ubiquitous computing, multimedia communication, real-time system and communication, quality of service provisioning, Dense Wavelength Division Multiplexing (DWDM) optical networks, optical burst switching, Grid computing, ultra-wide band, software defined radio, open spectrum access and cognitive radio networks, information theory, distributed signal processing, Semantic Web, RFID and medical/health informatics, organism and human cellular networks.

Lilin Yi, Associate Professor, Ph.D supervisor, received his BS(2002) and MS(2005) from Shanghai Jiao Tong University (SJTU). He achieved PhD degree from Ecole Nationale Supérieure des Télécommunications (ENST), France and SJTU, China, on Mar. and Jun. 2008, respectively, as a joint-educated PhD student. After graduation, he worked at Avanex R&D center as a product development manager, presided Alcatel-Lucent 100G novel optical amplifier and Avanex next generation optical amplification platform projects. Since 2010, he has joined the State Key Laboratory of Advanced Optical Communication Systems and Network, SJTU. His research interests are novel optical access networks and photonic information processing.

Zuqing Zhu received his PhD degree from the Department of Electrical and Computer Engineering, University of California, Davis, in 2007. From Jul. 2007 to Jan. 2011, he worked in the Service Provider Technology Group of Cisco Systems, San Jose, as a senior R&D engineer. In Jan. 2011, Dr. Zhu joined the University of Science and Technology of China (USTC), where he currently is an Associate Professor. His research interests are energy-efficient network designs, access network technologies, and optical communications and networks. He has published more than 80 papers in peer-reviewed journals and conferences of IEEE, IET, and OSA. Dr. Zhu has been in the Technical Program Committees (TPC) of INFOCOM, ICC, GLOBECOM, ICCCN, etc. He was a guest editor of the special issue on "Optical Networks in Cloud Computing" in IEEE Network. Dr. Zhu is also an editorial board member of Elsevier *Journal of Optical Switching and Networking* (OSN), Springer *Telecommunication Systems Journal* (TSMJ), Wiley *European Transactions on Emerging Telecommunications Technologies* (ETT), and etc. He is a Senior Member of IEEE and a Member of OSA.

Index